Library of
Davidson College
VOID

Miller's
COMPREHENSIVE
GAAP GUIDE

A comprehensive restatement
of all current promulgated
Generally Accepted Accounting Principles

Martin A. Miller, C.P.A.

1980

Harcourt Brace Jovanovich, Inc.
New York   Chicago   San Francisco   Atlanta   Dallas

The publisher has not sought nor obtained approval of this publication from any other organization, profit or non-profit, and is solely responsible for its contents.

Miller's Comprehensive GAAP GUIDE
is a trademark of Harcourt Brace Jovanovich, Inc.

Copyright © 1978, 1979 by Harcourt Brace Jovanovich, Inc.

All rights reserved. No part of this publication may be reproduced or transmitted in any form or by any means, electronic or mechanical, including photocopy, recording, or any information storage and retrieval system, without permission in writing from the publisher.

ISBN: 0-150-039573

Printed in the United States of America

Table of Contents

Foreword	i
Cross Reference–Original Pronouncements to GAAP Guide	iii
Accounting Changes	1.01
Accounting Policies	2.01
Business Combinations	3.01
Changes in Financial Position	4.01
Consolidated Financial Statements	5.01
Contingencies	6.01
Convertible Debt	7.01
Current Assets and Current Liabilities	8.01
Current Value Accounting	9.01
Deferred Compensation Contracts	10.01
Depreciable Assets and Depreciation	11.01
Development Stage Enterprises	12.01
Earnings Per Share	13.01
Equity Method	14.01
Extinguishment of Debt	15.01
Financial Reporting and Changing Prices	15.51
Foreign Operations and Exchange	16.01
General Price-Level Changes	17.01
Government Contracts	18.01
Income Taxes	19.01
Installment Method of Accounting	20.01
Intangible Assets	21.01
Interest on Receivables and Payables	22.01
Interim Financial Reporting	23.01
Inventory Pricing and Methods	24.01
Investment Tax Credit	25.01
Leases	26.01
Long-Term Contracts	27.01
Marketable Securities	28.01
Nonmonetary Transactions	29.01

Oil and Gas Producing Companies	30.01
Pension Plans	31.01
Quasi-Reorganizations	32.01
Real and Personal Property Taxes	33.01
Regulated Industries	34.01
Research and Development Costs	35.01
Results of Operations	36.01
Segmental Reporting	37.01
Stockholders' Equity	38.01
Stock Issued to Employees	39.01
Troubled Debt Restructuring	40.01
Disclosure Index	41.01
Topical Index	42.01

Foreword

This *Comprehensive GAAP Guide* contains all the promulgated and many of the nonpromulgated accounting principles in use today. Each promulgated pronouncement is thoroughly reviewed in a comprehensive format that is easy to assimilate and understand. Many chapters contain in-depth illustrations on the application of the specific accounting principle. Pronouncements covering the same subject matter have been compiled and incorporated in a single chapter regardless of the date of their origin.

Important nonpromulgated accounting principles have been integrated throughout the text in an effort to give the reader a more complete perspective of the specific subject matter.

Perhaps the most important feature of this comprehensive guide to accounting principles is its readability. The utmost care has been exercised to avoid incomprehensible language. Sentence structure has been deliberately simplified as much as possible to foster the maximum comprehension in a minimum period. Illustrations are used generously to demonstrate the applicability of specific concepts and principles, and observation paragraphs are utilized to stress important information.

No attempt is made to resolve apparent errors and conflicts in the promulgated pronouncements. However, these items are objectively brought to the reader's attention.

An innovative Disclosure Index has been provided which contains both required and recommended disclosures currently in use. This index has been designed to assist the preparer or reviewer of financial statements in determining whether necessary disclosures have been made.

Martin A. Miller

Cross-Reference

ORIGINAL PRONOUNCEMENTS TO COMPREHENSIVE GAAP GUIDE CHAPTERS

This locator provides instant cross-reference between an original pronouncement and the chapter(s) in this publication where such pronouncement appears. Original pronouncements are listed chronologically on the left and the chapter(s) in which the pronouncement appears in this GAAP GUIDE on the right. Where an original pronouncement has been superseded, cross-reference is made to the succeeding pronouncement.

ACCOUNTING RESEARCH BULLETINS

(Accounting Research Bulletins (ARB) 1-42 were revised, restated or withdrawn at the time ARB No. 43 was issued).

ORIGINAL PRONOUNCEMENT	GAAP GUIDE REFERENCE
ARB No. 43 (Restatement and Revision of Accounting Research Bulletins)	
Chapter 1-A:	
Unrealized Profit	Installment Method of Accounting, p. **20.01**
Capital Surplus	Stockholders' Equity, p. **38.01**
Consolidated Statements	Consolidated Financial Statements, p. **5.01**
Treasury Stock	Stockholders' Equity, p. **38.01**
Receivables—Officers & Employees	Current Assets and Current Liabilities, p. **8.01**
Donated Stock	Stockholders' Equity, p. **38.01**
Chapter 1-B:	
Profits or Losses—Treasury Stock	Stockholders' Equity, p. **38.01**
Chapter 2-A:	
Comparative Statements	Consolidated Financial Statements, p. **5.01**
Chapter 2-B:	
Combined Statement—Income & Surplus	Superseded by APB-9
Chapter 3-A:	
Current Assets and Current Liabilities	Current Assets and Current Liabilities, p. **8.01**
Chapter 3-B:	
Application of U.S. Government Securities to Federal Taxes	Superseded by APB-10
Chapter 4:	
Inventory Pricing	Inventory Pricing and Methods, p. **24.01**
Chapter 5:	
Intangible Assets	Superseded by APB-16 and 17

Cross-Reference

Chapter 6:
Contingency Reserves — Superseded by FASB-5

Chapter 7-A:
Quasi-Reorganizations — Quasi-Reorganizations, p. **32.01**

Chapter 7-B:
Stock Dividends and Splits — Stockholders' Equity, p. **38.01**

Chapter 7-C:
Business Combinations — Superseded by ARB-48

Chapter 8:
Income and Earned Surplus — Superseded by APB-9

Chapter 9-A:
Depreciation and High Costs — Depreciable Assets and Depreciation, p. **11.01**

Chapter 9-B:
Depreciation on Appreciation — Depreciable Assets and Depreciation, p. **11.01**

Chapter 9-C:
Emergency Facilities—Depreciation — Depreciable Assets and Depreciation, p. **11.01**

Chapter 10-A:
Accounting for Real and Personal Property Taxes — Real and Personal Property Taxes, p. **33.01**

Chapter 10-B:
Income Taxes — Superseded by APB-11

Chapter 11-A:
Cost-Plus-Fixed-Fee Contracts — Government Contracts, p. **18.01**

Chapter 11-B:
Renegotiations — Government Contracts, p. **18.01**

Chapter 11-C:
Terminated Defense Contracts — Government Contracts, p. **18.01**

Chapter 12:
Foreign Operations and Foreign Exchange — Partially superseded by FASB-8

Chapter 13-A:
Pension Plans—etc. — Superseded by APB-8

Chapter 13-B:
Compensation Involved in Stock Options — Stock Issued to Employees, p. **39.01**

Cross-Reference

Chapter 14:
Disclosure—Long-Term Leases   Superseded by APB-5

Chapter 15:
Unamortized Discount, Issue Cost, and Redemption Premium—Bonds   Superseded by APB-26

ARB No. 44
Declining Balance Depreciation   Superseded by ARB-44 (revised)

ARB No. 44 (revised)
Declining Balance Depreciation   Depreciable Assets and Depreciation, p. **11.01**

ARB No. 45
Long-Term Construction-Type Contracts   Long-Term Contracts, p. **27.01**

ARB No. 46
Discontinuance of Dating Earned Surplus   Quasi-Reorganizations, p. **32.01**

ARB No. 47
Accounting for Costs of a Pension Plan   Superseded by APB-8

ARB No. 48
Business Combinations   Superseded by APB-16

ARB No. 49
Earnings Per Share   Superseded by APB-9

ARB No. 50
Contingencies   Superseded by FASB-5

ARB No. 51
Consolidated Financial Statements   Consolidated Financial Statements, p. **5.01**

ACCOUNTING PRINCIPLES BOARD OPINIONS

ORIGINAL PRONOUNCEMENT   GAAP GUIDE REFERENCE

APB Opinion No. 1
New Depreciation Guidelines   Depreciable Assets and Depreciation, p. **11.01**

APB Opinion No. 2
Accounting for the Investment Credit   Investment Tax Credit, p. **25.01**

APB Opinion No. 2—Addendum
Accounting Principles for Regulated Industries   Regulated Industries, p. **34.01**

Cross-Reference

APB Opinion No. 3
The Statement of Source and Application of Funds — Superseded by APB-19

APB Opinion No. 4
Accounting for the Investment Credit — Investment Tax Credit, p. **25.01**

APB Opinion No. 5
Reporting of Leases in Financial Statements of Lessees — Superseded by FASB-13

APB Opinion No. 6
Status of Accounting Research Bulletins — Portions of this Opinion superseded by APB-11, 16, 17, 26 and FASB-8. The balance of this Opinion appears in the following chapters:

Stockholders' Equity, p. **38.01**
Current Assets and Current Liabilities, p. **8.01**
Depreciable Assets and Depreciation, p. **11.01**

APB Opinion No. 7
Accounting for Leases in Financial Statements of Lessors — Superseded by FASB-13

APB Opinion No. 8
Accounting for Costs of a Pension Plan — Pension Plans, p. **31.01**

APB Opinion No. 9
Reporting the Results of Operations — Portions of this Opinion superseded by APB-15, 16, 20, 30, and FASB-16. The balance of this Opinion appears in:

Results of Operations, p. **36.01**

APB Opinion No. 10
Omnibus Opinion—1966 — Portions of this Opinion superseded by APB-14, 16, and 18. The balance of this Opinion appears in the following chapters:

Income Taxes, p. **19.01**
Stockholders' Equity, p. **38.01**
Installment Method of Accounting, p. **20.01**

APB Opinion No. 11
Accounting for Income Taxes — Portions of this Opinion superseded by APB-23 and FASB-9. The balance of this Opinion appears in:

Income Taxes, p. **19.01**

APB Opinion No. 12
Omnibus Opinion—1967

Portions of this Opinion superseded by APB-14. The balance of this Opinion appears in the following chapters:
Depreciable Assets and Depreciation, p. **11.01**
Stockholders' Equity, p. **38.01**
Interest on Receivables and Payables, p. **22.01**

APB Opinion No. 13
Amending Paragraph 6 of APB-9, Application to Commercial Banks

Results of Operations, p. **36.01**

APB Opinion No. 14
Accounting for Convertible Debt and Debt Issued with Stock Purchase Warrants

Convertible Debt, p. **7.01**

APB Opinion No. 15
Earnings Per Share

Earnings Per Share, p. **13.01**

APB Opinion No. 16
Business Combinations

Business Combinations, p. **3.01**

APB Opinion No. 17
Intangible Assets

Intangible Assets, p. **21.01**

APB Opinion No. 18
The Equity Method of Accounting for Investments in Common Stock

Equity Method, p. **14.01**

APB Opinion No. 19
Reporting Changes in Financial Position

Changes in Financial Position, p. **4.01**

APB Opinion No. 20
Accounting Changes

Accounting Changes, p. **1.01**

APB Opinion No. 21
Interest on Receivables and Payables

Interest on Receivables and Payables, p. **22.01**

APB Opinion No. 22
Disclosure of Accounting Policies

Accounting Policies, p. **2.01**

APB Opinion No. 23
Accounting for Income Taxes—Special Areas

Income Taxes, p. **19.01**

APB Opinion No. 24
Accounting for Income Taxes—Investments in Common Stock Accounted for by the Equity Method

Income Taxes, p. **19.01**

Cross-Reference

APB Opinion No. 25
Accounting for Stock Issued to an Employee — Stock Issued to Employees, p. **39.01**

APB Opinion No. 26
Early Extinguishment of Debt — Extinguishment of Debt, p. **15.01**

APB Opinion No. 27
Accounting for Lease Transaction by Manufacturers or Dealer Lessors — Superseded by FASB-13

APB Opinion No. 28
Interim Financial Reporting — Interim Financial Reporting, p. **23.01**

APB Opinion No. 29
Accounting for Nonmonetary Transactions — Nonmonetary Transactions, p. **29.01**

APB Opinion No. 30
Reporting the Results of Operations — Results of Operations, p. **36.01**

APB Opinion No. 31
Disclosure of Lease Commitments by Lessees — Superseded by FASB-13

FINANCIAL ACCOUNTING STANDARDS BOARD (FASB)–STATEMENTS

ORIGINAL PRONOUNCEMENT — GAAP° GUIDE REFERENCE

FASB Statement No. 1
Disclosure of Foreign Currency Translation Information — Superseded by FASB-8

FASB Statement No. 2
Accounting for Research and Development Costs — Research and Development Costs, p. **35.01**

FASB Statement No. 3
Reporting Accounting Changes in Interim Financial Statements — Accounting Changes, p. **1.01**

FASB Statement No. 4
Reporting Gains and Losses from Extinguishment of Debt — Extinguishment of Debt, p. **15.01**

FASB Statement No. 5
Accounting for Contingencies — Contingencies, p. **6.01**

FASB Statement No. 6
Classification of Short-Term Obligations Expected to be Refinanced — Current Assets and Current Liabilities, p. **8.01**

Cross-Reference

FASB Statement No. 7
Accounting and Reporting by Development Stage Enterprises

Development Stage Enterprises, p. **12.01**

FASB Statement No. 8
Accounting for the Translation of Foreign Currency Transactions and Foreign Currency Financial Statements

Foreign Operations and Exchange, p. **16.01**

FASB Statement No. 9
Accounting for Income Taxes—Oil and Gas Producing Companies

Superseded by FASB-19

FASB Statement No. 10
Extension of "Grandfather" Provisions for Business Combinations

Business Combinations, p. **3.01**

FASB Statement No. 11
Accounting for Contingencies—Transition Method

Contingencies, p. **6.01**

FASB Statement No. 12
Accounting for Certain Marketable Securities

Marketable Securities, p. **28.01**

FASB Statement No. 13
Accounting for Leases

Leases, p. **26.01**

FASB Statement No. 14
Financial Reporting for Segments of a Business Enterprise

Segmental Reporting, p. **37.01**

FASB Statement No. 15
Accounting by Debtors and Creditors for Troubled Debt Restructuring

Troubled Debt Restructuring, p. **40.01**

FASB Statement No. 16
Prior Period Adjustments

Results of Operations, p. **36.01**

FASB Statement No. 17
Accounting for Leases—Initial Direct Costs

Leases, p. **26.01**

FASB Statement No. 18
Financial Reporting for Segments of Business Enterprises—Interim Financial Statements

Segmental Reporting, p. **37.01**

FASB Statement No. 19
Financial Accounting and Reporting by Oil and Gas Producing Companies

Oil and Gas Producing Companies, p. **30.01**

GAAP GUIDE / **ix**

Cross-Reference

FASB Statement No. 20
Accounting for Forward Exchange Contracts — Foreign Operations and Exchange, p. **16.01**

FASB Statement No. 21
Suspension of the Reporting of Earnings per Share and Segment Information by Nonpublic Enterprises — Earnings Per Share, p. **13.01**; Segmental Reporting, p. **37.01**

FASB Statement No. 22
Changes in the Provisions of Lease Agreements Resulting from Refunding of Tax-Exempt Debt — Leases, p. **26.01**

FASB Statement No. 23
Inception of the Lease — Leases, p. **26.01**

FASB Statement No. 24
Reporting Segment Information in Financial Statements That Are Presented in Another Enterprise's Financial Report — Segmental Reporting, p. **37.01**

FASB Statement No. 25
Suspension of Certain Accounting Requirements for Oil and Gas Producing Companies — Oil and Gas Producing Companies, p. **30.01**

FASB Statement No. 26
Profit Recognition on Sales-Type Leases of Real Estate — Leases, p. **26.01**

FASB Statement No. 27
Classification of Renewals or Extensions of Existing Sales-Type or Direct Financing Leases — Leases, p. **26.01**

FASB Statement No. 28
Accounting for Sales with Leasebacks — Leases, p. **26.01**

FASB Statement No. 29
Determining Contingent Rentals — Leases, p. **26.01**

FASB Statement No. 30
Disclosure of Information About Major Customers — Segmental Reporting, p. **37.01**

FASB Statement No. 31
Accounting for Tax Benefits Related to U.K. Tax Legislation Concerning Stock Relief — Income Taxes, p. **19.01**

FASB Statement No. 32

Specialized Accounting and Reporting Principles and Practices in AICPA Statements of Position and Guides on Accounting and Auditing Matters
Accounting Changes, p. **1.01**

FASB Statement No. 33

Financial Reporting and Changing Prices
Financial Reporting and Changing Prices, p. **15.51**

FINANCIAL ACCOUNTING STANDARDS BOARD (FASB)-INTERPRETATIONS

ORIGINAL PRONOUNCEMENT   GAAP GUIDE REFERENCE

FASB Interpretation No. 1

Accounting Changes Related to the Cost of Inventory
Accounting Changes, p. **1.01**

FASB Interpretation No. 2

Imputing Interest on Debt Arrangements Made Under the Federal Bankruptcy Act
Superseded by FASB-15

FASB Interpretation No. 3

Accounting for the Cost of Pension Plans Subject to the Employee Retirement Income Security Act of 1974
Pension Plans, p. **31.01**

FASB Interpretation No. 4

Applicability of FASB Statement No. 2 to Business Combinations Accounted for by the Purchase Method
Research and Development Costs, p. **35.01**

FASB Interpretation No. 5

Applicability of FASB Statement No. 2 to Development Stage Enterprises
Superseded by FASB-7

FASB Interpretation No. 6

Applicability of FASB Statement No. 2 to Computer Software
Research and Development Costs, p. **35.01**

FASB Interpretation No. 7

Applying FASB Statement No. 7 to Financial Statements of Established Operating Enterprises
Development Stage Enterprises, p. **12.01**

FASB Interpretation No. 8

Classification of a Short-Term Obligation Repaid Prior to Being Replaced by a Long-Term Security
Current Assets and Current Liabilities, p. **8.01**

Cross-Reference

FASB Interpretation No. 9

Applying APB Opinion Nos. 16 and 17 When A Savings and Loan Association or a Similar Institution is Acquired in a Business Combination Accounted for by the Purchase Method — Business Combinations, p. **3.01**

FASB Interpretation No. 10

Application of FASB Statement No. 12 to Personal Financial Statements — Marketable Securities, p. **28.01**

FASB Interpretation No. 11

Changes in Market Value After the Balance Sheet Date — Marketable Securities, p. **28.01**

FASB Interpretation No. 12

Accounting for Previously Established Allowance Accounts — Marketable Securities, p. **28.01**

FASB Interpretation No. 13

Consolidation of a Parent and Its Subsidiaries Having Different Balance Sheet Dates — Marketable Securities, p. **28.01**

FASB Interpretation No. 14

Reasonable Estimation of the Amount of a Loss — Contingencies, p. **6.01**

FASB Interpretation No. 15

Translation of Unamortized Policy Acquisition Costs by a Stock Life Insurance Company — Foreign Operations and Exchange, p. **16.01**

FASB Interpretation No. 16

Clarification of Definitions and Accounting for Marketable Equity Securities that Become Nonmarketable — Marketable Securities, p. **28.01**

FASB Interpretation No. 17

Applying the Lower of Cost or Market in Translated Financial Statements — Foreign Operations and Exchange, p. **16.01**

FASB Interpretation No. 18

Accounting for Income Taxes in Interim Periods — Income Taxes, p. **19.01**

FASB Interpretation No. 19

Lessee Guarantee of the Residual Value of Leased Property — Leases, p. **26.01**

Cross-Reference

FASB Interpretation No. 20
Reporting Accounting Changes under AICPA Statements of Position — Accounting Changes, p. **1.01**

FASB Interpretation No. 21
Accounting for Leases in a Business Combination — Leases, p. **26.01**

FASB Interpretation No. 22
Applicability of Indefinite Reversal Criteria to Timing Differences — Income Taxes, p. **19.01**

FASB Interpretation No. 23
Leases of Certain Property Owned by a Governmental Unit or Authority — Leases, p. **26.01**

FASB Interpretation No. 24
Leases Involving Only a Part of a Building — Leases, p. **26.01**

FASB Interpretation No. 25
Accounting for an Unused Investment Tax Credit — Investment Tax Credit, p. **25.01**

FASB Interpretation No. 26
Accounting for Purchase of a Leased Asset by the Lessee during the Term of the Lease — Leases, p. **26.01**

FASB Interpretation No. 27
Accounting for a Loss On a Sublease — Leases, p. **26.01**

FASB Interpretation No. 28
Accounting for Stock Appreciation Rights and Other Variable Stock Option or Award Plans — Stock Issued to Employees, p. **39.01**

FASB Interpretation No. 29
Reporting Tax Benefits Realized on Disposition of Investments in Certain Subsidiaries and Other Investees — Income Taxes, p. **19.01**

FASB Interpretation No. 30
Accounting for Involuntary Conversions of Nonmonetary Assets to Monetary Assets — Nonmonetary Transactions, p. **29.01**

GAAP GUIDE / xiii

ACCOUNTING CHANGES

Background

The promulgated GAAP on Accounting Changes are as follows:

    APB-20–Accounting Changes
    FASB-3–Reporting Accounting Changes in Interim Financial Statements
    FASB-32–Specialized Accounting and Reporting Principles and Practices in AICPA Statements of Position and Guides on Accounting and Auditing Matters.
    FASB Interpretation-1–Accounting Changes Related to the Cost of Inventory
    FASB Interpretation-20–Reporting Accounting Changes under AICPA Statements of Position

The promulgated GAAP apply to a full set of financial statements prepared in conformity with GAAP and, to the extent applicable, to regulated industries governed by rate-making regulations. In addition, the promulgated GAAP specifically do not alter or amend any accounting change made in conformity with Industry Audit Guides issued by the AICPA in the past or in the future.

> ***OBSERVATION:*** *Because the SEC rejected the successful efforts accounting method for oil and gas producing companies which is embodied in FASB-19, FASB-19 was subsequently amended in February 1979 by FASB-25.*
>
> *FASB-25 specifically states that for the purposes of the promulgated GAAP on Accounting Changes (APB-20) the provisions of FASB-19 pertaining to the successful efforts methods remain in effect. Therefore, since FASB-19 expresses a preference for the successful efforts method of accounting and rejects other methods, an enterprise that changes to any method other than the successful efforts will have the burden of justifying such change (APB-20).*

Types of Accounting Changes

Accounting changes are broadly classified as (1) changes in an accounting principle, (2) changes in an accounting estimate, and (3) changes in the reporting entity.

    The correction of an error in previously issued financial statements is not an accounting change.

Accounting Changes

Changes in Accounting Principles

There is a presumption that once adopted, an accounting principle should not be changed in accounting for events or for transactions of a similar nature. The pervasive principle of *consistency* enhances the utility of financial statements.

An accounting principle may be changed if the alternative principle is preferable (rule of preferability).

An accounting change should not be made for a single transaction or for a transaction or event in the past that has been terminated or is nonrecurring.

A change in an accounting principle is the result of changing from one acceptable accounting principle to another. A change in practice or in the method of applying an accounting principle or practice is also considered a change in accounting principle. Because the current or future effects of a change in an accounting estimate cannot be separated from an accounting principle, a change in an accounting estimate that is recognized in part or in whole by a change in an accounting principle should be reported as a change in an accounting estimate. For example, a change to expensing from deferring a cost because its future benefits have become doubtful involves both a change in an accounting principle and a change in an estimate, which are inseparable. These types of changes are reported as a change in an accounting estimate.

A change in, or a new, promulgated GAAP or the issuance of an industry audit guide by the AICPA constitutes sufficient support for a change in an accounting principle. Other changes in an accounting principle must be justified by the company making the change.

> **OBSERVATION:** *At the date this edition of the GAAP Guide was being printed, FASB-32 was promulgated, entitled "Specialized Accounting and Reporting Principles and Practices in AICPA Industry Accounting Guides, Industry Audit Guides, and Statements of Position". FASB-32 specifies that the accounting and reporting practices and principles appearing in AICPA Industry Accounting Guides, Industry Audit Guides and Statements of Position shall be designated as preferable accounting principles for purposes of justifying a change in accounting principle as required by APB-20.*

The following borderline areas are not considered a change in an accounting principle:

1. a principle, practice, or method adopted for the first time on new or previously immaterial events or transactions
2. a principle, practice, or method adopted or modified because of events or transactions that are clearly different in substance
3. changing from an accelerated depreciation method to straight line at a planned point in the life of an asset, provided the plan is made at the time of adoption of the accelerated method and the policy is consistently applied

A change in the composition of the elements of cost included in inventory is an accounting change that must be justified on the basis of the rule of preferability (FASB Interpretation-1).

The FASB has delegated to the AICPA the power to issue Statements of Position on how to report accounting changes (FASB Interpretation-20).

The following are the more common changes in accounting principles:

1. a change in the method of pricing inventory, such as LIFO to FIFO or FIFO to LIFO
2. a change in the method of depreciating previously recorded assets, such as from a straight line to an accelerated method or from an accelerated to a straight line method
3. a change in the method of accounting for long-term construction-type contracts, such as from the percentage-of-completion method to the completed-contract method or from the completed-contract method to the percentage-of-completion method

As mentioned earlier, a change in an accounting principle to effectuate a change in an accounting estimate is not considered a change in an accounting principle. It is considered a change in an accounting estimate.

Reporting a Change in an Accounting Principle

Although the presumption is that once an accounting principle has been adopted it should not be changed, when a change is necessary it should be recognized by including the cumulative effect in the net income of the period of change and not by restating the financial statements of prior periods. The cumulative effect of a change in an

Accounting Changes

accounting principle is equal to the total direct effects and any indirect effects recorded on the books, of the change on prior periods. The effect of the change in an accounting principle for the current period is not included in the cumulative effect, but the net income for the current period is reported on a basis that includes the newly adopted accounting principle.

Although the cumulative effect is not an extraordinary item, it is shown in the income statement net of related tax effects between extraordinary items and net income, as follows:

Income before extraordinary items (includes the effect of a change in an accounting principle for the current year	$XX,XXX
Extraordinary items (*Note:* _____)–net of related tax effects	X,XXX
Cumulative effect of a change in an accounting principle (includes the effect of a change in an accounting principle for prior years)–net of related tax effects	X,XXX
Net income	$XX,XXX

Earnings per share shown on the face of the income statement should include the per share amount attributable to the cumulative effects of the accounting change (net of related taxes).

At this juncture it may be well to establish the fact that the promulgated GAAP provides some exceptions to the rule of not restating prior-year financial statements in accounting for a change in an accounting principle. The following specific items are exceptions to the general rule, and prior-period financial statements must be restated for them in reporting a change in an accounting principle:

1. change from LIFO method of inventory pricing to another method
2. change in accounting for long-term construction-type contracts
3. change to or from the "full cost" method of accounting in the extractive industries
4. one-time change for closely held corporations in connection

with a public offering of its equity securities, or when such a company first issues financial statements (a) for obtaining additional equity capital from investors, (b) for effecting a business combination, or (c) for registering securities

In computing the cumulative effect of a change in an accounting principle, the *direct effects* are always included, but the *nondiscretionary effects* (indirect effects) are included only if they have been recorded on the books. Direct effects of a change in an accounting principle are those retroactive adjustments which are necessary to restate the financial statements of prior periods. Nondiscretionary effects are those which would have been recognized if the newly adopted accounting principle had been followed in prior period(s). In other words, nondiscretionary effects are those which were caused by the direct effects. For example, a change from an accelerated depreciation method to the straight line method will directly affect the net income of the prior periods in which the accelerated method was used. However, profit-sharing expense, incentive compensation costs and royalties based on net income are affected only if the base on which they were computed (net income, income before extraordinary items, etc.) is changed. Therefore, when a prior-period income from operations is changed by a direct effect of a change in an accounting principle, it may result in a nondiscretionary effect.

Direct effects are always included as part of the cumulative effect, but nondiscretionary effects are included only if they were recorded on the books in the prior period(s).

When an accounting change from FIFO to LIFO is made in pricing inventory, it may be impossible to compute the cumulative effect. In this and other situations where the cumulative effect cannot be determined, the disclosure of the cumulative effect is omitted. However, the amount of effect in the current year and its per share information should be disclosed in a footnote. The reason for omitting the cumulative effect should also be fully disclosed.

A new depreciation method may be adopted for newly acquired long-lived assets and all future assets of the same class. This does not constitute a change in an accounting principle under the promulgated GAAP. However, if the new depreciation method is applied to previously acquired long-lived assets of the same class, a change in an accounting principle occurs.

If an accounting change is considered immaterial in the year of change but is reasonably expected to become material in subsequent periods, it should be fully disclosed in the year of change.

Accounting Changes

In reporting the cumulative effect of a change in an accounting principle, two presentations for income before extraordinary items and for net income must be made. The regular presentation includes, in total amounts and amounts per share, for both primary and fully diluted EPS (1) the current year reflecting the new accounting principle and the cumulative effect on prior years and (2) any prior years as previously presented. The *pro forma* portion of the presentation includes, in total amounts and per share amounts, for both primary and fully diluted EPS (1) the current year reflecting the new accounting principle and (2) *pro forma* amounts for any prior years presented reflecting the effect of the new accounting principle. The following illustrates the regular and *pro forma* presentation that is required.

Regular portion:	1978	1977
Income before extraordinary item(s) and cumulative effect of a change in an accounting principle	$XX,XXX	$XX,XXX
Extraordinary item(s) [describe]	(X,XXX)	X,XXX
Cumulative effect on prior years (to December 31, 1977) of a change in an accounting principle	X,XXX	-
Net income	$XX,XXX	$XX,XXX
Per share amounts–no dilution:		
Income before extraordinary item(s) and cumulative effect of a change in an accounting principle	$X.XX	$X.XX
Extraordinary item(s)	(.XX)	.XX
Cumulative effect on prior years (to December 31, 1977) of a change in an accounting principle	.XX	-
Net income per share–primary	$X.XX	$X.XX
Per share amounts–fully diluted:		
Income before extraordinary item(s) and cumulative effect of a change in an accounting principle	$X.XX	$X.XX
Extraordinary item(s)	(.XX)	.XX
Cumulative effect on prior years (to December 31, 1977) of a change in an accounting principle	.XX	-
Net income per share-fully diluted	$X.XX	$X.XX

Pro forma portion:
Income before extraordinary item(s),
  assuming accounting change is
  applied retroactively $XX,XXX $XX,XXX
Earnings per share–no dilution $X.XX $X.XX
Earnings per share–fully diluted $X.XX $X.XX
Net income $XX,XXX $XX,XXX
Earnings per share–no dilution $X.XX $X.XX
Earnings per share–fully diluted $X.XX $X.XX

Note: As required by GAAP, extraordinary items and the cumulative effect on prior years are both shown on financial statements net of any related tax.

The nature, justification, and preferability (if applicable) of a change in an accounting principle and its effects on income should be clearly disclosed in the financial statements of the period in which the change is made.

For all changes in accounting principles where there is no restatement of prior financial statements, the following should be observed:

1. Prior-period comparative financial statements should be presented as previously reported.

2. The cumulative effect of changing to a new accounting principle should be made in net income of the period of the change and should be shown in the income statement between extraordinary items and net income. The effect of the change is *not* an extraordinary item, but should be reported in a similar manner.

    The amount of cumulative effect to be reported is the difference between (a) retained earnings at the beginning of the period of change and (b) retained earnings at the beginning of the period of change adjusted for the retroactive cumulative effect of the new accounting change, including related income tax effect.

3. The earnings per share information on the face of the income statement should include the per share amount of the cumulative effect of the change.

4. The earnings per share (primary and diluted) for income before extraordinary items and net income should be shown on the face of the income statement for all periods presented.

Reporting Accounting Changes–Interim Periods

The cumulative effect of an accounting change is always included in net income of the first interim period, regardless of which period during the year the accounting change occurs. If the accounting change occurs in other than the first interim period, the current and prior-period interim statements should be restated to include the newly adopted accounting principle. However, the cumulative effect of the change in an accounting principle is included only in the net income of the first interim period.

When the cumulative effects of a change in an accounting principle cannot be determined, the *pro forma* amounts cannot be computed. In this event, as mentioned earlier, the cumulative effect and *pro forma* amounts are omitted. However, the amount of effect of adopting the new accounting principle and its per share data for each interim period and year-to-date amounts must be disclosed in a footnote to the financial statements, along with the reasons for omitting the cumulative effect and *pro forma* information.

Publicly traded companies that do not issue separate fourth-quarter reports must disclose in a note to their annual reports any effect of an accounting change made during the fourth quarter. This is similar to other disclosure requirements of publicly traded companies that do not issue fourth-quarter interim reports.

The following disclosure concerning a cumulative effect type accounting change should be made in interim financial reports:

1. The nature and justification of the change should be made in the interim period in which the new accounting principle is adopted.
2. The effects of the accounting change on income from continuing operations, net income, and related per share data for both, should be made
   a. in the interim period in which the change is made
   b. in each, if any, prior interim period
   c. in each, if any, restated prior interim period
   d. in year-to-date and in last twelve-months-to-date financial reports that include the adoption of a new accounting principle
   e. in interim financial reports of the fiscal year, subsequent to the interim period in which the accounting change was adopted
3. The *pro forma* effects of the accounting change on income

from continuing operations, net income, and related per share data, should be made:
a. for the interim period in which the change is made
b. for any interim period of prior fiscal years for which financial information is presented
c. in year-to-date and last twelve-months-to-date financial reports that include the adoption of a new accounting principle

If no interim periods of prior fiscal years are presented, footnote disclosure for the corresponding interim period of the immediate fiscal year in which the accounting change occurred should be made for actual and *pro forma* income from continuing operations, net income, and related per share data.

Changes in an Accounting Estimate

A change in an accounting estimate is usually the result of new events, changing conditions, more experience, or additional information, any of which requires the revision of previous estimates.

Estimates are necessary in determining uncollectible receivables, salvage values, useful lives, provisions for warranty, and a multitude of other items involved in preparing financial statements.

A change in a depreciation method for a previously recorded asset is a change in an accounting principle, but a change in the estimated useful life or in the salvage value of a previously recorded asset is a change in an accounting estimate.

Reporting a Change in an Accounting Estimate

A change in an accounting estimate *should not* be accounted for by restatement of prior years' financial statements. The effect of the change in accounting estimates should be accounted for (1) in the period of change, if the change affects only that period, or (2) in the period of change and future periods, if the change affects both.

A change in an accounting estimate caused in part or in whole by a change in an accounting principle should be reported as a change in an accounting estimate.

Disclosure should be made in current-period financial statements of the effects of a change in an accounting estimate on income before extraordinary items, net income, and related per share data.

If a change in an accounting estimate affects future periods, the effect on income before extraordinary items, net income, and the related per share information should be disclosed in the income statement.

Ordinary accounting estimates for uncollectible accounts or inventory adjustments, made each period, do not have to be disclosed unless they are material.

Reporting a Change in an Entity

Restatement of prior years' financial statments is necessary when an accounting change results in financial statements that are actually statements of a different reporting entity.

All prior and current periods presented should be restated to reflect financial information for the new reporting entity.

Full disclosure should be made describing the nature of the change and the reason for it.

Changes in income before extraordinary items, net income, and related earnings per share should be adequately disclosed.

Reporting Corrections of Errors

Prior-period errors in financial statements discovered subsequently should be reported as prior-period adjustments. Recent promulgated GAAP (FASB-16) limits prior-period adjustments:

1. to corrections of errors in financial statements of prior periods
2. to adjustments resulting from the realization of income tax benefits of preacquisition operating-loss carryforwards of purchased subsidiaries

Errors result from mistakes in mathematics and application of an accounting principle or from misjudgment in the use of facts. A change in an accounting estimate is the result of new information, changing conditions, more experience, or additional information that requires the revision of previous estimates. A change from an unacceptable accounting principle to a generally accepted one is a correction of a prior-period error (APB-20).

The nature of the error and the effect of its correction on income before extraordinary items, net income, and the related per share data must be fully disclosed in the period the error is discovered and corrected.

Financial Summaries

The presentation of accounting changes, including *pro forma* amounts, in financial summaries, including five year summaries, should be presented in the same way as presented in the primary financial statements (APB-20).

Comprehensive Illustration

The following is a comprehensive illustration of presenting a change in an accounting principle.

At the end of 1977, a company decides to change from an accelerated method of recording depreciation on plant equipment to the straight line method. The direct effect of this change is $600,000 (1977–$100,000; 1976–$60,000; 1975–$100,000; 1974–$140,000; 1973 and prior–$200,000). The nondiscretionary items affected by the change in an accounting principle are an incentive bonus plan and royalties, which are 10% of the annual net income. Nondiscretionary items have been recorded on the books. Income tax rates are 50%. The company has 1,000,000 shares of common stock outstanding, and the comparative income statements for 1976 and 1977 reflect the following without any adjustments for the accounting change:

	1977	1976
Income before extraordinary item(s)	$2,400,000	$2,200,000
Less: Extraordinary item(s) (*Note:* ___)	70,000	—
Net income	$2,330,000	$2,200,000
Primary earnings per share before extraordinary item(s)	$ 2.40	$ 2.20
Extraordinary item(s)	(0.07)	—
Net Income	$ 2.33	$ 2.20

Adjustments needed in the previous information to account for the change in the accounting principle:

1. 1977 figures must be adjusted as follows:

1977 Direct effect (increases income)	$100,000
1977 Nondiscretionary effects (10%)	(10,000)
Total	$ 90,000
Less: Income taxes	45,000
Net effect on 1977	$ 45,000

2. The cumulative effect of the accounting change to be shown as a separate item between extraordinary income and net income in 1977 is:

1976 and prior years' direct effect	$500,000
1976 and prior years' nondiscretionary effects (10%) (decreases income)	(50,000)
Total	$450,000
Less: Income taxes	225,000
Net cumulative effect	$225,000

3. The 1976 figures must be adjusted as follows:

1976 direct effect (increases income)	$ 60,000
1976 nondiscretionary effects (10%)	(6,000)
Total	$ 54,000
Less: Income taxes	27,000
Net effect on 1976	$ 27,000

GAAP require two presentations of net income and EPS, as follows.

Regular Portion

1. The current year reflecting the new accounting principle and the cumulative effect on prior years.
2. Any prior years as previously presented.

Pro forma Portion

1. The current year reflecting the new accounting principle.
2. *Pro forma* amounts for any prior years presented reflecting the effect of the new accounting principle.

Accounting Changes

The statement presentation for our illustration, taking into consideration the effects of the change in using a different depreciation method, is:

	1977	1976
Income before extraordinary item(s) and cumulative effect of a change in accounting principle	$2,445,000	$2,200,000
Extraordinary item (*Note:___*)	(70,000)	—
Cumulative effect on prior years (to December 31, 1976) of changing to a different depreciation method (Note___)	225,000	—
Net income	$2,600,000	$2,200,000
EPS before extraordinary item(s)	$ 2.45	$ 2.20
Extraordinary item	(0.07)	—
Cumulative effect on prior years (to December 31, 1976) of changing to a different depreciation method	.22	—
Net income	$ 2.60	$ 2.20

Pro forma amounts assuming the new depreciation method is applied retroactively:

Income before extraordinary item(s)	$2,445,000	$2,227,000
Earnings per share	$ 2.45	$ 2.23
Net income	$2,375,000	$2,227,000
Earnings per share	$ 2.38	$ 2.23

The Company in the above illustration had no dilutive securities. Thus, the presentation for fully diluted EPS is omitted.

ACCOUNTING POLICIES

Background

The source of promulgated GAAP for Disclosure of Accounting Policies is APB-22. This promulgated GAAP specifically states that its provisions be followed by nonprofit entities and, in accordance with the Addendum to APB-2, companies in regulated industries would also have to comply. However, unaudited interim reports for companies which have not changed their accounting policies since the end of the preceding fiscal year need not disclose accounting policies in such interim reports.

> *OBSERVATION: Unaudited reports issued for internal use only and certain other special reports, apparently would not have to comply with APB-22.*
>
> *The promulgated GAAP states that it does not supersede any other promulgated GAAP issued previously.*

Overview

All financial statements covered by APB-22 that purport to present financial position, results of operations, and changes in financial position in accordance with GAAP must comply fully with the promulgated GAAP on disclosure of accounting policies.

Significant Accounting Policies

The preferable presentation of disclosing accounting policies is in the first footnote of the financial statements, under the caption Summary of Significant Accounting Policies. The promulgated GAAP (APB-22) specifically states this preference, but mentions the need for flexibility in the matter of formats.

The requirement of the promulgated GAAP is that a description of all significant accounting policies of a reporting entity should be included as an integral part of the financial statements. Basis of consolidation, depreciation methods, amortization of intangibles, inventory pricing, recognition of profit on long-term construction type contracts, and recognition of revenue from franchising and leasing operations are the examples described in the opinion. However, disclosure of accounting policies should not be duplicated if presented elsewhere as an integral part of the financial statements. In disclosing accounting policies it may become necessary to refer to items presented elsewhere in the report, such as in the case of a change in an accounting principle which requires specific treatment.

Disclosure

Both the accounting principle and the method of applying such a principle should be disclosed. Informed professional judgment is necessary to select for disclosure those principles which materially affect the financial position, results of operations, and changes in financial position. However, accounting principles and their method of application in the following areas are considered particularly important:

1. A selection from existing acceptable alternatives
2. The areas that are peculiar to a specific industry in which the entity functions
3. Unusual and innovative application of GAAP

Comprehensive Illustration

The following are comprehensive illustrations of the disclosure of significant accounting policies.

Principles of consolidation The consolidated financial statements include the assets, liabilities, revenues, and expenses of all significant subsidiaries. All significant intercompany transactions have been eliminated in consolidation. Investments in significant companies which are 20 to 50 percent owned are carried at equity in net assets and the corporation's share of earnings is included in income. All other investments are carried at cost or less.

Fixed assets and depreciation Fixed assets are carried at cost. Expenditures for replacements are capitalized, and the replaced items are retired. Maintenance and repairs are charged to operations. Gains and losses from the sale of fixed assets are included in income. Depreciation is calculated on a straight-line basis utilizing U.S. Internal Revenue Service guidelines lives. The Corporation and its subsidiaries use other depreciation methods (generally accelerated) for tax purposes where appropriate.

Accounting Policies

Inventories Inventory values are stated at the lower of cost or market using the last-in, first-out (LIFO) method for substantially all qualifying domestic inventories and the average cost method for other inventories.

Income taxes Provision has been made for deferred income taxes where differences exist between the period in which transactions, principally relating to depreciation, affect taxable income and the period in which they enter into the determination of income in the financial statements. The investment tax credit is deferred and amortized over the average life of the fixed assets by reductions in the provision for income taxes.

Pension plan It is the policy of the company and its consolidated subsidiaries to fund pension costs as accrued. Prior service costs are amortized over varying periods not exceeding 40 years.

Patents, trade marks, and goodwill Amounts paid for purchased patents and for securities of newly acquired subsidiaries in excess of the fair value of the net assets of such subsidiaries have been charged to patents, trade marks, and goodwill. The portion of such amounts determined to be attributable to patents is amortized over their remaining lives and the balance is amortized over the estimated period of benefit but not more than 40 years.

Translation of foreign currencies Accounts carried in foreign currencies are translated into U.S. dollars as follows: (a) inventories, fixed assets, investments, intangibles, and deferred credits at historical rates; (b) all other assets and liabilities at year-end rates; (c) income and expenses at monthly rates, except for depreciation and amortization of those balance sheet accounts translated at historical rates. Gains and losses resulting from exchange rate fluctuations are credited or charged to income currently.

Earnings per share Earnings per share is based on the weighted average number of shares of common stock outstanding in each year. There would have been no material dilutive effect on net income per share for 19XX or 19XX if convertible securities had been converted and if outstanding stock options had been exercised.

BUSINESS COMBINATIONS

Background

The promulgated GAAP for business combinations are covered by APB-16, Accounting for Business Combinations.

Both incorporated and unincorporated entities are covered by APB-16. However, certain types of transactions are not covered by APB-16, as follows:

1. acquisition of any minority interests in a subsidiary (APB-16 does require the use of the purchase method for this type of transaction)
2. creation by a corporation of a newly formed corporation for the purpose of transferring the corporation's net assets to the newly formed corporation
3. transfer of net assets or the exchange of shares of stock between companies under common control

Companies in regulated industries are specifically covered by APB-16, and must comply in accordance with the Addendum to APB-2.

Overview

A business combination occurs when one entity acquires part or all of another entity with the object of eliminating any duplication and of combining resources.

The purchase method of accounting for a business combination reflects the acquisition of one company by another. The difference, if any, between the fair value of the identifiable assets purchased and the amount paid is recorded as goodwill. The acquiring company reports the results of operations of the acquisition from the date it is acquired.

The pooling-of-interests method of accounting for a business combination reflects the union of ownership between the entities involved. The pooling is accomplished primarily by the issuance of common voting stock of the acquiring company. Goodwill is never recorded in a pooling of interests, because the assets and liabilities of the companies involved are carried forward at their recorded amounts. Results of operations are restated for prior periods as if the entities involved had always been combined.

Purchase Method

Business combinations accounted for by the purchase method are recorded at cost. The determination of cost is usually based on the fair value of the property acquired or the fair value of the property given up, whichever is more clearly evident. An asset acquired for cash is recorded at the amount disbursed. In an exchange of assets where no cash is involved, cost is determined by the fair value of the assets given up or received, whichever is more clearly evident. If stock is issued in exchange for assets, cost is determined by the fair value of the assets acquired, which is tantamount to the consideration received for the stock issued.

The cost of a liability assumed in a business combination is the present value of the amount that will eventually be paid. The difference between the fixed rate of debt securities assumed and the effective or current yield rate for comparable securities should be recorded as a premium or a discount (APB-21).

The market price of traded securities is usually clear evidence of fair value. However, the market price of a traded security issued in a business combination may have to be adjusted for the quantity issued, price fluctuations, and issue costs. A good barometer for fair value may be the average market price for a period before and after the business combination. In addition, independent appraisals are frequently useful in determining fair value.

Registration and issuing costs of equity securities issued in a business combination accounted for by the purchase method are deducted from the fair value of such securities. All direct costs of the acquisition are included as part of the total cost of the acquisition.

The recorded cost of an acquisition is equal to the determinable amount of cash and other net assets that are unconditionally surrendered at the date of acquisition. Any contingent additional consideration is fully disclosed in the financial statements but is not recorded as a liability. Contingently issuable debt or equity securities are not shown as outstanding until the contingency is definitely resolved. The fact that contingently issuable debt or equity securities are held by an independent escrow agent does not alter the treatment that such securities are not considered outstanding.

Contingent considerations may be based on maintaining or achieving specific earning levels over future periods or may be based on a security's maintaining or achieving a specific market price.

When a contingency consideration based on earnings is achieved, the acquiring company records the current fair value of the additional consideration. At this juncture, it is more than likely that the increase in the cost of the acquisition will be in the form of goodwill. In this event, the goodwill should be amortized over the remaining life of the acquired asset, but in no event more than 40 years (APB-17).

When a contingency consideration based on maintaining or exceeding a specific market price for the securities issued to consummate the acquisition is not achieved, the acquiring company will have to issue additional securities in accordance with the contingency arrangements. The issuance of the additional contingency securities is based on their then-current fair value but does not increase the overall cost of the acquisition, because the recorded cost of the original securities issued is reduced by the same amount. The only item that changes is the total number of shares issued for the acquisition. An example will clarify the situation.

A issues 1,000 shares of its common stock to a seller for an acquisition. The market price of the stock, at the date of the sale, was $12 per share, and A guarantees that, at the end of two years, if the market price is less than $12 per share, it will issue additional shares to make up any difference. Under the agreed-upon conditions A deposits 500 shares of stock with an independent escrow agent.

In accordance with the promulgated GAAP (APB-16), A records the acquisition at $12,000 ($12 per share × 1,000). At the end of the two years the market price of the stock is $10 per share, and the escrow agent delivers 200 shares to the seller in accordance with the seller's instructions. The remainder of the shares is returned to A.

A records the issuance of the 200 additional shares at the current market price of $10 per share for a total of $2,000, and correspondingly reduces the original stock issued to $10 per share, or a total of $10,000. The total acquisition price remains $12,000, and only the number of shares issued changes from 1,000 to 1,200.

In the event that debt securities are issued in an acquisition and that subsequently additional debt securities are issued as contingent consideration, the reduction in the value results in the necessity to record a discount on the debt securities. Discounts arising in this manner are amortized over the life of the securities, commencing from the date the additional securities are issued.

Contingent consideration that provides compensation for serv-

Business Combinations

ices or use of property are accounted for as expenses of the appropriate period on resolution of the contingency.

Interest or dividends paid or accrued on contingent securities during the contingency period are accounted for in the same manner as the underlying security. Therefore, interest expense or dividend distributions on contingent securities are not recorded until the contingency is resolved. In the event a contingency is resolved which results in the payment of an amount for interest or dividends on the contingent securities, that amount is added to the cost of the acquisition at the date of distribution.

When a savings and loan association is acquired in a business combination accounted for by the *purchase* method, the assets and liabilities acquired are recorded at their fair values on the date of acquisition. This is called the *separate valuation* method, as opposed to the *net spread* method, which values the purchase as a whole, based on the spread between interest rates received on the mortgage portfolio and interest rates paid on savings accounts. The net spread method is unacceptable for GAAP purposes.

In applying the separate valuation method, receivables are recorded at their present values, using appropriate current interest rates, less allowances for uncollectibility and collection. Payables are recorded at the present values of amounts to be paid, determined at appropriate current interest rates.

Any portion of the purchase price that cannot be assigned to specifically identifiable tangible and intangible assets acquired, less liabilities assumed, shall be recorded as goodwill. Goodwill must be amortized by the straight line method (APB-17), unless both the following conditions are met:

1. Part or all of the recorded goodwill includes one or more of the following factors which could not be separately determined:
    a. capacity of existing savings accounts and loan accounts to generate future income and/or additional business or new business
    b. nature of territory served
2. The anticipated benefits to be received from the factors in 1 above are expected to decline over their estimated lives.
    Only in those cases where both the above conditions are met can accelerated methods be used to amortize the purchased goodwill (FASB Interpretation 9).

Allocating cost The total cost of an acquisition must be allocated to the individual assets acquired. Each identifiable asset is assigned a cost equal to its fair value. Independent appraisals and/or subsequent sales of acquired assets may provide evidence of fair value. Some methods of determining values are:

1. Inventories—net realizable value less a reasonable profit, except raw material, which should be valued at current replacement cost
2. Receivables—present value of the amount that will be received, less an allowance for uncollectible accounts
3. Marketable securities—net realizable value
4. Plant and equipment—appraised values in accordance with intended use
5. Liabilities—present value of the amount to be paid

An acquiring corporation should allocate costs to assets received and liabilities assumed as follows:

1. All identifiable assets and liabilities should be assigned a portion of the total cost based on fair value at the date of acquisition.
2. Any excess of cost over the amount assigned to identifiable assets and liabilities should be recorded as goodwill.
3. In the event that the assignable fair values of net assets acquired exceed the cost (sometimes referred to as negative goodwill), the noncurrent assets acquired (excluding long-term investments in marketable securities) should be reduced proportionately. Excess of net assets over cost (negative goodwill) should not be recorded unless all the noncurrent assets acquired (excluding long-term investments in marketable securities) have been reduced to zero.

Disclosure for the Purchase Method

The following disclosures should be made in the period in which a business combination occurs and is accounted for by the purchase method:

Business Combinations

1. name, brief description, and total cost, of the acquisition
2. method of accounting, that is, the purchase method
3. period for which results of operations of the acquisition are included in the income statement (usually starts from the date of acquisition)
4. description of the plan for amortization of acquired goodwill
5. other pertinent information such as contingent payments, options, or other commitments
6. combining of several minor acquisitions for disclosure purposes is acceptable

The following supplemental information should be disclosed in the notes to the financial statements of an acquiring company in the year of acquisition:

1. Results of operations for the current period combining the acquisition as though it were acquired at the beginning of the period.
2. If comparative statements are presented, results of operations should include the acquisition as though it were acquired at the beginning of the comparative statement period.

Purchase versus Pooling of Interests

A purchase of assets is accounted for differently from a purchase of a stock interest. In both cases, however, goodwill or negative goodwill can arise. A pooling of interests is accounted for in the same way whether there is an exchange of stock for stock or of stock for net assets. In addition, goodwill or negative goodwill is never recorded in a pooling of interests.

Purchase of assets Each identifiable asset is assigned its fair value, liabilities assumed are deducted from the total assigned fair values, and the difference is either goodwill or negative goodwill.

On July 1, 1977, Jones Company sold all its net assets and business to Smith Corporation for $415,000. The following is Jones Company's balance sheet as at July 1, 1977:

BALANCE SHEET

Cash	$ 20,000
Accounts receivable	72,000
Allowance for doubtful accounts	(8,000)
Inventory	120,000
Plant and equipment	260,000
Total assets	$464,000
Accounts payable	$ 60,000
Accrued expenses	5,000
Mortgage payable–plant	120,000
Common stock	200,000
Retained earnings	79,000
Total liabilities and equity	$464,000

Additional information:

Confirmation of the accounts receivable revealed that $10,000 were uncollectible.

The physical inventory count was $138,000 (fair value).

The fair value of the plant and equipment was $340,000.

The journal entry to record the investment on the books of Smith Corporation is:

Investment in Jones Co. (100%) $415,000
    Cash $415,000

The computation of goodwill involved in the transaction is:

Computation of Goodwill

Assets	$464,000
Liabilities	
($60,000 + $5,000 + $120,000)	185,000
Total	$279,000
Additional uncollectibles	(2,000)
Increase in inventory	18,000
Increase in plant and equipment	80,000
Adjusted net assets	$375,000
Cost of purchase	415,000
Goodwill	$ 40,000

Business Combinations

Assume that the purchase price was $350,000.

Adjusted net assets	$375,000
Cost of purchase	350,000
Negative goodwill	$ 25,000

Negative goodwill does not get recorded, because noncurrent assets (plant and equipment) are reduced to $315,000.

Negative goodwill should never be recorded unless all the noncurrent assets acquired, except long-term investments in marketable securities, have been proportionately reduced to zero.

If after reducing the noncurrent assets (except long-term investment in marketable securities) to zero a credit still remains, it should be classified as a deferred credit—"excess of acquired stock over cost"—and should be amortized to income over the period that is expected to benefit, but not to exceed 40 years (APB-17).

Goodwill may not be written off as a lump sum to capital surplus or retained earnings, nor be reduced to a nominal amount, at or immediately after acquisition.

Purchase of a stock interest The percentage of book value acquired is subtracted from the purchase price, and any residue is goodwill or negative goodwill.

ABC Corporation purchased for $1,500,000 90% of the common stock and 50% of the preferred stock of XYZ Corporation. At the date of acquisition, XYZ Corporation's stockholders' equity was:

Stockholders' Equity

Common stock 100,000 shares, $5 par, all authorized, issued and outstanding	$ 500,000
5% preferred stock, 10,000 shares, all authorized, issued and outstanding	1,000,000
Paid-in capital	200,000
Retained earnings	300,000
Total stockholders' equity	$2,000,000

The computation of the goodwill involved in the transaction is:

Business Combinations

	Computation of Goodwill		
	Minority Interests (10%)	Preferred Stock	ABC Corporation (90%)
Common stock	$ 50,000		$ 450,000
Preferred stock		$500,000	500,000
Paid-in capital	20,000		180,000
Retained earnings	30,000		270,000
Totals	$100,000	$500,000	$1,400,000
Cost of 90% common and 50% preferred			1,500,000
Goodwill			$ 100,000

The journal entry to record the transaction is:

Investment in XYZ Corporation $1,500,000
   Cash $1,500,000

Goodwill of $100,000 was involved.

Goodwill is not necessarily the difference between cost and the book value of an investment, unless the book value is equal to the fair value of the underlying assets. The underlying assets represented by an investment must be individually assigned a fair value at the date of acquisition, and if the assigned fair values are less than the investment, the difference is goodwill. For consolidation purposes, the acquisition of a stock investment may be considered the purchase price paid for an interest in the underlying net assets of a business.

It must be remembered that if any excess of cost over acquired book value is allocated to depreciable or amortizable assets, the depreciation or amortization expense of subsequent periods must be increased to spread the amount of such excess over the remaining life of the assets.

If after assigning values to the underlying assets of an investment there is resulting goodwill, it must be amortized over a period of 40 years or less, starting from the date of the acquisition of the investment. However, since consolidating adjustments and eliminations are never posted on the books, it is necessary to reduce the

Business Combinations

beginning consolidated retained earnings, in the years subsequent to the first year, by the amount of depreciation or amortization of prior years.

Assuming that P was amortizing $10,000 of the excess of cost over book value (goodwill) over a 10-year period, the consolidated adjustment for the second full year would be:

Consolidated retained earnings	$1,000	
Amortization, current year	1,000	
Excess of cost over book value		$2,000

Goodwill should not be recorded where it is obvious that the underlying asset in a stock interest purchase or the net assets in a straight asset purchase are undervalued. Any excess cost over book value at the date of acquisition should be assigned specifically to these undervalued assets.

When any excess cost over book value (goodwill) is assigned to specific assets, it must be depreciated or amortized on the consolidated work papers.

Excess cost over book value of $25,000 is assigned (1) $5,000 to a parcel of land and (2) $20,000 to the building located on the land. The building has a 20-year life, and the following adjusting journal entry must be made on the consolidated work papers (assume one full year):

Land	$ 5,000	
Building	20,000	
Investment account		$25,000
Depreciation	$ 1,000	
Accumulated depreciation		$ 1,000

Since consolidated adjusting journal entries are never posted on the books, this journal entry must be repeated each year.

In the final year, when the building is completely depreciated, the following entry is made on the consolidated work papers:

Accumulated depreciation	$20,000	
Fixed asset–building		$20,000

The entry for the land remains and is repeated each year on the consolidated work papers as long as the land is part of the assets of the consolidated group.

If the residue in a purchase is negative goodwill, the noncurrent assets acquired, if any, (excluding long-term investments in marketable securities) must be reduced to zero before any negative goodwill can be recorded and amortized.

All transactions for cash or stock are purchases except the exchange, by the acquirer, of common voting stock for 90% or more of the common voting stock or all the net assets of the seller (pooling of interests).

In other words all transactions are purchases except those which qualify as a pooling of interests.

In a purchase, operations of the investee are taken into consideration by the investor, from the date of the purchase. There is no retroactive restatement of any financial statements.

Different Classes of Capital Stock

The main point to remember in computing a parent's investment in a subsidiary is to isolate those elements of the subsidiary's stockholders' equity to which the parent company is actually entitled. For instance, if the subsidiary had minority interests, they would have to be excluded in computing the parent's investment. Other items that must be considered are different classes of stock, dividends in arrears, and liquidating dividends. If another class of stock is participating, it must share in the retained earnings of the subsidiary to the extent of its participation. If another class of stock is cumulative as to dividends and dividends are in arrears, the amount of dividends in arrear must be deducted from retained earnings before determining the parent's interest in the subsidiary's stockholders' equity.

The following are guidelines for preferred stock issues:

1. Nonparticipating and noncumulative preferred stocks require no apportionment of retained earnings.

Business Combinations

2. Nonparticipating and cumulative preferred stocks require an apportionment only to the extent of any dividends in arrears.
3. Participating preferred stock requires an apportionment of retained earnings, under all circumstances. The apportion is made on the basis of the total dollar amount of the par or stated values of the securities involved.

On January 1, 1977, P acquires for $5,200,000 80% of the common stock and 60% of the 5% preferred stock of S. On the date of acquisition the stockholders' equity of S consisted of:

	Shares	Dollars
Common stock ($1 par)	1,000,000	$1,000,000
5% preferred stock ($100 par) nonparticipating and cumulative	50,000	5,000,000
3% preferred stock ($10 par) fully participating and noncumulative	200,000	2,000,000
Retained earnings		2,000,000

The 5% preferred stock has a liquiding preference value of $105 per share and dividends of $350,000 are in arrears. Determine the parent's share of the subsidiary's stockholders' equity as of the date of acquisition.

Apportionment of Retained Earnings

Total retained earnings	$2,000,000
Less: Dividends in arrears–preferred	350,000
Balance	$1,650,000
Less: Liquidating preference dividend $5	250,000
Balance	$1,400,000
Less: 20% minority interest	280,000
Balance to apportion	$1,120,000
3% preferred, 2/3	746,667
Balance to P Company	$ 373,333

The 3% preferred stock ($10 par) participates fully with the common stock ($1 par) in the earnings of the company. The apportionment is made on the basis of the total par or stated value dollars amount of the common and 3% preferred, which are $1,000,000 and $2,000,000 respectively. Therefore, the apportionment of retained earnings after all adjustments is 1/3 to common shareholders and 2/3 to the 3% participating preferred shareholders.

Business Combinations

	Computation of P's Investment			
	Minority Interests 20%	5% Preferred	Participating Preferred	P Company 80%
Common stock	$200,000			$ 800,000
5% preferred		$5,000,000		
3% preferred–participating			$2,000,000	
Retained earnings	280,000		746,667	373,333
Dividend–arrears		350,000		
Liquidating dividend		250,000		
Totals	$480,000	$5,600,000	$2,746,667	$1,173,333
60% of preferred to P		3,360,000		3,360,000
Totals	$480,000	$2,240,000	$2,746,667	$4,533,333
Cost of 80% of common and 60% of preferred				5,200,000
Goodwill				$ 666,667

Acquisition of Stock Directly from Subsidiary

Sometimes a stock interest is acquired directly from the investee. That is, a subsidiary will sell some of its own capital stock to another company. In this event, it must be remembered that the amount paid for capital stock must be added to the stockholders' equity before determining the acquirer's stock interest.

Company S had 100,000 shares of $1 par capital stock outstanding ($100,000) and $60,000 of retained earnings. On January 1, 1977, Company S authorized an additional 200,000 shares of capital stock $1 par and sold them to P Company for $250,000. Determine P Company's stock interest in S Company.

Computation of S Company's Stockholders' Equity	
Common stock $1 par (300,000 shares)	$300,000
Paid-in capital–common	50,000
Retained earnings	60,000
Total	$410,000

Business Combinations

<table>
<tr><td colspan="4" align="center">Computation of P's Investment in S</td></tr>
<tr><td></td><td></td><td>Minority
Interests
33⅓%</td><td>P
Company
66⅔%</td></tr>
<tr><td colspan="2">Common stock</td><td>$100,000</td><td>$200,000</td></tr>
<tr><td colspan="2">Paid-in capital</td><td>16,667</td><td>33,333</td></tr>
<tr><td colspan="2">Retained earnings</td><td>20,000</td><td>40,000</td></tr>
<tr><td colspan="2">Totals</td><td>$136,667</td><td>$273,333</td></tr>
<tr><td colspan="2">Cost of P's 66⅔%</td><td></td><td>250,000</td></tr>
<tr><td colspan="2">Negative goodwill</td><td></td><td>$ 23,333</td></tr>
</table>

Step-by-Step Acquisition

A corporation may acquire a subsidiary in more than one transaction. In this case, any goodwill or negative goodwill involved must be computed at the time of each step-by-step transaction. When control is achieved, it is necessary to adjust to the equity method any earlier step acquisition accounted for by the cost method. The result of this treatment is that the parent's portion of the undistributed earnings of the subsidiary for the period prior to achieving control is added to the investment account of the parent.

Assume that Company P acquired an interest in Company S in two steps: (1) acquired 20% of the outstanding common stock for $200,000; and (2) the following year acquired an additional 60% for $500,000. At the dates of acquisition, the equity book value for Company S was $900,000 and $1,100,000, respectively.

Computation of Excess of Cost over Book Value

First Acquisition
Cost of 20% acquired	$200,000
20% of equity book value of $900,000	180,000
Excess of cost over book value (goodwill)	$ 20,000

Second Acquisition
Cost of 60% acquired	$500,000
60% of equity book value of $1,100,000	660,000
Excess of book value over cost (negative goodwill)	($160,000)

Actually, as of the date of the second acquisition Company P had an investment of $700,000 for 80% of Company S. Company S at the second acquisition date had an equity book value of $1,100,000, and Company P's 80% is $880,000, for which it paid $700,000. If Company P had recorded its first acquisition of 20% by the equity method, it would have recorded its 20% of the $200,000 increase in Company S's book value (assuming that no dividends or other distributions were made to Company P by Company S). Thus the adjusted equity in Company S on the books of Company P would include the original $200,000 purchase price plus 20% of the $200,000 increase in book value (from $900,000 to $1,100,000) or a total of $220,000 ($180,000 + $40,000). The cost of the second acquisition of 60% for $500,000 and the adjusted basis for the 20% at $220,000 equals $720,000, which represents 80% of $1,100,000, or $880,000. The difference of $160,000 is the excess of book value over cost (negative goodwill) indicated by the computation for the second acquisition of 60%.

Pooling-of-Interests Method

The purchase method and the pooling-of-interests method are both acceptable in accounting for business combinations, but not as alternatives. A business combination either qualifies for the pooling-of-interest method or is treated as a purchase. *Part-purchase and part-pooling of the same business combination is unacceptable* (APB-16).

> **OBSERVATION:** *The promulgated GAAP requirements for using the pooling-of-interests method are detailed and quite restrictive.*

Conditions for the Pooling-of-Interests Method

1. Each of the combining companies must be autonomous and not have been a subsidiary or division of another corporation within two years before the plan of combination is initiated.

The initiation date is the *earlier:*

   a. of the date of public announcement, or notification to the shareholders of any one of the combining companies, the major terms of the plan including the ratio of exchange or a formula which provides for the ratio of exchange, or

b. of the date that shareholders of the company being acquired are notified directly or by newspaper advertisement of the exchange offer (APB Interpretation of APB-16).

A new company, incorporated within the last two years, qualifies unless it was in any way a successor to a company that would not have been considered autonomous.

It is irrelevant whether a parent company or any of its wholly owned subsidiaries distribute voting common stock to effect a combination, as long as the condition of autonomy is met.

> **OBSERVATION:** Although the promulgated GAAP specifically states "wholly owned subsidiary," an APB interpretation (nonpromulgated) suggests that substantially all the subsidiary's outstanding voting stock be owned by the parent and under no circumstances would less than 90% be considered substantially all.

A judicial order to divest is an exception to the rule and both the divesting company and the acquiring company will be considered autonomous.

2. At the date of initiation and at the date of consummation of the plan of combination, each combining company is independent of each other combining company. An intercorporate investment of 10% or less of the total outstanding voting common stock of any combining company is acceptable and will not impair the independence test.

> **OBSERVATION:** The promulgated GAAP provides that if a company held as an investment a minority interest of 50% or less on October 31, 1970, and initiates a plan of combination within five years after that date, the resulting combination could be accounted for as a pooling of interests provided all other provisions of the promulgated GAAP were complied with. This section is referred to as the "grandfather clause," and the five-year limitation was deleted by FASB-10.

3. After a plan is initiated, it must be completed within one

year, in accordance with a specific plan or completed in a single transaction.

> **OBSERVATION:** A pooling of interests is, in essence, a combining of existing shareholders' voting common stock in which the separate shareholder interests lose their identity, resulting in the mutual combination of risks and rights. Any change in the exchange ratio or terms thereof creates a new initiation date for the plan of combination. Any change in the relative voting rights that result in preferential treatment for some common stockholder groups is incompatable to a pooling of interests.

Litigation or proceedings of a governmental authority that delay the completion of a plan of combination are excepted from the one-year rule, providing they are beyond the control of any of the combining companies.

4. At the consummation date of the plan the acquiring company offers and issues its majority class of stock (voting rights) for no less than 90% of the *voting common stock interests* of the combining company being acquired. The 90% or more of the voting common stock interests being acquired is determined at the date the plan is consummated.

> **OBSERVATION:** An APB Interpretation, which is not promulgated GAAP, suggests that the consummation date is the date the assets are transferred to the issuing company.

This requirement of 90% or more of the voting common stock interests being acquired at consummation date can be related to the requirement that intercorporate investments of 10% or less, in any company being acquired, is acceptable for the independence rule (see condition 2 above).

The determination of whether the acquiring company acquires 90% or more of the outstanding voting common stock interests at the date of consummation excludes the following shares of the company being acquired:

a. any shares acquired for any form of consideration and held at

Business Combinations

the date of initiation of the plan of combination by the acquiring parent or its subsidiaries

b. any shares acquired, and held, after the date of initiation, by the acquiring parent or its subsidiaries, except those shares acquired by the issuance of the acquiring company's own voting stock

OBSERVATION: In other words, intercorporate investments in the company being acquired, except those acquired by the issuance of voting common stock after the date of initiation, are excluded in calculating the number of voting common stock interests that are exchanged at the consummation date.

The larger the intercorporate investment an acquirer has in an acquisition that was acquired prior to the initiation date, the more difficult the 90% will be to achieve.

An investment in the voting common stock of the acquiring company held by a company being acquired must be restated in an equivalent number of shares of the company being acquired. The equivalent number of shares is determined by the exchange ratio of the plan of combination and then deducted from the number of voting common shares actually exchanged on the consummation date. The resulting number of shares of the company being acquired must equal 90% or more of its total outstanding voting common shares at the date of consummation.

B has 100,000 shares of voting common stock outstanding and owns an investment in A of 1,000 shares of voting common stock. A initiated a plan of combination to acquire B by offering four shares of its voting common stock (majority class) for each share of B's voting common stock. At the date of consummation, 91,000 shares of B's stock are tendered to A. However, the 1,000 shares of voting common stock of A held by B must be restated into an equivalent amount of B's stock in accordance with the exchange ratio of 4 to 1, which equals 4,000 shares. In other words, at consummation date B is theoretically the owner of 4,000 shares of its own stock when restated in terms of the exchange ratio. The 4,000 shares are deducted from the 91,000 shares tendered, which equals 87,000 shares, and then compared to 90% of the outstanding

Business Combinations

voting common stock of B at the date of consummation, which in this case is 90,000 shares (90% of 100,000).

As a result, A's acquisition of 91,000 shares is restated to 87,000 shares, which does not meet the 90% requirement, and the transaction cannot be accounted for as a pooling of interests.

When two or more companies are being acquired in a plan of combination, each condition necessary for a pooling of interests must be met by each company.

However, 90% of each combining company must be exchanged for voting common stock of the acquiring company and intercompany investments between any of the combining companies are excluded in calculating whether 90% or more of the voting common stock interests are exchanged, but are included in computing the total amount of voting common stock interests outstanding.

A plan of combination may not include a pro rata cash distribution but may within limits include a cash distribution for fractional shares and for shares purchased from dissenting shareholders. Cash may also be used in a plan of combination to retire, or redeem, callable debt and equity securities.

A transfer of *all the net assets* at the date the plan is consummated in exchange for voting common stock (majority class) of the acquiring company qualifies as an exchange of substantially all (90% or more) of the *voting common stock interests.*

Although the requirement is for *all the net assets* of the company being acquired, temporary cash, receivables, and marketable securities may be retained to settle liabilities, disputed items, or contingencies. In a net asset transaction, both voting common stock and other stock may be issued by the acquiring company, if the company whose net assets are being acquired has both voting common stock and other stock outstanding. However, the voting common stock and other stock must be issued in proportion to the voting common stock and other stock outstanding, of the company being acquired, at the date of consummation of the plan of combination.

In determining the independence rule (see condition 2 above) in an exchange of voting common stock for net assets, intercorporate investments of 10% or less are evaluated in terms of the issuing company's voting common stock, as follows:

a. The number of voting common shares being issued at the

Business Combinations

date of consummation for all the net assets is allocated between outstanding voting common stock and other outstanding stock if any. The net assets being acquired should include any intercorporate investment in the acquiring company.

b. A ratio is computed between the number of shares of voting common stock outstanding, at the date of consummation, for the company whose net assets are being acquired, and the number of voting common shares of the acquirer allocated (in a above) to the acquisition of voting common stock interests.

c. An intercorporate investment of the issuer in the voting common stock of the company whose assets are being acquired is restated in equivalent shares of the ratio computed in b above.

d. An intercorporate investment in the issuing company by the company whose net assets are being acquired is not restated, because the number of shares is already stated in terms of the issuing company's stock.

e. In order to meet the 90% test, all intercorporate investments (when restated in terms of the stock of the issuing company) cannot exceed 10% of the number of issued shares of voting common stock allocated and issued for the acquisition of the voting common stock interests being acquired.

P owns 12,000 shares of S's voting common stock that was acquired prior to initiation date. P issues 100,000 shares of its voting common stock to acquire all the net assets of S, which includes 1,000 shares of P's voting common stock. The 100,000 shares of P's stock is allocated 70% to outstanding voting common stock and 30% to other outstanding stock. S has 210,000 shares of voting common stock outstanding.

P has allocated 70,000 (70% of 100,000) shares of its stock to acquire the 210,000 shares of S's voting common stock at the consummation date. This results in a ratio of 1 share of P for 3 shares of S.

The 12,000 shares of S that are owned by P are converted to 4,000 shares of P. The 1,000 shares of P that are owned by S are already stated in P's stock. The 4,000 equivalent shares and the 1,000 shares of P equal 5,000 shares and are compared to 10% of the 70,000 shares of P's voting common stock that have been allocated for the acquisition of the voting common stock interests in S. The 5,000 equivalent shares of P are less than the 10% of the 70,000 shares allocated by P for the acquisition and thus the combination qualifies for a pooling of interests.

---

5. No changes in the equity interests of the voting common stock of any combining company may be made in contemplation of a pooling of interests. This restriction is for a period beginning two years prior to the initiation date of the plan of combination and for the period between the initiation date and the consummation date.
   Normal distributions based on earnings and/or prior policy are permitted.
6. The reacquisition of voting common stock by any combining company is allowed except for purposes of business combinations. In addition, any reacquisition of voting common stock between the initiation and the consummation dates must be no more than a normal amount.
   A normal amount of reacquired shares is determined by reference to a company's pattern of reacquisition prior to the initiation of a plan of combination.
   A systematic pattern of reacquisition of voting common stock established for stock option or compensation plans is permitted.
   After a plan is initiated, the acquisition of voting common stock of the issuing company by any combining company is considered the same as if the issuing company reacquired its own shares.
   The important point of the provision of GAAP is that shares are not reacquired in substance or form to effectuate a business combination.
7. Each common stockholder to a plan of combination must receive a voting common stock interest exactly in proportion to his voting common stock interest prior to the combination.
8. The common stockholders to a plan of combination must receive the voting rights they are entitled to and must not be deprived or restricted in any way from exercising those rights.
9. The entire plan of combination must be effectuated on the date of consummation.
   This provision prohibits contingent shares that are to be issued at a later date, except for contingently issuable shares which will be used to adjust differences in amounts represented at consummation date by management. These differences are recorded as an adjustment to combined stockholders' equity and reflected in net income

of the period of resolution or as a prior-period adjustment of the correction of an error of a prior period.

10. After the combination is consummated, any transaction, implied or explicit, that is inconsistent with the combining of the interest of the common stockholders counteracts the effect of combining stockholders' interest.

Application of the Pooling-of-Interests Method

All the conditions for a pooling of interests must be met before a business combination can be accounted for as such. The mechanics of applying the pooling-of-interests method are:

1. At the date the combination is consummated, assets, liabilities, and stockholders' equity are combined and recorded at historical cost, in conformity with GAAP.

2. If an acquiring company issued treasury stock to effectuate part or all of a plan of combination, the treasury stock must first be treated as though it was retired (gain or loss is recorded), and then it is considered the same as any other previously unissued shares.

3. Intercorporate investments in the acquiring company are treated as treasury stock in combined financial statements. Intercorporate investments, other than in the acquiring company stock, are treated as retired stock of the combination.

4. All financial statements for the period in which the combination occurred should be reported as though the combination occurred at the beginning of the period.

5. Prior-year financial statements should be restated on a combined basis.

6. Expenses relating to the combination are expenses of the combined group and should be deducted from combined net income. Examples of such expenses are registration fees, finders and consultant fees, and costs and losses resulting from combining the separate companies.

7. If within two years after a combination, a material profit or loss results from the disposal of a significant portion of the assets of the previously separate companies, full disclosure, as an extraordinary item (net of tax effects), should be made in the combined financial statements.

8. Prior to the consummation date of a plan of combination, the investment on the books of the acquiring company (investor) should be accounted for by the equity method, if acquired for voting common stock, and at cost if the investment was acquired for cash.

Under the pooling-of-interests method, the cost of an acquisition is the total par or stated value of the capital stock issued by the acquirer to effectuate the combination. This amount is debited to an investment account and the appropriate capital stock account is credited. Fair values are ignored and goodwill is never recorded in a pooling of interests.

In a consolidated balance sheet the capital stock account will always be equal to the total par or stated value of the outstanding shares of the acquiring company. Therefore, the first adjustment to the investment account on the consolidated work papers is to eliminate the capital stock account of the acquired company. If the capital stock account of the acquired company exceeds the debit in the investment account (not usually likely), any balance is transferred to combined contributed capital by debiting the capital stock account and crediting combined contributed capital.

It is much more likely that the debit in the investment account will exceed the capital stock account of the acquired company. In this event, the excess is debited to any other contributed capital account of the acquired company and if an excess still exists, the balance is debited to consolidated retained earnings. Obviously, no amount should exist in the investment account after these adjustments.

Disclosure for Pooling-of-Interests Combinations

The following disclosures should be made to the financial statements in the period in which the pooling occurs:

1. brief description of the companies combined
2. method of accounting for the combination, that is, the pooling-of-interests method
3. description and amount of shares of stock issued to effect the combination
4. details of the results of operations for each separate company, prior to the date of combination, that are included in the current combined net income

5. description of the nature of adjustments in net assets of the combining companies to adopt the same accounting policies
6. If any of the combining companies changed their fiscal year as a result of the combination, full disclosure should be made of any changes in stockholders' equity that were excluded from the reported results of operations.
7. Revenue and earnings previously reported by the acquiring company should be reconciled with the amounts shown in the combined financial statements.
8. Any plan of combination that has been initiated but not consummated at a balance sheet date must be fully disclosed, including the effects of the plan on combined operations and any changes in accounting methods.

In the period that a pooling-of-interest is effectuated, recurring intercompany transactions should be eliminated to the extent possible from the beginning of the period. However, nonrecurring intercompany transactions involving long-term assets and liabilities need not be eliminated, but in that event they should be fully disclosed (APB-16).

CHANGES IN FINANCIAL POSITION

Background

The promulgated GAAP for Reporting Changes in Financial Position is APB-19. This promulgated GAAP applies to all profit-oriented business entities including those with unclassified balance sheets. Financial statements that present financial position and results of operations must include a statement of changes in financial position (hereinafter referred to as the Statement). In some circumstances, such as statements issued for internal use only, the Statement may be omitted.

Companies in regulated industries must comply with this promulgated GAAP in accordance with the Addendum to APB-2.

Overview

The Statement should be prepared on a broad concept and should include all the important changes in financial position. However, book entries such as for stock dividends and splits should not be included.

All important aspects of financing and investing activities, regardless of whether for cash or other elements of working capital, should be disclosed in the Statement.

Objectives of the Statement

The most informative disclosure of the Statement is the working capital provided from or used in operations for the period, providing that the effect of extraordinary items is disclosed separately from the effect of normal items.

The objectives of the Statement are:

1. to reflect the amount of working capital generated from or used in operations for the period
2. to summarize all the financing and investing activities of an enterprise during the period (whether or not for cash)
3. to disclose appropriately the net changes in each element of working capital for at least the current period

Gross Basis

All funds are reported on the Statement at their gross amounts. The only exception to this rule is normal trade-ins to replace equipment, which are shown on a net basis. That is, instead of showing the total equipment traded and the total equipment received, only the difference between the two is shown on the Statement.

> **OBSERVATION:** FASB-12 requires that both the current and noncurrent marketable security portfolios be shown on the balance sheet at their carrying amount, which is the lower of the aggregate cost or market. By doing this, the amount on the balance sheet is a net figure, which includes all debits and credits from sales, purchases, and changes in the valuation account.
>
> FASB-12 contradicts APB-19, because APB-19 requires that outlays for purchases, and proceeds from sales, of long-term investments be separately identified and shown on a "gross basis," whereas FASB-12 requires that both the current and noncurrent marketable security portfolios be shown at their carrying amount, which is the "net basis."
>
> Under FASB-12, it is possible, during a fiscal period, for a company to have in its noncurrent marketable security portfolio sales of $10 million, purchases of $15 million, and an increase in the valuation account of $5 million, and on its balance sheet there would be absolutely no change in carrying value from the preceding fiscal period!

Concept of Funds

Some of the definitions of funds are:

1. cash
2. cash and marketable securities
3. net quick assets
4. net working capital (excess of current assets over current liabilities)

Regardless of which concept of funds is used, GAAP require the inclusion of "all financial resources" in preparing the Statement.

"All financial resources" include cash, noncash, and nonworking capital transactions that are part of the financing and investing activities of a business, as follows:

1. funds used for the purchase of, or funds received from the sale of, long-term assets
2. conversion of preferred stock or long-term debt to common stock
3. issuance, assumption, redemption, or repayment of long-term debt
4. issuance, redemption, or purchase of capital stock for cash or noncash assets
5. distributions to shareholders, including dividends in cash or in property

Some entities do not distinguish between current and noncurrent assets and liabilities and would ordinarily indicate "cash" provided from, or used in, operations, instead of "working capital." Another alternative is the "net monetary concept," or "quick asset" approach, which reflects the changes in all nonquick assets and noncurrent liabilities. However, the preferable concept is the working capital approach, which reflects the changes in the noncurrent accounts that affect the movement of current items.

Each entity has the responsibility of utilizing the "statement format" that is most informative and complies with the objectives of the Statement.

Funds provided or used in operations To arrive at the *funds provided or used in operations* we generally start with net income and adjust it for noncash charges or credits, including:

1. depreciation expense
2. amortization expense
3. extraordinary items
4. deferred taxes
5. accrued income or loss from subsidiaries, joint ventures, etc.

If the *fund concept* being used is cash instead of working capital, net income on a cash basis must be adjusted for:

Changes in Financial Position

1. increases or decreases in receivables
2. increases or decreases in inventories
3. increases or decreases in accounts payable

Changes in each element of working capital The changes in each element of working capital are the increases or decreases in each current asset and current liability over the amounts in the preceding year, as follows:

Current Assets	1976	1977	Increase or (Decrease)
Cash	$10,000	$ 15,000	$ 5,000
Accounts receivable	25,000	35,000	10,000
Inventory	50,000	60,000	10,000
Prepaid expenses	1,000	500	(500)
Total current assets	$86,000	$110,500	$24,500
Current Liabilities			
Accounts payable	$10,000	$ 15,000	$ 5,000
Notes payable (current portion)	20,000	15,000	(5,000)
Accrued expenses	1,000	1,500	500
Total current liabilities	$31,000	$ 31,500	$ 500
Net working capital	$55,000	$ 79,000	
Increase or decrease in working capital			$24,000

Cash Format

The Statement may be prepared on a cash basis. However, the working capital basis is preferred. When preparing the Statement on a cash basis, the increase or decrease in cash during the period is computed instead of the increase or decrease in working capital.

1. The changes in the current accounts are presented in addition to the changes in the noncurrent accounts. (This is because we are starting with cash instead of working capital.)
2. Because all the changes in the current accounts appear on the Statement, there is no need for a separate schedule of changes in the elements of working capital.

Cash provided from (used in) operations should not be used unless all noncash items have been eliminated.

Per Share Amounts

Isolated statistics of working capital, or cash, especially per share information, should not be presented in annual reports to stockholders. If per share information is presented, it should show, as a minimum, amounts of inflow from operations, inflow from other sources, and total outflows, and each per share amount should be clearly identified.

Comprehensive Illustration

The following Consolidated Statements of Changes in Financial Position has been extracted from the 1977 Annual Report of Harcourt Brace Jovanovich, Inc.

Changes in Financial Position

Consolidated Statements of Changes in Financial Position
FOR THE YEARS ENDED DECEMBER 31, 1977 and 1976

	1977	1976
Funds provided by:		
Net income	$18,214,173	$16,471,195
Depreciation and amortization	11,390,220	6,143,537
Increase in unearned subscription and other income	1,789,455	3,144,882
Increase in deferred income taxes	1,493,471	37,194
Amortization of publication rights, copyrights, and other intangibles	376,663	229,773
Net income of The Harvest Life Insurance Company	(90,548)	(66,103)
Provided from operations	$33,173,434	$25,960,478
Long-term debt:		
Issued	$21,391,364	$47,472,000
Assumed in purchase of business (Note 2)	—	13,571,333
Deferred income taxes ($2,341,738) less other net noncurrent assets from acquisition of Sea World, Inc.	—	2,221,177
Equity (deficit) of pooled companies at dates of acquisition	844,622	(924,283)
(Decrease) increase in minority interests in subsidiaries (including $2,002,681 applicable to Sea World, Inc. in 1976)	(121,230)	2,093,536
Proceeds of sale on exercise of stock options	435,659	5,869
	$55,723,849	$90,400,110

Changes in Financial Position

Funds used for:		
Dividends declared	6,158,228	5,542,932
Additions to property and equipment:		
From acquisition of Sea World, Inc.	2,923,992	61,933,978
Other	25,988,856	9,139,148
Contribution to capital of The Harvest Life Insurance Company	500,000	—
Reduction of long-term debt	11,100,557	1,314,049
Purchase of minority interest in Sea World, Inc. (Note 2)	2,002,681	—
Increase in royalty advances to authors	575,730	1,587,681
Decrease (increase) in royalties payable after one year	552,574	(261,622)
Purchase of publication rights, copyrights, and other intangibles	6,314,425	541,803
Increase in other assets	1,855,333	2,365,609
	$57,972,376	$82,163,578
(Decrease) increase in working capital (Note 7)	($ 2,248,527)	$ 8,236,532

(7) The increases and (decreases) in the components of working capital are as follows:

	1977	1976
Current assets:		
Cash	$ (750,886)	$ 1,178,050
Marketable securities	(2,024,452)	3,013,724
Accounts receivable	13,363,681	8,790,762
Inventories	8,063,212	5,232,263
Prepaid expenses	596,955	512,590
	$19,248,510	$18,727,389
Current liabilities:		
Current portion of long-term debt	8,743,525	578,452
Accounts payable	4,397,579	5,945,871
Accrued liabilities	3,342,639	2,156,224
Royalties payable	697,262	1,860,449
Federal, state, and local income taxes payable	4,316,032	(50,139)
	$21,497,037	$10,490,857
(Decrease) increase in working capital	($ 2,248,527)	$ 8,236,532

The accompanying notes are an integral part of these statements.

CONSOLIDATED FINANCIAL STATEMENTS

Background

The promulgated GAAP for consolidated financial statements, including combined and comparative financial statements, are:

> ARB-43, Chapter 1A–Rules Adopted by Membership
> ARB-43, Chapter 2A–Comparative Financial Statements (as amended)
> ARB-51–Consolidated Financial Statements (as amended)

Since all the above promulgated GAAP are silent on coverage of companies in regulated industries, such companies should comply in accordance with the Addendum to APB-2.

Considerable nonpromulgated GAAP exists for consolidated financial statements, especially in the area of reporting and types of presentations.

Overview

Consolidated financial statements represent results of operation, changes in financial position, and financial position of a single entity. They are presumed to be more meaningful than separate statements and must be used when the parent controls voting interest of over 50% in a subsidiary. A subsidiary whose main business is leasing property to its parent must be consolidated. Investments of a temporary nature, foreign investments subject to controls and currency restrictions, and investments that are dissimilar and for which separate supplemental information would be more meaningful should not be consolidated.

Accounting and Reporting

Retained earnings of a purchased subsidiary at the date of acquisition are never treated as part of consolidated retained earnings. The retained earnings and capital stock of a purchased subsidiary at the date of acquisition represent the book value that must be eliminated in preparing consolidated statements.

The fact that a subsidiary has a different fiscal year does not justify not preparing consolidated statements. If a subsidiary's fiscal year is within three months or less of its parent's fiscal year, it is acceptable to use those fiscal-year statements for consolidation purposes, providing that disclosure is made of any material events occurring within the intervening period.

A subsidiary or net assets may be purchased (1) for book value, (2) in excess of book value, and (3) for less than book value. If purchased for more than book value, there may be resulting goodwill; if purchased for less than book value, there may be a resulting deferred credit, sometimes referred to as negative goodwill (see Business Combinations).

> **OBSERVATION:** *A subsidiary in legal reorganization or bankruptcy is controlled by the receiver or trustee and not by the parent company. Therefore, consolidated financial statements under these conditions would be inappropriate (ARB-43).*

There are situations where consolidated statements may be more meaningful if a particular subsidiary is not included. These situations exist where the activity of a particular subsidiary is completely unrelated to the rest of the affiliated group and its inclusion would be meaningless. Banks and insurance companies are examples of subsidiaries that may be excluded in a consolidation of a large group of manufacturing entities.

When a subsidiary is acquired by the purchase method in more than one transaction, each purchase should be determined on a step-by-step basis and consolidation usually not made until control (50%) is achieved. In the year that control is achieved, the percentage amount of net income from the purchased subsidiary will probably vary. For example, if a parent company purchased 25% of a subsidiary at the end of each quarter of a year, the income from the subsidiary that the parent would include in its income would be 0% at the end of the first quarter, 25% at the end of the second quarter, 50% at the end of the third quarter, and 75% at the end of the last quarter. (Income from a purchased acquisition accrues subsequent from the date of acquisition.) The promulgated GAAP suggest two methods for the inclusion of income from a subsidiary in periods where there are several purchases. The preferable method usually is to include the subsidiary in the consolidation as if it had been acquired at the beginning of the period, and to deduct at the bottom of the consolidated income statement the net income of the subsidiary that does not accrue to the parent.

OBSERVATION: *Apparently, when using this method, all the revenue and expense accounts of the subsidiary remain in the consolidated income statement, since only the net income that the parent is not entitled to is deducted from the consolidated net income at the bottom of the statement.*

The other method suggested is to include in the parent's consolidated income statement only the subsidiary's revenue and expenses subsequent to the date of acquisition.

In disposal of a subsidiary during the year, the promulgated GAAP suggest that it may be preferable to omit from the consolidated income statement all details of the operation of the subsidiary and to show only the equity of the parent in the earnings of the subsidiary, prior to disposal, as a separate item in the consolidated income statement (the equity method).

Consolidated financial statements are prepared in the same manner for a pooling of interests as they are for a purchase. In the purchase method, fair values are assigned to identifiable assets and any excess cost is recorded as goodwill. In a pooling of interests, the cost of an acquisition is the total par or stated value of the capital stock issued by the acquiring company and goodwill is never recorded. (For further discussion see Business Combinations.)

The equity method (APB-18) should be used for all subsidiaries not consolidated unless the subsidiary is a temporary investment, a foreign investment subject to control and currency restrictions, or where the consolidated statements would be more meaningful if the subsidiary was excluded from consolidation (banks, insurance companies, etc., as members of a large manufacturing group). If the equity method is not used for reasons cited herein, then the cost method should be used. However, when the cost method is used, the consolidated statements should disclose the following:

1. cost of the investment
2. underlying equity in the investment
3. dividends received in the current period
4. equity of the parent in the net income of the subsidiary for the current period

When the cost method is utilized for unconsolidated subsidiaries, consideration must be given to the other elements of consolidating

if it had been used. For example, appropriate recognition should be made of the difference between the cost of the subsidiary and the underlying equity in the net assets at the date of acquisition. As a result, it may be necessary to adjust consolidated depreciation or amortization. Intercompany gains or losses between the consolidating group and the unconsolidated subsidiary must also be reviewed. The intercompany gain or loss on sales made by the unconsolidated subsidiary to members of the consolidated group should be eliminated in determining the equity in the undistributed earnings of the unconsolidated subsidiary. The disclosure requirement of the equity in the undistributed earnings of the unconsolidated subsidiary has been mentioned previously. Intercompany gains or losses on sales to unconsolidated subsidiaries need not be eliminated unless they exceed the unrecorded equity in undistributed earnings of the unconsolidated subsidiary. In any event, if such sales are material, they should be appropriately disclosed. Further disclosure summarizing the assets, liabilities, and operating results is necessary if the total unconsolidated subsidiaries are material in relationship to the consolidated statements.

Combined Financial Statements

Consolidated financial statements are usually justified on the basis that one of the consolidating entities exercises control over the affiliated group. When there is no such control, combined financial statements may be used to accomplish the same results. A commonly controlled group of companies, or a group of unconsolidated subsidiaries that could otherwise not be consolidated, should utilize combined financial statements. Combined financial statements are prepared on the same basis as consolidated financial statements, except that a controlling interest is not included.

Comparative financial statements Comparative financial statements reveal much more information than noncomparative statements and furnish useful data about differences in the results of operations for the periods involved or in the financial position at the comparison dates.

Consistency is a major factor in creating comparability. Prior-year amounts and classifications must be, in fact, comparable with the current period presented, and exceptions must be clearly disclosed.

Consolidation versus Equity Method

The only difference between the equity method of accounting for investments in common stocks and consolidated financial statements is the amount of detail reported. Under both methods all intercompany transactions are eliminated. In consolidated financial statements the details of all entities to the consolidation are reported in full. In the equity method the investment is shown as a single amount in the investor balance sheet, and earnings or losses are generally shown as a single amount in the income statement. This is the reason why the equity method is frequently referred to as "one-line consolidation."

Consolidated Work Papers

The difference between regular work papers for a single business and consolidated work papers is that the adjustments on the regular work papers will be journalized and posted to the books, whereas eliminations and adjustments made on consolidated work papers *are never posted to the books of the individual companies.*

Intercompany Transactions

Sales and purchases The gross amount of intercompany sales and/or purchases is eliminated on the consolidated work papers. When the adjustment has already been made in the trial balance for ending inventory the eliminating entry is made against cost of sales. When the adjustment has not been made for ending inventory the eliminating entry is made against the purchase account.

Receivables and payables Intercompany receivables and payables include:

1. accounts receivable and accounts payable
2. advances to and from affiliates
3. notes receivable and notes payable
4. interest receivable and interest payable

The gross amount of all intercompany receivables and payables is eliminated on the consolidated work papers. Care must be exercised where a receivable is discounted with one of the consolidated companies (no contingent liability). If the balance sheet reflects a discounted receivable with another affiliate, it must be eliminated by a debit to discounted receivables and a credit to receivables. However, if one affiliate discounts a receivable to another affiliate, who in turn discounts it to an outsider, a real contingent liability exists, which must be shown on the consolidated balance sheet.

Unrealized profits in inventory Regardless of any minority interests, all (100%) of any intercompany profits in inventory must be eliminated on the consolidated work papers if such inventory profits are represented by assets within the group. If the inventory containing intercompany profits has been disposed of to outsiders, no adjustment need be made. If the adjustment for intercompany profits in inventory is not made, consolidated net income is overstated and the consolidated ending inventory is overstated.

P company purchased $200,000 and $250,000 of merchandise in 1976 and 1977, respectively, from its subsidiary S at 25% above cost. As of December 31, 1976 and 1977, P had on hand $25,000 and $30,000 of merchandise purchased from S. What is the consolidated adjusting entry on December 31, 1977?

Computation of Intercompany Profits

Beginning inventory	$25,000	=	125%
Cost to S	20,000	=	100%
Intercompany profit	$ 5,000		25%
Ending inventory	$30,000	=	125%
Cost to S	24,000	=	100%
Intercompany profit	$ 6,000		25%

The adjustment is different for a consolidated balance sheet than for a consolidated income statement, because a consolidated balance sheet reflects only the ending inventory, whereas a consolidated income statement usually shows both the beginning and ending inventories. For a consolidated balance sheet only, the consolidated adjusting entry is:

Retained earnings	$6,000	
Inventory		$6,000

Consolidated Financial Statements

For a consolidated income statement the following adjustments are necessary:

Sales–S Company	$250,000	
Purchases–P Company		$250,000
To eliminate intercompany sales and purchases.		
Consolidated retained earnings	$ 5,000	
Purchases or cost of sales		$ 5,000
To reverse consolidated adjustment of 12/31/76.		
Purchases or cost of sales	$ 6,000	
Inventory–ending		$ 6,000
To eliminate intercompany profit in ending inventory.		

The adjustment to consolidated retained earnings was necessary because on the prior year's consolidated work papers the intercompany profit was eliminated. Remember, consolidated adjustments and eliminations are never posted to the books of the individual companies. Therefore the beginning inventory for P still reflected the prior year's intercompany inventory profits from S.

If merchandise containing an intercompany inventory profit is reduced from the purchase price to market value and the reduction is equal to, or more then, the actual intercompany inventory profit, no further reduction is made. For example, if merchandise costing one affiliate $10,000 is sold to another affiliate for $12,000, who reduces it to market value of $11,000, the consolidated working paper adjustment for unrealized intercompany inventory profits should be only $1,000.

Minority interests do not affect the adjustment for unrealized intercompany profits in inventories. However, consolidated net income and minority interests in the net income of a subsidiary are affected, because the reduction or increase in beginning or ending inventory of a partially owned subsidiary does affect the determination of net income.

Unrealized intercompany losses in inventory are accounted for in the same manner as unrealized profits, except that they have the opposite effect.

Consolidated Financial Statements

Profits or losses on sales and/or purchases prior to an affiliation are never recognized as a consolidated adjustment.

Unrealized profits in long-lived assets Regardless of any minority interests, all (100%) of any intercompany profits on the sale and/or purchase of long-lived assets between affiliates is eliminated on the consolidated work papers.

When one affiliate constructs or sells a long-lived asset to another affiliate at a profit, the profit must be eliminated on the consolidated work papers. As with unrealized intercompany profits or losses in inventory, minority interests do not affect any consolidated adjustment for profits in intercompany sales of long-lived assets between affiliates. However, net income of the subsidiary involved in the intercompany profit on a long-lived asset is affected, which in turn affects consolidated net income and minority interests.

In consolidating a subsidiary in a regulated industry, intercompany profits are not eliminated on manufactured or constructed facilities for other members of the consolidated group, to the extent that they are equivalent to a reasonable return on investment as established by industry practice.

If a nondepreciable asset is involved in an intercompany profit on a long-lived asset, the profit is eliminated by a debit to either retained earnings, in the case of an adjusted consolidated balance sheet, or to gain on sale, in the case of a consolidated income statement.

Depreciable assets require the same adjustment for intercompany profit as nondepreciable long-lived assets, and an adjustment must also be made for any depreciation recorded on the intercompany profit.

An 80%-owned subsidiary sells to its parent for $100,000 a piece of machinery that cost $80,000. The sale was made on July 1, 1977, and consolidated statements are being prepared for December 31, 1977. The parent depreciates machinery over 10 years on a straight line basis and recorded one-half a year's depreciation on the purchased machinery.

The first entry eliminates the $20,000 of intercompany profit, as follows:

```
    Gain on sale of machinery      $20,000
        Machinery                              $20,000
```

Consolidated Financial Statements

Since the parent company has recorded one-half a year's depreciation on the machinery, the following additional entry is made:

Accumulated depreciation	$ 1,000	
Depreciation expense		$ 1,000

Because consolidated eliminations and adjustments are never posted to any books, in the second year the following entries are made:

Retained earnings	$20,000	
Machinery		$20,000
To eliminate intercompany profit on prior year's sale of machinery.		

Accumulated depreciation	$ 3,000	
Retained earnings		$ 1,000
Depreciation expense		2,000
To eliminate the $2,000 depreciation expense on intercompany profit on the sale of machinery and to eliminate the $1,000 depreciation expense for prior year's depreciation.		

The process of eliminating the depreciation expense on the intercompany profit on the sale of long-lived assets continues until the asset is fully depreciated, and then thereafter until the asset is disposed of or retired. In our example, the following entry would be made every year on the consolidated work papers after the asset is fully depreciated and before it is disposed of or retired.

Accumulated depreciation	$20,000	
Retained earnings		$20,000

An affiliate that makes an intercompany profit on the sale of long-lived assets to another affiliate may pay income taxes on the gain. This occurs usually when the affiliated group does not file consolidated tax returns and the gain cannot be avoided for tax purposes. In such cases, the intercompany profit on the sale should be reduced by the related tax effects in computing the consolidated adjusting entry.

Intercompany bondholdings Intercompany bonds purchased by an affiliate are treated in the year of acquisition as though they have been retired. Any gain or loss is recognized in the consolidated income statement for the year of acquisition.

The amount of gain or loss on an intercompany bond purchase is the difference between the unamortized bond premium or discount on the books of the issuer and the amount of any purchase discount or premium.

An intercompany gain or loss on bonds cannot occur when an affiliate makes the purchase direct from the affiliated issuer, because the selling price will be exactly equal to the cost.

An affiliate purchases $20,000 face value 6% bonds from an affiliated issuer for $19,500.

On the affiliated investor's books the following entry is made:

Investment in bonds	$19,500	
Cash		$19,500

On the affiliated issuer's books the entry is:

Cash	$19,500	
Discount on bonds payable	500	
Bonds payable		$20,000

The consolidated elimination is:

Bonds payable	$20,000	
Discount on bonds payable		$ 500
Investment in bonds		19,500

An intercompany gain or loss on bonds cannot occur when the purchase price is exactly the same as the carrying value on the books of the affiliated issuer.

The following conditions must exist for an affiliated investor to realize a gain or loss on intercompany bondholdings:

1. The bonds are already outstanding.
2. The bonds are purchased outside the affiliated group.
3. The price paid is different from the carrying value of the affiliated issuer.

Company S acquires $50,000 of face amount 6% bonds from an outsider. These bonds were part of an original issue of $300,000 made by the parent of Company S. The purchase price was $45,000, and the bonds mature in four years and nine months. Interest is payable on June 30 and December 31, and the purchase was made on March 31.

The journal entry on the books of Company S to record the purchase is:

Investment in bonds	$45,000	
Accrued interest receivable	750	
Cash		$45,750

On the consolidated working papers at the end of the year the following entries are made:

Investment in bonds	$ 5,000	
Gain on intercompany bondholdings		$ 5,000
To adjust the investment in bonds to face amount and record the gain.		
Bonds payable–Co. P.	$50,000	
Investment in bonds–Co. S		$50,000
To eliminate intercompany bondholdings.		
Interest income–Co. S	$ 2,250	
Interest expense–Co. P		$2,250
To eliminate intercompany interest on bonds that was actually earned.		

Consolidated Financial Statements

Interest income—Co. S	$ 788	
Investment in bonds		$ 788

To eliminate amortization of $5,000 discount on bonds recorded on Co. S books. ($9/_{57}$ of $5,000 = $788)

Accrued interest payable	$ 1,500	
Accrued interest receivable		$ 1,500

To eliminate accrued interest payable on 12/31/XX by Co. P, and the accrued interest receivable on 12/31/XX by Co. S.

This example contains all the possible adjustments except for an issuer's premium or discount. Assume the following additional information on the original issue:

Face amount	$300,000
Issued at 96	288,000
Date of issue	1/1/70
Maturity date	1/1/80

Company S had purchased its $50,000 face amount when the issue had four years and nine months left to maturity.

On the parent company's books this discount is being amortized over the life of the bond issue at the rate of $1,200 per year ($12,000 discount divided by 10 years).

An adjustment must be made on the consolidated work papers to eliminate the portion of the unamortized bond discount existing at the date of purchase that is applicable to the $50,000 face amount purchased by Company S.

Total discount on issue	$12,000
1/6 applicable to Co. S purchase	$ 2,000
Amount of discount per month	
($2,000 divided by 120 months)	$ 16.67
Four years and nine months	
equal 57 months × $16.67	$ 950

The amount of unamortized bond discount on Co. P books applicable to the $50,000 purchase made by Company S was $950 at the date of purchase. This $950 would have entered into the computation of the gain or loss on intercompany bondholdings. In the example the gain or loss on intercompany bondholdings of $5,000 would have been reduced by $950 ($4,050) and the following additional consolidated elimination would have been made:

Gain or loss on intercompany bondholdings	$950	
Unamortized bond discount		$950

Intercompany Dividends Intercompany dividends must be eliminated on the consolidated work papers. Consolidated retained earnings should reflect the accumulated earnings of the consolidated group arising since acquisition which has not been distributed to the shareholders of, or capitalized by, the parent company. In the event that a subsidiary capitalizes earnings arising since acquisition by means of a stock dividend, or otherwise, a transfer to capital surplus is not required in consolidating.

Intercompany Stockholdings If a subsidiary holds stock of its parent, it is treated as "treasury stock" on the consolidated balance sheet and subtracted from consolidated stockholders' equity.

The "Entity Theory"

Consolidated financial statements prepared on the basis of the "entity theory" show both the majority and minority interests with equal prominence. The assumption of the "entity theory" is that both the majority and minority interests have proprietary rights, and consolidated statements should be prepared on that basis. The stockholders' equity section of the consolidated balance sheet should not reflect minority interests as a liability but should disclose minority interests separately on the statements, as follows:

Consolidated Financial Statements

Stockholders' Equity

Majority class:	
Capital stock	$ XX,XXX
Retained earnings	XX,XXX
Minority class:	
Capital stock	X,XXX
Retained earnings	X,XXX
Total stockholders' equity	$XXX,XXX

Income Tax Considerations

Income taxes must be deferred on any intercompany profits where the asset still exists within the consolidated group. However, if consolidated tax returns are filed, no adjustment need be made for deferred income taxes, because intercompany profits are eliminated in computing the consolidated tax liability.

Minority Interests

Consolidated financial statements are prepared primarily for the benefit of creditors and shareholders.

Minority interests in net income are deducted to arrive at consolidated net income. However, minority interests are theoretically limited to the extent of their equity capital, and losses in excess of minority interest equity capital are charged against the majority interest. Subsequently, when the losses reverse, the majority interests should be credited with the amount of minority interest losses previously absorbed before credit is made to the minority interests.

Minority interests are shown in the consolidated balance sheet under a separate caption within the consolidated stockholders' equity section.

Computing minority interests in a complex father-son-grandson affiliation may be demonstrated by using the following diagram.

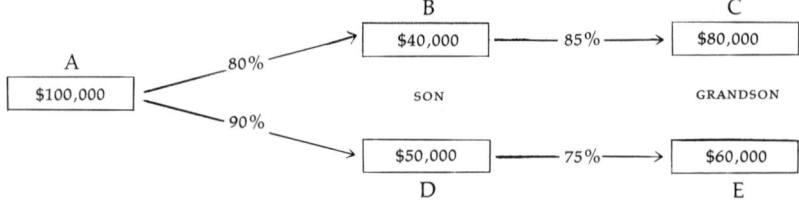

Consolidated Financial Statements

The computations of minority interests and consolidated net income follows:

	E	D	C	B	A
Net income	$60,000	$50,000	$80,000	$ 40,000	$100,000
75% to D	(45,000)	45,000			
		$95,000			
90% to A		85,500			85,500
85% to B			(68,000)	68,000	
				$108,000	
80% to A				86,400	86,400
Minority interests	$15,000	$ 9,500	$12,000	$ 21,600	
Consolidated net income					$271,900

In a situation where a subsidiary owns shares of the parent company, consolidated net income may be found algebraically, as the following illustration depicts:

Company	Unconsolidated Income	
A	$40,000	A, the parent, owns 80% of B
B	20,000	B owns 70% of C
C	10,000	C owns 20% of A

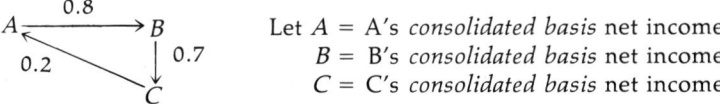

Let A = A's *consolidated basis* net income
B = B's *consolidated basis* net income
C = C's *consolidated basis* net income

The figures and relationships can be put into algebraic form so as to compute *consolidated net income.*

$$A = 40,000 + 0.8B$$
$$B = 20,000 + 0.7C$$
$$C = 10,000 + 0.2A$$

Consolidated Financial Statements

Solving for A, we have:

$$A = 40{,}000 + 0.8\,(20{,}000 + 0.7C)$$
$$A = 40{,}000 + 16{,}000 + 0.56C$$
$$A = 56{,}000 + 0.56C$$
$$A = 56{,}000 + 0.56\,(10{,}000 + 0.2A)$$
$$A = 56{,}000 + 5{,}600 + 0.112A$$
$$0.888A = 61{,}600$$
$$A = 63{,}369$$

Since 20% of the parent, A, is owned by an outsider, C, only 80% of A is used as consolidated net income.

$63{,}369 \times 0.8 =$ <u>$50,695</u> = consolidated net income

Disclosure

The consolidation policy should be fully disclosed on the financial statements or in footnotes to the statements.

CONTINGENCIES

Background

Accounting for contingencies is covered in FASB-5 and FASB Interpretation 14. FASB-11, Accounting for Contingencies—Transition Method, is no longer relevant.

The conditions for accrual of loss contingencies in this promulgated GAAP (FASB-5) do not amend any other requirement to accrue a particular type of loss expense in any other existing promulgated GAAP. In particular, the following items are specifically excluded from the scope of FASB-5:

1. APB-8–Accounting for Pension Plans
2. APB-12–as it pertains to Deferred Compensation
3. APB-25–Accounting for Stock Issued to Employees
4. Accounting for other employment-related costs, such as group insurance, vacation pay, workmen's compensation, and disability benefits

This promulgated GAAP (FASB-5) specifically covers companies in regulated industries, in accordance with the Addendum to APB-2, and requires certain additional disclosures by these companies, which are discussed later in this Chapter.

Overview

A contingency is an existing condition, situation, or set of circumstances involving varying degrees of uncertainty that may, through a related future event, result in the acquisition or loss of an asset or the incurrence or avoidance of a liability, usually with the concurrence of a gain or a loss. The resulting gain or loss is referred to as a "gain contingency" or a "loss contingency."

Not all uncertainties in the accounting process are contingencies, as that term is used in FASB-5. Depreciable assets have a reasonably estimated life, and depreciation expense is used to systematically allocate the cost of the asset over its estimated useful life. Estimates, such as depreciation and accrued amounts, are not uncertainties as described in FASB-5.

Contingencies

Classification of Contingencies

GAAP classifies contingencies as follows:

1. *Probable:* likely to materialize
2. *Reasonably possible:* halfway between probable and remote
3. *Remote:* slight chance of materializing

Loss contingencies may arise from the risk of exposure of:

1. collectibility of receivables
2. property loss by fire, explosion, or other hazards
3. appropriation of assets
4. pending or threatened litigation
5. product warranties or defects
6. claims and assessments
7. catastrophes

This list is not all-inclusive.

Accrual of Loss Contingency

Provision for a loss contingency should be accrued by a charge to income, providing that both of the following conditions exist:

1. It is *probable* that as at the date of the financial statements an asset has been impaired or a liability incurred, based on subsequent available information prior to the issuance of the financial statements.
2. The amount of loss can be reasonably estimated.

If a loss contingency is probable and only a range of possible loss (similar to a minimum-maximum) can be established, then the minimum amount in the range should be accrued, unless some other amount within the range appears to be a better estimate (FASB Interpretation-14).

No Accrual of Loss Contingency

In the event that both the above conditions are not met and a loss contingency is at least *reasonably possible,* financial statement disclosure is necessary. The disclosure should describe the nature of the loss contingency and the range of possible loss (similar to a minimum-maximum), or include a statement that no estimate can be made.

It may be desirable to disclose losses arising after the date of the financial statements that can be reasonably estimated, by supplementing the historical financial statements with pro forma statements reflecting the loss as if it occurred at the date of the financial statements.

Unasserted Claims

Unless it is *probable* that a claim will be asserted and there is a *reasonable possibility* of an unfavorable outcome, disclosure is not required for unasserted claims or assessments where apparently the potential claimant has no knowledge of the claim's existence.

Disclosure of Reasonably Possible Losses

It may be necessary to disclose a reasonably possible loss to avoid misleading statements. These types of events occur after the balance sheet date and before the issuance of the statements that indicate a reasonably possible loss but do not qualify as an accrual of a loss contingency. Disclosure should include the nature of the loss or loss contingency and an estimate of the amount of loss or a statement that an estimate cannot be determined.

Disclosure of Remote Losses

Loss contingencies on guarantees and similar items, even if they have a *remote possibility* of materializing, should be disclosed.

Guarantees to repurchase, obligations of banks under letters of credit, and the guarantee of the indebtedness of another are examples of these types of remote losses.

The disclosure shall contain the nature and amount of the guarantee.

Regulated Industries

Companies in regulated industries that accrue estimated losses for reporting purposes that are contrary to this promulgated GAAP (FASB-5) shall disclose the following information in the financial statements:

Contingencies

1. The accounting policy, the nature of the accrual, and the basis for reaching the estimated amount.
2. The amount of any related liability or asset valuation account included in each balance sheet presented.

Gain Contingencies

Gain contingencies should be disclosed in the financial statements but should not be reflected in income, because to do so might be to recognize revenue prior to its realization. Care should be exercised in the case of gain contingencies to avoid misleading implications as to the recognition of revenue prior to its realization (ARB-50).

Contingency Reserves

The two broad types of contingency reserves are:

1. general contingency reserves whose purposes are not specific
2. reserves designed to set aside a part of current income to absorb losses anticipated in connection with inventories on hand or future purchases of inventory

If a provision for a reserve is made against current revenue and is not properly chargeable thereto, net income for the period is understated by the amount of the provision. If a reserve so created is used to increase the income of subsequent periods, the income of such subsequent periods is overstated. By use of a reserve in this manner, profits may be unjustifiably increased or decreased for a given period. This type of practice impairs the integrity of the financial statements and makes them misleading.

When inventories have been properly measured (valuation principle) in accordance with GAAP, further writedowns through the use of a contingency reserve result in not matching current revenues and costs for the period, and charges to future operations are correspondingly reduced. This results in shifting income from one period to another in violation of the principle that reserves should not be used for the purpose of equalizing reported income.

The principles regarding the creation of these types of reserves are:

1. Reserves should be created only by a segregation or appropriation of retained earnings.

2. No costs or losses should be charged to the reserve, and no part of the reserve should be transferred to income or in any way used to affect the determination of net income for any year.
3. The reserve should be restored to retained earnings directly when any part or all of the reserve is no longer considered necessary.
4. The reserve should preferably be classified in the balance sheet as part of shareholders' equity.

Disclosure of Noninsurance

The promulgated GAAP (FASB-5) does not require the disclosure of noninsurance or underinsurance of possible losses, but specifically states that it does not discourage this practice.

CONVERTIBLE DEBT

Background

The existing promulgated GAAP on Convertible Debt and Debt Issued with Stock Purchase Warrants is APB-14.

Any debt security not explicitly discussed herein should be accounted for in accordance with the substance of the transaction (APB-14).

The time of issuance of a debt security for the purpose of applying the promulgated GAAP is the date on which an agreement as to the terms of the debt security is reached and announced, even though the agreement may be subject to subsequent approval by the stockholders and/or directors.

Companies in regulated industries should comply with promulgated GAAP in accordance with the Addendum to APB-2.

Overview

A convertible debt security is one which can be converted into an equity security at the option of the holder. The characteristics of convertible debt include:

1. The issue price is not significantly greater than the face amount.
2. The interest rate is lower than the interest rate on an equivalent, but not convertible, security.
3. The initial conversion price is greater than the market value of the underlying security.
4. The conversion price does not change (except pursuant to certain antidilutive considerations).
5. The security is usually callable by the issuer.
6. The debt is usually subordinate to nonconvertible debt.

Accounting and Reporting

A conversion feature that is attached to a security cannot be accounted for separately and a value cannot be assigned to it.

A conversion feature that is separate from a security, such as a detachable stock purchase warrant, should be accounted for separately and a value assigned to it. The value assigned to a separate

Convertible Debt

conversion feature is the relative fair value of the conversion feature at the time of issue. Any resulting premium or discount to the security must be accounted for. Any amount assigned to the conversion feature is credited to paid-in capital.

It is important to remember that a value is assigned to a conversion feature only if it is detachable and has its own market price.

The convertible security itself is credited at par or face value, the detachable warrant is credited at market value, and the discount or premium is the residual amount required to balance the cash received.

Xeta Corporation issues $10,000 of 5% convertible preferred stock with a detachable common stock warrant to purchase one share of Xeta's common stock at a specified price. At the time of issuance the quoted market price of the convertible stock was $97 per share, and the stock warrants were quoted at $2 each. The proceeds of the sale to Xeta Corporation were $9,900. The transaction is accounted for as follows:

Cash	$9,900	
Discount on 5% convertible preferred	300	
5% convertible preferred stock		$10,000
Paid-in capital, stock warrants		200

The proceeds of the sale of one share of the 5% convertible preferred stock was allocated:

Payment for the 5% convertible preferred stock (at market)	$97
Payment for one stock warrant	2
Total	$99

Other Considerations

Convertible debt and convertible preferred stock are considered common stock equivalents (CSE) if their cash yield, based on the market price at the date of issuance, is less than two-thirds the then-current bank prime interest rate (APB-15).

CURRENT ASSETS AND CURRENT LIABILITIES

Background

The primary source of promulgated GAAP concerning current assets and current liabilities is ARB-43, Chapter 3A. Other related promulgated GAAP included in this chapter are:

> ARB-43, Chapter 1A–Receivables from Officers, Employees, or Affiliated Companies
> FASB-6–Classification of Short-Term Obligations Expected to Be Refinanced
> FASB Interpretation-8–Classification of a Short-Term Obligation Repaid Prior to Being Replaced by a Long-Term Security

Since the promulgated GAAP is silent as to its coverage, it is assumed that companies in both regulated and unregulated industries must comply.

Operating Cycle

In the ordinary course of business there is a continuing *circulation of capital* within the current assets. For example, with a manufacturer, cash is expended for materials, labor, and factory overhead that are converted into finished inventory. After being sold, the inventory is usually converted into a trade receivable and, on collection of the receivable, is converted back to cash. The average time elapsing between expending the cash originally and receiving the cash back from the trade receivable is called an *operating cycle*. *One year* is used as a basis for segregating current assets when the operating cycle occurs more frequently than once a year. When the operating cycle is *longer than one year,* as with the lumber, tobacco, and distillery businesses, then the longer period should be used as the operating cycle. *In the event that a business clearly has no operating cycle, the one-year rule is used.*

The classification of current assets and current liabilities for a specific company is directly related to the company's operating cycle.

Frequently, businesses have a *natural business year,* at the end of which the company's activity, inventory, and trade receivables are at their lowest point.

Current Assets

Resources that are reasonably expected to be realized in cash, sold, or consumed (prepaid items) during the normal operating cycle of a business are classified as current assets. Current assets are sometimes called circulating or working assets, and cash that is restricted as to withdrawal or use for other than current operations should not be classified as a current asset.

There are several basic categories of current assets:

Cash Includes money in any form, for example, cash on deposit, cash awaiting deposit, and cash funds available for use.

Secondary cash resources The most common type of secondary cash resources are marketable securities.

Inventories Includes all types of inventories including merchandise, raw materials, work in process, finished goods, operating supplies, and ordinary maintenance material and parts.

Receivables Includes accounts receivable, notes receivable, and receivables from officers and employees. To be classified as current assets all these must become due within the current operating cycle.

Prepaid expenses Includes prepaid insurance, interest, rents, taxes, advertising, and operating supplies. Prepaid expenses will not be converted into cash, but if they were not paid in advance, they would require the use of current assets during the operating cycle.

Current assets do not always represent their present realizable cash value. Accounts receivable, net of allowances for uncollectible accounts, are effectively stated at the amount of cash estimated as realizable. Supplementary information should be disclosed that reveals the basis on which current assets are stated and an indication of the method of determining the cost.

Current Liabilities

Current liabilities are obligations whose liquidation is reasonably expected to require the use of current assets or the creation of other current liabilities.

Current Assets and Current Liabilities

There are several basic types of current liabilities:

Obligations for items that have entered the operating cycle, which include trade payables and accrued liabilities such as wages and taxes.

Other debt that is expected to be liquidated during the current operating cycle, which include short-term notes and the currently maturing portion of long-term debt.

Prepayments that include collections received in advance of services, for example, prepaid subscriptions and other deferred revenues.

Accruals which include estimates of accrued amounts that are expected to be required to cover expenditures within the year for known obligations (1) when the amount can be determined only approximately (provision for accrued bonuses payable) or (2) where the specific person(s) to whom payment will be made is (are) unascertainable (provision for warranty of a product).

Current liabilities should not include a contractual obligation falling due at an early date that is expected to be refinanced or refunded and is not reasonably expected to require the use of current assets or the creation of other current liabilities.

When appropriate, current liabilities should be recorded at their present values of the amounts to be paid.

Working Capital

Working capital is the excess of current assets over current liabilities, and it indicates the relative liquidity of an enterprise.

The statement of changes in financial position is a mandatory part of a complete set of financial statements prepared in conformity with GAAP (APB-19). One of the major purposes of the statement of changes in financial position is to report the increase or decrease in working capital during the period and the changes in each element of working capital.

Changes in each element of working capital The changes in each element of working capital are the increases or decreases in each current asset and current liability over the amounts in the preceding year, as follows:

Current Assets and Current Liabilities

Current Assets	1976	1977	Increase or (Decrease)
Cash	$10,000	$ 15,000	$ 5,000
Accounts receivable	25,000	35,000	10,000
Inventory	50,000	60,000	10,000
Prepaid expenses	1,000	500	(500)
Total current assets	$86,000	$110,500	$24,500
Current Liabilities			
Accounts payable	$10,000	$ 15,000	$ 5,000
Notes payable-current	20,000	15,000	(5,000)
Accrued expenses	1,000	1,500	500
Total current liabilities	$31,000	$ 31,500	$ 500
Net working capital	$55,000	$ 79,000	
Increase or decrease in working capital			$24,000

The *current ratio,* or *working capital ratio,* is a measure of current position and is useful in analyzing short-term credit.

The current ratio is computed by dividing the total current assets by the total current liabilities.

	1977	1976
Current assets	$650,000	$525,000
Current liabilities	250,000	225,000
Working capital	$400,000	$300,000
Current ratio	2.6 : 1	2.3 : 1

The *acid-test ratio* is determined by dividing the "cashlike" assets by total current liabilities. The cashlike assets consist of cash, receivables, and marketable securities. Only receivables and securities *convertible into cash* should be included, and restricted cash and securities should be excluded.

	1977	1976
Cash	$ 200,000	$ 150,000
Marketable securities	400,000	350,000
Receivables, net	800,000	600,000
Total cashlike assets	$1,400,000	$1,100,000
Total current liabilities	$ 600,000	$ 500,000
Acid-test ratio	2.3 : 1	2.2 : 1

Receivables

Accounts receivable, net of allowances for uncollectible accounts, are effectively stated at the estimated amount of cash that will be realized. This is accomplished by calculating the estimated amount of uncollectible accounts based either on prior experience or an industry average. Two acceptable procedures of accounting for bad debts are (1) the direct write-off method and (2) the allowance method.

Direct write-off method This method recognizes a bad debt expense only when a specific account is determined to be uncollectible. The weaknesses of the direct write-off method are:

1. Bad debt expense is not "matched" with the related sales.
2. Accounts receivable are always overstated, because no attempt is made to account for the unknown bad debts included therein.

Allowance method A percentage of each period's sales or ending accounts receivable is estimated to eventually prove uncollectible. Consequently, the amount determined is charged to bad debts of the period and the credit is made to a valuation account such as allowance for doubtful accounts. When specific accounts are written off, they are debited to the allowance account, which is periodically recomputed.

Bad debts may be estimated as a percentage of sales or of accounts receivable. For financial statement purposes, unearned interest and finance charges are deducted from the related receivable. This is necessary in order to state the receivable at its current realizable value.

Discounted notes receivable arise when the holder endorses the note (with or without recourse) to a third party and receives a sum of cash. The difference between the amount of cash received by the holder and the maturity value of the note is called the discount. If the note is discounted with recourse, the assignor remains contingently liable for the ultimate payment of the note when it becomes due. If the note is discounted without recourse, the assignor assumes no further liability.

The account called discounted notes receivable is a contra account which is deducted from the related receivables for financial statement purposes.

Current Assets and Current Liabilities

The following is the procedure for computing the proceeds of a discounted note:

1. Compute the total maturity value of the note, including interest due at maturity.
2. Compute the discount amount (the maturity value of the note multiplied by the discount rate for the time involved).
3. The difference between the two amounts (1 minus 2) equals the proceeds of the note.

A $1,000 90-day 10% note is discounted at a bank at 8% when 60 days are remaining to maturity.

Maturity—$1,000 × 102.5% ($1/4$ of 10% plus face)	$1,025.00
Discount—$1,025 × 1.333% ($1/6$ of 8%)	13.66
Proceeds of note	$1,011.34

Factoring

Factoring is a process by which a company can convert its receivables into cash by assigning them to a factor either with or without recourse. "With recourse" means that the assignee can return the receivable to the company and get back the funds paid if the receivable turns out to be uncollectible. "Without recourse" means that the assignee assumes the risk of any losses on collections. Under factoring arrangements, the customer may or may not be notified.

Pledging

Pledging is the process whereby the company uses existing accounts receivable as collateral for a loan. The company retains title to the receivables but pledges that it will use the proceeds to pay the loan.

Cash Surrender Value of Life Insurance

Unless management intends to cash in a life insurance policy in which it is the beneficiary, the cash surrender value, if any, is classified as a *noncurrent asset*.

Computing Life Insurance Expense

The insurance expense is always the difference between the premium paid (cash) and the increase in the cash surrender value of the policy.

Disclosure

Current assets and current liabilities should be clearly identified in the financial statements, and the basis of determining the amounts stated should be fully disclosed. The following are the more common disclosures that should be made for current assets and current liabilities in the financial statements or in footnotes thereto:

1. method of valuing current marketable securities (FASB-12)
2. classification of inventories and the method used (FIFO, LIFO, average cost, etc.)
3. restrictions on current assets
4. current portions of long-term obligations
5. description of accounting policies relating to current assets and current liabilities

Accounts receivable and notes receivable from officers, employees, or affiliated companies, if material, must be reported separately in the financial statements (ARB-43, Chapter 1A).

Current Obligations Expected to Be Refinanced

FASB-6 and FASB Interpretation-8 establish the promulgated GAAP for reclassifying a short-term obligation (current liability) that is expected to be refinanced into a long-term liability, or stockholders' equity. In other words, if a company intends to refinance a short-term obligation into a classification other than current liability, prior to the issuance of the financial statements, it may be allowed to do so at the balance sheet date, even though the refinancing has not occurred. The actual intent to refinance, supported by an agreement which meets certain requirements (discussed below) are prerequisites for the reclassification.

The promulgated GAAP (FASB-6) applies only to those companies that issue classified balance sheets. A classified balance sheet reflects current assets and current liabilities separately for easy determination of working capital and to make the financial presentation more meaningful. Because of the specialized nature of some industries (stock brokers, real estate agents, stock life insurance companies, etc.) unclassified balance sheets are presented and therefore are not affected by the promulgated GAAP.

A short-term obligation should be excluded from current liabilities if the company intends to refinance it on a long-term basis and the intent is supported by either of the following conditions:

1. The actual issuance, after the date of the balance sheet but prior to the issuance of the financial statements, of a long-term obligation or equity security whose proceeds are used to retire the short-term obligation—in essence, the conversion of a short-term obligation into a long-term obligation or equity.

    The amount of short-term obligations which can be reclassified cannot exceed the actual proceeds received from the issuance of the new long-term obligation.

    If equity securities are issued, the short-term obligation is excluded from current liabilities but is not included in stockholders' equity.

    OBSERVATION: *The promulgated GAAP (FASB-6) is silent on what classification to use to report the newly issued equity securities on the financial statements.*

2. Prior to the issuance of the financial statements the company has entered into an agreement that enables it to refinance a short-term obligation on a long-term basis. The terms of the agreement must be clear and unambiguous and must contain the following provisions:
    a. The agreement is noncancelable as to all parties and extends beyond the normal operating cycle of the company (if the company has no operating cycle or the operating cycle occurs more than once a year, then the one-year rule is used).
    b. At the balance sheet date and at its issuance, the company was not in violation, nor was there any information that indicated a violation, of the agreement.
    c. The lender or investor is expected to be financially capable of honoring the agreement.

The amount of short-term obligation which can be excluded from the current liabilities cannot exceed the amount of available refinancing covered by the established agreement. The amount must be adjusted for any limitations in the agreement which indicate that the full amount obtainable will not be available to retire the short-term obligations. In addition, if the agreement indicates that the amount available for refinancing will fluctuate, then the most conservative estimate must be used. If no reasonable estimate can be made, then the agreement does not fulfill the necessary requirements and the full amount of current liabilities must be presented.

An enterprise may seek alternative financing sources besides those in the established agreement. However, if alternative sources do not materialize, the company must intend to borrow from the source in the agreement.

> **OBSERVATION:** *If the terms of the agreement allow the prospective lender or investor to set interest rates, collateral requirements, or similar conditions that are unreasonable to the company, the intent to refinance may not exist.*

Any "roll over" agreements or "revolving credit agreements" must meet the above provisions to enable a company to reclassify the related short-term obligations.

Disclosure

The financial statements must contain a footnote disclosing the amount excluded from current liabilities and a full description of the financial agreement and new obligations incurred or expected to be incurred or the equity securities issued or expected to be issued.

CURRENT VALUE ACCOUNTING

Background

There is no promulgated GAAP on current value accounting, and its general use for basic financial statements is prohibited under existing GAAP. However, like general price-level information, current value data may be utilized to supplement the historical cost financial statements required by GAAP.

> **OBSERVATION:** FASB-33 requires the application of some Current Value and General Price-Level Accounting techniques (see Financial Reporting and Changing Prices).

Overview

Current value accounting deals with the measurement of profits, and the valuation of a business entity, during periods of inflation.

In current value accounting, historical costs are replaced by current values that attempt to measure what a company would receive if it disposed of its assets. Thus, current value accounting violates the going-concern concept of GAAP in that it is based on liquidation values.

Current Value Methods

The major problem in current value accounting is the measurement of current values. The two most commonly used methods are the entry value system and the exit value system.

The entry value system is based on cost of replacement or reproduction. Replacement cost is the estimated cost of acquiring new and equivalent property at current prices after adjusting for depreciation, and may be approximated through the use of a specific price index. Reproduction cost is the estimated cost of producing new and equivalent property at current prices after adjusting for depreciation.

The exit value system is usually based on net realizable value in the ordinary course of business or sometimes on discounted future cash flow. Net realizable value is the estimated selling price of the asset less any costs to complete or dispose. Discounted future cash flow is the present value of estimated cash inflows, or cost savings, discounted at an appropriate rate of interest.

Monetary and Nonmonetary Items

To apply current value accounting methods, it is necessary to separate assets and liabilities into monetary and nonmonetary, in the same manner as in general price-level information.

Monetary assets or liabilities are fixed in terms of currency and are usually contractual claims. Since these amounts are fixed, there is usually no need to restate monetary assets and liabilities. Examples of monetary assets and liabilities are cash, accounts and notes receivable, and accounts and notes payable.

Nonmonetary assets or liabilities are those other than monetary assets or liabilities. Nonmonetary assets are generally restated for changes in current value. Examples of nonmonetary assets and liabilities are inventory, investments in common stock, property, plant and equipment, liability for advance rent collected, and common stock.

Because monetary assets are stated in fixed amounts of currency, they represent the amount of cash that is expected to be realized by them in the near future. Therefore, monetary assets are effectively stated at their net realizable value and do not usually have to be restated for current value financial statements.

Nonmonetary assets are not stated in fixed amounts of currency and thus do not reflect their net realizable value. Therefore, nonmonetary assets must be restated to their present current worth for current value financial statements.

Holding Gains

Regardless of the current value method used, holding gains will arise.

A holding gain is the difference between the current value of an asset and its historical cost. Realized holding gains result from the disposal of an asset, either by sale or use, during an accounting period. Unrealized holding gains result from increases in current values of assets during an accounting period in which such assets are retained by the entity.

Controversy exists as to whether holding gains should be reported in the current value income statement or in a separate statement of changes in holding gains.

Current Value Income

Under the current value concept, current operating income is the result of deducting from actual revenues the cost of goods sold and

Current Value Accounting

other expenses based on current values. Realized income is determined by adding realized holding gains to net operating income (current operating income less income taxes). Current value income is obtained by adding unrealized holding gains to realized income. The following illustration shows the steps required to determine current value income.

Revenues (actual)
Less: Current value of cost of goods sold and other expenses
Current operating income
Less: Income taxes
Net operating income
Plus: Realized holding gains
Realized income
Plus: Unrealized holding gains
Current value income

The following example illustrates the computation of current value income.

Fair Value, Inc., paid $1,200,000 in December 1976 for certain of its inventory. In December 1977, one-half the inventory was sold for $1,000,000, when the replacement cost of the original inventory was $1,400,000. *Ignoring income taxes,* what amount should be shown as the total gain resulting from the above facts in a current fair value accounting income statement for 1977?

The computation of current value income is as follows:

Proceeds of sale	$1,000,000
Less: Current value of inventory sold (½ of $1,400,000)	700,000
Current operating income	$ 300,000
Plus: Realized holding gain–Inventory ($700,000 current value − $600,000 historical cost)	100,000
Realized income	$ 400,000
Plus: Unrealized holding gain–Inventory	100,000
Current value income	$ 500,000

Comprehensive Illustration

This comprehensive illustration compares traditional historical cost accounting to the current value method of accounting.

Current Value Accounting

Balance Sheet

Assets	Historical Cost	Current Value
Current Assets:		
Cash	$ 1,700	$ 1,700
Accounts receivable	5,500	5,500
Investments	200	200
Inventory	2,500	3,000
Fixed Assets:		
Plant	4,000	5,000
Accumulated depreciation	(400)	(500)
Total Assets	$13,500	$14,900
Liabilities		
Current liabilities	$ 5,000	$ 5,000
Stockholders' Equity:		
Common stock	4,000	4,000
Retained earnings	4,500	2,900
Revaluation reserve		3,000
Total Liabilities and Stockholders' Equity	$13,500	$14,900

Comments:

Under the current value accounting method the monetary assets and liabilities are not restated, because they represent amounts fixed in terms of currency. However, the nonmonetary assets and liabilities (inventory, plant, and stockholders' equity) are restated to their net realizable values.

Current Value Accounting

Statement of Income

	Historical Cost		Current Value	
Sales		$13,000		$13,000
Cost of goods sold		4,000		5,500
Gross Margin		$ 9,000		$ 7,500
Less Expenses:				
Depreciation	$200		$ 250	
Others	600	800	600	850
Income before taxes		$ 8,200		
Current operating income				$ 6,650
Less: Provision for taxes		4,100		4,100
Net income		$ 4,100		
Net operating income				$ 2,550
Realized holding gains applicable to:				
Sale of inventory			$1,500	
Depreciation on plant			50	1,550
Realized income				$ 4,100
Unrealized holding gains applicable to:				
Replacement at cost of inventory at year end			$ 500	
Undepreciated value of plant			950	1,450
Current value income				$ 5,550

Comments:

Under the traditional historical cost method, net income is $4,100, whereas current value income is $5,550. Both methods use actual sales, but the current value method uses current values (replacement cost) in computing cost of goods sold and other expenses. In periods of inflation, gross margins will usually be less than under historical cost accounting, because current values are used.

Net income under historical cost accounting is always equal to realized income under current value accounting. In other words, historical cost accounting net income always includes realized holding gains. Holding gains are always separately identified in current value income statements. The only difference in dollar amounts between the two methods is unrealized holding gains. A current value income statement will reflect all unrealized holding

Current Value Accounting

gains, whereas these unrealized gains are never included in a historical cost income statement.

The provision for income taxes is the same for both historical cost and current value income statements. Depreciation expense is computed on the current value of an asset for current value accounting, whereas historical cost is used for historical cost purposes.

Statement of Changes in Revaluation Reserve
(Holding Gains)

Revaluation reserve (holding gains)–beginning of the year:		—
Realized holding gains applicable to:		
Inventory sold	$1,500	
Depreciation on plant (5% of $1000)	50	$1,550
Unrealized holding gains applicable to:		
Inventory at year end	$ 500	
Undepreciated value of plant	950	1,450
Total revaluation reserve (holding gains)		$3,000

Comments:

The revaluation reserve (which is shown on the balance sheet as $3,000) is a stockholders' equity account which reflects the difference between historical cost and current worth.

Statement of Retained Earnings

	Historical Cost	Current Value
Beginning balance	$ 400	$ 400
Add: Net income	4,100	
Current value income		5,550
Total	$4,500	$5,950
Less: Backlog depreciation		50
Revaluation reserve		3,000
Ending retained earnings	$4,500	$2,900

Comments:

Backlog depreciation (sometimes referred to as the "amortization gap") is the difference between accumulated depreciation under historical cost and accumulated depreciation based on current value.

DEFERRED COMPENSATION CONTRACTS

Background

The main source of promulgated GAAP for Deferred Compensation Contracts is APB-12, paragraphs 6-8.

If individual deferred compensation contracts, as a group, are tantamount to a pension plan, they should be accounted for as pension plans, under the GAAP–Accounting for the Cost of Pension Plans.

Overview

Deferred compensation contracts should be accounted for on an individual basis for each employee. If a deferred compensation contract is based on current and future employment, only the amounts attributable to the current portion of employment should be accrued.

If a deferred compensation contract contains benefits payable for the life of a beneficiary, the total liability should be based on the beneficiary's life expectancy or on the estimated cost of an annuity contract that would provide sufficient funds to pay the required benefits.

The total liability for deferred compensation contracts is determined by the terms of each individual contract. The amount of the periodic accrual, computed from the first day of the employment contract, must total no less than the then present value of the benefits provided for in the contract. The periodic accruals should be made systematically over the active term of employment.

Comprehensive Illustration

A deferred compensation contract provides for the payment of $50,000 per year for five years, beginning one year after the end of the employee's 10-year contract. A 10% interest rate will be assumed.

We must find the present value for the five $50,000 payments at the end of 10 years, as follows:

Deferred Compensation Contracts

Present value of $50,000 in five years	$ 31,045
Present value of $50,000 in four years	34,150
Present value of $50,000 in three years	37,565
Present value of $50,000 in two years	41,320
Present value of $50,000 in one year	45,455
Total present value of benefits at end of employment	$189,535

We now know that $189,535 must be accumulated over 10 years to have available the funds required to pay the benefits in accordance with the contract. We must find the amount of the annual accrual that earning 10% interest will total $189,535 at the end of 10 years. This may be found by using the formula for the value of an annuity due, as follows:

$$A = R\,[\Sigma\,(1 + i)^n]$$
$$\$189,535 = \$10,811$$

The annual accrual is $10,811.

DEPRECIABLE ASSETS AND DEPRECIATION

Background

This chapter brings together the promulgated GAAP relating to depreciable assets and depreciation, in addition to nonpromulgated GAAP of importance.

The following is the promulgated GAAP discussed in this chapter:

> ARB-43 Chapter 9A–Depreciation and High Costs
> ARB-43 Chapter 9C–Emergency Facilities
> ARB-44 (Revised)–Declining-Balance Depreciation
> APB-1–New Depreciation Guidelines and Rules
> APB-6, paragraph 17–Depreciation on Appreciation
> APB-6, paragraph 20–Declining-Balance Depreciation
> APB-12, paragraphs 4 and 5–Disclosure of Depreciable Assets and Depreciation

Companies in regulated industries should comply with the above promulgated GAAP in accordance with the Addendum to APB-2.

Overview

The basic principle of matching revenue and expenses is applied to long-lived assets that are not held for sale in the ordinary course of business. The systematic and rational allocation used to achieve "matching" is usually accomplished by depreciation, amortization, or depletion, according to the type of long-lived asset involved.

Asset Cost

The basis of accounting for depreciable fixed assets is cost, and all normal expenditures of readying an asset for use should be capitalized. However, unnecessary expenditures that do not add to the utility of the asset should be charged to expense. An expenditure for repairing a piece of equipment that was damaged during shipment should be charged to expense.

Razing and removal costs (less salvage value) of structures located on land purchased as a building site are added to the cost of the land. Land itself is never depreciated.

Depreciable Assets and Depreciation

> **OBSERVATION:** *Promulgated GAAP (ARB-43) requires that assets be recorded at cost, except in the case of quasi-reorganizations (corporate readjustments) in which it is permissible to write up or write down assets to market values (APB-6).*
>
> *When price-level accounting methods are used as supplemental statements, the distortion of assets and related depreciation resulting from inflation is somewhat ameliorated.*

Salvage Value

Salvage or residual value is an estimate of the amount that will be realized at the end of the useful life of a depreciable asset. Frequently, depreciable assets have little or no scrap value at the end of their estimated useful life and, if immaterial, the amount(s) may be ignored.

Estimated Useful Life

The estimated useful life of a depreciable asset may differ from company to company or industry to industry. A company's maintenance policy will affect the longevity of a depreciable asset.

> **OBSERVATION:** *Total utility of an asset, expressed in time, is called the* physical life. *The utility of an asset to a specific owner, expressed in time, is called the* service life.

Valuation of Assets

Under specific circumstances, assets may be valued in the following ways:

Historical cost The actual amount paid at the date of acquisition, including all normal expenditures of readying an asset for use.

Replacement cost The amount that it would cost to replace an asset. Frequently, replacement cost is the same as fair value.

Fair market value The price at which a willing seller would sell to a willing buyer, neither under any compulsion to buy or to sell.

Present value   The value today of something due in the future.

General price-level restatement   The value of an asset restated in terms of current purchasing power.

Self-Constructed Fixed Assets

When a business constructs a long-lived fixed asset for its own use, the following procedure should be observed:
1. All *direct costs* should be included in the total cost of the asset, which should be capitalized.
2. *Fixed overhead costs* should not be included unless they are increased by the construction of the asset.
3. *Interest costs* may or may not be capitalized as part of the construction cost of the fixed assets.

> **OBSERVATION:**   An FASB Exposure Draft entitled "Capitalization of Interest Costs" was issued on December 15, 1978. At the date of publication of this edition of the GAAP Guide, the Exposure Draft had not yet been promulgated. The following is a brief summary of the provisions of the Exposure Draft on "Capitalization of Interest Costs."
>
> Certain interest costs may be capitalized and added to the acquisition cost of assets which require longer than one year to complete for their intended use. The cost of assets to which capitalized interest may be allocated include the cost of both those assets acquired for a company's own use and those acquired for sale in the ordinary course of business. Thus, inventory items which require a long time to produce, such as aged whiskey, qualify for capitalization of interest costs.
>
> Imputing interest costs on equity funds is specifically prohibited by the Exposure Draft.
>
> The interest capitalization period commences with the first expenditure for the asset and continues through the acquisition period. Interest is not capitalized during delays or interruptions, other than brief, which occur during the acquisition or development stage of the qualifying asset. When the qualifying asset is substantially complete and ready for its intended use, the capitalization of interest ceases.
>
> A portion of the actual interest costs incurred on bor-

rowed funds during the capitalization period is allocated as capitalized interest and added to the historical cost of the qualifying asset. The following guidelines are recommended in the Exposure Draft:

a. During any monthly period, the interest cost allocated should be based on the average accumulated expenditures outstanding for the qualifying asset and shall not exceed the actual interest cost incurred during the same period.

b. Where a qualifying asset is related to a specific new borrowing, the allocated interest cost is equal to the amount of interest incurred on the new borrowing. However, if the average accumulated expenditures outstanding for the period exceed the amount of the related specific new borrowing, interest cost must be computed on the excess. The rate used to compute interest costs on the excess is the rate on any other recent unrelated borrowings, and if there are none, then the rate on older borrowings is used.

c. Weighted-average interest rates for older borrowings may be used or an overall interest rate may be applied to the accumulated expenditures. Reasonable estimates may also be used as long as the results approximate the provisions of the Exposure Draft.

Write-Up of Assets to Appraisal Values

GAAP prohibit the write-up of fixed assets to market or appraisal values. However, although prohibiting such a procedure, GAAP state that if fixed assets are written up to market or appraisal values, depreciation should be based on the written-up amounts (ARB-43).

Improvement of Depreciable Assets

Expenditures that increase the capacity or operating efficiency of an asset, if they are substantial, should be capitalized. Minor expenditures are usually treated as period costs even though they may have the characteristics of capital expenditures. When the cost of improvements is substantial or when there is a change in the estimated useful life of an asset, depreciation charges for future periods should be revised on the basis of the new book value and the new estimated remaining useful life.

The revision of the estimated useful life of an asset is measured prospectively and accounted for in the current and future periods. No adjustment is made to prior depreciation.

A machine that originally cost $100,000 was being depreciated (no salvage value) over ten years, using the straight line method. At the beginning of the fifth year $20,000 was expended, which considerably improved the operating efficiency of the machine and extended its useful life four years.

Original cost	$100,000
Less: Four years' depreciation	40,000
Balance/(adjusted)	$ 60,000
New expenditure	20,000
New depreciable base	$ 80,000
Useful life (6 + 4) in years	10
Amount of annual depreciation	$ 8,000

Kinds of Depreciation

Physical depreciation is related to a depreciable asset's wear and deterioration over a period.

Functional depreciation arises from obsolescence or inadequacy of the asset to perform efficiently. Obsolescence may arise when there is no further demand for the product that the depreciable asset produces or from the availability of a new depreciable asset that can perform the same function for substantially less cost.

Depreciation Methods

The goal of a depreciation method should be to provide for a reasonable, consistent matching of revenue and expense, by systematically allocating the cost of the depreciable asset over its estimated useful life.

The actual accumulation of depreciation in the books is accomplished by using a *contra* account, called accumulated depreciation or allowance for depreciation.

Depreciable Assets and Depreciation

The amount subject to depreciation is the difference between cost and residual or salvage value and is called the *depreciable base*.

Straight line *Straight line depreciation* is determined by the formula:

$$\frac{\text{Cost less salvage value}}{\text{estimated useful life}} = \text{annual depreciation}$$

Estimated useful life is usually stated in time periods, such as years or months.

Units of production The *units-of-production method* relates depreciation to the estimated production capability of an asset and is expressed in a rate per unit or hour.

The formula is:

$$\frac{\text{Cost less salvage value}}{\text{estimated units or hours}} = \text{rate per unit}$$

A machine is purchased at a cost of $85,000 and has a salvage value of $10,000. It is estimated that the machine has a useful life of 750,000 hours.

$$\frac{\$85,000 - \$10,000}{750,000} = \$0.10 \text{ per hour depreciation}$$

The units-of-production method is used in situations where the usage of the depreciable asset varies considerably from period to period, and in those circumstances in which the service life is more a function of use than passage of time.

Sum of the years' digits The *sum-of-the-years'-digits method* is one of the accelerated methods of depreciation that provides higher depreciation expense in the early years and lower charges in later years.

To find the sum of the years' digits, the digit of each year is progressively numbered and then added up. The sum of the years' digits for a five-year life would be:

$$5 + 4 + 3 + 2 + 1 = 15$$

For four years:

$$4 + 3 + 2 + 1 = 10$$

For three years:

$$3 + 2 + 1 = 6$$

When dealing with an asset with a long life, it is necessary to use the general formula for finding the sum of the years' digits:

$$S = \left(N \, \frac{N + 1}{2}\right)$$

To find the sum of the years' digits for an asset with a 50-year life:

$$S = 50 \left(\frac{50 + 1}{2}\right)$$

$$S = 50(25^{1}/_{2})$$

$$S = 1{,}275 \text{ sum of the years' digits for 50 years}$$

The sum of the years' digits becomes the denominator, and the digit of the highest year becomes the first numerator. For example, the first year's depreciation for a five-year life would be $5/15$ of the depreciable base of the asset.

Assume that an asset cost $11,000, has a salvage value of $1,000, and has an estimated useful life of four years.

The first step is to determine the depreciable base:

Cost of asset	$11,000
Less salvage value	1,000
Depreciable base	$10,000

Depreciable Assets and Depreciation

The sum of the years' digits for four years is:

$$4 + 3 + 2 + 1 = 10$$

The first year's depreciation is ⁴/₁₀, the second year's ³/₁₀, the third year's ²/₁₀, and the fourth year's ¹/₁₀, as follows:

$$
\begin{aligned}
&{}^4/_{10} \text{ of } \$10{,}000 = \$\,4{,}000 \\
&{}^3/_{10} \text{ of } \$10{,}000 = 3{,}000 \\
&{}^2/_{10} \text{ of } \$10{,}000 = 2{,}000 \\
&{}^1/_{10} \text{ of } \$10{,}000 = \underline{1{,}000} \\
&\text{Total depreciation} \quad \underline{\$10{,}000}
\end{aligned}
$$

When an asset is placed in service during the year, the depreciation expense is taken only for the portion of the year that the asset is used. For example, if an asset (of a company on a calendar-year basis) is placed in service on July 1, only six months' depreciation is taken. In our preceding illustration the six months' depreciation expense would be $1/2$ of $4/10$, or $2,000. If this occurs, then the second year's depreciation expense is calculated as follows:

$$
\begin{aligned}
&{}^1/_2 \text{ of } {}^4/_{10} \text{ of } \$10{,}000 = \$2{,}000 \\
&{}^1/_2 \text{ of } {}^3/_{10} \text{ of } \$10{,}000 = \underline{1{,}500} \\
&\text{Depreciation expense second year} \quad \underline{\$3{,}500}
\end{aligned}
$$

Declining balance The most common of these accelerated methods is the *double-declining-balance method,* although other alternative (lower than double) methods are acceptable. Under double-declining balance, the first year's depreciation is double the straight line rate. In succeeding years, the same percentage is applied to the remaining book value. No allowance is made for salvage, because the method always leaves a remaining balance, which is treated as salvage value. However, the asset should not be depreciated below the estimated salvage value.

An asset costing $10,000 has an estimated useful life of 10 years. Using the double-declining-balance method, the expense is computed as follows.

First, the regular straight line method percentage is determined,

Depreciable Assets and Depreciation

which in this case is 10% (10-year life). This amount is doubled to 20% and applied each year to the remaining book value, as follows:

Year	Percentage	Remaining Book Value	Depreciation Expense
1	20	$10,000	$2,000
2	20	8,000	1,600
3	20	6,400	1,280
4	20	5,120	1,024
5	20	4,096	819
6	20	3,277	655
7	20	2,622	524
8	20	2,098	420
9	20	1,678	336
10	20	1,342	268
Salvage value		1,074	

Had the preceding illustration been 1½ times declining balance (150%), the rate would have been 15% of the remaining book value.

In the illustration above, if the asset (of a company on a calendar-year basis) had been placed in service on July 1, the first year's depreciation would have been $1,000 (½ of $2,000), and the second year's depreciation would have been 20% of $9,000 (remaining value after the first year), or $1,800.

The declining-balance method is sometimes referred to as the "fixed-percentage-on-book-value method."

Cost-Recovery Method

The cost-recovery method, also known as the sunk-cost theory, is used in situations where recovery of cost is undeterminable or very questionable. The procedure is simply that all cost is recovered before any gain is recognized. The cost-recovery method is also used for questionable receivables.

Other Types of Depreciation

Replacement depreciation The original cost is carried on the books, and the replacement cost is charged to expense in the period the replacement occurs.

Retirement depreciation The cost of the asset is charged to expense in the period it is retired.

Present-value depreciation Depreciation is computed so that the return on the investment of the asset remains constant over the period involved.

Promulgated GAAP dictates that depreciation should systematically and rationally allocate the cost of an asset over its estimated useful life. Straight line, sum-of-the-years'-digits, and declining-depreciation methods are considered acceptable, providing they are systematic and rational (ARB-44). For financial accounting purposes, companies should not use depreciation guidelines or other tax regulations issued by the IRS, but should estimate useful lives and calculate depreciation expense according to generally accepted procedures. When depreciation for tax purposes differs from depreciation for financial accounting purposes, income tax allocation (APB-11) should be used.

In periods of inflation, depreciation charges based on historical cost of the original fixed asset may not reflect current price levels, and hence may not be an appropriate matching of revenues and expenses for the current period. In 1953, promulgated GAAP (ARB-43) took the position that it was acceptable to provide an appropriation of retained earnings for replacement of fixed assets, but not acceptable to depart from the traditional cost method in the treatment of depreciation, because a radical departure from the generally accepted procedures would create too much confusion in the minds of the readers of financial statements. Although inflation has become quite serious in recent years, depreciation based on historical cost remains the official, promulgated accounting principle.

Depletion

Cost depletion is the basic method of computing a deduction for depletion. An estimate is made of the amount of natural resources to be extracted, in units or tons, barrels, or any other measurement. The estimate of total recoverable units is then divided into the total cost of the depletable asset, to arrive at a depletion rate per unit. The annual depletion expense is the rate per unit times the number of units extracted during the fiscal year. If at any time there is a revision of the estimated number of units that are expected to be

Depreciable Assets and Depreciation

extracted, a new unit rate is computed. The cost of the natural resource property is reduced each year by the amount of the depletion expense for the year.

Disclosure

Allowances for depreciation and depletion should be deducted from the assets to which they relate (APB-12).

The following disclosures of depreciable assets and depreciation should be made in the financial statements or notes thereto:

1. depreciation expense for the period
2. balances of major classes of depreciable assets by nature or function
3. accumulated depreciation allowances by classes or in total
4. the methods used, by major classes, in computing depreciation

> **OBSERVATION:** Promulgated GAAP (APB-12) requires that the above disclosures be made in the financial statements or in footnotes. In addition, the effect of a change from one depreciation method to another must be disclosed (APB-20).

DEVELOPMENT-STAGE ENTERPRISES

Background

FASB-7 establishes the current promulgated GAAP for Accounting and Reporting by Development Stage Enterprises in all industries. Its application to regulated industries should be made in compliance with the Addendum to APB-2. It supersedes FASB Interpretation-5 in the area of research and development for development-stage enterprises, and does not alter or amend any other promulgated or nonpromulgated GAAP. Promulgated GAAP in this area specifically states that FASB-7 does not alter nonpromulgated GAAP with respect to:

a. an established business in expansion phases
b. extractive industries in exploration or development stages
c. real estate firms developing properties

Applying FASB-7 to financial statements of established operating companies is covered by FASB Interpretation-7, which is covered later in this chapter.

Overview

A development-stage company is one in which principal operations have not commenced or principal operations have generated an insignificant amount of revenue. During the development stage, a company devotes most of its activities toward establishing a new business. (For example, building production facilities or acquiring operational assets, training personnel, developing markets, etc.)

Accounting and Reporting

A development-stage company must issue the same basic financial statements as any other enterprise, and such statements should be prepared in conformity with GAAP. A development-stage company should follow GAAP in determining whether operating costs should be expensed, capitalized, or deferred. In the case of a subsidiary or a similar type of enterprise, this determination is made within the context of the entity presenting the financial statements. Thus, it would be possible to expense an item on the financial statements of a subsidiary and capitalize the same expense on the financial statements of the parent company (FASB Interpretation-7). For example, if a subsidiary purchases a machine that will be used only for research and development, it would expense the cost of the item in the year of acquisition. However, the parent company could capitalize the same machine, if in its normal course of business such a machine has an alternative future use.

Disclosure

The bulk of FASB-7 concentrates on establishing the disclosure requirements for a development-stage company. The financial statements must disclose the following:

1. Accumulated losses should be described as "deficit accumulated during the development stage."
2. The income statement should show revenues and expenses for each period being presented and should also present a running cumulative total of both amounts from the company's inception. This provision also applies to dormant companies that have been reactivated at the development stage. In such cases, the totals begin from the time that development-stage activities are initiated.
3. The statement of changes in financial position should reflect a cumulative total of the sources and uses of funds from the company's inception and amounts for the current period.
   The statement of changes in financial position need be presented only when required by promulgated GAAP. That is, it can be omitted if the financial statements are for internal use only or if they are prepared for a special purpose.
4. A separate statement of stockholders' equity shall be issued and shall contain the following information:
   a. The date and number of shares of stock (or other securities) issued for cash or other consideration and the dollar amounts assigned
   b. for each issuance of capital stock involving noncash consideration, a description of the nature of the consideration and the basis for its valuation.

   A company can combine separate transactions of equity securities, providing that the same type of securities and amount of consideration are involved.
   Modification of the statement of stockholders' equity may be required for a combined group of companies that form a

development-stage company or for an unincorporated development-stage entity.

> **OBSERVATION:** Promulgated GAAP does not indicate the types of modifications that might be necessary.

5. The financial statements shall be identified as those of a development-stage company and contain a description of the proposed business activities.
6. The first year that the company is no longer in the development stage, the financial statements shall indicate that in the prior year it was in the development stage. If the company includes prior-year figures for comparative purposes, the cumulative amounts required in 2 and 3 above should not appear.

When a development-stage company which is a subsidiary adopts a new accounting principle, the parent should also reflect this accounting change by making the necessary adjustments on its financial statements in compliance with APB-20 (FASB Interpretation-7). Any such adjustments and related income tax effects should be recorded and disclosed.

EARNINGS PER SHARE

Background

The main source of promulgated GAAP for Earnings per Share is APB-15. The presentation of the components that make up EPS are discussed in APB-9, Reporting the Results of Operations.

The promulgated GAAP apply to financial statements of corporations prepared in conformity with GAAP whose capital structure comprises common stock, including common stock equivalents, and/or senior securities. In this respect, the promulgated GAAP excludes mutual companies that do not have common stock, such as mutual savings banks, credit unions, cooperatives, and other similar entities. Also specifically excluded from the promulgated GAAP are registered investment companies, government-owned corporations and nonprofit entities.

In addition, statements prepared for special purposes, wholly owned subsidiaries and parent companies that accompany consolidated financial statements are not covered by the promulgated GAAP for obvious reasons.

Companies subject to government regulations for setting rates are not specifically referred to in the promulgated GAAP. Therefore, in accordance with the Addendum to APB-2, regulated companies should comply with the provisions of the promulgated GAAP (APB-15) for reporting earnings per share.

Nonpublic Enterprise (FASB-21)

A nonpublic enterprise is an enterprise other than one:

1. whose debt or equity securities are traded in a public market
2. that is required to file financial statements with the SEC

An enterprise loses its status as nonpublic when it issues financial statements in preparation for the sale of any class of securities in a public market.

A public market is a foreign or domestic stock exchange or an over-the-counter market.

A nonpublic enterprise is not required to disclose earnings per share (APB-15), or segment information (FASB-14), in a complete set of separately issued financial statements. The nonpublic enterprise may be a subsidiary, a joint venture, or any other investee.

Earnings Per Share

If the nonpublic enterprise elects to disclose earnings per share or segment information, it must comply with the disclosure requirements of GAAP. It may not disclose this information on an arbitrary basis.

Overview

Earnings per share (EPS) or loss per share (LPS) is an important measure of performance for all users of financial statements, and should appear prominently on the face of the income statement for all periods presented. Earnings-per-share data should be consistent with the captions shown on the income statement, but EPS for continuing operations and EPS for net income are mandatory.

> **OBSERVATION:** Although EPS for extraordinary items is not required, it is strongly recommended by APB-15 and APB-30. EPS for discontinued operations and the resulting gain or loss on the disposal of a segment may or may not be presented (APB-30).
>
> EPS for the cumulative effects of an accounting change is required by APB-20 and APB-30.

If prior-period dollar amounts on an income statement have been restated as a result of a prior-period adjustment, the EPS data must also be restated, and the *effects* of such a restatement in per share amounts should be disclosed in the financial statements in the year of restatement.

When common stock equivalents or other dilutive securities cause a dilution in one of the EPS data presented on the face of the income statement, and at the same time cause an antidilutive effect in another EPS data presented on the same income statement, all the EPS data presented should be computed using the common stock equivalents or other dilutive securities, regardless of the dilution (APB-30).

In reporting the cumulative effects of an accounting change, two presentations of EPS data for each caption presented are required. The regular presentation includes the primary and fully diluted EPS (1) for the current year reflecting the new accounting principle and its cumulative effect on prior years and (2) for any prior years as previously presented. The *pro forma* presentation includes the primary and fully diluted EPS (1) for the current year reflecting the new accounting principle and (2) for any prior years presented, restated to include the effect of the new accounting principle (APB-20). (See Accounting Changes chapter for illustration of presentation.)

A "dual presentation" is the presentation of EPS data for both primary and fully diluted earnings per share. This information indicates the minimum and maximum levels of dilution for current earnings. GAAP requires that primary and fully diluted EPS be given equal prominence on the income statement.

If a conversion takes place during or after a current period (up to the issuance date of the financial report) that would have materially affected primary EPS if such conversions were included in primary EPS from the beginning of the period or from the date of issuance, if later, supplemental information reflecting the retroactive effect should be furnished in a footnote. Under no circumstances should such retroactive effect be included in EPS data on the face of the income statement.

Common Stock Equivalents

The concept of common stock equivalents (CSE) is essential to an understanding of reporting EPS in accordance with GAAP. The concept is based on the principle of *substance over form,* in that, although certain securities are not actually common stock, the terms and/or conditions under which they were issued usually contain provisions that enable the holder to become a common stockholder. For example, the holder of participating preferred stock is usually entitled to share in the earnings of a corporation when the earnings exceed a specified level. If the corporation has excellent earnings, the value of the participating preferred stock will undoubtedly increase, and its owner has a share in the earnings potential of the business. At the same time, the earnings potential of the common stockholder is decreased, usually as to dividends and possible price appreciation on his shares. This is the concept of *dilution.*

Consequently, the auditor wishes to identify and disclose the substance of these dilutive securities by disclosing their effect on the earnings of the common shareholder. Neither the conversion to common stock nor the imminence of conversion is a prerequisite to a security being considered a CSE.

The determination that a security is (or is not) a CSE is made at the time the security is issued and is based on conditions that existed at the time of issuance. Once a security has been classified as a CSE, it should not be changed thereafter as long as the security is outstanding. If a security is deemed to be a CSE and identical securities are subsequently issued, the identical securities must be classified as CSE.

Earnings Per Share

> **OBSERVATION:** *In determining the "time of issuance" of a security for the purposes of CSE, all pertinent facts must be considered. The time of issuance is generally the date on which the terms of the offering were reached and announced even though they are subject to the approval of directors, stockholders, or others.*

If a security is not classified as a CSE at the time of issuance but is subsequently reclassified as a CSE, it is excluded from primary EPS but included in computing fully diluted EPS (primary EPS and fully diluted EPS are discussed below).

Common stock equivalents are used only in respect to EPS, and the designation does not effect any other accounting treatment or financial statement presentation.

The following are common types of CSE:

Stock options, warrants, and similar instruments Stock options, warrants, and other similar instruments should be considered CSE *at all times.* These types of security arrangements usually have no cash yield and their right to obtain common stock usually dictates their value.

Convertible debt and convertible preferred stock If at the time of issuance, a convertible security has terms or conditions that make it a CSE and its cash yield based on its market price at the date of issuance is less than $66^{2}/_{3}\%$ of the then current bank prime interest rate, the convertible security should be considered a CSE.

In the event that there is no market price available, the determination should be based on the fair value of the security.

If the cash yield on the security changes within the first five years of its life, the lowest rate during that period should be used in determining its status as a CSE.

Participating securities If a participation feature includes a share in the earnings potential of the corporation on substantially the same basis as that of the common shares, such participating securities are generally classified as CSE.

Contingent shares Contingent issuable shares depend on some future event or on certain conditions being met.

Earnings Per Share

Generally, contingently issuable shares should not be considered CSE unless the contingent event has been attained as at the reporting date for the EPS. The following general rules apply to contingent issuable shares.

Attainment or maintenance of a certain level of earnings (1) If the level is currently being attained, the contingent shares should be considered CSE for both primary and fully diluted earnings. (2) If the attainment or maintenance contingency is above the present level of earnings, the contingent shares should be considered CSE only for the purpose of fully diluted earnings, in which case earnings for the period are adjusted to the specified earning level before computing EPS. Prior-period EPS should not be restated to reflect the year-to-year effect of the above changes.

Contingent on future market price CSE for both primary and fully diluted earnings should be considered only for the number of contingent shares that would be issued based on the market price at the close of the period being reported on. Prior-period EPS is restated to reflect the market price changes from year to year.

Both future earnings and future market price Some contingent issuable shares are conditioned on both future earnings and a future market price. Under these conditions only the number of shares that would be issuable by meeting both conditions at the end of the period being reported on should be considered CSE for both primary and fully diluted earnings. Prior-period EPS is restated to reflect the change in the number of shares from year to year.

Some options, warrants, and other CSE are not convertible until some future date. Usually these securities receive no cash dividends, derive their worth solely from their conversion feature, and thus can be considered CSE depending on the time they become directly convertible. If they can be converted within five years after the period being presented, they are CSE for both primary and fully diluted EPS; if they can be converted before ten years but after five, they are used only in fully diluted EPS calculations; any conversion after ten years can be ignored on the basis of its questionable relevance to the current period (APB-15).

Shares placed in escrow accounts that are contingently returnable shall be accounted for in the same manner as contingently issuable shares, for the purposes of computing EPS.

Sometimes subsidiaries issue convertible securities, options, warrants, or common stock that are in the hands of the public, which should be considered CSE from the standpoint of consolidated and parent company financial statements for the purpose of computing EPS. In this event, the subsidiary should compute its EPS in accordance with the promulgated GAAP, and then the consolidated group or parent company would compute its proportionate share of the subsidiary's primary and/or fully diluted EPS based on the number of shares held. In other words, the consolidated group or parent company would include as income from the subsidiary only an amount equal to the number of shares held in the subsidiary multiplied by the subsidiary's primary and/or fully diluted EPS computed in accordance with GAAP.

Sometimes a subsidiary will issue a security that is convertible into parent company stock, or issue options or warrants to purchase parent company stock. In this case, the options and warrants should be considered CSE by the parent company in computing consolidated and parent company primary and fully diluted EPS. However, subsidiary securities convertible into parent company stock must be evaluated to determine whether they are CSE and enter into the computation of the parent company's primary EPS, or whether they are not CSE and enter only into the parent company's computation of fully diluted EPS. The test for CSE in this case is the same as that for any other convertible security: If at the time of issuance, a convertible security has terms or conditions that make it a CSE, and its cash yield based on its market price at the date of issuance is less than $66^2/3\%$ of the then current bank prime interest rate, the convertible security should be considered a CSE.

Although most dividends are reported as historical facts for the purposes of EPS, stock dividends, splits or reverse splits should be presented in terms of the current equivalent number of common shares outstanding at the date of declaration. When this procedure is used, the basis for reporting such dividends should be fully disclosed. In this connection, presenting data as to dividends per share following a pooling of interest creates a disclosure problem. Therefore, in such cases it is usually preferable to disclose the dividends per share by the principal constituent on a historical basis, and in addition, the amount per equivalent share, or the total amount, for the other constituents in the pooling for each period, along with adequate disclosure of all pertinent facts. In all cases, where dividends are reported on other than a historical basis, full disclosure of such basis should be made in the financial statements or footnotes thereto.

CSE Materiality

If the dilution in EPS from all CSE is less than 3%, the dilution may be ignored (APB-15). This is an application of the basic principle of materiality.

The rule is that "common stock equivalents that in the aggregate dilute EPS by less than 3% need not be taken into consideration." However, in order to determine the 3% rule, primary and fully diluted EPS must be computed without and with the CSE.

Antidilution

If the inclusion of a CSE has the effect of increasing EPS or of decreasing LPS (loss per share), such CSE should be excluded from the EPS computation. As a result, a CSE may enter into the determination of primary EPS in one year and not another, because once a security has been classified as a CSE it always retains that status.

The following example illustrates the effects of antidilution.

During January the XYZ Company issued 10,000 shares of 100 par value 5% preferred stock when the bank prime interest rate was 7%. The preferred shares were sold for $110 per share and were convertible into five shares of common stock. XYZ Company also had 300,000 shares of common stock outstanding at the beginning of the year. Net income was $220,000. What was the EPS for XYZ Company for the year?

Computation of Weighted Average Shares

Common stock outstanding, beginning of year	300,000
CSE–Preferred stock (issued for less then $2/3$ bank prime)	50,000
Weighted average shares	350,000

Adjustments to Net Income

Net income	$220,000
Less: Preferred dividends	50,000
Adjusted	$170,000
EPS, assuming conversion ($220,000 ÷ 350,000)	$ 0.63
EPS, assuming no conversion ($170,000 ÷ 300,000)	$ 0.59

Note: EPS with conversion is antidilutive and is not used.

Earnings Per Share

Computation of Preferred Stock Yield

The cash yield (effective rate) is determined by dividing the initial issuance price into the stated amount of interest. The preferred stock was sold at issuance for $110 per share and the stated interest was 5%:

$$\$5 \div \$110 = 0.0454 = 4.5\%$$

The result of this computation indicates that the cash yield at the date of issuance was 4.5%. The cash yield is compared to $2/3$ of the current bank prime rate at the date of issuance, which was 7%:

$$2/3 \text{ of } 7\% = 0.0466 = 4.7\%$$

The cash yield of 4.5% was less than $2/3$ of the 7% bank prime rate (4.7%) at the date of issuance, which makes the preferred stock a CSE. However, because of its antidilutive effect, the preferred stock is not used.

Simple Capital Structures

A corporation with a simple capital structure is one that consists of only capital stock, or which includes no potentially dilutive CSE that could dilute EPS by more than 3% in the aggregate.

For organizations with simple capital structures, the presentation of EPS in the income statement should appear as follows:

	19XX	19XX
Income before extraordinary items	$XX,XXX	$XX,XXX
Extraordinary items (describe)	XXX	—
Net income	$XX,XXX	$XX,XXX
Earnings per common share:		
Income before extraordinary items	$ X.XX	$ X.XX
Extraordinary item (note 1)	.XX	—
Net income per share	$ X.XX	$ X.XX

Earnings Per Share

EPS data are presented before and after extraordinary items. The per share amounts for extraordinary items are arrived at simply by subtraction.

Complex Capital Structures

For organizations with complex capital structures the procedure for determining EPS requires that the auditor gather information regarding various outstanding securities, use that information in computing two EPS figures (which is called a dual presentation), and then present the two EPS amounts with equal prominence on the face of the income statement. The captions for the two EPS figures are "Earnings per common share and common stock equivalents" and "Earnings per common share–assuming full dilution."

The first of these captions is referred to as *primary earnings* and the second as *fully diluted earnings.* The difference between primary EPS and fully diluted EPS is that primary EPS considers only securities that are common stock or CSE, whereas fully diluted EPS indicates the maximum dilution.

Under both methods, antidilutive securities are excluded. Antidilutive securities are those which have the effect of increasing EPS or reducing loss per share.

Three types of securities that might enter into the computation of fully diluted EPS are:

1. senior stock or debt that is convertible but not a CSE
2. options or warrants
3. contingently issuable shares

The difference between primary and fully diluted EPS is whether the securities are CSE. Only CSE enter into primary EPS, whereas all potentially dilutive securities are part of fully diluted EPS.

Dual Presentation of Net Income

A dual presentation includes primary EPS and fully diluted EPS. Only CSE enter into the computation of primary EPS, whereas CSE plus any other dilutive securities enter into the computation of fully diluted EPS.

Any securities that increase EPS are excluded from all computa-

Earnings Per Share

tions. These types of securities are called "antidilutive" and either increase EPS or decrease a LPS (loss per share).

    Primary EPS = common stock + CSE
Fully diluted EPS = primary EPS + any additional dilutive securities

Weighted Average Shares

Computations of EPS are based on the weighted number of shares outstanding for each period presented. A separate computation of the weighted number of shares outstanding must be made for primary EPS and fully diluted EPS.

The following example for ABC Company demonstrates how the weighted average shares are determined.

Common stock outstanding, 1/1/77	200,000 shares
Preferred stock (convertible into 2 shares of common stock), outstanding 1/1/77	50,000 shares
Convertible debentures (convertible into 100 shares of common stock for each $1,000 bond)	$100,000

On March 31, ABC reacquired 5,000 shares of its own common stock.

On May 1, ABC converted 20,000 shares of preferred stock into common.

On July 1, ABC converted $50,000 of convertible debentures into common stock.

On September 30, ABC reacquired 5,000 shares of its common stock.

Computation of Weighted Average Shares

1.	Common stock outstanding, 1/1/77	200,000
2.	Common stock reacquired, 3/31/77	(3,750)
3.	Conversion of preferred stock on 5/1/77	26,667
4.	Conversion of convertible debentures on 7/1/77	2,500
5.	Common stock reacquired on 9/30/77	(1,250)
	Total weighted average shares, 1977	224,167

1. Common stock outstanding   Since the 200,000 shares of common stock were outstanding for the entire year, all the shares are included in the weighted average shares.

13.10 / *GAAP GUIDE*

Earnings Per Share

2. **Common stock reacquired** 5,000 shares were reacquired on March 31, 1977, which means that $^9/_{12}$ of the year they were not outstanding. Since the 5,000 shares are already included in the 200,000 shares (1 above), we must deduct that portion which was not outstanding during the full year. Thus, $^9/_{12}$ of the 5,000 shares, or 3,750 shares, should be excluded from the computations, which means that only 196,250 of the 200,000 shares were outstanding for the full year.

3. **Conversion of preferred** On May 1, 1977, 20,000 shares of the preferred were converted into common stock. Since the conversion rate is 2 for 1, an additional 40,000 shares were outstanding from May 1 to the end of the year. Thus, $^8/_{12}$ of the 40,000 shares, or 26,667 shares, should be included in the weighted average shares outstanding for the year.

4. **Conversion of convertible debentures** On July 1, 1977, $50,000 of the convertible debentures were converted into common stock. The conversion rate is 100 shares for each $1,000 bond, which means that the $50,000 converted consisted of fifty $1,000 bonds, or 5,000 shares of common stock. Since the conversion was on July 1, only $^6/_{12}$ of the 5,000 shares (2,500) are included in the weighted average shares outstanding for the year.

5. **Common stock reacquired** 5,000 additional shares out of the 200,000 shares outstanding at the beginning of the year were reacquired on September 30, which means that for $^3/_{12}$ of the year they were not outstanding. Thus, $^3/_{12}$ of 5,000 shares, or 1,250 shares, must be excluded from the computation of weighted average shares outstanding for the year.

The weighted average number of shares must be used so as to reflect the period in which each security affected operations.

Any stock splits or stock dividends (or reverse splits or dividends) must be retroactively recognized in all periods presented in the financial statements. A stock split or stock dividend should be recognized if it occurs after the close of the period but before issuance of the financial statements. If this situation occurs, it must be fully disclosed in the statements. Also, as mentioned previously, the dividends per share must be reported in terms of the equivalent number of shares outstanding at the time the dividend is declared.

Earnings Per Share

Before computing EPS a company must subtract from net income any earnings pledged to senior security holders. If such a security is cumulative preferred, all dividends, whether the company has earnings to cover them or not, must be deducted from net income. In the case of a net loss, the loss is increased by the amount of cumulative dividends in arrears. If the senior security stipulates that dividends are limited to earnings, then adjustments are obviously made to the extent of available earnings.

A company adjusts noncumulative interest or dividends only to the extent they are accruable or declared.

All the above adjustments must be given adequate disclosure in the financial statements or footnotes thereto.

As mentioned earlier, it is possible for a security to be dilutive with respect to one of the EPS figures presented in the financial statements and at the same time be antidilutive to another. In such an instance the effects of such a security should be included in all EPS calculations.

Treasury Stock Method

When potential dilution from stock options and similar instruments is less than 20% of the number of common shares outstanding, the treasury stock method is used to compute the dilution.

Stock options and similar instruments are not CSE until the market price of the underlying stock exceeds the exercise price for three consecutive months. In that event, the treasury stock method is used to determine the amount of dilution.

The treasury stock method assumes that the stock options or similar instruments are exercised and the money received by the company is used to purchase as much common stock on the open market as possible. The average market price is used for primary EPS and the ending market price is used for fully diluted EPS, unless the average market price is higher. The amount of stock that cannot be purchased because of the lack of money is considered additional outstanding shares, which could have a dilutive effect on EPS. The computations are made by quarters in the year, unless the market price is relatively stable during the year, in which case one computation for the year can be used. The formula to compute CSE for stock options and similar instruments is:

Earnings Per Share

$$\text{Number of shares} - \left[\frac{\text{number of shares} \times \text{exercise price}}{\begin{array}{c}\text{average market price}^* \\ \text{or} \\ \text{ending market price}^{**}\end{array}} \right] = \text{additional shares outstanding}$$

*Average market price is used for primary EPS.
**Ending market price is used for fully diluted EPS, unless average market price is higher.

> **OBSERVATION:** Frequently an option or similar instrument is excluded from the computation of primary EPS, but must be included in the determination of fully diluted EPS.

The following problem illustrates how the incremental shares by quarters is computed for stock options and similar instruments.

A company has 10,000 stock options outstanding, which are exercisable at $60 each. Given the market prices below, determine the incremental shares by quarters, and the number of shares that should be included for both primary and fully diluted EPS.

	\multicolumn{4}{c}{Quarters}			
	1	2	3	4
Average market price	56	64	70	68
Ending market price	60	68	72	64

The formula for determining the incremental shares by quarters for primary EPS using the *average market price* is as follows:

1st quarter $\quad 10,000 - \dfrac{10,000 \times \$60}{\$56} = 0^*$

2nd quarter $\quad 10,000 - \dfrac{10,000 \times \$60}{\$64} = 625$

3rd quarter $\quad 10,000 - \dfrac{10,000 \times \$60}{\$70} = 1,429$

4th quarter $\quad 10,000 - \dfrac{10,000 \times \$60}{\$68} = 1,176$

Total incremental shares by quarters $= \underline{3,230}$

Divided by 4 quarters $= \underline{\underline{808}}$

*The exercise price of $60 is higher than the average market price.

Earnings Per Share

The reason why we divide by four quarters is that four quarters entered into our computation. The 808 shares must be included in the computation of primary EPS.

The computation of fully diluted EPS uses the *ending market price* unless the average market price is higher.

1st quarter	$10{,}000 - \dfrac{10{,}000 \times \$60}{\$60}$	=	0*
2nd quarter	$10{,}000 - \dfrac{10{,}000 \times \$60}{\$68}$	=	1,176
3rd quarter	$10{,}000 - \dfrac{10{,}000 \times \$60}{\$72}$	=	1,667
4th quarter	$10{,}000 - \dfrac{10{,}000 \times \$60}{\$68 \text{ (note 1)}}$	=	1,176
Total incremental shares by quarters			4,019
Divided by 4 quarters			1,005

*The exercise price of $60 is the same as the ending market price.

Note 1. Since the average market price is higher in the fourth quarter, it is used.

The computation of the incremental shares by quarters when divided by the number of quarters involved gives us the number of shares that could not be purchased with the proceeds from the hypothetical exercise of all the stock options. The computation could be determined by just dividing either the average or ending market price (whichever is applicable) into the hypothetical funds received by the exercise of the stock options, and whatever number of shares cannot be purchased are considered additional outstanding shares.

Under the treasury stock method, the funds that would have been received from the exercise of the options or similar instruments are calculated and:

1. The amount calculated as received is applied as if the funds were used to purchase common stock at the *average market price during the period,* except that for *fully diluted EPS* the market price at the end of the year is used, *if it is higher than the average market price.*

2. All options are considered to be exercised as at the beginning of the period (or time of issuance, if later).
3. Any remaining shares of common stock that theoretically could not be purchased because of the lack of funds are considered outstanding and are added to the total outstanding shares of common stock used to compute EPS.

The theory behind the treasury stock method is that any number of shares of common stock that could have been purchased on the open market with the exercised price funds from the options or similar instruments are not additional outstanding stock and have no dilutive effect on EPS.

The treasury stock method is not used for options and similar instruments that contain a provision which permits or requires the holder to pay part or all of the exercise price by tendering debt or other security of the issuer. The amount of dilution caused by these options and similar instruments is determined by the "if converted" method, which is discussed later in this chapter.

Modified Treasury Stock Method

When the number of shares of common stock that can be purchased with the hypothetical funds from the exercise of the options or similar instruments exceeds 20% of the number of common shares outstanding, the modified treasury stock method is used to determine the dilution, if any.

A maximum of 20% of the outstanding number of common shares may be purchased with the money received from the hypothetical exercise of all the stock options and similar instruments involved.

If any hypothetical money is still left after purchasing the 20% maximum, it is applied as follows (hypothetically):

1. reduction of any existing debt
2. investment in short-term paper

Net income is adjusted for any interest expense (income) saved or created by 1 and 2, and the related tax effects are taken into consideration.

The following problem demonstrates how the modified treasury stock method is used in those situations where the stock options outstanding exceed 20% of the authorized and issued common stock.

Earnings Per Share

Assume the following data:

Common stock	500,000 shares
Stock options (exercisable at $28)	120,000 shares
6% debt outstanding	$500,000
Net income	$400,000
Average and year-end market price of common stock	$30
Tax rate	50%

What is the primary EPS?

Since the number of stock options exceeds 20% of the total outstanding shares before exercise, the modified treasury stock method must be used.

The first step is to assume that all the outstanding stock options are exercised.

Proceeds of exercise of options (120,000 × $28) $3,360,000

The next step is to apply the proceeds as follows:

1. To purchase the maximum (20%) amount of common stock in the open market at either (a) the average market price in the case of primary EPS computation or (b) the ending market price or the average market price, whichever is higher, in the case of fully diluted EPS computations.
2. If any of the hypothetical funds remain after purchasing the maximum (20%) amount of common stock on the open market, they are applied:
   a. first, to reduce any long-term debt of the enterprise,
   b. secondly, to purchase short-term paper (hypothetically)

In this problem the application of the proceeds would be:

Application of Proceeds

Purchase of maximum 100,000 shares (20%)	$3,000,000
Reduction in 6% debt	360,000
Total application of proceeds	$3,360,000

Earnings Per Share

After the excess funds are applied to the reduction of $360,000 of 6% long-term debt, we must compute what effect this has on net income, because interest expense is hypothetically reduced by the reduction of the long-term debt.

Adjustment to Income

Net income	$400,000
Add: Net reduction of interest on 6% debt, less 50% taxes (0.06 × $360,000 × 0.5)	10,800
Adjusted net income	$410,800

Since 120,000 stock options were outstanding and we were restricted to purchasing 100,000 (20% maximum), the remaining 20,000 shares must be considered outstanding for the computations of both primary and fully diluted EPS.

Adjustment to Common Stock

Common stock outstanding	500,000
Additional shares (120,000 − 100,000)	20,000
Adjusted common stock	520,000
Primary EPS ($410,800 ÷ 520,000)	$ 0.79

The last item we must check is whether the addition of the stock options to the computation of primary EPS has had an antidilutive effect. This is determined by computing primary EPS without the stock options, as follows:

Primary EPS before options ($400,000 ÷ 500,000) $0.80

Since primary EPS excluding the stock options is higher than it is including them, there is no antidilutive effect. However, in this case the antidilutive effect is less than the 3% materiality rule and can be ignored.

The following is a summary of the steps in the modified treasury stock method:

1. The regular treasury stock method is followed except that a maximum of 20% of the outstanding number of common shares may be theoretically purchased.

2. The regular steps are followed for the treasury stock method.
3. Any remaining theoretical funds are applied in the following order:
   a. reduction of any borrowings
   b. investment in short-term government or commercial paper
   c. recognition of any tax effect of a and b
4. The total effect of all steps are aggregated; if the net effect is dilutive, it is recognized in EPS.

If-Converted Method

Convertible debt and convertible preferred stock are considered common stock equivalents (CSE) if their cash yield, based on the market price at the date of issuance, is less than two-thirds the then current bank prime interest rate.

When convertible debt or convertible preferred stock is CSE and enter into primary EPS, or when these same types of securities are not CSE but enter into the computation of fully diluted earnings, the *if-converted* method is used to determine dilution.

The principle objective of the if-converted method is to adjust net income for the effects of including a security in primary or fully diluted EPS. These adjustments are usually preferred dividends or interest on convertible securities.

> **OBSERVATION:** Nondiscretionery items that would have been made on the basis of net income, such as profit-sharing expense, royalties, and investment credits, must also be taken into consideration.

The if-converted method assumes that convertible issues are converted at the beginning of the year or at issuance date, if later.

Some convertible debt and preferred stock require the holder to pay a stipulated amount of cash on conversion. The treasury stock method is used to account for any cash received when the if-converted method is used. However, theoretical stock purchases are assumed only if the market price exceeds the exercise price or if the exercise price is less than market because the convertible security is selling at a discount.

It stands to reason that if you are going to consider one of these

Earnings Per Share

types of securities a CSE, the applicable dividend and interest must be added back to net income, *if either was previously deducted.*

The following example illustrates the application of the if-converted method.

X Company has outstanding 100,000 shares of common stock and $500,000 in 6% debentures convertible into 10 shares for each $1,000 bond. The convertible debentures are CSE, and net income for the year was $100,000. What is primary EPS, assuming a 50% tax rate?

Primary shares outstanding:
Common stock	100,000
Convertible debentures (500 × 10)	5,000
Total primary shares—outstanding	105,000

Primary net income:
Net income	$100,000
Add back interest on bonds, less tax effects (0.06 × $500,000 × 0.5)	15,000
Total primary net income	$115,000

Primary EPS (with conversion) ($115,000 ÷ 105,000 shares)	$ 1.10

Once again we must check to see whether the inclusion of the convertible debentures in the computation of primary EPS is antidilutive, by comparing primary EPS computed with the bonds to primary EPS computed without the bonds, as follows:

Primary EPS (without conversion) ($100,000 ÷ 100,000 shares)	$1.00

Primary EPS with conversion of the convertible bonds ($1.10) is more than primary EPS without the conversion ($1) and is therefore antidilutive.

In the above example, assume that instead of the convertible debenture, there were 10,000 shares of 3% preferred stock ($100 par) convertible into five shares for each share of preferred. What is the primary EPS?

Earnings Per Share

Primary shares outstanding:
Common stock	100,000
Convertible preferred (10,000 × 5)	50,000
Total primary shares	150,000

Primary net income (with conversion) $100,000

No adjustment is made when considering preferred stock as CSE, because dividends are deducted from net income.

Primary net income (without conversion):
($100,000 − $30,000 for preferred dividends) $70,000

Primary EPS (with conversion):
($100,000 ÷ 150,000 shares) $ 0.67

Primary EPS (without conversion)
($70,000 ÷ 100,000 shares) $ 0.70

Primary EPS with conversion is *not antidilutive* and is therefore used.

The *if-converted method* recognizes that the holders of a convertible bond or other debt instrument may share in equity (through conversion to common stock) or in debt (from holding the bond), but not in both. Many convertible securities are such that in order to convert to common stock, the holder must surrender his security.

In summary, convertible issues of this type that are CSE are assumed to be converted as at the beginning of the period (or at the date of issuance, if later), and the following steps are taken:

1. Net income must be recomputed to reflect the conversion of these securities from the beginning of the period. Interest charges and other expenses attributable to the convertible issues, along with any preferred dividends, must be taken into consideration in recomputing net income.

2. EPS is computed on the basis of the amount of common stock that would have been outstanding if these types of convertible securities were converted as at the beginning of the period (or at the date of issuance, if later).

Some warrants and convertible securities require a cash payment on conversion. In these cases, if the market price of the underlying stock exceeds the exercise price or if the security being converted is selling for a discount that results in an exercise price lower than the market price of the underlying common stock, then (1) the theoretical proceeds should be applied in accordance with the treasury stock method *and* (2) the if-converted method should apply as to the retirement or conversion of such warrants or convertible securities.

Two-Class Method

Although the *two-class method* is considered inappropriate when other acceptable methods can be used, it may be necessary in the case of *participating securities and two classes of common stock.*

Under the *two-class method,* CSE are treated as common stock, but with a dividend rate different from that of the common stock, there is no conversion of any convertible securities, and:

1. No use of theoretical proceeds is considered.
2. All required distributions to senior securities, CSE, and common stock are assumed to be deducted from net income.
3. The remaining amount is divided by the CSE and common shares, after adding back distributions under 2 above to arrive at primary EPS.

Loss per Share

Loss per share is generally based on the number of outstanding common shares, and any assumption of conversion would be antidilutive because the loss is spread over more shares, thereby reducing the loss per share.

Business Combinations

Shares issued in a combination accounted for by the *purchase method* are accounted for in the EPS calculation from the date of the acquisition. When the *pooling method* is used, the calculation is based on the total weighted average number of shares of the constituent firms, adjusted to the equivalent shares of the surviving company.

Earnings Per Share

The difference in treatment is based on the difference between the purchase method, in which results of operations appear in the parent's net income only from the date of acquisition, and the pooling method, in which results are "pooled" for all periods presented.

> **OBSERVATION:** As mentioned previously, data as to dividends per share following a pooling of interests may create a disclosure problem. In such cases, it is usually preferable to disclose on a historical basis the dividends per share paid by the principal constituent of the pooling and the amount of dividends per equivalent share, or the total amount of dividends, for the other constituents in the pooling. This type of presentation should be made for each period presented, along with adequate disclosure of all the pertinent facts.
>
> In all cases, where dividends are reported on other than a historical basis, full disclosure of such basis is required in the financial statements or footnotes thereto.

Disclosure

Disclosure should be made of all pertinent rights and privileges of the various security holders, including dividend and liquidation preferences, participation rights, call prices and dates, and conversion and exercise prices.

The bases on which primary and fully diluted EPS have been calculated should be disclosed in a schedule or a footnote to the financial statements. This disclosure should include the identification of any CSE in determining primary and fully diluted EPS, describe all assumptions used, and reveal the number of shares issued on conversion, exercise, or otherwise during the most recent annual fiscal period and any subsequent periods presented.

It may be desirable to provide clear-cut computations or reconciliations of each security entering into the computation of primary and fully diluted EPS. However, this type of information which shows the historical amount of outstanding common shares should not be shown on the face of the income statement.

A company should also disclose, preferably in a footnote, the effect of any recapitalization. For instance, if common stock is sold and the proceeds are used to retire preferred stock or bonds, supplemental EPS information should be supplied, showing the

Earnings Per Share

effects of such a transaction if it had occurred at the beginning of the period.

The following specific disclosures mentioned in this chapter are repeated here for convenience:

1. EPS should appear prominently on the face of the income statement for all periods presented.
2. The effects of prior-period EPS restated in per share amounts should be disclosed in the financial statements in the year of restatement.
3. If CSE or conversions occur during or after a current period that would have materially affected primary EPS, supplemental information reflecting the retroactive effect should be furnished in a footnote, if such CSE had been included in the computation of EPS for the current period. Under no circumstances should such retroactive effect be actually included in EPS data on the face of the income statement.
4. When stock dividends, splits, or reverse splits are presented in terms of the current equivalent number of common shares outstanding, as they should be, the basis for reporting such dividends should be fully disclosed.
5. A stock dividend, split, or reverse split that occurs after the close of a period but before issuance of the financial statements should be retroactively recognized in all periods presented in the financial statements. Full disclosure of the fact must be made in the financial statements or footnotes thereto.
6. All adjustments made to net income for the computation of EPS must be adequately disclosed.

Comprehensive Illustration

The following problem illustrates the application of all the components of determining EPS in accordance with the promulgated GAAP (APB-15).

Assume the following information for Black Corporation for 1977 and 1976. On the basis of this information compute the primary and fully diluted EPS for 1977 and 1976. Show your computation by supporting schedules in good form.

Earnings Per Share

Common stock ($1 par) issued prior to 1976	1,000,000 shs.
Common stock ($1 par) issued for cash, 7/1/77	100,000 shs.
Stock options to acquire one share of $1 common for $50 issued 1/1/70 expire 1/1/80.	100,000 shs.
3% Preferred stock ($100 par) convertible into 1.5 shares of $1 common. Sold at par (3/1/71) when the bank prime rate was 7%.	200,000 shs.
6% Debentures issued at par 4/1/77, convertible into 15 shares of $1 common for each $1,000 bond. Bank prime rate at date of issue was 7%.	$ 500,000

Market price of common stock ($1 par):

	Average	Ending
1977	64	66
1976	48	47

Income tax rate: 50%

	1977	1976
Income before extraordinary item	$3,200,000	$2,600,000
Extraordinary item	(400,000)	(600,000)
Cumulative effect of a change in accounting for depreciation	100,000	—
Net income	$2,900,000	$2,000,000

Computation of Weighted Average Shares

	1977	1976
Common stock ($1 par)	1,000,000	1,000,000
Common stock ($1 par) issued 7/1/77 equivalent shares (100,000 × 6/12)	50,000	—
Stock option (CSE) (Schedule A)	21,875	—
3% Preferred stock (CSE) (Schedule B)	300,000	300,000
Primary weighted average shares	1,371,875	1,300,000
Stock options (schedule A)	2,368	—
Convertible debentures (schedule C)	5,625	—
Fully diluted weighted average shares	1,379,868	1,300,000

Schedule A—Computation of CSE, Stock Options

1977–Primary EPS (use average market price = 64)

$$100{,}000 - \frac{100{,}000 \times \$50}{\$64} = 21{,}875$$

1977–Fully diluted EPS (use ending market price = 66, unless average is higher = 64)

$$100{,}000 - \frac{100{,}000 \times \$50}{\$66} = 24{,}243$$

Less included in primary EPS (above)	21,875
Additional shares for fully diluted EPS	2,368

1976–The average and ending market prices are less than the $50 exercise price, which results in no CSE.

Schedule B–Computation of CSE, Preferred Stock

Because the yield rate (3%) is less than $2/3$ of the bank prime rate of 7% ($2/3$ of 7% = 4.67%) at the date of issue, the preferred stock is CSE.

$$200{,}000 \text{ shares} \times 1.5 \text{ (conversion rate)} = 300{,}000$$

Schedule C–Convertible Debenture Dilution

The 6% convertible debentures are not CSE, because they were issued to yield 6%, which is more than $2/3$ of the bank prime rate of 7% ($2/3$ of 7% = 4.67%). However, they do enter into the computation of fully diluted EPS because of their potential dilution (convertibility).

Issued 4/1/77 and convertible into 15 shares per $1000.

Fully converted (500 × 15)	7,500
Issued 4/1/77 (7,500 × 9/12)	5,625

Earnings Per Share

Antidilution test–3% preferred stock:

	1977	1976
Without preferred:		
Net income	$2,900,000	$2,000,000
Less: Preferred dividends ($3 × 200,000)	600,000	600,000
Adjusted	$2,300,000	$1,400,000
Weighted average shares (1,000,000 + 50,000 + 21,875)	1,071,875	1,000,000
Primary EPS without conversion	$ 2.15	$ 1.40
With preferred:		
Net income	$2,900,000	$2,000,000
Weighted average shares	1,371,875	1,300,000
Primary EPS, with conversion	$ 2.11	$ 1.54

Antidilution test–6% convertible debentures:

	1977
Without conversion:	
Net income	$2,900,000
Weighted average shares (1,000,000 + 50,000 + 21,875 + 300,000 + 2,368)	1,374,243
Fully diluted EPS without conversion	$2.11
With conversion:	
Net income	$2,900,000
Plus: interest expense ($500,000 × 6% × 9/12 × 50% tax rate)	11,250
Adjusted net income	$2,911,250
Weighted average shares (1,374,243 + 5,625)	1,379,868
Fully diluted EPS with conversion	$2.11

Statement Presentation

	1977	1976
Income before extraordinary item	$3,200,000	$2,600,000
Extraordinary item (Note ____)	(400,000)	(600,000)
Cumulative effect of change in accounting principle (depreciation)	100,000	
Net income	$2,900,000	$2,000,000

Earnings per share and common stock equivalents:

Income before extraordinary item	$ 2.33	$ 2.00
Extraordinary item (Note _____)	(0.29)	(0.60)
Cumulative effect of change in accounting for depreciation	0.07	—
Net income	$ 2.11	$ 1.40
Shares outstanding	1,371,875	1,000,000

Earnings per share assuming full dilution:

Income before extraordinary item	$ 2.33	$ 2.00
Extraordinary item (Note _____)	(0.29)	(0.60)
Cumulative effect of change in accounting for depreciation	0.07	—
Net income	$ 2.11	$ 1.40
Shares outstanding	1,379,868	1,000,000

Comments:

1. In 1976 the preferred stock was excluded from primary and fully diluted EPS because it was antidilutive ($1.40 versus $1.54).
2. Any CSE that in the aggregate dilutes EPS (primary or fully diluted) by less than 3% can be ignored (materiality rule). In this comprehensive illustration the aggregate dilution of the CSE included in the computation of EPS was greater than 3% ($2.19 − $2.11 = $.08 or 3.65%).

NOTE: The pro-forma presentation required for a change in an accounting principle has been excluded from the above illustration for the sake of brevity.

EQUITY METHOD

Background

The promulgated GAAP for the Equity Method of Accounting for Investments in Common Stock is APB-18 (as amended).

FASB-13, paragraph 31, requires that subsidiaries whose principal business is leasing property to its parent company should be consolidated and the equity method is unacceptable.

The promulgated GAAP extends the use of the equity method to investments in common stock of corporate joint ventures and to investments included in parent company financial statements which are prepared for stockholders. The promulgated GAAP does not cover investment companies registered under, or those which would be included in, the Investment Company Act of 1940, or nonbusiness entities, such as individuals, trusts, and estates.

Since the promulgated GAAP (APB-18) is silent on its application to companies in regulated industries, such companies should comply in accordance with the Addendum to APB-2.

Overview

Domestic and foreign unconsolidated subsidiaries and corporate joint ventures should be presented in consolidated financial statements on the *equity basis* by an investor (usually the parent company), whose investment in the voting stock gives it the ability to *exercise significant influence over the operating and financial policies* of the unconsolidated subsidiary, although control may be less than majority.

Under the equity basis of accounting for investments in common stock, consolidated net income during a time period includes the parent company's proportionate share of the net income reported by the subsidiary or affiliate for the periods subsequent to acquisition. *The effect of this treatment is that net income for the period and stockholders' equity at the end of the period are the same as if the companies had been consolidated.* Any dividends received are treated as adjustments of the amount of the investment under the equity basis.

The equity method of accounting for investments in common stock is not a substitute for consolidated statements when circumstances indicate that consolidation is more meaningful and appropriate.

Equity Method

When appropriate, investors should use the equity method to account for investments in common stock, in all unconsolidated subsidiaries, in corporate joint ventures, and in other common stock investments (domestic and foreign).

Generally, a subsidiary whose principal business is leasing property to its parent must be consolidated and the equity method is unacceptable for a fair presentation (FASB-13, paragraph 31).

It is presumed, absent evidence to the contrary, that an investment (directly or indirectly) of less than 20% of the voting stock of an investee indicates lack of significant influence, and the use of the equity method or consolidated statements is not required.

It is assumed, absent evidence to the contrary, *that an investment (directly or indirectly) of 20% or more of the voting stock of an investee indicates the ability to exercise significant influence and control, and the equity method or consolidated statements, whichever is more meaningful, is required for a fair presentation.*

The 20% ownership is based on current outstanding securities that have voting privilege. Potential ownership and voting privileges should be disregarded.

Cost Method

The cost method is generally used when ownership is less than 20%. The original investment under the cost method is recorded at cost, and income is recognized from dividends received out of accumulated earnings earned after the date of acquisition.

Dividends received out of accumulated earnings prior to the date of acquisition are recorded as a return on investment and reduce the cost of the investment.

Certain factors, such as continuing operating losses, may indicate that a substantial decline in the value of the investment has occurred. If such a decline is not temporary, it should be recognized in the accounts.

Special rules apply to the cost method when it is used to account for unconsolidated subsidiaries (see chapter on Consolidated Financial Statements).

Equity Method

Under the equity method the original investment is recorded at cost and is adjusted periodically to recognize the investor's share of earnings or losses after the date of acquisition. *Dividends received reduce the basis of the investment.* Continuing operating losses from

Equity Method

the investment may indicate the necessity for an adjustment in the basis of the investment in excess of those recognized by the application of the equity method.

An investor's share of earnings or losses from its investment is usually shown as a *single amount* (called a *one-line consolidation*) in the income statement, after the following adjustments:

1. Intercompany profits and losses are eliminated, unless realized, in the same manner as if the investee were consolidated.
2. Any difference between the underlying equity in net assets of the investee and the cost of the investment should be accounted for on a consolidated basis. Therefore, goodwill should be amortized over a period of 40 years or less.
3. The investment should be shown in the investor's balance sheet as a single amount and earnings or losses should be shown as a single amount (one-line consolidation) in the income statement, *except for the investor's share of (a) extraordinary items and (b) prior-period adjustments, which should be shown in the income statement separately.*
4. Capital transactions of the investee that affect the investor's share of stockholders' equity should be accounted for on a consolidated basis.
5. Gain or loss is recognized when an investor sells the common stock investment, *equal to the difference between the selling price and the carrying amount of the investment at the time of sale.*
6. If the investee's financial reports are not timely enough for an investor to apply the equity method, the investor should use the most recent available financial statement, and the lag in time created should be consistent from period to period.
7. Other than temporary declines, a decrease in an investment should be recognized in the books of the investor.
8. Losses on an investment decrease the basis of the investment, which may not be reduced below zero, at which point the use of the equity method should be discontinued, unless the investor has guaranteed obligations of the investee or is committed to provide financial support. The investor should resume the equity method when the investee subsequently

Equity Method

reports net income and the net income exceeds the investor's share of any net losses not recognized during the period of discontinuance.

9. Dividends for cumulative preferred stock of the investee must be deducted first before the investor's share of earnings or losses is computed, whether the dividend was declared or not.

10. An investor who acquires more than 20% ownership in an investee after having had less than 20% *must retroactively adjust its accounts to the equity method on the basis of a step-by-step acquisition of a subsidiary.* In this event, at the date of each step in the acquisition, the carrying value of the investment must be compared with the underlying net assets of the investee to determine whether goodwill (positive or negative) is involved.

11. If an investment in voting stock falls below the 20% level, the presumption is that the investor has lost the ability to exercise significant influence and control, in which case the equity method should be discontinued. The carrying amount at the date of discontinuance becomes the cost of the investment. Subsequent dividends are accounted for by the cost method from the date the equity method was discontinued.

12. An investor's share of earnings or losses from an investment accounted for by the equity method is based on the outstanding shares of the investee without regard to common stock equivalents (APB-15).

13. The equity method should not be used for investments of a temporary nature, for foreign investments subject to controls and restrictions, and for those investments that are dissimilar and for which separate, supplemental information would be more meaningful.

OBSERVATION: This criterion is the same as that used for consolidated financial statements.

OBSERVATION: It is interesting to note that the cost method and the equity method are both bookkeeping and reporting methods. For example, a company may account for an investment by the cost method and prepare financial statements on the equity method. On the other hand,

Equity Method

consolidation would more likely be classified as a reporting method. The amount of detail reported in the financial statements is the main difference between the equity method and consolidation.

Disclosure

Full disclosure must be made for investments accounted for by the equity method and should include:

1. the name of the investment
2. the percentage of ownership
3. the accounting policies of the investor in accounting for the investment
4. the difference between the carrying value of the investment and the underlying equity in the net assets, and the accounting treatment of such difference
5. the quoted market price of the investment, except if it is a subsidiary
6. if material, a summary of the assets, liabilities, and results of operations presented as a footnote or as separate statements
7. the material effect on the investor of any convertible securities of the investee

If the equity method is not used for an investment of 20% or more, disclosure should be made of the name of the investment and reason(s) why the equity method was not used. Conversely, if the equity method is used for an investment of less than 20%, disclosure should be made of the name of the investment and reason(s) why the equity method was used.

In evaluating the extent of disclosure, the investor must weight the significance of the investment in relation to its financial position and results of operations.

Conclusion

The basis of recording income from investments accounted for by the cost method is dividends arising from earnings after the date of acquisition. Dividends are frequently unrelated to the earnings or losses of an investment, because some companies pay dividends in

Equity Method

excess of earnings and sometimes when there are no earnings at all. These types of shortcomings of the cost method make it difficult to relate earnings to the proper periods.

The market value method recognizes both dividends received and changes in the market price of the investment. Dividends received are included as income from the investment, as is the increase or decrease in the market value of the investment. The carrying amount of the investment in the balance sheet is the market value of the investment on that date. Thus the market value method more clearly reports the economic substance of holding the investment.

The promulgated GAAP requires that the equity method be used for domestic and foreign unconsolidated subsidiaries and noncontrolled investments in voting common stock. The equity method is used in those situations where the investor can exercise significant influence over the investee, which is presumed to occur when the investment is 20% or more of the investee. Under the equity method, dividends are credited to the investment account and are not considered income, and after all the necessary eliminating entries are made, the investor periodically records its share of the investee's net income as a debit to the investment account and a credit to income from the investment. The eliminating entries are the same as would be made for consolidated financial statements, including amortization of goodwill, if necessary. The equity method is usually called "one-line consolidation," because the investment is shown in the balance sheet as one amount and the income is likewise shown in the income statement, except for extraordinary items and prior period adjustments. Gain or loss on an investment accounted for by the equity method is the difference between the sales price and the carrying value of the investment on the date of sale. If a decline of the value of an investment accounted for under the equity method is other than temporary, it is recorded as a loss in the period it occurs.

The basic difference between consolidation and the equity method is the amount of detail reported in the financial statements.

Comprehensive Illustration

Cost method The original investment is recorded at cost in an investment account. Additions to, or returns of, the original investment are also recorded at cost in the investment account. Dividends received out of accumulated earnings prior to acquisition are recorded as a return of investment. *All other dividends are recorded as dividend income.*

The recording of dividends as dividend income is the major difference between the cost and the equity methods.

Equity method This method is exactly the same as the cost method except:

1. Dividends received are credited to the investment account and are not considered income.
2. The investor periodically records its share of the investee's net income by a debit to the investment account and a credit to income from subsidiary. Goodwill is amortized over a period of 40 years or less.

On December 31, 1976, LKM Corporation acquired a 90% interest in Nerox Company for $700,000. Total stockholders' equity on the date of acquisition consisted of capital stock (common $1 par) of $500,000 and retained earnings of $250,000. During 1977, Nerox Company had net income of $90,000 and paid a $40,000 dividend.

Cost method:

Investment in Nerox (90%)	$700,000	
Cash		$700,000
Cash	$ 36,000	
Dividend income		$ 36,000

On December 31, 1977, the investment account on the balance sheet would show $700,000 and the income statement would show $36,000 dividend income.

Equity method:

Investment in Nerox (90%)	$700,000	
Cash		$700,000
Cash	$ 36,000	
Investment in Nerox (90%)		$ 36,000

Equity Method

Investment in Nerox (90%)	$ 81,000	$ 625
Net income from 90% subsidiary	625	81,000

The debit of $81,000 to the investment account represents 90% of the $90,000 of net income for Nerox Company for 1977. The credit of $625 to the investment account represents amortization of goodwill of $25,000 which is assumed to be amortized over the maximum period of 40 years ($700,000 purchase price less 90% of $750,000 ($675,000) book value = $25,000 goodwill).

On December 31, 1977, the investment account on the balance sheet would show $744,375 ($700,000 + $81,000 − $625 − $36,000), and the income statement would show $80,375 net income from 90% subsidiary.

The basic difference between the cost and equity methods of accounting for a stock investment is that the cost method records dividends as dividend income and the equity method does not record dividend income, but does record as income the proportionate share of the investee's net income.

Converting from Cost Method to Equity Method

Under the cost method the investment account is debited only with the cost of the stock acquired. Dividends received on the stock acquired are credited to dividend income and are reported in net income for the period. An exception occurs when dividends are received out of accumulated earnings prior to the date of the acquisition of the investment, which are recorded as a reduction of the investment and not as dividend income. Under the equity method the investment account changes to reflect the book value that the stock acquired actually represents. The difference between the two methods will always be the actual book value that the stock acquired represents less any dividends received that were reported as dividend income.

P acquires a 30% stock interest in S for $45,000. Stockholders' equity of S at the date of acquisition consisted of $100,000 of capital stock and retained earnings of $50,000, for a total of $150,000. During the year, S had net income of $30,000 and paid to P a dividend of $3,000 out of current earnings.

Cost method:

P will record in an investment account its investment in S of $45,000, and will report the $3,000 dividend as dividend income in determining its net income for the year. P's investment account at the end of the year will still show a balance of $45,000, the original investment.

Equity method:

P will record as income 30% of the $30,000, or $9,000, as its share of the net income of S for the year, as follows:

Investment in S	$9,000	
Subsidiary income		$9,000

When the $3,000 dividend was received during the year, the entry was:

Cash	$3,000	
Investment in S		$3,000

P's investment in S at the end of the year was $51,000, as follows:

Original investment	$45,000
Add 30% of S's net income	9,000
Total	$54,000
Less: dividend received	3,000
Investment at end of year	$51,000

The $51,000 investment at the end of the year should exactly agree with P's 30% interest in S at the end of the year, as follows:

Stockholders' equity, beginning of year	$150,000
Add net income for year	30,000
Total	$180,000
Less: Dividend paid (P received $3,000, which represents 30%; thus 100% = $10,000)	10,000
Stockholders' equity, end of year	$170,000
P's investment of 30% of $170,000	$ 51,000

EXTINGUISHMENT OF DEBT

Background

APB-26 is the current promulgated GAAP for early extinguishment of debt. Gain or loss from the early extinguishment of debt or at scheduled maturity is covered by FASB-4. Early extinguishments of debt through troubled debt restructurings are covered by FASB-15. APB-26 covers the early extinguishment of all debt, including convertible debt, but does not alter accounting for the issuance of convertible debt with detachable stock purchase warrants (APB-14). Companies in regulated industries are covered by APB-26 in accordance with the Addendum to APB-2.

Overview

An early extinguishment of debt is the reacquisition of any form of debt prior to scheduled maturity. The only exception to this definition is the conversion of existing convertible debt. Refunding is the term used when other debt is substituted for existing debt.

The main problem in accounting for any extinguishment of debt is the difference between the amount paid to reacquire the debt and the net carrying amount of the debt at the date of acquisition.

Accounting for Extinguishments of Debt

All extinguishments of debt, prior to maturity, are basically alike, and accounting for such transactions should be the same regardless of the method used to achieve the extinguishment.

There are three methods for accounting for the difference between the redemption price of an outstanding debt and the net carrying book value:

1. amortize over the remaining original life
2. amortize over the life of the new issue
3. recognize gain or loss in the current period of redemption

The only acceptable method (GAAP) is to recognize any difference in the extinguishment of debt immediately in the year of redemption.

Net carrying amount the amount due at maturity, adjusted for unamortized premium or discount and for cost of issuance (legal, accounting, underwriter's fees).

Extinguishment of Debt

Reacquisition price the amount paid for the extinguishment. Includes call premium and any other costs of reacquisition.

Note: When extinguishment is achieved through the exchange of securities, the reacquisition price is the total present value of the new securities being issued.

Gain or Loss

Gain or loss on the extinguishment of debt is the difference between the reacquisition price and the net carrying amount.

The gain or loss is recognized immediately, in the year of extinguishment, and, if material, is reported as an extraordinary item, net of related tax effects. Gains or losses from cash purchases of debt made to satisfy current or future sinking fund requirements should be identified and reported separately (FASB-4).

Appropriate accounting recognition should be given to any stated or unstated rights or privileges arising from an extinguishment of debt.

Gains or losses on the extinguishment of debt should not be amortized over future periods.

In the early extinguishment of a debt, the recorded value of the new debt should not be affected in any way by the amount of the old debt.

Frequently, a refunding is made to avoid higher future interest rates or to take advantage of low current interest rates.

Refunding of Tax Exempt Debt (FASB-22)

If a change in a lease occurs as a result of a refunding by the lessor of tax-exempt debt and (1) the lessee receives the economic advantages of the refunding, (2) the revised lease qualifies and is classified either as a capital lease by the lessee or as a direct financing lease by the lessor, the change in the lease shall be accounted for on the basis of whether or not an extinguishment of debt has occurred, as follows:

1. Accounted for as an extinguishment of debt
    a. The lessee adjusts the lease obligation to the present value of the future minimum lease payments under the revised agreement, using the effective interest rate of the new lease agreement. Any gain or loss shall be treated as a gain or loss on an early extinguishment of debt.

b. The lessor adjusts the balance of the minimum lease payments receivable and the gross investment in the lease (if affected) for the difference between the present values of the old and new or revised agreement. Any gain or loss shall be recognized in the current period.
2. Not accounted for as an extinguishment of debt
   a. The lessee accrues any costs connected with the refunding that it is obligated to reimburse to the lessor. The interest method is used to amortize the costs over the period from the date of the refunding to the call date of the debt to be refunded.
   b. The lessor recognizes as revenue any reimbursements to be received from the lessee for costs paid related to the debt to be refunded over the period from the date of the refunding to the call date of the debt to be refunded.

Disclosure

Gains or losses from the early extinguishment of debt which are classified as extraordinary items should be disclosed in the financial statements or in properly cross-referenced footnotes thereto, as follows:

1. a description of the transaction, including the sources, if identifiable, of any funds used to extinguish the debt
2. the income tax effect for the period of extinguishment
3. the gain or loss per share net of any related income taxes

Comprehensive Illustration

On December 31, 1975, a corporation decides to retire $500,000 of an original issue of $1,000,000 8% debentures, which were sold on December 31, 1970, at a price of 98 and are callable at 101. The legal and other costs for issuing the debentures was $30,000. Both the original discount and the issue costs are being amortized over the 10-year life of the issue. What gain or loss is recognized on this early extinguishment of debt?

Extinguishment of Debt

Amount of original expenses of issue	$30,000
Amount of original discount (2% of $1,000,000)	$20,000
Amount of premium paid for redemption (debentures callable at 101, 1% of $500,000)	$ 5,000
Date of issue	12/31/70
Date of maturity	12/31/80
Date of redemption	12/31/75

Interest on debentures is irrelevant.

Computation discussion If the original legal and other expenses of $30,000 are being amortized over the 10-year life of the issue and five years have elapsed since that date, one-half of these expenses have already been amortized, leaving a balance of $15,000 at the date of redemption. However, only one-half of the outstanding debentures is being retired, which leaves $7,500 to account for in the computation of gain or loss.

The original discount of $20,000 (debentures sold at 98) is handled exactly the same as the legal and other expenses. Since one-half of the discount has already been amortized, leaving a $10,000 balance at the date of redemption, and since only one-half of the issue is being redeemed, this leaves $5,000 more that must go into the computation of gain or loss.

Obviously, any time that a security is redeemed at a premium, the amount of premium must also enter into the computation of gain or loss. In this case, the premium is $5,000.

Since there is no other relevant information in the problem relating to gain or loss, the following items enter into the final computation:

Original-issue expenses relating to retired debentures	$ 7,500
Original discount relating to the retired debentures	5,000
Premium paid for redemption	5,000
Loss on redemption of $500,000 of debentures	$17,500

FINANCIAL REPORTING AND CHANGING PRICES

(Editor's Note: Because it was issued just a few days before our press date, the restatement and review of FASB-33 in this chapter does not contain the extent of coverage and analysis that the Author generally prefers. In addition, some last minute clarification was made by telephone with the FASB.)

Background

FASB-33 entitled "Financial Reporting and Changing Prices", requires that certain large publicly held companies disclose specific minimum information concerning the effects of changing prices. The specific minimum information, in supplementary form, must accompany the basic financial statements of an enterprise. FASB-33 is effective for fiscal years ending on or after December 25, 1979, for publicly held companies which fall into one of the following two categories:

a. inventories, and property, plant and equipment (exclusive of any depreciation), which amounts to $125 million or more (NOTE: Land, natural resources, and capitalized leaseholds are considered property for the purposes of FASB-33.)

b. total assets of $1 billion or more (net of depreciation)

Both of the above conditions must be determined in accordance with GAAP and be computed as at the beginning of the fiscal year. The required supplementary information must be presented for consolidated financial statements, but does not have to be presented for the individual entities which make up the consolidated group.

> **OBSERVATION:** Apparently, if a company meets the requirements of FASB-33 at the end of its fiscal year, but not at the beginning of its fiscal year, the supplementary information need not be disclosed. However, FASB-33 specifically encourages all enterprises, publicly held or not, to provide the supplementary information. Furthermore, the FASB also encourages the reporting of the supplementary information for fiscal years prior to the December 25, 1979 effective date.

The provisions of FASB-33 need not be applied to:

1. interim financial statements
2. foreign publicly held enterprises whose basic financial statements are not prepared in U.S. currency

Terminology

The following definitions are quoted from FASB-33:

1. *Constant dollar accounting.* A method of reporting financial statement elements in dollars each of which has the same (i.e., constant) general purchasing power. This method of accounting is often described as accounting in units of general purchasing power or as accounting in units of current purchasing power.
2. *Current cost accounting.* A method of measuring and reporting assets and expenses associated with the use or sale of assets, at their current cost or lower recoverable amount at the balance sheet date or at the date of use or sale.
3. *Current cost/constant dollar accounting.* A method of accounting based on measures of current cost or lower recoverable amount in terms of dollars, each of which has the same general purchasing power.
4. *Current cost/nominal dollar accounting.* A method of accounting based on measures of current cost or lower recoverable amount without restatement into units, each of which has the same general purchasing power.
5. *Historical cost/constant dollar accounting.* A method of accounting based on measures of historical prices in dollars, each of which has the same general purchasing power.
6. *Historical cost/nominal dollar accounting.* The generally accepted method of accounting, used in the primary financial statements, based on measures of historical prices in dollars without restatement into units, each of which has the same general purchasing power.
7. *Income from continuing operations.* Income after applicable income taxes but excluding the results of discontinued operations, extraordinary items, and the cumulative effect of accounting changes.
8. *Public enterprise.* A business enterprise (a) whose debt or equity securities are traded in a public market on a domestic stock exchange or in the domestic over-the-counter market (including securities quoted only locally or regionally) or (b) that is required to file financial statements with the Securities and Exchange Commission.

An enterprise is considered to be a public enterprise as soon as its financial statements are issued in preparation for the sale of any class of securities in a domestic market.

> **OBSERVATION:** Constant dollar accounting is more commonly known as general price-level accounting, and current cost accounting is generally referred to as current value accounting.

Overview

The degree of inflation or deflation in an economy may become so great that conventional statements lose much of their significance, and general price-level statements clearly become more meaningful.

The unit of measure is the basic difference between historical and general price-level financial statements. General price-level financial statements do not represent replacement cost or an appraisal value, but merely represent what historical-cost statements reflect in general purchasing power, as at a specific date. GAAP used in historical-cost financial statements are also used in general price-level financial statements. Changes in the general price level are measured in terms of index numbers; the base year is given the index number of 100, and changes are expressed as percentages of the base year.

Current value accounting deals with the measurement of profits, and the valuation of a business entity, during periods of inflation.

In current value accounting, historical costs are replaced by current values that attempt to measure what a company would receive if it disposed of its assets. Thus, current value accounting violates the going-concern concept of GAAP in that it is based on liquidation values.

> **OBSERVATION:** Elsewhere in this publication are separate chapters on General Price-Level Changes and on Current Value Accounting. For a more complete understanding of FASB-33, it is strongly recommended that both of the above chapters be read.

Monetary Assets and Liabilities

For purposes of general price-level accounting assets and liabilities are called *monetary items* if their amounts are fixed by contract or otherwise in terms of numbers of dollars. Cash, accounts and notes receivable in cash, and accounts and notes payable in cash are examples of monetary items.

Monetary items automatically gain or lose general purchasing power during inflation or deflation as a result of changes in the general price-level index. For example, a holder of a $10,000 promissory note executed 10 years ago and due today will receive exactly $10,000 today, in spite of the fact that $10,000 in cash today is worth a lot less than $10,000 in cash was worth 10 years ago!

For the purposes of FASB-33, foreign currency on hand, claims to foreign currency, foreign currency obligations, and deferred income tax items are all treated as monetary items.

Nonmonetary Assets and Liabilities

Assets and liabilities that are not monetary items are called *nonmonetary items* for purposes of general price-level accounting. Inventories, investments in common stocks, property, plant, equipment, and deferred charges are examples of nonmonetary items. Holders of nonmonetary items may lose or gain with the rise or fall of the general price-level index if the nonmonetary item does not rise or fall in proportion to the change in the price-level index. In other words, a nonmonetary asset or liability is affected (1) by the rise or fall of the general price-level index and (2) by the increase or decrease of the fair value of the nonmonetary item. For example, the purchaser of 10,000 shares of General Motors common stock 10 years ago was subject (1) to the decrease in purchasing power and (2) to the rise in the fair value of his stock. If the decrease in purchasing power exactly offsets the increase in the price of the stock, the purchaser is, in effect, in the same position today as he was 10 years ago (that is, monetarily).

Net Monetary Position

The difference between monetary assets and monetary liabilities, at any specific date, is the net monetary position. The net monetary position may be either positive (monetary assets exceed monetary liabilities) or negative (monetary liabilities exceed monetary assets).

In periods in which the general price-level index is rising (inflation), it is advantageous for a business to maintain a net negative monetary position. The opposite is true during periods in which the general price-level index is falling (deflation). In periods of inflation, a business which has a net negative monetary position will experience general price-level gains, because it can pay its liabilities in a fixed number of dollars that are getting cheaper as time goes by. A net positive monetary position during periods of inflation results in a general price-level loss, because the value of the dollar is declining.

Some assets and liabilities have characteristics of both monetary and nonmonetary items. Convertible debt, for example, is monetary in terms of its fixed obligation, but nonmonetary in terms of its conversion feature.

The determination of whether an item is monetary or nonmonetary is made as at the balance sheet date. Therefore, if convertible debt has not been converted as of that date, it should be classified as a monetary item. Additionally, a bond receivable held for speculation would be classified as nonmonetary, because the amount that will be received when the bond is sold is no longer fixed in amount, as it would be if the same bond was held to maturity.

The following table reflects the monetary-nonmonetary classification of most assets and liabilities:

	Monetary	Nonmonetary
Cash (in most forms)	X	
Accounts and notes receivable	X	
Allowance for receivables	X	
Inventories		X
Inventories - under fixed contract price	X	
Employee loans	X	
Prepaid expenses	X	
Advances to subsidiaries	X	
Fixed assets		X
Accumulated depreciation		X
Cash surrender value of life insurance	X	
Intangible assets		X
Accounts and notes payable	X	
Accrued expenses	X	
Accrued losses on firm commitments	X	
Refundable deposits	X	
Taxes payable	X	
Most long-term liabilities	X	
Unamortized premium or discount on long-term liabilities	X	
Obligations under warranties		X

	Monetary	Nonmonetary
Deferred income tax credits	X	
Deferred investment tax credits		X
Capital stock (common)		X
Retained earnings		X
Minority interest		X

Minimum Supplementary Information

The promulgated GAAP (FASB-33) requires that the minimum supplementary information be presented both on a current cost basis (Current Value Accounting), and on an historical cost/constant dollar basis (General Price-Level Accounting). In other words, the same supplementary information must be disclosed using two different methods of accounting.

FASB-33 further requires that information based on the historical cost/constant dollar basis must be included in financial statements with fiscal years ending on or after December 25, 1979. However, the supplementary information based on the current cost basis for the fiscal year ending on or after December 25, 1979 need not be included in the supplementary information until the next fiscal year.

Companies in regulated industries must comply with FASB-33 in accordance with the Addendum to APB-2. However, a regulated company may be limited to a specific return on its assets. In this event, the basic historical financial statements may already reflect recoverable amounts for assets. In any event, for the purposes of FASB-33, cost of goods sold, and depreciation expense must be restated to constant dollars, or at current costs if replacement of the service potential of the related assets is contemplated. If replacement is not contemplated then expenses should be disclosed at recoverable amounts.

Certain terms and information in FASB-33 are applicable to both the constant dollar method and the current cost method, as follows:

Depreciation Depreciation methods, useful lives and salvage value should be the same for restatement purposes (constant dollars or current costs) as those used for historical cost purposes. If historical cost computations already include an allowance for changing prices, then a different method may be used for restatement purposes. However, any material differences must be disclosed in the explanatory notes to the supplementary information.

Also, if depreciation expense is allocated to several expense categories in the supplementary information presentation of "income from continuing operations", then the total amount of constant dollar and current cost depreciation expense for the current period must be disclosed by footnote.

Recoverable amounts Reductions to recoverable amounts represent additional write-downs during a current period, from the restated amount (constant dollar or current cost) to a lower recoverable amount. These reductions reflect a permanent decline in the value of inventory, or property, plant and equipment. Recoverable amounts may be determined by reference to net realizable values or values in use. Net realizable value and value in use are discussed later in this Chapter.

Constant Dollar Disclosures

FASB-33 specifies that the Consumer Price Index for All Urban Consumers (CPI-U) be used to determine the constant dollar supplementary information. The CPI-U is reproduced, in full, at the end of this Chapter.

Although comprehensive restatement of the basic historical and financial statements is not required, it is strongly recommended by the promulgated GAAP. If only the minimum supplementary information is disclosed, inventory, property, plant, equipment, cost of goods sold, depreciation, depletion, amortization expense and any reductions of these items to a lower recoverable cost shall be restated to constant dollars by the use of the average price index. However, if comprehensive restatement of the historical cost financial statements is made, then an enterprise may use either the average price index or the price index at the end of the period.

Items which are stated in foreign currency must be translated to U.S. dollars in accordance with GAAP before being restated into constant dollars.

The minimum supplementary information required by FASB-33, which must be disclosed for the current year by the historical cost/constant dollar accounting method (General Price-Level Accounting) is as follows:

Income from continuing operations should be presented for revenue and expense using the same categories of revenue and expense as those appearing in the basic historical cost financial statements. The presentation should be either in a "statement format", or in a "reconciliation format", which discloses all adjustments between the supplementary information and the basic historical cost financial statements (see illustrations at the end of this Chapter).

Accounting classifications may be combined if they are not individually significant for restating purposes, or if the restated amounts are approximately the same as the historical cost amounts.

For purposes of complying with the *minimum disclosure,* only the following items need be restated:

a. inventory
b. property, plant and equipment (does not include intangibles or goodwill)
c. cost of goods sold
d. depreciation, depletion and amortization

All other financial statement items need not be restated and may be disclosed as one amount in the constant dollar presentation of "income from continuing operations."

Purchasing power gain or loss on net monetary items should not be included in the determination of "income from continuing operations", but should be reported as a separate item on the same schedule as that of "income from continuing operations."

In addition to the current fiscal year information (condensed statement or reconciliation of "income from continuing operations" and purchasing power gain or loss on net monetary items) an enterprise must disclose supplementary information in a five year summary. The same constant dollars (average or year-end) used in the condensed statement or reconciliation of "income from continuing operations" must also be used in the five-year summary, or alternatively, the restatement may be to the Consumer Price Index base year (1967).

The five-year summary must contain the following *minimum disclosures* restated in constant dollars:

Net operating revenue is presented as one restated amount for each of the five years.

Financial Reporting and Changing Prices

Income from continuing operations is presented as one restated amount (compared to the statement or reconciliation format required for the current year).

Purchasing power gain or loss on net monetary items is disclosed as one restated amount.

Net assets at end of fiscal period is disclosed as one restated amount and is equal to all of the net assets appearing on the basic historical cost financial statements except inventories, property, plant and equipment, which are included at their restated amounts or at a lower recoverable amount. (Total net assets at historical cost minus inventories, property, plant and equipment at historical cost, plus inventories, property, plant and equipment at restated amounts or lower recoverable amounts equals net assets as required by FASB-33.)

Income per common share from continuing operations is disclosed as one restated amount for each of the five years, and is found by dividing the outstanding number of shares of common stock into the total restated "income from continuing operations."

Cash dividends declared per common share are disclosed as one restated amount for each of the five years.

Market price per common share at end of year is disclosed as one restated amount for each of the five years.

The five-year summary should include a note disclosing the constant dollars (average or year-end) used in the presentation.

Although disclosure of all supplementary information is encouraged, for fiscal years prior to the effective December 25, 1979 date, the five-year summary need only contain (1) net sales and other operating revenue, (2) cash dividends declared per common share, and (3) market price per common share at end of year.

Current Cost Disclosures

Natural resources and income producing real estate may be excluded from the current cost supplementary information presentation

Financial Reporting and Changing Prices

until fiscal years ending on or after December 25, 1980. The FASB intends to issue an exposure draft in the near future dealing with these items for current cost presentation purposes.

The minimum supplementary information required by FASB-33, which must be disclosed for the current period by the current cost accounting method (Current Value Accounting), is as follows:

Income from continuing operations should be presented for revenue and expense using the same categories of revenue and expense as those appearing in the basic historical cost financial statements. The presentation should be either in a "statement format", or in a "reconciliation format", which discloses all adjustments between the supplementary information and the basic historical cost financial statements (see illustrations at end of this Chapter).

Account classifications may be combined if they are not individually significant for restating purposes, or if the restated amounts are approximately the same as the historical cost amounts.

The current cost presentation of "income from continuing operations" shall be before any increase or decrease for the year in current costs in inventory, property, plant and equipment (holding gains or losses).

Inventory, property, plant and equipment at end of year must be disclosed at current costs or a lower recoverable amount at the end of the current period.

Increase or decrease in inventory, property, plant and equipment the increase or decrease for the current period in current cost amounts must be disclosed. (Total beginning current costs minus ending current costs equals increase or decrease in current costs for the year.)

In addition to the current fiscal year information (condensed statement or reconciliation of "income from continuing operations", current cost amounts of inventory and property, plant and equipment at end of year, and the increase or decrease in current costs of inventory, property, plant and equipment during the year), an enterprise must disclose supplementary information in a five-year summary on a current cost basis. However, all current cost information on the five-year summary must be restated again into constant dollars using the same constant dollars as were used in restating "income from continuing operations" or alternatively by restating the amounts to the purchasing power of the Consumer Price Index base year (currently 1967). In other words, this restatement process can be either to current purchasing power or to purchasing power of a prior year (base-year).

The five-year summary must contain the following minimum disclosures in terms of current costs, restated in constant dollars:

Income from continuing operations is presented as one restated amount (compared to the statement or reconciliation format required for the current year). The current cost amount is restated to constant dollars.

Income per common share from continuing operations is disclosed as one restated amount, for each of the five years, and is found by dividing the outstanding number of shares of common stock into the total restated "income from continuing operations." The current cost amount is restated to constant dollars.

Net assets at end each fiscal year should be disclosed on the five-year summary and is equal to all of the net assets appearing on the basic historical cost financial statements except inventories, property, plant and equipment, which are included at their current costs or at a lower recoverable amount. (Total net assets at historical cost minus inventories, property, plant and equipment at historical cost, plus inventories, property, plant and equipment at current costs, or lower recoverable amount, equals net assets as required by FASB-33.)

The current cost or lower recoverable amount of net assets is then restated in terms of constant dollars.

Increase or decrease in inventory, property, plant and equipment at current costs the increase or decrease, net of inflation, in current costs for inventory, property, plant and equipment in each of the five-years must be restated in terms of constant dollars and disclosed in the five-year summary.

Although disclosure of all supplementary information is encouraged, for fiscal years prior to the effective December 25, 1979 date, the five-year summary need only contain (1) net sales and other operating revenue, (2) cash dividends declared per common share, and (3) market price per common share at end of year.

Where comprehensive restatement of financial statements is made in lieu of the minimum supplementary information, net assets for the five-year summary may be stated at the same amount shown in the comprehensive restated financial statements.

FASB-33 also requires that explanatory statements accompany the supplementary information. These explanatory statements should be sufficiently detailed so that a user who possesses reasonable business acumen will be able to understand the information presented.

In disclosing the specific minimum supplementary information under the current cost accounting method (Current Value Accounting) the promulgated GAAP (FASB-33) requires that assets and expenses be measured as follows:

1. *Inventories* - at current cost, or lower recoverable amount.
2. *Property, plant and equipment* - at current cost, or lower recoverable amount. Property, plant and equipment includes land and capitalized leases. Current cost of leasing may be used by lessees instead of current cost of purchasing.
3. *Cost of goods sold* - at current cost, or lower recoverable amount. If sales occur evenly throughout the year, the average current cost for the year may be used.
4. *Depreciation, depletion and amortization* - at the average current cost for the year, or lower recoverable amount.

Other items of revenue and expense not included above may be included in the current cost "income from continuing operations", at the same amounts appearing in the primary historical cost financial statements.

> **OBSERVATION:** As mentioned previously, all natural resources and income producing real estate may be excluded from current cost supplementary information until further notice from the FASB.

FASB-33 describes specific criteria for net realizable value, value in use, and current costs, as follows:

Net realizable value is the expected amount of net cash or other net equivalent to be received from the sale of an asset in the regular course of business. For the purposes of FASB-33, net realizable value may be used only if the specific asset is about to be sold.

Value in use is the total net present value of all future cash inflows which are expected to be received from the use of an asset. For the purposes of FASB-33, value in use may be used only if there are no immediate intentions to sell or otherwise dispose of the asset. Value in use shall be estimated by taking into consideration an appropriate discount rate that includes an allowance for the risk involved in the circumstances.

Current cost is the current cost to purchase or reproduce the specific asset. Current reproduction cost must contain an allocation for current overhead costs (direct costing not permitted).

Current cost of property, plant and equipment which is owned, is the current cost of acquiring an asset that will perform or produce similar to the owned asset.

Current cost of purchase or reproduction which is stated in foreign currency must be translated either at the current rate of exchange for depreciation and cost of goods sold, or at the exchange rate in effect at the balance sheet date in the case of inventory, and property, plant and equipment.

Evidence must be obtained to support all of the current costs used. Evidence may be obtained internally or externally, including independent appraisals, and may be applied to a single item or to groups of items. An enterprise must disclose, in its supplementary explanatory notes, the major types of evidence used to support its calculations of current costs.

FASB-33 lists the following types and sources of evidence:

1. current invoice prices
2. vendors' firm price lists, quotations, or estimates
3. standard manufacturing costs which reflect current costs
4. unit pricing, which is a method of determining current cost for assets, such as buildings, by applying a unit price per square foot of space to the total square footage in the building.
5. revision of historical cost by the use of:
    (i) externally generated price indexes for the services or goods being restated
    (ii) internally generated indexes for the services or goods being restated
    (Note: This method is sometimes referred to as indexation.)

Income tax expense and the provision for deferred taxes, if any, are not restated in terms of current cost and are presented in the supplementary information at their historical cost. Disclosure must be made in the supplementary information to the effect that income tax expense for the current period is presented at its historical cost.

Comprehensive Illustrations

The FASB has established an advisory group to develop illustrations of formats for presenting the supplementary information required by FASB-33. In the interim, companies are urged to experiment with different types of presentations.

Because the required information is complex and not easily understood by users of financial statements, it is absolutely necessary that companies utilize simple and comprehensible presentations, accompanied by clear explanatory notes, in order to present meaningful information.

The following illustrations may be useful in assisting those who must prepare the supplementary information required by FASB-33:

Financial Reporting and Changing Prices

Condensed Statement of Income and Other Data Restated in Terms of the Average Purchasing Power of the 1979 Dollar*

For the Year Ended December 31, 1979

Net revenue from operations	$100,000
Cost of goods sold	$ 46,000
Depreciation and amortization	4,000
Other operating expenses	32,000
Interest expense	8,000
Total	$ 90,000
Income from continuing operations - before taxes	$ 10,000
Less: Provision for income taxes	4,800
Income from continuing operations	$ 5,200
Inflation gain or (loss) on net monetary items	$ (1,600)

*Cost of goods sold, depreciation and amortization are restated in terms of their historical costs.

Reconciliation of Income From Continuing Operations as Reported in the Statement of Income to Income From Continuing Operations Restated in Terms of the Average Purchasing Power of the 1979 Dollar

For the Year Ended December 31, 1979

Income from continuing operations - per income statement	$ 11,300
Adjustments for restatements:	
Net revenue from operations	$ 3,000
Cost of goods sold	(2,100)
Depreciation and amortization	(3,400)
Other operating expenses	(1,500)
Interest expense	(500)
Provision for income taxes*	—
Total	$ 4,500
Restated income from operations	$ 5,200
Inflation gain or (loss) on net monetary items	$ (1,600)

*The provision for income taxes is not restated.

Five-Year Comparison of Selected Financial Data
For the Five Years Ended December 31, 1979

	1975	1976	1977	1978	1979
(1) Net revenue from operations					$100,000
(1) Restated income from operations					$ 5,200
(1) Per common share					0.26
(1) Inflation gain or (loss) on net monetary items					$ (1,600)
(2) Net assets at end of year					$462,500
(1) Cash dividends - per common share					$ 0.20
(1) Market price at end of year - per common share					$ 2.70
Average consumer price index					205.0

(1) In average 1979 dollars
(2) Restated from historical costs

As mentioned previously, detailed explanatory statements should accompany the supplementary information required by FASB-33. The explanatory material should explain the process of restating the purchasing power of one year into that of another in order to obtain information which is adjusted for the effects of inflation or deflation. General Price-Level Restatement and Current Value Accounting should be explained in lay terms so that the user of the supplementary information may reasonably comprehend the data.

Condensed Statement of Income
Restated to Reflect the Effects of Inflation
For the Year Ended December 31, 1979

	Historical	Restated*
Net revenues from operations	$900,000	$900,000
Cost of goods sold	700,000	715,131
Gross margin	$200,000	184,869
Operating expenses:		
Depreciation and amortization	$ 20,000	$ 23,478
Interest	6,000	6,000
All other	74,000	74,000
Total	$100,000	$103,478
Income from continuing operations	$100,000	$ 81,391
Less: Provision for income taxes	20,000	20,000
Income from continuing operations	$ 80,000	$ 61,391
Less: Inflation loss on net monetary items		6,887
Income from continuing operations - restated		$ 54,504

Other Selected Financial Data:

Income from continuing operations - per common share	$ 0.80	$ 0.61
Inflation loss on net monetary items - per common share	—	$ 0.06
Income from continuing operations - after inflation loss - per common share	—	0.55
Cash dividends per common share	$ 0.30	$ 0.27
Market price at end of year - per common share	$ 12.00	$ 11.70
Net assets at end of year	$462,500	$612,719

* Restatement is made to 1979 average dollars using the Consumer Price Index (base year 1967).

Consumer Price Index for All Urban Consumers (CPI-U)
(1967 = 100)

YEAR	JAN.	FEB.	MAR.	APR.	MAY	JUNE	JULY	AUG.	SEP.	OCT.	NOV.	DEC.	AVG.
1946	54.5	54.3	54.7	55.0	55.3	55.9	59.2	60.5	61.2	62.4	63.9	64.4	58.5
1947	64.4	64.3	65.7	65.7	65.5	66.0	66.6	67.3	68.9	68.9	69.3	70.2	66.9
1948	71.0	70.4	70.2	71.2	71.7	72.2	73.1	73.4	73.4	73.1	72.6	72.1	72.1
1949	72.0	71.2	71.4	71.5	71.4	71.5	71.0	71.2	71.5	71.1	71.2	70.8	71.4
1950	70.5	70.3	70.6	70.7	71.0	71.4	72.1	72.7	73.2	73.6	73.9	74.9	72.1
1951	76.1	77.0	77.3	77.4	77.7	77.6	77.7	77.7	78.2	78.6	79.0	79.3	77.8
1952	79.3	78.8	78.8	79.1	79.2	79.4	80.0	80.1	80.0	80.1	80.1	80.0	79.5
1953	79.8	79.4	79.6	79.7	79.9	80.2	80.4	80.6	80.7	80.9	80.6	80.5	80.1
1954	80.7	80.6	80.5	80.3	80.6	80.7	80.7	80.6	80.4	80.2	80.3	80.1	80.5
1955	80.1	80.1	80.1	80.1	80.1	80.1	80.4	80.2	80.5	80.5	80.6	80.4	80.2
1956	80.3	80.3	80.4	80.5	80.9	81.4	82.0	81.9	82.0	82.5	82.5	82.7	81.4
1957	82.8	83.1	83.3	83.6	83.8	84.3	84.7	84.8	84.9	84.9	85.2	85.2	84.3
1958	85.7	85.8	86.4	86.6	86.6	86.7	86.8	86.7	86.7	86.7	86.8	86.7	86.6
1959	86.8	86.7	86.7	86.8	86.9	87.3	87.5	87.4	87.7	88.0	88.0	88.0	87.3
1960	87.9	88.0	88.0	88.5	88.5	88.7	88.7	88.7	88.8	89.2	89.3	89.3	88.7

Financial Reporting and Changing Prices

Year	Jan	Feb	Mar	Apr	May	Jun	Jul	Aug	Sep	Oct	Nov	Dec	Annual
1961	89.3	89.3	89.3	89.3	89.3	89.4	89.8	89.7	89.9	89.9	89.9	89.9	89.6
1962	89.9	90.1	90.3	90.5	90.5	90.5	90.7	90.7	91.2	91.1	91.1	91.0	90.6
1963	91.1	91.2	91.3	91.3	91.3	91.7	92.1	92.1	92.1	92.2	92.3	92.5	91.7
1964	92.6	92.5	92.6	92.7	92.7	92.9	93.1	93.0	93.2	93.3	93.5	93.6	92.9
1965	93.6	93.6	93.7	94.0	94.2	94.7	94.8	94.6	94.8	94.9	95.1	95.4	94.5
1966	95.4	96.0	96.3	96.7	96.8	97.1	97.4	97.9	98.1	98.5	98.5	98.6	97.2
1967	98.6	98.7	98.9	99.1	99.4	99.7	100.2	100.5	100.7	101.0	101.3	101.6	100.0
1968	102.0	102.3	102.8	103.1	103.4	104.0	104.5	104.8	105.1	105.7	106.1	106.4	104.2
1969	106.7	107.1	108.0	108.7	109.0	109.7	110.2	110.7	111.2	111.6	112.2	112.9	109.8
1970	113.3	113.9	114.5	115.2	115.7	116.3	116.7	116.9	117.5	118.1	118.5	119.1	116.3
1971	119.2	119.4	119.8	120.2	120.8	121.5	121.8	122.1	122.2	122.4	122.6	123.1	121.3
1972	123.2	123.8	124.0	124.3	124.7	125.0	125.5	125.7	126.2	126.6	126.9	127.3	125.3
1973	127.7	128.6	129.8	130.7	131.5	132.4	132.7	135.1	135.5	136.6	137.6	138.5	133.1
1974	139.7	141.5	143.1	143.9	145.5	146.9	148.0	149.9	151.7	153.0	154.3	155.4	147.7
1975	156.1	157.2	157.8	158.6	159.3	160.6	162.3	162.8	163.6	164.6	165.6	166.3	161.2
1976	166.7	167.1	167.5	168.2	169.2	170.1	171.1	171.9	172.6	173.3	173.8	174.3	170.5
1977	175.3	177.1	178.2	179.6	180.6	181.8	182.6	183.3	184.0	184.5	185.4	186.1	181.5
1978	187.2	188.4	189.8	191.5	193.3	195.3	196.7	197.8	199.3	200.9	202.0	202.9	195.4
1979	204.7	207.1	209.1	211.5	214.1	216.6	218.9	221.1					

FOREIGN OPERATIONS, AND EXCHANGE

Background

The major promulgated GAAP on Foreign Currencies, Operations and Exchanges is FASB-8, which has been amended by FASB-20, Accounting for Forward Exchange Contracts.

Companies in regulated industries should comply with this promulgated GAAP in accordance with the Addendum to APB-2.

> *OBSERVATION:* The promulgated GAAP also applies to companies whose reporting currency is in other than U.S. dollars, providing that the financial statements have been prepared in conformity with GAAP.

Overview

Business transactions and foreign operations that are recorded in a foreign currency must be restated in U.S. dollars in accordance with GAAP.

Transactions occur at various dates, and since the abandonment of the gold standard, exchange rates have tended to fluctuate considerably. Before an attempt is made to translate the records of a foreign operation, the records should be in conformity with GAAP. In addition, if the foreign statements have any accounts stated in a currency other than their own, they must be converted into the foreign statement's currency before translation into U.S. dollars.

The three major areas concerned with foreign operations are:

1. accounting for a single transaction or several isolated transactions, such as a sale or a purchase
2. restating financial statements to or from a foreign currency
3. accounting for foreign exchange contracts

Single or Several Transactions

If the exchange rate changes between the time a purchase or sale is contracted for and the time actual payment is made, a foreign exchange gain or loss will result.

If goods were purchased for 100,000 pesos when the rate of exchange was 10 pesos to a dollar, the journal entry in dollars would be:

Purchases	$10,000	
Accounts payable		$10,000

Assuming that when the goods are paid for, the exchange rate is 12:1, the journal entry in dollars would be:

Accounts payable	$10,000	
Cash		$ 8,334
Foreign exchange gain		1,666

The $8,334, at a 12:1 exchange rate, can purchase 100,000 pesos. The difference between the $8,334 and the original recorded liability of $10,000 is a foreign exchange gain.

A foreign exchange gain or loss must be computed at each balance sheet date on all recorded foreign transactions that have not been settled. The difference between the exchange rate used in recording the transaction in dollars and the exchange rate at the balance sheet date (current exchange rate) is the gain or loss on foreign currency exchange.

Restating Financial Statements

Foreign financial statements must conform with GAAP before they can be translated into dollars and, prior to their inclusion in a company's financial statements, by consolidation, combination, or the equity method.

There are two categories of exchange rates that may be used in translating financial statements. Historical exchange rates are those which existed at the time of the transaction, and the current exchange rate is the rate that is current at the date of translation.

Monetary assets and liabilities are those which are fixed in amount, such as cash, accounts receivable, and most liabilities. Under the present promulgated GAAP, all monetary assets and liabilities are translated at the current rate of exchange. All other assets, liabilities, and stockholders' equity are translated by reference to money price exchanges based on the type of market and time. The promulgated GAAP describes the four types of money price exchanges as follows:

1. *Past purchase exchange*–the historical or acquisition cost, because it is based on the actual past purchase price
2. *Current purchase exchange*–the replacement cost, because it is measured by the current purchase price of a similar resource
3. *Current sale exchange*–the market price, because it is based on the current selling price of the resource
4. *Future exchange*–the present value of future net money receipts, discounted cash flow, or the discounted net realizable value, because it is based on a future resource

All other assets, liabilities, and stockholders' equity are translated, based on the four money price exchanges, as follows:

1. Accounts based on past purchase exchanges (historical or acquisition cost) are translated at historical exchange rates.
2. Accounts based on current purchase, current sale, and future exchanges are translated at the current exchange rate.

Revenue and expense transactions are translated at the average exchange rate for the period, except those expenses related to assets and liabilities, which are translated at historical exchange rates. For example, depreciation and amortization are translated at historical exchange rates, the rate that existed at the time the underlying related asset was acquired.

> **OBSERVATION:** *An easier way of stating the exchange rate to be used in accordance with the promulgated GAAP is:*
> *All accounts on the financial statement that are based on historical or acquisition cost are translated at historical exchange rates; all other accounts are translated at the current rate.*

The following is a comprehensive list of assets, liabilities, and stockholders' equity items and their corresponding translation rates:

Foreign Operations, and Exchange

	Translation Rates	
	Current	Historical
Cash (in almost all forms)	X	
Marketable securities–at cost		X
Marketable securities–at market	X	
Accounts and notes receivable	X	
Allowance for receivables	X	
Inventories–at cost		X
Inventories–at market, net realizable value, selling price	X	
Inventories–under fixed contract price	X	
Prepaid expenses		X
Refundable deposits	X	
Advances to subsidiaries	X	
Fixed assets		X
Accumulated depreciation		X
Cash surrender value–life insurance	X	
Intangible assets (all)		X
Accounts and notes payable	X	
Accrued expenses	X	
Accrued losses on firm commitments	X	
Taxes payable	X	
All long-term liabilities	X	
Unamortized premium or discount on long-term liabilities	X	
Obligations under warranties	X	
Deferred income		X
Capital stock		X
Retained earnings		X
Minority interests		X

As previously mentioned, revenue and expenses not related to any balance sheet items are translated at the average currency exchange rate for the period. The average may be based on a daily, weekly, monthly, or quarterly basis or on the weighted average rate for the period, which will probably result in a more meaningful conversion. Revenue and expense items that are related to a balance sheet account, such as deferred income, depreciation, and beginning and ending inventories are translated at the same exchange rate as the related balance sheet item.

In translating the lower-of-cost-or-market rule, the translated historical cost is compared to the translated market, and whichever is lower in dollars is used. This may require a write-down in dollars from cost to market, which was not required in the foreign currency financial statements. On the other hand, if market was used on the foreign statements and in translating to dollars market exceeds historical cost, the write-down to market on the foreign statements will have to be reversed before translating, which would then be done at the historical rate. Once inventory has been written down to market in translated dollar statements, the resulting carrying amount is used in future translations until the inventory is sold or a further write-down is necessary. This same procedure is used for assets, other than inventory, that may have to be written down from historical cost.

The reason for the above procedure in applying the lower-of-cost-or-market rule in translating foreign financial statements is that exchange gains and losses are a consequence of translation and not of applying the lower-of-cost-or-market rule (FASB Interpretation 17). This means that translated market is equal to replacement cost (market) in the foreign currency translated at the current exchange rate, except that:

1. Translated market cannot exceed net realizable value in foreign currency translated at the current exchange rate.
2. Translated market cannot be less than (1) above, reduced by an approximate normal profit translated at the current exchange rate.

All this really means is that the lower of cost or market is determined after everything is translated into dollars.

In translating unamortized policy acquisition costs by a stock life insurance company, historical exchange rates are used, because under GAAP such costs are considered deferred charges. Translation of a liability for future policy benefits is made at the current exchange rate. In order for the dollar financial statements to be in conformity with GAAP, a computation of the reserve for the actuarially determined liability for future benefits on insurance policies in force must be made after translation into dollars. If the computation results in a reserve adjustment in dollars, it is made in the translated dollar statements by a decrease or an increase to current earnings. This may require a charge to current earnings in the foreign statements to be reversed in whole or in part in preparing the dollar statements if the translated charge exceeds the reserve deficiency computed in dollars (FASB Interpretation 15).

Business combinations accounted for by the pooling-of-interests method are translated as if the foreign operation had always been a subsidiary. Therefore, historical exchange rates are those recognized for specific transactions by the foreign subsidiary. Under the purchase method, assets and liabilities of a foreign operation are adjusted to their fair values at the date of acquisition and then translated at the exchange rate in effect at that date. The difference between the related net assets and the dollar purchase price of the acquisition is goodwill or negative goodwill.

For translation purposes, the current exchange rate is the one in effect as of the balance sheet date of the foreign statements. Therefore, if the parent company's financial statements are at a date different from the date(s) of its foreign operation(s), the exchange rate in effect at the date of the foreign subsidiary's balance sheet is used for translation purposes.

> **OBSERVATION:** The date of the balance sheet affects only the current exchange rate and does not usually affect the historical exchange rates.

Foreign Exchange Contracts

A foreign exchange contract is an agreement to exchange, at a future specific date and rate, currencies of different countries. A foreign exchange contract may be entered into for the following reasons:

1. to hedge a foreign currency,
   a. commitment
   b. net asset position
   c. net liability position
2. to speculate

Gain or loss on most foreign exchange contracts is recognized in current net income of the period in which the exchange rate changes. The exception is a hedge of an identifiable foreign currency commitment or exposed net asset or net liability position that meets all the following conditions:

1. The life of the contract extends from the identifiable foreign

Foreign Operations, and Exchange

currency commitment date to the anticipated transaction date(s), or to a later date if successive contracts are involved.

> **OBSERVATION:** A contract that exceeds the amount of commitment and/or extends beyond the transaction date(s) still qualifies for the exception. However, the excess amount over the commitment and/or any amount pertaining to a period after the transaction date(s) may be included only to the extent that the foreign exchange contract is intended to provide a hedge on an after-tax basis.
>
> A hedge on an after-tax basis provides assurance that the gain or loss on the forward contract offsets the effect of an exchange rate change related to the foreign currency commitment, after taking into consideration the net tax effects.
>
> Where gain or loss pertaining to amounts in excess of the foreign currency commitment is deferred, it is included as an offset to the related tax effects in the period in which such tax effects are recognized. In addition, these deferred gains or losses which are treated as offsets to a related tax effect are excluded from the disclosure requirement of the aggregate exchange gain or loss included in determining net income for a period.

2. The contract is for the same currency as the foreign currency commitment, in the same or a less amount.
3. The foreign currency commitment is firm and noncancelable.

Gain or loss on a hedge of an identifiable foreign currency commitment, or exposed net asset or net liability position, that meets all the above conditions is deferred and included in the overall gain of the identifiable foreign currency transaction. However, a loss shall not be deferred if the identifiable transaction is reasonably expected to result in a loss, including the deferred loss on the foreign exchange contract.

Deferred gain or loss on a hedge of a foreign currency commitment that is sold or terminated is not recognized until the related identifiable transaction is consummated.

The promulgated GAAP (FASB-8) specifies two separate methods of determining gain or loss on foreign exchange contracts depending upon whether or not gain or loss is deferred.

Deferred. Gain or loss is the difference between the balance sheet date spot rate and the spot rate at inception of the contract multiplied by the principal amount of foreign currency.

Not deferred. Gain or loss is the difference between the contracted forward rate and the forward rate available for the remaining maturity of the contract, multiplied by the principal amount of foreign currency.

Note: The spot or forward rate last used to measure a gain or loss on the contract for an earlier period may be used if necessary.

The discount or premium involved in a foreign exchange contract is the difference between the contract rate and the spot rate on the date of purchase multiplied by the principal amount of foreign currency. Discounts and premiums are disposed of as follows:

Identifiable hedges. No separate accounting is necessary, because discounts and premiums are recognized as part of the results of the identifiable transaction.

Speculative contracts. No separate accounting is necessary, because discounts and premiums are recognized as part of the total gain or loss.

All other contracts. Discounts and premiums are separately accounted for and amortized to net income over the life of the forward exchange contract.

Since detail compliance may require significant record keeping, the promulgated GAAP suggests the use of averages and/or reasonable approximations, providing the results do not differ materially from the prescribed standards. In addition, if multiple exchange rates exist at the same time, the following should be used:

Restating financial statements. The rate applicable to dividend remittances should be used.

All other. The rate that can be used to settle the transaction.

Income Taxes

Foreign exchange gains or losses, resulting from currency transactions, create a timing difference when included in financial accounting income of one period and in taxable income of a different period. A timing difference necessitates the use of tax allocation between periods (APB-11).

The tax effect of a taxable exchange gain or loss of a foreign operation on a foreign currency transaction should be included in the translated financial statements of the period in which the rate change occurs.

Under the promulgated GAAP, the objective of translating financial statements is to reproduce the same results that each individual transaction would have produced if each were translated into dollars on the date it occurred. Because of the many individual transactions that are usually involved, the promulgated GAAP permits the use of an average rate for most revenue and expense items except those directly related to balance sheet accounts, which are translated at historical rates.

The use of historical rates in translating some revenue and expense items (inventories and depreciation) does not require interperiod allocation, because timing differences do not arise from translating assets or liabilities at historical rates. Because of this, the effective tax rate in the foreign statements may differ from that of the translated dollar statements. Also, the use of historical rates may change other relationships between the foreign statements and the translated dollar statements, such as the gross profit percentage. The promulgated GAAP attributes these types of changes to the use of the dollar as the unit of measure to comply with GAAP.

In translating deferred taxes in accordance with the promulgated GAAP, the following applies:

1. Deferred taxes relating to statement accounts that are translated at the current exchange rate are translated at the current exchange rate.

A foreign operation has an accrued warranty obligation of FC 2,000, and FC 1,600 at the beginning and end of the year, respectively. The operation is on the accrual basis for financial statements and on a cash basis for tax purposes. The currency exchange rate at the beginning of the year was FC 10 = $1, and at the end of the year FC 8 = $1. The foreign tax rate of 50% remained the same throughout the year.

The deferred tax on accrued warranty obligation in dollars at the beginning of the year is $100 (FC 2,000 × 50% ÷ 10); and at the end of the year it is also $100 (FC 1,600 × 50% ÷ 8). The warranty obligation in dollars did not change in spite of the fact that the foreign currency decreased by FC 400.

2. Deferred taxes relating to statement accounts that are translated at historical rates are based on whether the gross change or net change method is used, as follows:
   a. *Gross change.* Deferred taxes are translated at historical rate.
   b. *Net change.* Deferred taxes are measured in dollars by adding or deducting from the dollar balance at the beginning of the period, the current period's deferred tax translated at the average exchange rate for the period.

A foreign operation uses the net change method of deferred tax allocation for timing differences arising from the use of accelerated depreciation for tax purposes and the straight line method for financial statements. At the beginning of the year the deferred tax credit in dollars was $200,000, and the current period's deferred tax expense is FC 20,000. The average currency exchange rate for translating income tax expense during the current period is FC 10 = $1.

The deferred tax credit in dollars at the end of the year is the $200,000 balance at the beginning of the year, plus the FC 20,000 current period's deferred tax expense translated at the average rate for the year (FC 20,000 divided by 10), which is $2,000. Therefore, the deferred tax credit in dollars at the end of the period is $202,000.

The above procedures result in translating deferred income taxes of a foreign operation in accordance with the objectives of the promulgated GAAP.

If a foreign investment is accounted for by the equity method, the foreign financial statements must be translated before applying the equity method.

If exchange gains or losses arising from the translation of foreign investments and subsidiaries are not included in current U.S. taxable income, the need for deferred taxes should be determined by reference to APB-23, Accounting for Income Taxes–Special Areas, and APB-24, Accounting for Income Taxes–Investments in Common Stock Accounted for by the Equity Method. (APB-23 and APB-24 are covered in this publication in the Income Taxes chapter.)

Exclusion of Foreign Operations

Conditions may exist where it will be prudent to exclude a foreign operation from consolidated financial statements. Disruption of a foreign operation caused by internal strife or severe exchange restrictions may make it impossible to compute meaningful exchange rates. Under these conditions it is best to include earnings of a foreign operation only to the extent that the cash has been received in unrestricted funds.

Adequate disclosure should be made of any foreign subsidiary or investment that is excluded from the financial statements of the parent or investor. This may be accomplished by separate supplemental statements or a summary describing the important facts and information.

Disclosure

Disclosure in the financial statements or footnotes thereto should be made of the following:

1. the aggregate exchange gain or loss included in determining net income for the period
2. a description and quantification of the effects of rate changes on reporting results of operations, excluding 1 above
3. significant rate changes and related effects that occur subsequent to the balance sheet date

If a foreign statement has a date different from that of the parent company's statements, and a rate change occurs that affects the foreign statement, no adjustment shall be made. However, full disclosure as stated above should be made.

Conclusion

The promulgated GAAP (FASB-8) establishes accounting and reporting standards for foreign currency transactions and for translation of foreign currency financial statements that are included by consolidation, combination, or the equity method in a parent company's financial statements. Foreign financial statements must conform to U.S. generally accepted accounting principles before they can be translated into dollars.

The exchange gain or loss is usually determined by translating the ending balance sheet and income accounts at either historical, current, or average exchange rates. Balance sheet accounts that are based on historical exchange rates are translated at historical rates; all other balance sheet accounts, including monetary assets and liabilities, are translated at the current exchange rate (rate at date of balance sheet). Revenue and expense accounts are translated at the average exchange rate for the period, except those accounts directly related to historical cost balance sheet accounts, which are translated at historical rates.

Special procedures are necessary to determine the lower of cost or market and deferred income taxes.

When translation of a foreign statement is complete, the ending trial balance in dollars will not balance, because the difference in dollars required to balance is the gain or loss on currency exchange translation.

Exchange gain or loss can be deferred on a hedge of an identifiable foreign currency commitment or an exposed net asset or net liability position, which meets certain special conditions.

The objective of translating financial statements is to approximate the same results that each individual underlying transaction would have produced on the date of occurrence.

GENERAL PRICE-LEVEL CHANGES

Background

Most information about restating financial statements for general price-level changes is contained in APB Statement 3, which was issued in June 1969. APB Statements are not considered promulgated GAAP.

> ***OBSERVATION:*** *FASB-33 requires the application of some Current Value and General Price-Level Accounting techniques (see Financial Reporting and Changing Prices).*

Overview

The degree of inflation or deflation in an economy may become so great that conventional statements lose much of their significance, and general price-level statements clearly become more meaningful.

The unit of measure is the basic difference between historical and general price-level financial statements. General price-level financial statements do not represent replacement cost or an appraisal value, but merely represent what historical-cost statements reflect in general purchasing power, as at a specific date. GAAP used in historical-cost financial statements are also used in general price-level financial statements. Changes in the general price level are measured in terms of index numbers; the base year is given the index number of 100, and changes are expressed as percentages of the base year.

General

It is important to remember that general price-level adjusted statements are based on historical cost. The process of restatement simply converts the historical dollars into dollars of current purchasing power. Statements are adjusted to reflect the price level at the *end* of the current period.

Historically, the rate of inflation in the United States has not been significant enough to cause serious erosion of the *unit of measure principle*. However, the double-digit inflation of recent years has caused some to question the usefulness of historical-cost financial statements.

General Price-Level Changes

The price-level adjustment process consists of restating historical-cost financial statements into common dollars.

Monetary Assets and Liabilities

For purposes of general price-level accounting assets and liabilities are called *monetary items* if their amounts are fixed by contract or otherwise in terms of numbers of dollars. Cash, accounts and notes receivable in cash, and accounts and notes payable in cash are examples of monetary items.

Monetary items automatically gain or lose general purchasing power during inflation or deflation as a result of changes in the general price-level index. For example, a holder of a $10,000 promissory note executed 10 years ago and due today will receive exactly $10,000 today, in spite of the fact that $10,000 in cash today is worth a lot less than $10,000 in cash was worth 10 years ago! Such losses or gains of this nature are called *general price-level gains or losses*. Although monetary assets and liabilities are *not restated* on a general price-level balance sheet, the general price-level gains and losses are calculated and are recognized in the general price-level income statement.

Nonmonetary Assets and Liabilities

Assets and liabilities that are not monetary items are called *nonmonetary items* for purposes of general price-level accounting. Inventories, investments in common stocks, property, plant, equipment, and deferred charges are examples of nonmonetary items. Holders of nonmonetary items may lose or gain with the rise or fall of the general price-level index if the nonmonetary item does not rise or fall in proportion to the change in the price-level index. In other words, a nonmonetary asset or liability is affected (1) by the rise or fall of the general price-level index and (2) by the increase or decrease of the fair value of the nonmonetary item. For example, the purchaser of 10,000 shares of General Motors common stock 10 years ago was subject (1) to the decrease in purchasing power and (2) to the rise in the fair value of his stock. If the decrease in purchasing power exactly offsets the increase in the price of the stock, the purchaser is, in effect, in the same position today as he was 10 years ago (that is, monetarily).

By means of the general price-level index nonmonetary items are *restated* to current purchasing power at the end of the reporting period. The difference produced by the restatement of nonmonetary items does not represent replacement cost or current values, but presents the historical cost in terms of current purchasing power.

Inventory purchased at the end of a period, although a nonmonetary item, may well be already stated at approximately the general purchasing power at the end of a period.

Net Monetary Position

The difference between monetary assets and monetary liabilities, at any specific date, is the net monetary position. The net monetary position may be either positive (monetary assets exceed monetary liabilities) or negative (monetary liabilities exceed monetary assets).

In periods in which the general price-level index is rising (inflation), it is advantageous for a business to maintain a net negative monetary position. The opposite is true during periods in which the general price-level index is falling (deflation). In periods of inflation, a business which has a net negative monetary position will experience general price-level gains, because it can pay its liabilities in a fixed number of dollars that are getting cheaper as time goes by. A net positive monetary position during periods of inflation results in a general price-level loss, because the value of the dollar is declining.

Some assets and liabilities have characteristics of both monetary and nonmonetary items. Convertible debt, for example, is monetary in terms of its fixed obligation, but nonmonetary in terms of its conversion feature.

The determination of whether an item is monetary or nonmonetary is made as at the balance sheet date. Therefore, if convertible debt has not been converted as of that date, it should be classified as a monetary item. Additionally, a bond receivable held for speculation would be classified as nonmonetary, because the amount that will be received when the bond is sold is no longer fixed in amount, as it would be if the same bond was held to maturity.

Price Indexes

Price-level changes are measured by price indexes. Price indexes are stated in percentages to a base year, which is assigned a value of 100.

By using a price index, dollars of general purchasing power in one period can be restated to dollars of general purchasing power of another period. The formula for restating dollars of one period to those of another is:

$$\frac{\text{new index (converting to)}}{\text{old index (converting from)}}$$

For example, assume that the current ending price index is 120, and a parcel of land was purchased for $10,000 in a year when the price index was 80. The conversion would be:

$$\frac{120}{80} \times \$10,000 = \$15,000$$

This conversion should not be interpreted to mean that the land is worth $15,000. What it means is that, historically, the purchasing power needed to buy the land is equal to $15,000 in terms of the dollar represented by the new price index.

Restating can be made in either direction—to current purchasing power or to purchasing power of a prior year.

In the United States the best price index for restating financial statements is the Gross National Product Implicit Price Deflator, which is *not* a specific-goods price index, but a broad index of general price changes.

General Price-Level Gain or Loss

Monetary items automatically gain or lose general purchasing power as a result of changes in price indexes. Assume that a comparative balance sheet showed cash of $10,000 and notes payable of $20,000 at both balance sheet dates in a year when the price index went from 110 to 117. Obviously, the current year's $10,000 in cash cannot purchase what the prior year's $10,000 in cash could. Using our formula the conversion of the current year to general price levels would be:

$$\frac{117}{110} \times \$10,000 = \$10,636$$

The $636 is a loss in the general purchasing power of the cash as measured by the change in the price indexes.

On the other hand, the current year's $20,000 of notes payable will be paid with cheaper dollars than the prior year's $20,000 in notes payable:

$$\frac{117}{110} \times \$20,000 = \$21,272$$

The $1,272 ($21,272 − $20,000) is a gain in the general purchasing power, because the liability will be paid with dollars of less general purchasing power.

If our hypothetical company had no other monetary assets and liabilities besides the cash of $10,000 and notes payable of $20,000, it would have a net general price-level gain of $636 ($1,272 − $636 = $636) for the year.

A change in the price index from one period to another can be expressed as a percentage. When the index moves from 110 to 117, it has increased 7 points, or 6.36% ($7/110$ = 6.36). Applying this percentage increase to the $10,000 cash and $20,000 notes payable in the preceding example:

$10,000 × 6.36% =   ($ 636)
$20,000 × 6.36% =   1,272
Net price level gain
  for the period $ 636

Note that price-level increases arising from assets cause a price-level *loss,* whereas price-level increases arising from liabilities cause a price-level *gain.*

Instead of computing a gain or loss on each individual monetary item, it is easier to calculate the net monetary position. In our last example, the net monetary position (negative) was $10,000 ($10,000 in cash less $20,000 notes payable). We can now restate the beginning net monetary position for the change in the price index and then subtract the actual net monetary position at the end of the period, as follows:

Net monetary position (negative)

$10,000 × $\frac{117}{110}$ $10,636

Less: Ending net monetary position   10,000*
Net general price-level gain $ 636

*$10,000 cash less the $20,000 notes payable on the current year's balance sheet.

General Price-Level Changes

Advantages of Restatement

Advantages of general price-level financial statements are:

1. The dollar is not stable, and changes in its monetary value should be reflected in financial statements in order to produce more realistic information.
2. General price-level financial statements provide more meaningful information in terms of current economic conditions.
3. Management's effectiveness in periods of inflation or deflation can be more readily determined.
4. General price-level balance sheets more clearly approximate current values.

Disadvantages of Restatement

Disadvantages of general price-level financial statements are:

1. Historical-dollar financial statements are based on verifiable information.
2. There is no general agreement as to which price-level index to use and how it should be applied.
3. Most assets and liabilities that have been recently acquired are already valued close to current price levels.
4. Historical costs have been employed traditionally over many years with satisfactory results.

Schedule of General Price-Level Gain or Loss

Our previous discussion has been oversimplified in order to demonstrate the nature of general price-level gains or losses.

In reality, a business will have many transactions that cause a change in net monetary assets or liabilities. Cash and credit sales increase the net monetary position; purchases, operating expenses, and cash dividends decrease the net monetary position. Depreciation and amortization have no effect on the net monetary position. The procedure for preparing a schedule of general price-level gain or loss is:

1. Determine the net monetary position (positive or negative) at the beginning of the period (usually the monetary assets less

the monetary liabilities at the end of the prior period) adjusted to the general price-level index at the end of the period.

2. Add all increases in net monetary items from all sources (sales, miscellaneous revenue, proceeds from the sale of fixed assets, proceeds from the issuance of debt or stock, etc.), adjusted to the general price-level at the end of the period.

3. Deduct all decreases in net monetary items from all sources (expenditures for purchases, operating expenses, acquisition of assets, miscellaneous expenses, and the retirement of debt or stock), adjusted to the general price-level index at the end of the period.

4. Arrive at the *estimated* net monetary position at the end of the period, which is the difference between steps 1, 2, and 3 above.

   (1 + 2 − 3) = estimated net monetary position at the end of the period

5. Compute the *actual* net monetary position at the end of the period (monetary assets less monetary liabilities), and subtract this from the estimated net monetary position calculated in step 4.

   Note: The difference between the estimated net monetary items at the end of the period and the actual net monetary items at the end of the period is the general price-level gain or loss for the period. If the estimated net monetary items exceed the actual, a loss results. If the estimated net monetary items are less than the actual, a gain results.

This price-level gain or loss is shown in the income statement as the item immediately preceding net income.

General Price-Level Financial Statements

The following are general rules for preparing price-level adjusted financial statements:

1. All financial statements presented, including those of prior years, are restated to the purchasing power of the dollar at the most recent balance sheet date. This is called "rolling over" the previously restated statements. The prior restated statements are simply restated again to the current price

General Price-Level Changes

level. This serves two purposes. It converts last year's statements into current-year dollars (comparability), and it translates last year's ending retained earnings into current-year dollars for use in the current-year statement of retained earnings.

2. Sales and expenses incurred evenly throughout the year are converted by using the average general price index for the year.
3. The inventory method (FIFO, LIFO, etc.) will dictate the price index to use for restating inventory.
4. Depreciation is restated by using the price index of the related asset.
5. Buildings, equipment, and other fixed assets are restated by using the price index existing at the time of their purchase.
6. Common stock is restated by using the price index existing at the time the stock was issued.

Comprehensive Illustration

The following comprehensive problem illustrates how financial statements are restated for general price-level changes.

ABC Corporation's financial statements for the year ended December 31, 1977, are shown below:

ABC Corporation
BALANCE SHEET
As of December 31, 1977

Cash	$100,000
Accounts receivable	200,000
Inventory (FIFO)	50,000
Fixed assets	250,000
Total assets	$600,000
Accounts payable	$ 70,000
Common stock	200,000
Retained earnings	330,000
Total liabilities and equity	$600,000

General Price-Level Changes

ABC Corporation
INCOME STATEMENT
For the year ended December 31, 1977

Sales		$900,000
Cost of goods sold:		
Beginning inventory	$ 50,000	
Add: Purchases	700,000	
Total	$750,000	
Less: Ending inventory	50,000	
Cost of goods sold		700,000
Gross profit		$200,000
Operating expenses:		
Depreciation		$ 20,000
Other		80,000
Total operating expenses		$100,000
Income before taxes		$100,000
Income tax expense		20,000
Net income		$ 80,000

Relevant price indexes:

Beginning of year	104
End of year	108
Average	106
Fixed assets acquired	92
Formation of company	90

Additional data:
  The company's net monetary position at December 31, 1976, was $130,000. Inventories are priced on a FIFO basis.

The first step is to compute the amount of the general price-level gain or loss.

The essence of creating the schedule of general price-level gain or loss is to compare the monetary items at year end with the amount at which the items would have been stated if they were nonmonetary items.

The steps in preparing this schedule for ABC Corporation are illustrated below.

1. The net monetary position at the beginning of the year

(December 31, 1976) is given as $130,000. Restate this to current dollars as follows:

$$\$130{,}000 \times \frac{108}{104} = \$135{,}000$$

The beginning index of 104 is used because this is the net monetary position at the *beginning* of the period.

2. Assemble all increases in monetary items and convert them, using the appropriate index.

Increases:

Sales	$900,000
Total increases	$900,000
Factor	108/106
Adjusted sales	$916,981

The average index of 106 is used because sales are assumed to occur evenly through the year.

3. Assemble all decreases in monetary items and convert them, using the appropriate index.

Decreases:

Purchases	$700,000
Other expenses	80,000
Income tax expense	20,000
Total decreases	$800,000
Factor:	108/106
Adjusted expenses	$815,094

The average index of 106 is used because purchases and expenses, including income tax expense, are assumed to be incurred evenly through the year.

General Price-Level Changes

4. The net estimated monetary position at year end is calculated as follows:

Net monetary position–beginning	$135,000
Plus: Increases	916,981
Less: Decreases	(815,094)
Net estimated monetary position–ending	$236,887

5. The actual net monetary position at the end of the period is calculated from actual amounts appearing on the balance sheet for the end of the period, as follows:

Monetary assets:

Cash	$100,000
Accounts receivable	200,000
Total actual monetary assets	$300,000

Monetary liabilities:

Accounts payable	$ 70,000
Total actual monetary liability	$ 70,000
Net monetary position (positive)	$230,000

The general price-level gain or loss can now be calculated as follows:

Actual net monetary items	$230,000
Estimated net monetary items	236,887
General price-level gain (loss)	$ (6,887)

Since the estimated net monetary position exceeds the actual net monetary position, there is a loss.

The work papers for the restatement of the financial statements of ABC Corporation follow:

General Price-Level Changes

ABC Corporation
INCOME STATEMENT
For the year ended December 31, 1977

	Historical	Conversion Factor	Adjusted
Sales	$900,000	108/106	$916,981
Cost of goods sold:			
Beginning inventory	$ 50,000	108/104	$ 51,923
Add: Purchases	700,000	108/106	713,208
Total	$750,000		$765,131
Less: Ending inventory	50,000	108/108	50,000
Cost of goods sold	$700,000		$715,131
Gross profit	$200,000		$201,850
Operating expenses:			
Depreciation	$ 20,000	108/92	$ 23,478
Other	80,000	108/106	81,509
Total	$100,000		$104,987
Net income before taxes	$100,000		$ 96,863
Income tax expense	20,000	108/106	20,377
Net income	$ 80,000		$ 76,486
General price-level gain (loss)			($ 6,887)
Net income—adjusted for changes in general price levels			$ 69,599

17.12 / GAAP GUIDE

General Price-Level Changes

Schedule of General Price-Level Gain (Loss)

Historical		Converted for Price-Level Changes
$130,000	Beginning net monetary position [index at beginning of year (104) index at end of year (108) = conversion factor 108/104]	$135,000
900,000	Increases in monetary items during the year: sales $900,000 [average index during the year (106), index at end of year (108) = conversion factor 108/106]	916,981
(800,000)	Decreases in monetary items during the year: purchases $700,000, other expenses $80,000, income tax expense $20,000 [average index during the year (106), index at end of year (108) = conversion factor 108/106]	(815,094)
$230,000	Ending net estimated monetary position	$236,887
230,000	Ending actual net monetary position*	230,000
—	General Price-Level Gain or (Loss)	$ (6,887)

*Monetary assets–end of period $300,000
Less: Monetary liabilities–end of period 70,000
Actual net monetary position–end of period $230,000

General Price-Level Changes

ABC Corporation
BALANCE SHEET
As of December 31, 1977

	Historical	Conversion Factor	Adjusted
Cash	$100,000	108/108	$100,000
Accounts receivable	200,000	108/108	200,000
Inventory	50,000	108/108	50,000
Fixed assets	250,000	108/92	293,478
Total assets	$600,000		$643,478
Accounts payable	$ 70,000	108/108	$ 70,000
Common stock	200,000	108/90	240,000
Retained earnings	330,000		333,478
Total liabilities and equity	$600,000		$643,478

Note: Only the nonmonetary assets and liabilities are restated on the general price-level balance sheet. The changes in the net monetary assets and liabilities have already been taken into account in the general price-level income statement as a general price-level gain or loss.

GOVERNMENT CONTRACTS

Background

The promulgated GAAP which addresses itself to Government Contracts is as follows:

> ARB-43, Chapter 11A–Cost-Plus-Fixed-Fee Contracts
> ARB-43, Chapter 11B–Renegotiation
> ARB-43, Chapter 11C–Terminated War and Defense Contracts

Since the above promulgated GAAP is silent on the extent of its coverage, it is assumed that companies in regulated industries would be included in accordance with the Addendum to APB-2.

Overview

More frequently than not, government contracts are performed under a cost-plus-fixed-fee (CPFF) arrangement which provides for possible renegotiation, if the contracting officer for the government believes that excess profits were made by the contractor. These contracts usually also provide that the government may terminate the contract for its convenience at any time.

CPFF Contracts

Cost-plus-fixed-fee contracts generally provide that the government pay a fixed fee in addition to all costs involved in fulfilling the contract. The contract may include the manufacture of a product or only the performance of services, and the government may or may not withhold a specified percentage of the interim payments until completion of the entire contract. Furthermore, CPFF contracts are usually cancellable by the government, and when such contracts are terminated the contractor is entitled to reimbursement for all costs, plus an equitable portion of the fixed fee.

One of the main problems in accounting for CPFF contracts is when profits should be recognized. As a general rule, profits should not be recognized until the right to full payment becomes unconditional, which is usually when the product has been delivered and accepted or the services fully rendered (completed-contract method).

However, when CPFF contracts extend over several years the

completed-contract method may be utilized; the percentage-of-completion method is acceptable, provided that costs and profits can be reasonably estimated and realization of the contract is reasonably assured.

An advance payment by the government may not be offset as a payment on account, unless it is expected to be applied as such with reasonable certainty. A distinction should be made in the balance sheet between unbilled costs and fees and billed amounts. In the event that an advance is offset, it must be clearly disclosed.

Renegotiation

Renegotiation involves the adjustment of the original selling price or contract. Since the government makes renegotiation adjustments an integral part of a contract, a provision for such probable adjustments is necessary. This provision for renegotiation should be based on the contractor's past experience or on the general experience of the particular industry, and it is shown in the income statement as a reduction of the related sales or income. If a reasonable estimate cannot be made, disclosure of the inability to provide for renegotiation should be fully disclosed in the financial statements or footnotes thereto. The provision for renegotiation is reported as a current liability in the balance sheet.

In those unusual cases where collection is not reasonably assured, it may be preferable to employ the installment-sale or cost-recovery method in accounting for a government contract.

When a provision for renegotiation is made in a particular year and the subsequent final adjustment differs materially, the difference should be shown in the income statement of the year of final determination.

Disclosure

When a significant part of a company's business is derived from government contracts, such disclosure should be made in the financial statements or footnotes thereto, indicating the uncertainties involved and the possibility of renegotiation in excess of the amount provided. In addition, the basis of determining the provision for renegotiation should be disclosed (prior experience, industry experience, etc.).

Terminated War and Defense Contracts

This section of the promulgated GAAP deals with both fixed-price and cost-plus-fixed-fee contracts. It addresses the problems involved in the termination of a government contract by the government but does not cover terminations resulting from default of the contractor.

The determination of profit or loss on a terminated government contract is made as of the effective date of termination. This is the date that the contractor accrues the right to receive payment on that portion of the contract which has been terminated.

Although most government contracts provide for a minimum profit percentage formula in the event agreement cannot be reached, the amount of profit to be reported in the case of termination for the convenience of the government is the difference between all allowable costs incurred and the amount of the termination claim.

If it is impossible to determine a reasonable estimate of the termination claim for reporting purposes, full disclosure of this fact should be made by footnote to the financial statements, which should describe the uncertainties involved. In other words, those parts of the termination claim which can be reasonably ascertained should be reported, and those which cannot be reasonably ascertained should be described in a footnote to the financial statements.

Termination claims should be classified as current assets. Prior to termination notice, advances received should be deducted from termination claims receivable for reporting purposes. Loans received on the security of the contract or termination claim should be separately shown as current liabilities.

The cost of items included in the termination claim that are subsequently reacquired by the contractor should be recorded as a new purchase, and the amount should be applied as a reduction of the termination claim. These types of reductions from the termination claim are generally referred to as *disposal credits.*

Disclosure

Material amounts of termination claims should be classified separately from other receivables in the financial statements.

Termination claims should be stated at the amount estimated as collectible, and adequate provision or disclosure should be made for items of a controversial nature.

Claims against the government, if material, should be segregated from other receivables.

INCOME TAXES

Background

The present promulgated GAAP on income taxes, which is covered herein, consists of the following:

    APB-10, paragraph 6–Tax Allocation Accounts–Discounts
    APB-10, paragraph 7–Offsetting of Securities Against Taxes Payable
    APB-11–Accounting for Income Taxes
    APB-23–Accounting for Income Taxes–Special Areas
    APB-24–Accounting for Income Taxes–Investments in Common Stocks Accounted for by the Equity Method
    FASB Interpretation-18–Accounting for Income Taxes in Interim Periods
    FASB Interpretation-22–Applicability of Indefinite Reversal Criteria to Timing Differences
    FASB Interpretation-29–Reporting Tax Benefits Realized on Disposition of Investments in Certain Subsidiaries and Other Investees
    FASB-31–Accounting for Tax Benefits Related to U.K. Tax Legislation Concerning Stock Relief

    Note: APB-11 is considered the main source for general income tax GAAP. Accounting for Income Taxes–Oil and Gas Producing Companies. (FASB-19) and Accounting for the Investment Credit (APB-2) are discussed elsewhere in this publication.

Overview

One of the basic principles in accounting is that business entities are presumed to continue in existence unless liquidation is imminent (going-concern principle). Therefore, a business currently subject to income taxes will ordinarily continue to pay such taxes in the future. Income tax expense is an important determinant of net income, and must be identified to, and measured with, the appropriate accounting periods.

Income for federal tax purposes and financial accounting income frequently differ. Obviously, income for federal tax purposes is computed in accordance with the prevailing tax laws, whereas financial accounting income is determined in accordance with GAAP. In such a case, a company will have two different income tax liabilities: one for income tax purposes and the other for financial accounting purposes. This disparity is caused by timing differences.

Timing Differences

Timing differences are merely transactions that do not appear in financial accounting income and taxable income in the same reporting period. For example, accelerated depreciation for tax purposes and straight line depreciation for financial accounting purposes create a timing difference in that taxable income will be different from financial accounting income in the same period. There are two types of timing differences:

1. those which always reverse themselves in one or more future periods
2. those which never reverse themselves, or permanent differences

Comprehensive interperiod income tax allocation includes the effects of timing differences in computing income tax expense for a period. This process balances the tax liability and income tax expense for a period by the use of tax deferrals and accruals.

Transactions that cause timing differences There are four basic causes of timing differences:

1. income that is included in taxable income, after it had already been included in financial accounting income
   (*Example:* Installment sales are reported for tax purposes as they are collected, but in financial accounting the total income is recognized in the period the sale is made, so collections on the installment sale are included in taxable income, after the entire sale was recognized by financial accounting in the year of sale.)
2. income that is included in taxable income before it is included in financial accounting income
   (*Example:* Rents collected in advance must be included in taxable income, but in financial accounting such rents are recognized only in the periods in which they are earned.)
3. expenses deducted for taxable income after they have already been deducted for financial accounting income
   (*Example:* Provision for estimated product warranty is not

deductible in computing taxable income, but such provision is made in financial accounting at the time a sale is made.)
4. expenses deducted for taxable income before they are deducted for financial accounting purposes
(*Example:* Accelerated depreciation is allowed in computing taxable income, but in financial accounting the straight line method is usually used to more properly match revenue with its expired costs.)

Some timing differences reduce income taxes that would otherwise have to be paid, whereas other timing differences may increase income taxes.

Permanent differences Permanent differences arise from special tax laws regarding exempt income, dividend received exclusions, and certain other special deductions that, after taken, are permanent. Since permanent differences do not affect subsequent periods, no interperiod tax allocation need be made to account for them.

Permanent differences are either (a) nontaxable, (b) nondeductible, or (c) special tax allowances. Examples are:

1. tax-exempt interest (municipal, state)
2. proceeds from life insurance on officers
3. amortization of goodwill
4. life insurance premiums when corporation is beneficiary
5. certain fines, bribes, kickbacks, etc.
6. dividends-received deduction for corporations
7. excess percentage depletion over cost depletion

Bad debt allowances of savings and loan associations, and policyholders' surplus of stock life insurance companies that create a difference between taxable income and pretax financial accounting income are usually considered permanent differences, because the company controls the events that create the tax consequence. However, if circumstances dictate that income taxes will be paid because of a reduction in the bad debt allowance or in policyholders' surplus, a tax expense should be accrued on such reductions in the period they occur. In effect, these reductions do create a timing difference when they occur and should not be accounted for as an extraordinary item.

Income Taxes

Disclosure of bad debt allowances and policyholders' surplus should be made in the financial statements or in footnotes, as follows:

Bad debt allowance (reserves):

1. the purpose of the allowance account and the rules and regulations pertaining thereto
2. the fact that income taxes may become payable if the allowance account is used for other purposes
3. the total amount of the allowance account for which income taxes have not been accrued

Policyholders' surplus:

1. treatment of the policyholders' surplus under the provisions of the IRC
2. the fact that income taxes may become payable if the company takes specific action, which should be appropriately described
3. the total amount of policyholders' surplus for which income taxes have not been accrued

These disclosure requirements also apply to the parent company of the savings and loan association or the stock life insurance company.

Operating Losses

Under present tax regulations an operating loss of a period may be carried back or forward and may be applied as a reduction of income in those periods permitted by the tax laws. In such a case, the taxable income and the financial accounting income will change for the periods that the loss is carried back or forward.

If an operating loss is carried forward, the tax effects are not recognized because there is no assurance that they will be realized. For example, a loss carryforward would decrease the amount of taxes due in a certain future period, but if the company continues to lose money, there will be no profits to offset the carryforward and it may never be utilized. However, when the tax benefits of a loss carryforward are recognized in full or in part in subsequent periods, it is reported as an extraordinary item.

If an operating loss is carried back, the tax effect will certainly be realized in the form of a claim for taxes previously paid.

There is only one exception to not recognizing the effects of a loss carryforward. The tax effects of a loss carryforward may be realized in the books of accounts *providing that the realization is assured beyond any reasonable doubt.* In this event, in determining the results of operations for those periods the potential tax benefit (deferred tax credit) is recognized in the period(s) that gave rise to the loss. Estimates of the tax benefit should be based on the tax rates that are expected to exist at the time of realization. Any difference between the estimated amount and that received is applied as an adjustment of the tax expense of the period in which the benefit is received. Realization of a loss carryforward is assured beyond any reasonable doubt if the following conditions exist:

1. The company has been reasonably profitable over a long period or has experienced occasional losses which were subsequently offset by taxable income.
2. The loss carryforward is the result of an isolated, nonrecurring, and identifiable source.
3. Realization of future taxable income is large enough to offset the loss carryforward and will occur within the period allowed under tax law.

If tax benefits of loss carryforwards have not been recognized by a purchased subsidiary prior to the date of acquisition, they are recorded as assets purchased if realization is assured beyond any reasonable doubt. If they have not been recognized prior to the acquisition date, they are recognized when actually realized and treated as a retroactive adjustment of the purchase transaction. In this event, operating results for periods subsequent to the purchase may have to be retroactively adjusted if the affected balance sheet items have been subject to amortization.

A similar situation arises for loss carryforwards arising prior to a quasi-reorganization where realization is assured beyond a reasonable doubt. Under these circumstances, a previously unrecognized loss carryforward is recorded as an asset at the date of reorganization. If realization is not assured, the tax benefits of a loss carryforward are recognized when actually realized, and added to contributed capital, on the basis that the benefits are attributable to loss periods prior to the quasi-reorganization.

All other unused tax deductions and/or credits that may be carried back and forward in determining taxable income except

Income Taxes

investment tax credits are handled in the same manner as operating losses. That is, if realization is assured beyond any reasonable doubt, the tax deduction or credit is recognized for financial accounting purposes (books). As a general rule, investment tax credits may not be recognized even though their realization is assured beyond any reasonable doubt. However, in using the "with and without" method of computing deferred taxes, investment tax credits are recognized for financial accounting purposes (books) prior to their realization for tax return purposes (see- Investment Tax Credits).

The tax effects of any realizable loss carryback should be recognized in the determination of the loss period net income. A claim of refund for past taxes will result and is shown on the balance sheet as a separate item (from other deferred taxes) and classified as either current or noncurrent. In the income statement, the claim of refund for past taxes is shown as a reduction of income tax expense for the current period.

When the tax effects of a carryback loss are not recognized (when prior years already are losses) and at the same time a net deferred tax credit exists, an adjustment may have to be made. In such a case, the deferred tax credits should be (1) eliminated to the extent of the tax effect of the resulting loss carryforward or (2) amortized over the period of the resulting loss carryforward. If in subsequent periods the loss carryforward is realized, in part or in whole, the prior adjustments to the deferred tax credits will have to be readjusted or reinstated at the then current tax rates. This procedure is similar to the offsetting of unused investment tax credits against existing net deferred tax credits required by FASB Interpretation-25 (see- Investment Tax Credits).

Timing Differences—Special Areas

There is a presumption that all undistributed earnings of a subsidiary (domestic and foreign) will eventually be transferred to the parent. Unless the presumption is overcome, the undistributed earnings included in a parent's consolidated income will result in a timing difference, which should be recognized in the accounts. In addition, corporate joint ventures and investments in common stocks accounted for by the equity method present the same problem as a subsidiary in regard to timing differences and should be accounted for in the same manner.

> **OBSERVATION:** Undistributed earnings of a subsidiary include those of a domestic international sales corporation (DISC) that qualify for tax deferral.

An investor's proportionate share of operating losses from a subsidiary which files separate income tax returns, a joint venture, or an investment in common stock accounted for by the equity method, is accounted for in the same manner as other operating losses (see 19.04). As a result, an operating loss of this type is included in the investor's income or loss for the period, but is not treated as a timing difference unless it is realizable beyond any reasonable doubt. The journal entry to record the investor's proportionate share of an investee's operating loss is a debit to a loss account which appears on the income statement and a credit to the investment account. As a result, a difference is created between the accounting and tax basis of the investment. In addition, no deferred taxes are provided for, unless the operating loss is realizable beyond a reasonable doubt. Should the operating loss become realizable beyond a reasonable doubt a tax benefit is realized at that time. Because of the difference between the accounting and tax basis, a tax benefit will also be realized upon the ultimate disposition of the investment. FASB Interpretation-29 requires that these tax benefits be included as part of the gain or loss on the disposition of the investment. The result is that the tax benefit is given the same classification as the gain or loss on the investment (continuing operations, extraordinary item, disposal of a segment, etc). Any significant variation in the usual relationship between income tax expense and pretax accounting income must be disclosed in the financial statements (APB-11).

> **OBSERVATION:** There is a mistake in paragraph 3 of FASB Interpretation-29. The reference to paragraph 63(c) of APB-11, should be paragraph 62(c). There is no paragraph 63(c).

Indefinite reversal criteria The presumption that all undistributed earnings of a subsidiary or corporate joint venture will be eventually distributed to the parent may be overcome by sufficient evidence that the subsidiary or corporate joint venture has invested or will invest such earnings indefinitely, or that they will be remitted in a tax-free liquidation—all in accordance with a specific plan. In the event the plans change and earnings will be remitted in the

Income Taxes

foreseeable future, the parent company should accrue as an expense of the current period the appropriate income tax expense. If the reverse occurs, where income taxes were accrued and the undistributed earnings will not be distributed in the foreseeable future, the parent company should adjust income tax expense of the current period. In either case, the adjustment of income tax expense should not be accounted for as an extraordinary item.

The indefinite reversal criteria for investments in common stock accounted for by the equity method depends upon those interests that control the investment. Only the controlling interest(50% or more) of an investment in common stocks accounted for by the equity method, can determine that undistributed earnings will be reinvested for an indefinite period. The fact that the equity method presumes that an investor has the ability to exercise significant influence over the investee if the investor owns 20% or more control, is irrelevant in considering the indefinite reversal criteria.

Corporate joint ventures may be permanent or have a limited life depending on the nature of the venture. GAAP (APB-18) requires that corporate joint ventures, of less than 50% control, be accounted for by the equity method.

Changes in investment An investment (usually 50% or more) in a subsidiary may change to the extent that a subsidiary relationship no longer exists, and the equity method (20% to 49% control) or the cost method (less than 20% control) must be applied. In the event that a subsidiary changes to an investment in common stock accounted for by the equity method, the investor should recognize income taxes on its share of the current earnings of the investee in accordance with the equity method. If, previous to the change in an investment from a subsidiary to one accounted for by the equity or cost method, the parent had not accrued income taxes because of the indefinite reversal criteria, it should then accrue income taxes on the undistributed earnings in the period that it becomes apparent that part or all of the undistributed earnings will be remitted. This accrual should not be accounted for as an extraordinary item.

Deferred income taxes resulting from undistributed earnings of a subsidiary, corporate joint venture, and an investment in common stock accounted for by the equity method should be considered in accounting for a sale or other disposition of the underlying investment.

Income Taxes

An investment in common stock accounted for by the equity method may fall below the 20% ownership that is presumed to indicate significant control, or may rise to 50% or more, which indicates that it has become a subsidiary. If the investment becomes a subsidiary, the deferred income taxes, if any, previously accrued should be included in the income of the parent only as dividends are received that exceed the parent's share of earnings subsequent to the date of becoming a subsidiary. If the investment falls below 20% ownership, the deferred income taxes previously accrued should be included in income only as dividends are received that exceed the allocable share of earnings subsequent to the date the investment fell below 20%.

In the event of a sale or other disposition of an investment in common stock accounted for by the equity method, deferred taxes attributable to the investment should be taken into consideration.

Railroad gradings and tunnel bores Income tax benefits resulting from the amortization of railroad gradings and tunnel bores are timing differences for which comprehensive interperiod tax allocation must be made (FASB Interpretation-18).

U.S. steamship companies Present promulgated GAAP does not cover deposits in capital construction funds or statutory reserves of U.S. steamship companies complying with the Merchant Marine Act of 1970.

Measuring timing differences Difficulties in measuring timing differences in these special areas do not jusitfy ignoring the accrual of income taxes. Estimates and assumptions should be used that include all available related tax planning, tax credits, and deductions. Parent companies' income tax expense should also include a provision, if any, for taxes that would have been withheld if the undistributed earnings had been remitted as dividends.

The determination of whether the undistributed earnings of an investment in common stock accounted for by the equity method will be realized in dividends, the sale or other disposition, or a combination of both, must be made on the basis of the facts and circumstances of each individual investment. If it is determined that the undistributed earnings will be realized in dividends, the accrued income taxes should be based on any available dividend-received deduction, foreign-tax credit, and other tax credits or deductions that may be applicable in the circumstances. On the other hand, if the ultimate disposition will be realized by the sale of the investment, the accrued income taxes should be based on capital gain rates, if applicable, recognizing all other available credits and deductions.

The operating losses of a subsidiary, a joint venture, and an investment in common stock accounted for by the equity method are accounted for in the same manner as other operating losses previously mentioned.

Deferred Tax Method

The deferred tax method of allocating income taxes should be used (APB-11) and is considered the most useful and practical approach to interperiod allocation. The promulgated GAAP (APB-11) has rejected the use of other methods.

Under the deferred tax method, income taxes payable are computed twice: once on the amount that excludes any transaction causing a timing difference and once on the amount that includes the transaction causing a timing difference. The difference between the two income taxes payable is the deferred income tax for the period for that particular timing difference.

The promulgated GAAP (APB-11) states that "The tax effect of a timing difference should be measured by the differential between income taxes computed with and without inclusion of the transaction creating the difference between taxable income and pretax accounting income." Taxable income is further defined as "the excess of revenues over deductions or the excess of deductions over revenue to be reported for income tax purposes for a period . . . except that deductions do not include loss carryforwards or loss carrybacks."

The following is an illustration of the "with and without" method of computing deferred income taxes as required by APB-11.

Assume the following facts for the XYZ Corporation for its calendar year ended December 31, 19XX:

- $250,000 allowable investment tax credit for the current year
- $1,000,000 of pretax financial accounting income (books)
- $200,000 of net timing differences which reduce taxable income
- 40% tax rate for the current period

Income Taxes

- The maximum investment tax credit may not exceed the taxpayer's first $25,000 of tax liability, plus 60% of the tax liability over $25,000.

Discussion

Income tax expense is computed on all taxable items included in pretax financial accounting income. In this example, all items included in financial accounting income are eventually taxable.

There are no permanent differences in this example. In any event, permanent differences do not affect subsequent periods because they do not reverse in future periods, and no interperiod tax allocation need be made to account for them. Therefore, if a permanent difference is taxable, it is included in computing income tax expense (books) for the period. If a permanent difference is nontaxable, it is excluded in computing income tax expense for financial accounting purposes.

The first computation in solving this example illustration is to determine income tax expense on pretax financial accounting income (books) and the current income tax liability on taxable income (tax return), as follows:

Income Tax Expense on Pretax Financial Accounting Income:	
Pretax financial accounting income	$1,000,000
Rate of tax	40%
Income tax expense before allowable investment tax credit	$ 400,000
Allowable investment tax credit [$25,000 plus 60% of ($400,000 less $25,000)]	250,000
Income tax expense (books)	$ 150,000
Current Income Tax Liability on Taxable Income:	
Pretax financial accounting income	$1,000,000
Less: Timing difference	200,000
Taxable income	$ 800,000
Rate of tax	40%
Income tax liability before allowable investment tax credit	$ 320,000
Allowable investment tax credit [$25,000 plus 60% of ($320,000 less $25,000)]	202,000
Current income tax liability	$ 118,000

The $32,000 difference between income tax expense of $150,000 (books) and the current income tax liability of $118,000 (tax return)

Income Taxes

is the deferred tax expense on the net timing difference of $200,000, computed as follows:

Net timing difference	$ 200,000
Rate of tax	40%
Income tax expense before allowable investment tax credit	$ 80,000
Allowable investment tax credit (60% of $80,000)	48,000
Deferred tax expense on timing difference	$ 32,000

The journal entry to record the income tax expense for the current period and the deferred taxes is:

Income tax expense-current	$118,000	
Income tax expense-deferred	32,000	
Current tax liability		$118,000
Deferred taxes		32,000

The provision for income taxes in the income statement for the current period would appear as follows:

Provision for income taxes:	
Current	$118,000
Deferred	32,000
Total provision for income taxes	$150,000

Analysis of Solution:
From a practical standpoint, interperiod tax allocation is basically an accrual or prepayment process. In the above example, XYZ Corporation had $200,000 more pretax financial accounting income (books) than it showed on its tax return. Perhaps the reason for the difference was that for book income the straight-line method of depreciation was being used and for tax return purposes they used an accelerated method. The fact is that they showed $200,000 more income per books than on their tax return and for that reason taxes computed on book income was $32,000 more than that reflected on

the tax return. The credit of $32,000 to deferred taxes is actually an accrual of income taxes which will have to be paid in the future when the timing difference reverses itself.

It must be realized that a timing difference can either increase or decrease taxable income. In the illustration of the XYZ Corporation, suppose that the $200,000 timing difference arose because of rental income collected in advance. Advance rental income is taxable when received for tax purposes, but would be excluded from financial accounting income (books) because it would not be income for the current period. In that case, pretax financial accounting income would only be $800,000 and taxable income $1,000,000. Instead of accruing the tax on the $200,000 timing difference, XYZ would in fact have to prepay it. The computations using the "with and without" method follows:

Income Tax Expense on Pretax Financial Accounting Income:	
Pretax financial accounting income	$ 800,000
Rate of tax	40%
Income tax expense before allowable investment tax credit	$ 320,000
Allowable investment tax credit	
[$25,000 plus 60% of ($320,000 less $25,000)]	202,000
Income tax expense	$ 118,000
Current Income Tax Liability on Taxable Income:	
Pretax financial accounting income	$ 800,000
Add: Timing difference	200,000
Taxable income	$1,000,000
Rate of tax	40%
Income tax liability before allowable investment tax credit	$ 400,000
Allowable investment tax credit	
[$25,000 plus 60% of ($400,000 less $25,000)]	250,000
Current income tax liability	$ 150,000

The $32,000 difference between income tax expense of $118,000 (books) and the current income tax liability of $150,000 (tax return) is the deferred tax expense on the net timing difference of $200,000. However, this time the journal entry will reflect that the $32,000 of deferred taxes is actually a prepayment of future taxes, as follows:

Income Taxes

Income tax expense-current	$150,000	
Deferred taxes	32,000	
Income tax expense-deferred		$ 32,000
Current tax liability		150,000

The provision for income taxes in the income statement for the current period would appear, as follows:

Provision for income taxes:		
Current		$150,000
Deferred		(32,000)
Total provision for income taxes		$118,000

The "short cut" approach which determines the deferred tax by applying the current tax rate to the transaction causing the timing difference works most of the time. However, in some instances involving the effect of the investment credit, foreign tax credit, and operating losses, the "short cut" approach does not theoretically work.

Timing differences may be considered individually, or in groups of similar timing differences which may be further determined by the gross change or net change method. However, the tax effect in all cases is based on a differential calculation of taxes involved.

> **OBSERVATION:** *Where a company is subject to more than one tax rate, the U.S. tax rate is usually increased by a percent equivalent, to take into consideration taxes imposed by other jurisdictions.*

Individual method The tax effect of a timing difference is computed separately on each timing difference.

Gross change method For each group of similar timing differences a computation is made for the tax effects of originating differences based on the current tax rate, and for the tax effects of reversing differences at the tax rate reflected in the account.

Net change method A single computation is made at current tax rates for the net cumulative tax effect of both originating and reversing differences occurring during a period for a particular similar group.

Groups of similar timing differences are determined on the basis of those arising from the same kind of transaction, such as depreciation, installment sales, and warranties.

Once a method for determining the tax effects of timing differences is selected, it must be consistently applied, because a change would probably require a consistency exception in the auditor's report.

Deferred taxes are amortized as the timing differences reverse in periods subsequent to their origination.

The total of all deferred federal income tax charges and all deferred federal income tax credits should be offset and the resulting net figure used for balance sheet purposes. (This does not include a claim of refund or offsets to future taxes arising from net operating loss carrybacks and carryforwards, which should be shown in separate accounts and classified as either current or noncurrent.)

Matching Concept

The principle of matching income tax expense with the related financial accounting income is the objective of comprehensive interperiod tax allocation.

ABC Construction Co. uses the completed contract method for tax purposes and the percentage-of-completion method for financial accounting purposes. The realized gross profit recognized on one four-year contract was $5,000, $6,000, $7,000 and $12,000. Assuming a 50% tax rate in effect for the four years, tax allocation would be:

	1	2	3	4
Income	$5,000	$6,000	$7,000	$12,000
50% taxes	2,500	3,000	3,500	6,000
Net income	$2,500	$3,000	$3,500	$ 6,000

The journal entry the first three years was:

Income tax expense $XXX
    Deferred taxes $XXX

Income Taxes

In the fourth year, when the contract was completed and appeared on the tax return, the journal entry was:

Income tax expense	$6,000	
Deferred taxes	9,000	
Income tax liability		$15,000

The matching concept includes accruing deferred taxes on undistributed earnings of subsidiaries, corporate joint ventures, and investments in common stock accounted for by the equity method. There is a presumption that these types of undistributed earnings will be paid, and deferred taxes should be accrued in the period such earnings are earned.

Control over the subsidiary, joint venture, or investment can determine that distributions of earnings will not be made or postponed indefinitely. Under these circumstances, deferred taxes need not be accrued.

Intraperiod Tax Allocation

Existing promulgated GAAP (APB-11) requires intraperiod tax allocation to contain the relationship between income tax expense and

1. income before extraordinary items
2. extraordinary items
3. prior-period adjustments
4. direct entries to other stockholders' accounts

Intraperiod tax allocation merely involves associating the income tax expense involved with each of the above categories, which are usually shown "net of tax" in the income statement.

When an operating loss occurs, the tax effects should be associated with it in the period of occurrence.

Discounting Tax Allocation Accounts

Under present promulgated GAAP (APB-10), deferred taxes should not be accounted for on a discounted basis.

Offsetting—Taxes Payable

As a general rule the offsetting of assets and liabilities in the balance sheet is unacceptable unless a right of offset exists.

When securities that are specifically acceptable as payment for taxes are purchased, a right of offset exists, and such securities may be deducted from the related taxes payable on the balance sheet.

Income Taxes—Interim Periods

The promulgated GAAP for Interim Financial Reporting (APB-28) requires that taxes for interim periods be determined in accordance with the existing promulgated GAAP for accounting for income taxes (APB-11). In addition, it requires that an estimated annual effective tax rate be established and used, which includes anticipated investment tax credits, foreign tax credits, percentage depletion, capital gain rates, and all other available tax planning alternatives used in determining ordinary income or loss. At the end of each interim period during the year, this effective tax rate is revised, if necessary, to the best current estimates of the annual effective tax rate.

The interim-period tax is determined by applying the established estimated annual effective tax rate to the year-to-date ordinary income or loss, and subtracting the previous interim year-to-date tax on the ordinary income or loss. Ordinary income or loss is defined as income or loss from continuing operations before a provision for income taxes, excluding significant unusual or nonrecurring items. This excludes extraordinary items, discontinued operations, and cumulative effects of changes in an accounting principle. Income tax is defined to include both current and deferred taxes.

The estimated annual effective tax rate shall include only the tax benefit of a loss that has already been realized, or future realization is assured beyond any reasonable doubt. Therefore the year-to-date tax benefit of a loss shall not exceed benefits that have already been realized or those for which future realization is assured beyond any reasonable doubt.

The estimated annual effective tax rate should include an adjustment for existing net deferred credits, if an estimated ordinary loss is projected for a fiscal year or the year-to-date ordinary loss exceeds the entire projected loss for the year, and if all or part of the tax benefit of the loss will not be realized or realization is not

Income Taxes

assured beyond a reasonable doubt. The adjustment to the existing net deferred credits is the lesser of:

1. the unrecognized tax benefits of the loss
2. the net deferred tax credits that would otherwise be amortized during the carryforward period of the loss

Adjustments to net deferred credits should be included in computing the maximum tax benefit for year-to-date amounts.

The adjustment to the net deferred credits should be cumulatively reinstated in subsequent periods at the then-current tax rates when the loss carryforward is realized in whole or in part.

The following illustration reflects the computation of the estimated annual effective tax rate and its application.

A business estimates $1,000,000 of ordinary income for the year and anticipated realizable tax credits of $100,000. The income tax rate is 50%. Seasonable patterns in the fourth quarter assure the realization of the tax benefits beyond any reasonable doubt.

Tax on ordinary income (50%)	$500,000
Less: Anticipated credits	100,000
Net tax to be provided	$400,000
Estimated annual effective tax rate ($400,000 required tax divided by $1,000,000 income)	40%

Based on the estimated annual effective tax rate, the quarterly computations of taxes might appear as:

Period	Estimated Results Quarter	Estimated Results Cumulative	Estimated Tax Rate	Provision for Taxes Quarter	Provision for Taxes Cumulative
1	($200,000)	($200,000)	40%	($80,000)	$(80,000)
2	100,000	(100,000)	40%	40,000	(40,000)
3	150,000	50,000	40%	60,000	20,000
4	950,000	1,000,000	40%	380,000	400,000
	$1,000,000			$400,000	

If a reliable estimate cannot be made for the annual effective tax rate, the actual year-to-date annual effective tax rate should be used. If a reliable estimate of part of the ordinary income or loss, or of the related tax (or benefit), cannot be made, it should be reported in the interim period in which it actually occurs.

Significant, unusual, or extraordinary items that are reported separately net of their related tax effects are recognized in the interim period in which they occur. The related tax on these items is the difference between the tax on year-to-date ordinary income including the item, and the tax on year-to-date ordinary income excluding the item.

Assume the same facts as those in the preceding illustration; assume also that the business incurs a tax-deductible significant unusual extraordinary loss in the third quarter of $200,000 the benefit (50%) for which is assured beyond any reasonable doubt, because the loss can be carried back.

Since the estimated annual effective tax rate is unaffected under these circumstances, the tax on ordinary income or loss is the same, and the computation of the estimated annual effective tax rate is not reproduced.

	Income		Provision for Taxes	
Period	Ordinary	Extraordinary	Ordinary	Extraordinary
1	($200,000)		($80,000)	
2	100,000		40,000	
3	150,000	($200,000)	60,000	($100,000)
4	950,000		380,000	
	$1,000,000	($200,000)	$400,000	($100,000)

If the $200,000 tax-deductible unusual extraordinary loss in the third quarter was not realizable beyond any reasonable doubt, it would appear only in the third and succeeding periods to the extent that it could offset ordinary income for the year to date.

The tax benefit of a loss from significant, unusual, and extraordinary items or discontinued operations shall not be recognized until it is realized or realization is assured beyond a reasonable doubt. Realization is assured beyond a reasonable doubt by:

1. offsetting year-to-date ordinary income
2. offsetting taxable income from unusual, extraordinary, discontinued operations, or items credited directly to stockholders' equity accounts
3. carrying back the loss to prior years

Income Taxes

4. future taxable income that is almost certain to occur shortly, especially from seasonal patterns of revenue

If all or part of such losses are not realized, and previously reported net deferred tax credits exist that would have been amortized during the carryforward period, the net deferred tax credits should be amortized in the same manner as previously stated.

The provision for taxes on income or loss from operations of a discontinued segment prior to measurement date, and the gain or loss on disposal of the discontinued operations, is determined (as stated earlier) by the difference between the tax on year-to-date ordinary income or loss including such items and the tax on year-to-date ordinary income or loss excluding the items. Thereafter the provision for taxes shall not be recomputed, but should be divided into two components: (1) for the remaining ordinary income or loss and (2) for the income or loss from operations of the discontinued segment. A revised estimated annual effective tax rate and resulting tax benefits is then recomputed for the remaining ordinary income or loss.

The following illustration depicts how a discontinued segment is accounted for:

A business estimates ordinary income of $1,000,000 for the year and tax credits of $100,000 that are realizable beyond any reasonable doubt. Income tax rates are 50%. The estimated annual effective tax rate is as follows:

Tax on pretax ordinary income (50%)	$500,000
Less: Anticipated credits	(100,000)
Net tax to be provided	$400,000
Estimated annual effective tax rate	
($400,000 ÷ $1,000,000)	40%

The first two quarters appear as:

	Estimated Results			Provision for Taxes	
Period	Quarter	Cumulative	Rate	Quarter	Cumulative
1	$200,000	$200,000	40%	$ 80,000	$ 80,000
2	250,000	450,000	40%	100,000	180,000

Income Taxes

During the third quarter the decision to discontinue a division of the company was made. The results of operations for the continuing divisions of the company and for the discontinued division are as follows:

	Revised	Discontinued Division	
Quarter	Ordinary Income	Operations	Loss on Disposal
1	$ 250,000	($ 50,000)	
2	350,000	(100,000)	
3	500,000	(100,000)	($550,000)
4 (estimated)	500,000		
Total for Year	$1,600,000	($250,000)	($550,000)

The only assumptions that have changed for the estimated annual effective tax rate is that $20,000 of the $100,000 in tax credits was related to the discontinued operations. The recomputation of the estimated annual effective tax rate is:

Tax on ordinary income (50% of $1,600,000)	$800,000
Less: Anticipated tax credits	80,000
Net tax to be provided	$720,000
Estimated annual effective tax rate ($720,000 ÷ $1,600,000)	45%

The quarterly amounts, based on the revised ordinary income and estimated annual effective tax rate, are:

	Estimated Results			Provision for Taxes	
Period	Quarter	Cumulative	Rate	Quarter	Cumulative
1	$ 250,000	$ 250,000	45%	$112,500	$112,500
2	350,000	600,000	45%	157,500	270,000
3	500,000	1,100,000	45%	225,000	495,000
4	500,000	1,600,000	45%	225,000	720,000
	$1,600,000			$720,000	

The computation of the tax benefit attributable to the discontinued division for the first two quarters is the difference between the tax on year-to-date ordinary income or loss including the discontinued division, and the tax on the year-to-date ordinary income or loss, excluding the discontinued division, as follows:

Income Taxes

	Tax on Ordinary Income		
Quarter	Previously Computed	Recomputed	Tax Benefit, Discontinued Div.
1	$ 80,000	$112,500	($32,500)
2	100,000	157,500	(57,500)
Totals	$180,000	$270,000	($90,000)

The third-quarter tax benefits for (1) the loss from operations and (2) the provision for the disposal of the discontinued division are computed on the revised estimated annual income with and without the effects of the discontinued division, as follows:

	Discontinued Division	
	Loss on Operations	Loss on Disposal
Estimated revised ordinary income	$1,600,000	$1,600,000
Discontinued division loss on operations	250,000	
Discontinued division loss on disposal		550,000
Total	$1,350,000	$1,050,000
Tax at regular tax rate (50%)	$ 675,000	$ 525,000
Anticipated credits–continuing operations	(80,000)	(80,000)
Taxes–after effect of discontinued division	$ 595,000	$ 445,000
Previously computed taxes for year	720,000	720,000
Tax benefit–discontinued division	$ (125,000)	$ (275,000)
Less: Tax benefits recognized in first two quarters	(90,000)	—
Tax benefit for third quarter	$ (35,000)	$ (275,000)

The $20,000 in tax credits related to the discontinued division have not been recognized on the assumption that they will not be realized.

The tax benefit of a prior year's operating loss carryforward is recognized as an extraordinary item (APB-11) to the extent that offsetting income is available in each interim period.

The cumulative effect of a change in an accounting principle on the beginning-of-the-year retained earnings is reported in the first interim period of the fiscal year (FASB-3). The related income tax effects are computed as though the new accounting principle had been applied retroactively to all affected prior periods (APB-20). When the change is made in other than the first interim period, the prechange interim periods are restated, by applying the newly adopted accounting principle to those prechange interim periods. The tax or tax benefits for the prechange interim periods is then recomputed on the year-to-date and annual estimated amounts, modified only for the effect of the change in accounting principle.

Businesses subject to tax in more than one taxing jurisdiction shall compute one overall estimated annual effective tax rate, except that:

1. ordinary income (loss) and related tax (benefit) shall be excluded in computing the estimated annual effective tax rate and interim-period tax (benefit), in any jurisdiction that anticipates an ordinary loss for the year, or has an ordinary loss for the year-to-date, for which a tax benefit cannot be recognized.

2. ordinary income (loss) and related tax (benefit) shall be excluded in computing the estimated annual effective tax rate and interim-period tax (benefit) in any foreign jurisdiction where reliable estimates cannot be made. In this event, the tax (benefit) on ordinary income (loss) shall be recognized in the interim period in which it is reported.

Changes resulting from new tax laws should be reflected in a revised estimated annual effective tax rate for the first interim period affected.

Full disclosure should be made of any significant difference in the usual relationship between income tax expense and pretax accounting income, arising from the application of the promulgated GAAP for accounting for income taxes in interim periods.

Disclosure

Balance sheet accounts relating to tax allocations are of two types:

1. deferred charges and deferred credits arising from timing differences
2. claim of refunds for past taxes or offsets to future taxes arising from the tax effects of carrybacks and carryforwards

Deferred charges and credits arising from timing differences represent the cumulative recognition of their tax effects and are classified on a net basis as either current or noncurrent according to their related asset or liability. For example, if a provision for warranties is classified as a current liability, any related deferred charge should also be classified as current.

Claims for refunds and offsets to future taxes from the tax effects of carrybacks and carryforwards are classified as current or noncurrent on the basis of their expected realization during the current operating cycle.

The amounts and expiration dates of all operating-loss carryforwards not previously recognized should be disclosed, including those amounts which will be credited to deferred tax accounts.

All other significant unused deductions or credits including expiration dates should be fully disclosed.

The components of income tax expense for the period should be disclosed in the results of operations as

1. taxes estimated to be payable
2. tax effects arising from timing differences
3. tax effects of operating losses

In addition, as stated earlier, the income tax expense should be allocated to (1) income before extraordinary items, (2) extraordinary items, and (3) tax effects of any prior-period adjustments (see Intraperiod Tax Allocation section).

The tax benefit of an operating-loss carryforward that has not been recognized previously should be reported as an extraordinary item in the period in which it is realized.

The amount of tax effects of prior-period adjustments and direct entries to stockholders' equity should be disclosed.

Deferred taxes should not be included in the stockholders' equity section of a balance sheet or in the valuation of assets or liabilities.

Significant differences between taxable income and pretax accounting income and material variations between income tax expense and pretax accounting income should be fully disclosed unless apparent in the financial statements or from the nature of the entity's business activities.

Where income taxes have not been accrued on undistributed earnings because of the indefinite reversal criteria, the financial statements should contain a declaration of intention to reinvest the undistributed earnings or a statement that they will be remitted in the form of a tax-free liquidation, whichever is applicable. In addition, the cumulative amount of undistributed earnings for which income taxes have not been recognized should be disclosed.

United Kingdom Tax Benefits (FASB-31)

Recent changes in the tax law of the United Kingdom has created a potential six year recapture period for the "stock relief" deduction. For companies affected by this new legislation, any tax benefits arising from the "stock relief" deduction shall be deferred, unless it is "probable" that recapture of the tax benefits will not occur during the six year recapture period (FASB-31). If, in a subsequent period, it is determined that a previously recorded deferred tax benefit will not be recaptured because of a change in circumstances, then the tax benefit should be recognized in that period as a reduction of income tax expense. The reverse is also true. If, in a subsequent period, it is determined that a previously recognized tax benefit will be recaptured because of a change in circumstances, it should be deferred in that period by increasing income tax expense (FASB-31).

When the above requirements are initially included in interim financial statements, the recognition of previously deferred tax benefits shall be reported as an item of income tax expense for that interim period only, and shall not be classified as an extraordinary item. For subsequent interim reporting periods, adjustments due to changed circumstances shall be included as an adjustment of the estimated annual effective tax rate for the interim period in which circumstances change.

Full disclosure must be made in the financial statements or footnotes thereto if a significant variation in the customary relationship between income tax expense and pretax accounting income occurs as a result of compliance with FASB-31.

GLOSSARY

Deferred taxes Tax effects to be charged to expense in subsequent periods.

Income tax expense That amount of income tax chargeable to the current period, whether or not currently payable (or refundable).

Income Taxes

Income tax liability The amount of income tax due as calculated under the provision of the U.S. Internal Revenue Code.

Income taxes Taxes based on income as determined by the provisions of the U.S. Internal Revenue Code, as well as other foreign, franchising, state, and local taxes based on income.

Indefinite reversal criteria Sufficient evidence that a subsidiary has invested or will invest its undistributed earnings indefinitely, or such earnings will be remitted in a tax-free liquidation. In this event, income taxes need not be accrued on the undistributed earnings.

Interperiod tax allocation The process of using tax deferrals and accruals to balance the tax liability and expense among periods.

Intraperiod tax allocation The process of apportioning the tax expense within a period to the proper accounts, namely, income before extraordinary items, extraordinary items, prior-period adjustments, and direct entries to equity accounts.

"Net of tax" presentation Tax effects recognized under interperiod tax allocation are considered to be adjustments of the valuation of the related asset or liability.

Permanent differences Differences between the taxable income and the pretax accounting income that are caused by different rules of recognition of items affecting net income. Permanent differences do not reverse themselves in subsequent periods.

Pretax accounting income Profit or loss for a period, exclusive of income tax expense, as determined under the guidelines of GAAP.

Tax carrybacks or carryforwards Losses in years other than the current year that can be applied to prior years (carrybacks) or future years (carryforwards) to reduce net taxable income.

Tax effects Differences between the tax liability and the tax expense that are caused by timing differences. Included in tax effects are tax carrybacks and carryforwards and taxable adjustments to equity accounts.

Taxable income Net excess (or deficiency) of revenues over deductions (not including tax carrybacks or carryforwards) as specified in the Code.

Timing differences Differences between the taxable income and the pretax accounting income that are caused by different periods of recognition of items affecting net income. Timing differences reverse themselves in subsequent periods, so that the net long-term timing difference is zero.

INSTALLMENT METHOD OF ACCOUNTING

Background

APB-10, paragraph 12, and ARB-43, Chapter 1A paragraph 1, constitute the promulgated GAAP for the installment method of accounting and unrealized profit.

The promulgated GAAP is silent on its coverage of companies in regulated industries. Thus, in accordance with the Addendum to APB-2, companies in regulated industries should comply with this promulgated GAAP.

Overview

Promulgated GAAP prohibits accounting for sales by any form of installment accounting except under exceptional circumstances where collectibility cannot be reasonably estimated or assured. The doubtfulness of collectibility can be caused by the length of an extended collection period or because no basis of estimation can be established. In such cases a company can use either the cost recovery method or the installment sales method of accounting (APB-10).

Cost Recovery Method

The cost recovery method, also known as the sunk-cost theory, is used in situations where recovery of cost is undeterminable or extremely questionable. The procedure is simply that all cost is recovered before any gain is recognized. Once all cost has been recovered, any other collections are recognized as revenue. The only expenses remaining to be charged against such revenue are those relating to the collection process.

For example, if a company sells for $100 an item that cost $40, and receives no down payment, the first $20 collected, regardless of the year collected, would be considered recovery of one-half the cost. The next $20 collected would be recovery of the balance of the cost, regardless of the year collected. The remaining $60 (all gross profit) would be recognized as income when received. The only additional expenses that could be charged against the remaining $60 would be those directly related to the collection process.

Installment Method of Accounting

Recording Installment Sales

Under the installment sales method of accounting, each payment collected consists of part recovery of cost and part recovery of gross profit, in the same ratio that these two elements existed in the original sale. For example, assume that a furniture dealer sells for $100 a chair that cost him $70. The gross profit percentage for this sale is 30%. The dealer would recognize 70% of any payment as a recovery of cost and 30% as realized gross profit.

The entries to record the initial sale, assuming the use of a periodic inventory system and no down payment, are:

Accounts receivable–installment sales	$100	
Installment sales		$100
Cost of installment sales	$ 70	
Inventory		$ 70

At the end of the period, the company closes out the installment sales account and the cost of installment sales to unrealized gross profit on installment sales account, which in this example is $30. The entry is:

Installment sales	$100	
Cost of installment sales		$ 70
Unrealized gross profit on installment sales		30

In the period that the company collects $40, the entries are:

Cash	$40	
Accounts receivable–installment sales		$40
Unrealized gross profit on installment sales	$12	
Realized gross profit on installment sales		$12

The $40 collected include $28 recovery of cost and $12 of realized gross profit on installment sales (70%/30% relationship).

Installment Method of Accounting

Since gross profit ratios are different for most products and departments and fluctuate between years, it is necessary to keep a separate record of sales by year, product lines, and department. Separate accounts and records must be kept for receivables, realized gross profit, unrealized gross profit, and repossessions for each category of product. Under the installment sales method, selling and administrative costs are charged to expense in the period incurred.

Generally, the seller will protect its interest in an installment sale by retaining title to the goods through a conditional sales contract, lease, mortgage, or trustee. In the event of a default on an installment sales contract, the related account receivable and unrealized gross profit are written off. In many cases of default, the goods are repossessed by the seller. The loss (or gain) on a default of an installment sales contract is determined as follows:

$$\text{Loss (or Gain)} = \begin{bmatrix} \text{balance of} \\ \text{account} \\ \text{receivable} \end{bmatrix} \text{less} \begin{bmatrix} \text{unrealized} \\ \text{gross} \\ \text{profit} \end{bmatrix} \text{less} \begin{bmatrix} \text{inventory value of} \\ \text{repossessed} \\ \text{merchandise} \\ \text{(if any)} \end{bmatrix}$$

For example, continuing the preceding illustration, if the first payment of $40 was the only payment the company received and the goods were not repossessed, the journal entry to record the default and loss would be:

Unrealized gross profit	$18	
Loss on installment sales	42	
Accounts receivable–installment sales		$60

If the goods were repossessed and had an inventory value of $25, the journal entry would be:

Unrealized gross profit	$18	
Loss on installment sales	17	
Inventory	25	
Accounts receivable–installment sales		$60

Installment Method of Accounting

When goods are repossessed, one of the major problems is determining the value of these inventory goods. Some of the methods of determining the value include:

1. fair market value
2. unrecovered cost (results in no gain or no loss)
3. resale value less reconditioning costs plus a normal profit (net realizable value)
4. no value–a good method when no other method is appropriate, particularly when the actual value is minor

Deferred Income Taxes

The installment sales method is acceptable for tax purposes, because the government attempts to collect taxes when the taxpayer has the cash on hand rather than basing collection on a theoretical analysis of accounting principles. The use of installment accounting for tax purposes and normal accrual accounting for financial reporting purposes results in a timing difference and creates a deferred tax liability.

Disclosure

Accounts receivable on installment sales are shown separately in the balance sheet. They are classified as current assets in accordance with the normal operating cycle of the entity, which frequently extends for more than one year. Resources that are reasonably expected to be realized in cash, sold, or consumed (prepaid items) during the normal operating cycle of a business are classified as current assets. The amounts maturing each period for each class of installment receivable should also be disclosed.

Unrealized gross profit is presented in the balance sheet as a separate caption, immediately above stockholders' equity or as a contra account to the related installment receivable.

Since realized gross profit is recognized as a portion of each cash collection, a percentage relationship will always exist between the installment accounts receivable balance for a particular sales category and the related unrealized gross profit for that category. The percentage relationship will be the same as the gross profit ratio on the initial sale.

INTANGIBLE ASSETS

Background

The promulgated GAAP for Accounting for Intangible Assets is APB-17. A good source of nonpromulgated GAAP is Accounting Research Study No. 10, Accounting for Goodwill (AICPA).

The promulgated GAAP (APB-17) covers both internally developed intangibles and those acquired in a business combination. However, the promulgated GAAP (APB-17) does not cover research and development costs included in FASB-2.

All enterprises, whether regulated or nonregulated, are included in the scope of the promulgated GAAP (APB-17).

Overview

The term *intangible asset* refers to certain long-lived legal rights and competitive advantages developed or acquired by a business enterprise.

Intangible assets differ considerably in their characteristics, useful lives, and relationship to operations of an enterprise and may be classified as follows.

Identifiability Patents, copyrights, franchises, trademarks, and other similar intangible assets that can be specifically identified with reasonably descriptive names. Other types of intangible assets lack specific identification, the most common being goodwill.

Manner of acquisition Intangible assets may be purchased or developed internally and may be acquired singly, in groups, or in business combinations.

Determinate or indeterminate life Patents are issued to inventors for a period of 17 years. Copyrights and most franchises also expire within a definite period. Other intangible assets such as organizational costs, secret processes, and goodwill have no determinable term of existence, or the expected period of benefit cannot be ascertained at the time of acquisition.

Transferability The rights to a patent, copyright, or franchise can be separately identified and bought or sold. Organizational costs are an inseparable part of a business, and it is unlikely that a purchaser would purchase the organizational costs without the

Intangible Assets

business. Similarly, goodwill is inseparable from a business and is transferable only as an inseparable intangible asset of an enterprise.

Cost of Intangibles

A company should record as assets the cost of intangible assets acquired from other enterprises or individuals. Costs of developing, maintaining, or restoring intangible assets that are not specifically identifiable, have indeterminate lives, or are inherent in a continuing business and related to an enterprise as a whole, such as goodwill, should be deducted from income when incurred.

> **OBSERVATION:** *The promulgated GAAP (APB-17) apparently does not cover identifiable intangible assets that are purchased. Therefore, expenses of large advertising campaigns that might benefit several accounting periods may very well be capitalized and amortized over the periods that are expected to benefit.*

Cost is measured by (1) the amount of cash disbursed or the fair value of other assets distributed, (2) the present value of amounts to be paid for liabilities incurred, and (3) the fair value of consideration received for stock issued (cost may be determined either by the fair value of the consideration given or by the fair value of the property acquired, whichever is more clearly evident).

The cost of unidentifiable intangible assets is measured by the difference between the cost of the group of assets or of the enterprise acquired and the sum of the assigned costs to identifiable assets acquired, less liabilities assumed. Cost of identifiable assets should not include goodwill.

The cost of an intangible asset, including goodwill acquired in a business combination, may not be written off as a lump sum to capital surplus or to retained earnings, or be reduced to a nominal amount at or immediately after acquisition (ARB-43, Chapter 5).

Amortization

The cost of each type of intangible asset should be amortized by systematic charges to income over the period estimated to be benefited, but not to exceed 40 years.

Usually, all methods of amortizing goodwill are criticized as

Intangible Assets

arbitrary, because the life of goodwill is indefinite and an estimated period of existence is not measurable.

Amortizing the cost of intangible assets, on arbitrary bases, in the absence of evidence of limited lives or decreased values may recognize expenses and decreases of assets prematurely, but delaying amortization of the cost until a loss is evident may recognize the decreases after the fact.

Even if the estimated useful life of an intangible asset is more than 40 years, it must be amortized over 40 years or less.

A business enterprise should evaluate the periods of amortization continually to determine if later circumstances warrant revision of estimated useful lives. If estimates are changed, the unamortized cost should be allocated to the number of years in the revised useful life, but not to exceed 40 years after date of acquisition.

Method The straight line method of amortization should be applied unless a company demonstrates that another systematic method is more appropriate. The method and estimated useful lives of intangible assets should be adequately disclosed in the financial statements.

Income tax effect Amortization of acquired intangible assets not deductible in computing income taxes payable does not create a timing difference, and allocation of income taxes is inappropriate. Goodwill only acquired after November 1, 1970, should be amortized, and retroactive amortization of previously unamortized goodwill acquired prior to November 1, 1970, is prohibited (APB-17).

Negative Goodwill

The measurement or valuation of cost in financial accounting usually means the historical or acquisition cost. The sum of the market or appraised values of identifiable assets less liabilities assumed may sometimes exceed the cost of the assets or business enterprise being acquired. Under these circumstances, the values assigned to the noncurrent assets being acquired should be reduced proportionately (except long-term investments in marketable securities) to absorb the excess value. A deferred credit for an excess of assigned values of identifiable assets over cost (*negative goodwill*) should not be recorded unless the noncurrent assets have been reduced to zero. If, after reducing the noncurrent assets (except long-term investments in marketable securities) to zero, a deferred

Intangible Assets

credit still remains, it should be classified as a deferred credit—excess of acquired net assets over cost, and amortized systematically to income over the period expected to benefit, but not in excess of 40 years. The method and period of amortization should be adequately disclosed in the financial statements. No part of the excess of acquired net assets over cost (negative goodwill) should be credited directly to stockholders' equity at the date of acquisition.

Disposal of Goodwill

Goodwill is unidentifiable apart from a business and cannot be disposed of separately from the enterprise as a whole. However, a large segment or a separable group of assets of an acquired company may be sold or otherwise liquidated, and all or a portion of the unamortized cost of goodwill recognized in the acquisition should be included in the cost of the assets sold.

Step-by-Step Acquisitions

If an enterprise purchases, on a step-by-step basis, a subsidiary that is consolidated or an investment that is accounted for under the equity method, the fair value of the underlying assets acquired and the goodwill for each step purchased must be separately identified.

Assume that Company P acquired an interest in Company S in two steps: (1) It acquired 20% of the outstanding common stock for $200,000. (2) The following year it acquired an additional 60% for $500,000. At the dates of acquisition, the equity book value for Company S was $900,000 and $1,100,000 respectively.

Computation of Excess of Cost over Book Value
First Acquisition

Cost of 20% acquired	$200,000
20% of equity book value of $900,000	180,000
Excess of cost over book value (goodwill)	$ 20,000

Second Acquisition

Cost of 60% acquired	$500,000
60% of equity book value of $1,100,000	660,000
Excess of book value over cost (negative goodwill)	($160,000)

Actually, as of the date of the second acquisition Company P had

Intangible Assets

an investment of $700,000 for 80% of Company S. Company S at the second acquisition date had an equity book value of $1,100,000, and Company P's 80% is $880,000, for which it paid $700,000. Had Company P been recording its first acquisition of 20% on the equity method, it would have recorded its 20% of the $200,000 increase in Company S's book value (assuming that no dividends or other distributions were made to Company P by Company S), so that the adjusted equity in Company S on the books of Company P would include the original $200,000 purchase price plus 20% of the $200,000 increase in book value (from $900,000 to $1,100,000), or a total of $220,000 ($180,000 + $40,000). The cost of the second acquisition of 60% for $500,000 and the adjusted basis for the 20% at $220,000 equals $720,000, which represents 80% of $1,100,000, or $880,000. The difference of $160,000 is the excess of book value over cost (negative goodwill), indicated by the computation for the second acquisition of 60%.

Disclosure

A description of intangible assets, method of amortization, and estimated useful lives should be appropriately disclosed in the financial statements or in footnotes.

In the event that a large part or all of the unamortized cost of an intangible asset is included as an extraordinary charge in the determination of net income, the reasons for the extraordinary deduction should be fully disclosed.

Savings and Loan Associations

The two methods available to record the acquisition of a savings and loan association are the net-spread method and the separate-valuation method. Under the net-spread method, the spread between interest paid on deposits and interest received on mortgages is used to evaluate whether the difference is normal, subnormal, or above normal for a particular market area. If the spread is normal, the principal assets and liabilities that are being acquired are recorded at the carrying amounts shown on the financial statements of the association being acquired. If the spread is subnormal or above normal, an adjustment is made to compensate for the difference. In other words, the acquisition is viewed as the purchase of an entire business and not of separate individual assets. The net-spread method is not acceptable for the purposes of GAAP.

Intangible Assets

The separate-valuation method is based on recording the acquired identifiable assets at fair value at the date of purchase (APB-16), which is the usual method called for by GAAP. Any difference between the fair value of assets acquired less liabilities assumed is recorded as purchased goodwill.

Fair value of assets is influenced by the ability of the assets to generate future income and/or new business within the territory served. Therefore, if the amount paid for the assets to generate future income or new business can be separately determined, it shall not be recorded as goodwill, but recorded as a separate identified intangible asset and amortized over its estimated life. Any portion of the purchase price that cannot be specifically allocated to identifiable tangible or intangible assets shall be recorded as goodwill.

Goodwill recorded in an acquisition of a savings and loan association may be amortized by accelerated methods (contrary to the general rule) if both of the following circumstances exist:

1. Included in goodwill is an indeterminable amount for the acquired assets to generate future income or new business, but these factors cannot be separately valued.
2. The expected benefits from such factors are expected to decline over their useful lives.

Comprehensive Illustrations

The following examples depict the computation of goodwill using different facts.

---

1. Company P acquires for $725,000 an 80% interest in the outstanding common stock of Company S. At the date of acquisition Company S has capital stock of $600,000 and retained earnings of $150,000.

Intangible Assets

As at the Date of Acquisition

Cost of investment in Company S		$725,000
Company S stockholders' equity:		
Capital stock	$600,000	
Retained earnings	150,000	
Total	$750,000	
Acquired by Company P	80%	
Equity acquired by Company P		600,000
Excess of cost over book value (goodwill)		$125,000

2. Company P acquires for $500,000 cash all the assets and liabilities of Company S. An appraisal at the date of acquisition reflects the following values.

Accounts receivable (net)	$ 75,000
Inventories	125,000
Fixed assets	400,000
Long-term marketable securities	100,000
Total	$700,000
Liabilities assumed (present values)	250,000
Value of underlying assets	$450,000
Cost of assets acquired	500,000
Excess of cost over assets acquired (goodwill)	$ 50,000

If the cost of the assets acquired was $400,000, creating negative goodwill of $50,000, only noncurrent assets, *except long-term marketable securities,* should be adjusted downward, but not below zero. The result in this case is that fixed assets are reduced to $350,000, and *no negative goodwill is recorded.* However, negative goodwill would have been recorded on the books if all the noncurrent assets (except long-term marketable securities) had been reduced to zero and a balance of the excess of book value over cost still remained.

Intangible Assets

3. When preferred stock is involved in an acquisition of a subsidiary, caution must be taken when (a) dividends are in arrears or (b) there is any preference in liquidation.

Company P acquires for $900,000, 75,000 shares of Company S common stock. At the date of acquisition Company S has 100,000 shares of common stock outstanding with a stated value of $1,000,000, 5,000 shares of 5% preferred stock $100 par outstanding with dividends in arrears of $50,000; the preferred stock is entitled to $105 per share in the event of liquidation.

Computation of Excess of Cost over Book Value

	Preferred	Common
5,000 shares of preferred stock, par $100	$500,000	
Stated value of common stock		$1,000,000
Dividends in arrears	50,000	(50,000)
Liquidation preference on preferred stock	25,000	(25,000)
Retained earnings		225,000
Paid-in capital		100,000
Totals	$575,000	$1,250,000
75% of common equity acquired by P		$ 937,500
Cost of 75%		900,000
Excess of book value over cost (negative goodwill)		$ 37,500

INTEREST ON RECEIVABLES AND PAYABLES

Background

APB-21 is the main source of GAAP on imputing, if necessary, interest on receivables and payables. However, APB-21 excludes the following types of receivables and payables:

1. Arising in the ordinary course of business which are due in approximately one year or less
2. Whose terms of payments are in property or services and not in cash
3. Representing security or retainage deposits
4. Arising in the ordinary course of business of a lending institution
5. Arising from transactions between a parent and its subsidiaries, or between subsidiaries of a common parent.
6. Whose interest rate is determined by a governmental agency

The promulgated GAAP does not specify whether its provisions must or must not be followed by companies in regulatory industries subject to the rate-making process. Therefore, the Addendum to APB-2 should be followed, which means that the provisions of APB-21 do apply to companies in regulatory industries subject to the rate-making process.

In reading this promulgated GAAP it is important to keep in mind the types of transactions that are specifically excluded.

> **OBSERVATION:** The FASB has issued an Exposure Draft entitled "Capitalization of Interest Costs," which at the date of this publication has not been promulgated. A brief summary of this Exposure Draft appears in Chapter 11.00, Depreciable Assets and Depreciation under the caption "Self-Constructed Fixed Assets."

Overview

Those receivables and payables which are not excluded from APB-21 and which are contractual rights to receive or pay money at a fixed or determinable date must be recorded at their present value, if (1) the interest rate is not stated or (2) the stated interest rate is unreasonable. This is an application of the basic principle of substance over form.

A note issued or received solely for cash equal to its face amount is presumed to earn the interest stated. However, if rights or privileges are attached to the note, they must be evaluated separately. For example, a beer distributor lends a customer who wishes to purchase bar equipment $5,000 for two years at no interest. There is, of course, a tacit agreement that the customer will buy the distributor's products. In this event, a present value must be established for the note receivable, and the difference between the face of the note ($5,000) and its present value must be considered an additional cost of doing business for the beer distributor.

There is a general presumption that the interest stated on a note, resulting from a business transaction entered into at arm's length, is fair and adequate. However, if no interest is stated or the interest stated appears unreasonable, the substance of the transaction must be recorded.

A note issued or received in a noncash transaction contains two elements to be valued: (1) the principal amount for the property, goods, or services exchanged and (2) an interest factor for the use of funds over the time period of the note. These types of notes must be recorded at their present value. Any difference between the face amount of the note and its present value is a discount or premium that must be amortized over the life of the note.

Determining Present Value

There is no predetermined formula for computing an appropriate interest rate. *However, the objective is to approximate what the rate would have been, using the same terms and conditions, if it had been negotiated by an independent lender.* The following guidelines are recommended:

1. credit rating of the borrower
2. restrictive covenants or collateral involved
3. prevailing market rates
4. rate at which the debtor could borrow funds

The appropriate interest rate will frequently depend upon a combination of the above factors.

Amortization of Discount or Premium

The difference between the present value and the face amount of the receivable or the payable represents the amount of premium or discount. A discount exists if the present value of the total eventual proceeds of the note (face amount plus stated interest), using the appropriate rate of interest, is less than the face amount of the note. A premium exists if the present value of the total eventual proceeds of the note (face amount plus stated interest), using the appropriate rate of interest, is more than the face amount of the note.

The premium or discount should be amortized over the life of the note, using a constant rate on any outstanding balance. This method is called the *interest method* and is reviewed in the comprehensive illustration at the end of this Chapter.

Statement Presentation of Discount or Premium

The premium or discount that arises from the use of present values on cash and noncash transactions is inseparable from the related asset or liability. Therefore, such premiums or discounts are deducted from their related asset or liability on the balance sheet. Discounts or premiums resulting from imputing interest must not be classified as deferred charges or credits.

Disclosure

A full description of the receivable or payable, the effective interest rate, and the face amount of the note should be disclosed in the financial statements or footnotes thereto.

Issue costs should be reported separately in the balance sheet as deferred charges.

Comprehensive Illustrations

The following example indicates how interest is imputed on a non-interest-bearing note.

A manufacturer sells a machine for $10,000 and accepts a $10,000 note receivable bearing no interest for five years; 10% is an appropriate interest rate. The initial journal entry would be:

Interest on Receivables and Payables

Note receivable	$10,000.00	
Sales (present value at 10%)		$6,209.00
Deferred interest income		3,791.00
End of 1st year:		
Deferred interest income	$ 620.90	
Interest income		$ 620.90
(10% of $6,209)		
End of 2nd year:		
Deferred interest income	$ 682.99	
Interest income		$ 682.99
(10% of $6,829.90)		
End of 3rd year:		
Deferred interest income	$ 751.29	
Interest income		$ 751.29
(10% of $7,512.89)		
End of 4th year:		
Deferred interest income	$ 826.42	
Interest income		$ 826.42
(10% of $8,264.18)		
End of 5th year:		
Deferred interest income	$ 909.06	
Interest income		$ 909.06
(10% of $9,090.60)		

   In the example the manufacturer records the note at its face amount but records the sale at the present value of the note because that is all the note is worth today. The difference between the face amount of the note and its present value is recorded as "deferred interest income." This deferred interest income is payment for the use of the manufacturer's funds for the five years.

   The *interest method* is used to produce a constant rate which is applied to any outstanding balance. In the above example the present value of $6,209 was recorded for the $10,000 sale using the appropriate interest rate of 10% for the five year term of the note. The difference between the $10,000 sale and its present value of $6,209 is $3,791, which was recorded as deferred interest income. Since the present value was determined by using the 10% rate for five years, it stands to reason that the same 10% rate, when applied to each annual outstanding balance for the same five years, will result in full amortization of the deferred interest income, as follows:

		Amortization of Deferred Interest Income
Original balance	$6,209.00	$3,791.00
Year 1, 10%	620.90	620.90
Remaining balance	$6,829.90	$3,170.10
Year 2, 10%	682.99	682.99
Remaining balance	$7,512.89	$2,487.11
Year 3, 10%	751.29	751.29
Remaining balance	$8,264.18	$1,735.82
Year 4, 10%	826.42	826.42
Remaining balance	$9,090.60	$ 909.40
Year 5, 10%	909.05	909.05
*Remaining balance	$9,999.65	$ 0.35

*Difference of $0.35 due to rounding.

The next example illustrates how a note with an unreasonable rate of interest should be recorded.

A company purchases a $10,000 machine and issues for payment a $10,000 four-year note bearing 2% compound interest per year; 10% is considered an appropriate rate of interest. The initial journal entry is:

Machine (present value of $10,824 @ 10%)	$7,393	
Deferred interest expense	3,431	
Note payable		$10,000
Deferred interest payable		824

1st year:
| Interest expense | $739 | |
| Deferred interest expense | | $739 |

2nd year:
| Interest expense | $813 | |
| Deferred interest expense | | $813 |

3rd year:
 Interest expense $895
  Deferred interest expense $895

4th year:
 Interest expense $984
  Deferred interest expense $984

In the fourth year, when the note and the 2% interest are paid, the following journal entry is made:

 Note payable $10,000
 Deferred interest payable   824
  Cash $10,824

In the above example the company records a note payable ($10,000) and the deferred interest ($824) at their face amount. The total due in four years is $10,824, and the machine is valued at the present value of this amount ($7,393). This is because today the $10,824 is worth only $7,393, which is all that the sale should be recorded at. The difference between the total amount due in four years ($10,824) and its present value ($7,393) must be considered deferred interest ($3,431) for the use of the seller's funds.

INTERIM FINANCIAL REPORTING

Background

APB-28 covers the general promulgated GAAP for accounting and reporting on interim periods. This opinion provides the accounting and disclosure requirements necessary for interim reporting and establishes the minimum disclosures for interim reports of publicly traded companies.

Since the promulgated GAAP (APB-28) is silent on the extent of its coverage, it is assumed that both unregulated and regulated companies must comply with its provisions.

Income taxes for interim reporting are discussed in the chapter on Income Taxes; accounting changes for interim reporting are discussed in the chapter on Accounting Changes. Financial reporting for segments of a business enterprise is not required in interim financial statements (FASB-18).

Overview

Interim financial reports may be issued quarterly, monthly, or at other intervals, and may include complete financial statements or summarized data. In addition, they usually include the current interim period and a cumulative year-to-date period with comparative reports on the corresponding periods of the immediately preceding fiscal year.

The procedures and disclosures expressed in the promulgated GAAP (APB-28) are applicable whenever an entity issues interim financial reports.

Accounting and Reporting

Each interim period must be viewed as an integral part of the annual period, and accounting principles and reporting practices should be based on those of the latest annual reports of the entity, unless there has been a change in an accounting principle. A change in an accounting principle during an interim period is discussed in the chapter on Accounting Changes.

The accounting and reporting on the results of operation for interim financial statements is discussed in the following paragraphs.

Revenues are recognized as earned on the same basis as that for fiscal periods.

As closely as possible product costs are determined as those for the fiscal period with some exceptions for inventory valuation, as follows:

1. Companies using the gross profit method to determine interim inventory costs, or other methods different from those used for annual inventory valuation, should disclose the method used at the interim date and any material difference from the reconciliation with the annual physical inventory.
2. A liquidation of a base-period LIFO inventory at an interim date that apparently will be corrected by the end of the annual period should be valued at the expected cost of replacement. Cost of sales for the interim period should include the expected cost of replacement and not the cost of the base-period LIFO inventory.
3. Inventory losses from market declines should be included in the interim period in which they occur, and gains in subsequent interim periods should be recognized in such interim period but should not exceed the losses included in prior interim periods.

    Temporary market declines that are expected to be made up by the end of the annual period need not be recognized in interim periods.
4. Inventory and product costs computed by the use of a standard cost accounting system should be determined by the same procedures used at the end of a fiscal year. Variances from standard costs that are expected to be made up by the end of the fiscal year need not be included in interim-period statements.

Other costs and expenses should be charged or allocated to produce a fair presentation of the results of operation, changes in financial position, and financial position for all interim periods. The following should apply in accounting for other costs and expenses:

1. The general rule in preparing interim-period financial statements is that costs and expenses that clearly benefit more than one period should be properly allocated to the periods affected. This procedure should be consistently applied.

2. Companies that have material seasonal revenue variations must avoid the possibility that interim-period financial statements become misleading. Disclosure of material seasonal revenue variations should be made in the interim-period financial statements. In addition, it is desirable to disclose results for a full year, ending at the interim date.
3. Unusual and infrequent transactions that are material and not designated as extraordinary items, such as the effects of a disposal of a segment of business, should be reported separately in the interim periods in which they occur.
4. All other pertinent information, such as accounting changes, contingencies, seasonal results, and purchase or pooling transactions, should be disclosed to provide the necessary information for the proper understanding of the interim financial statements.

Interim reports should not contain arbitrary amounts of costs or expenses. Estimates should be reasonable and should be based on all available information applied consistently from period to period. An effective tax rate is used for income tax provision in interim periods. Income taxes for interim-period reports are discussed in the chapter on Income Taxes.

Material contingencies and other uncertainties that exist at an interim date must be disclosed in interim reports in the same manner as that required for annual reports. However, these contingencies and uncertainties, at an interim date, should be evaluated in relation to the annual report. The disclosure for such items must be repeated in every interim and annual report until the contingency is resolved or becomes immaterial.

Summarized Interim Financial Statements

Publicly traded companies reporting summarized financial information at interim dates should include the following minimum information:

1. gross revenues, provision for income taxes, extraordinary items, effects of accounting changes (principles or practice), and net income
2. primary and fully diluted earnings-per-share data
3. material seasonal variations of revenues, costs, or expenses

4. contingent items and effects of the disposal of a segment of a business
5. material changes in financial position

Summarized interim financial statements based on these minimum disclosures *do not* constitute a fair presentation of financial position and results of operations in conformity with GAAP.

In the event that fourth-quarter results are not issued separately, the annual report should include disclosures for the fourth quarter on the aggregate effect of material year-end adjustments and infrequently occurring items, extraordinary items, and disposal of business segments that occurred in the fourth quarter.

When summarized interim financial data are not presented, significant changes in liquid assets, working capital, long-term liabilities, and stockholders' equity should be disclosed and disseminated to the public.

INVENTORY PRICING AND METHODS

Background

The main source of promulgated GAAP for inventories is ARB-43, Chapter 4 (as amended). Other promulgated GAAP relating to the subject of inventory are FASB Interpretation-1, Accounting Changes Related to the Cost of Inventory, and FASB Interpretation-17, Applying the Lower of Cost or Market Rule in Translated Financial Statements.

In addition to the above and other areas of promulgated GAAP, this chapter includes most of the nonpromulgated GAAP on inventories.

Overview

Inventories of goods must be periodically compiled, measured, and recorded in the books of accounts of a business. Inventory includes the total amount of tangible personal property and is usually classified as (1) finished goods, (2) work in process, and (3) raw materials.

Inventories exclude long-term assets that are subject to depreciation or assets that will be classified as such.

Inventories are classified as current assets, except when there are excessive quantities which may not reasonably be expected to be used or sold within the normal operating cycle of a business. In this event, the excess inventory is classified as noncurrent.

The periodic preparation of financial statements requires that revenues and costs be matched (one of the basic [pervasive] principles of GAAP), and the valuation of inventories is a major objective in that matching principle.

Inventory Systems

Periodic System The inventory is determined by a physical count as of a specific date. As long as the count is made frequently enough for reporting purposes, it is not necessary to maintain extensive inventory records. The inventory shown on the balance sheet is determined by the physical count and is priced in accordance with the inventory method used. The net change between the beginning and ending inventories enters into the computation of the cost of goods sold.

Inventory Pricing and Methods

Perpetual System. With this system, inventory records are maintained and updated regularly. The system has the advantage of providing inventory information on a timely basis, but requires the maintenance of a full set of inventory records. Theoretically physical counts are not necessary, but they are normally taken to verify the inventory records. GAAP require that a physical check of perpetual inventory records be made periodically. The maintenance of the inventory information consists of posting each individual transaction.

Title to Goods

Legal title to merchandise usually determines whether or not it is included in the inventory of an enterprise. According to the Uniform Commercial Code, title to goods passes from the seller to the buyer in any manner and on any conditions explicitly agreed on by the parties. If no conditions are explicitly agreed on, title to goods passes from the seller to the buyer at the time and place at which the seller completes his performance with reference to the physical delivery of the goods. Title passes to the buyer at the time and place of shipment if the seller is required only to send the goods. However, if the contract requires delivery at destination, title passes when the goods are tendered at the destination. The following is the most commonly used terminology in passing title from the seller to the buyer:

> *F.O.B.*–means "free on board" and requires the seller, at his expense, to deliver the goods to the destination indicated as F.O.B.
>
> *F.A.S.*–means "free alongside" and is usually used in conjunction with a dock or a seaport. The seller must at his expense deliver the goods to the vessel indicated on the F.A.S.
>
> *C.I.F.*–means that the price of the goods includes the cost of the goods and the insurance and freight to the named destination.
>
> *C & F*–means that the price of the goods includes the cost of the goods and the freight to the named destination.
>
> *C.O.D.*–means "collect on delivery" and requires the buyer to pay for the goods at the time and place of delivery.

Costs

The basis of accounting for inventories is cost (basic principle), which has been defined as the price paid or consideration given to acquire an asset. In inventory accounting, cost is the sum of the expenditures and charges, direct and indirect, in bringing goods to their existing condition or location.

The principles of measuring inventory costs can be easily stated, but the application of the principles, particularly to items in work in process and finished goods, is difficult because of the problem involved in allocating the various costs and charges. For example, idle factory expense, excessive spoilage, double freight, and rehandling costs can be so abnormal that they may have to be charged to the current period, rather than as a portion of the inventory costs. Selling expenses should not be considered as any part of inventory costs. *The exclusion of all overhead from inventory costs is an unacceptable accounting procedure* (direct or variable costing).

Departure from the Cost Basis

When the utility of the goods, in the ordinary course of business, is no longer as great as their cost, a departure from the cost basis principle of measuring the inventory is required. Whether the cause be from obsolescence, physical deterioration, changes in price levels, or any other, the difference should be recognized as a loss of the current period. This is usually accomplished by stating such goods at a lower level designated as market (lower of cost or market principle).

Lower of Cost or Market

In the phrase *lower of cost or market,* the term market means current replacement cost, whether by purchase or by reproduction, *but is limited to the following maximum and minimum amounts:*

1. *Maximum:* cannot exceed the estimated selling price less any costs of completion and disposal. The maximum cost is also the net realizable value.

2. *Minimum:* the maximum less an allowance for normal profit.

Inventory Pricing and Methods

Item	Cost	Replacement Cost	(1) Selling Price	(2) Costs of Completion	(1 − 2) Maximum*	(3) Normal Profit	[(1 − 2) − 3] Minimum
1	$20.50	$ 19.00	$ 25.00	$ 1.00	$ 24.00	$ 6.00	$ 18.00
2	26.00	20.00	30.00	2.00	28.00	7.00	21.00
3	10.00	12.00	15.00	1.00	14.00	3.00	11.00
4	40.00	55.00	60.00	6.00	54.00	4.00	50.00
	$96.50	$106.00	$130.00	$10.00	$120.00	$20.00	$100.00

*The maximum is equal to the net realizable value.

The lower of cost or market for the above four items is:

Item 1	$19.00	Item 3	$10.00
Item 2	$21.00	Item 4	$40.00

If the lower of cost or market is applied to each individual item in the above illustration, items 1 and 2 must be written down by $1.50 and $5.00, respectively, or a total of $6.50. However, if the lower of cost or market is applied to the entire inventory, there is no write-down, because total cost of $96.50 is lower than market of $106.00.

The correct procedure in applying the lower-of-cost-or-market principle is first to determine what market is and then to compare it to cost. Market can be either replacement cost or the maximum or minimum restriction on replacement cost.

When market is lower than cost, the purposes of the maximum and minimum limitation are:

1. The maximum prevents a loss in future periods by at least valuing the inventory at its estimated selling price less costs of completion and disposal.

2. The minimum prevents any future periods from realizing any more than a normal profit.

The write-down of inventory to market is usually reflected in cost of goods sold, unless the amount is unusually material, in which case the loss should be identified separately in the income statement.

The journal entry to record the write-down to a separate account is:

| Inventory loss due to decline in market | $XXX | |
| Inventory | | $XXX |

The lower-of-cost-or-market principle may be applied to a single item, a category, or the total inventory, provided that the method most clearly reflects periodic income.

The purpose of reducing inventory to the lower of cost or market is to reflect fairly the income of the period (matching-of-revenue-and-cost principle).

The basic principle of consistency must be applied in the valuation of inventory, and the method should be disclosed in the financial statements.

In the event that a significant change occurs in the measurement of inventory, adequate disclosure of the nature of the change and, if material (materiality principle), the effect on income should be disclosed in the financial statements.

Exceptions Exceptional cases, such as precious metals having a fixed determinable monetary value with no substantial cost of marketing, may be stated at such monetary value. Where inventory is stated at a value in excess of cost, this fact should be fully disclosed in the financial statements.

The prerequisites of this exception are (1) immediate marketability at quoted prices and (2) cost difficult to obtain.

Cost Methods

For inventory purposes, cost may be determined by specific identification or by the association of the flow of cost factors—first-in, first-out (FIFO), last-in, first-out (LIFO), and average.

In selecting an inventory cost method the primary objective is the selection of the method that under the circumstances most clearly reflects periodic income. When similar goods are purchased at different times, it may not be possible to identify and match the specific costs of the item sold. Frequently, the identity of goods and their specific related costs are lost between the time of acquisition and the time of sale. This has resulted in the development and general acceptance of several assumptions with respect to the flow of cost factors (FIFO, LIFO, and average cost) to provide practical bases for the measurement of periodic income.

Inventory identification In some lines of business specific items or lots of inventory are clearly identifiable from the time of purchase through the time of sale and are costed on this basis. Usually, the identity of goods is lost between the time of acquisition and the time of sale, and inventories are identified on the flow-of-cost factors. When a flow-of-cost method is used, the actual physical movement of the inventory is irrelevant.

Standard Costs

The use of standard costs is a management tool that identifies favorable or unfavorable variances from predetermined estimates established by past performance or time and motion studies. Inventory valuation by the use of standard costs is acceptable, if adjusted at reasonable intervals to reflect the approximate costs computed under one of the recognized methods, and adequate disclosure is made in the financial statements.

At the end of the reporting period the physical inventory is costed at LIFO, FIFO, or some other generally accepted method. Any variation between this result and the carrying value of the inventory at standard cost must be closed out to cost of goods sold and ending inventory such that the reported figure represents that which the generally accepted method would yield.

First-in, First-out Method (FIFO)

The *FIFO method* of identifying inventory is based on the assumption that costs should be charged against revenue in the order in which they occurred. The inventory remaining on hand is presumed to consist of the most recent costs. In other words, the first goods acquired are the first goods out, and the last goods acquired are in the ending inventory (assuming that there is an ending inventory).

Theoretically, FIFO approximates the results that would be obtained by the specific identification method.

Last-in, First-out Method (LIFO)

The last-in first-out method of determining inventory (LIFO) requires that records be maintained as to the base year layer and additional layers that may be created or used up. An additional LIFO layer is created in any year in which the ending inventory is more than the beginning inventory. An additional LIFO layer is priced at the earliest or average costs of the year in which it was created, because the LIFO method matches the last costs incurred with current revenue, leaving the first cost incurred to be included in any inventory increase.

After an original LIFO layer is created (base year), it may

decrease or additional layers may be created each year according to the quantity of ending inventory.

When the ending inventory is less than the beginning inventory, one or more LIFO layers may be used up. It is important to remember that once a LIFO layer is used up, any future new LIFO layer is priced at the costs of the year in which it is created, and not by reference to a prior LIFO layer cost.

In addition to the disclosure of significant accounting policies (APB-22) and of composition of inventories (ARB-43, Chapter 4), a business using the LIFO method of reporting inventory must disclose the following:

1. current replacement value of the LIFO inventories at each balance sheet date presented
2. the effect on the results of operations for any reduction of a LIFO layer

> **OBSERVATION:** Certain restrictions on LIFO inventory disclosure are imposed by the IRS. An election (FORM 970) must be made to use the LIFO method for tax purposes. If the LIFO method is used for tax purposes, the IRS requires that it also be used for financial reporting purposes.

Dollar-Value LIFO

A variation of the conventional LIFO method is the dollar-value LIFO method. Under the regular LIFO method, units of inventory are priced at unit prices. Under the dollar-value LIFO method, the base-year inventory is priced in dollars; for inventories of all subsequent years, price indices are used, with the base year as 100.

Year	Inventory at Base-Year Prices	Price Index	$ LIFO Inventory Amount
1	$100,000	100	$100,000
2	20,000	105	21,000
3	10,000	110	11,000
4	20,000	120	24,000
5	20,000	125	25,000
Totals	$170,000		$181,000

Inventory Pricing and Methods

Weighted Average Method

The weighted average method of inventory valuation assumes that costs are charged against revenue on the basis of an average of the number of units acquired at each price level. The resulting average price is applied to the ending inventory to find the total ending inventory value. The weighted average is determined by dividing the total costs of the inventory available, including any beginning inventory, by the total number of units, as follows:

	Units	Cost per Unit	Total Cost
Beginning inventory	10,000	4.00	$ 40,000
Purchase, July 25	8,000	4.20	33,600
Purchase, August 15	5,000	4.13	20,650
Purchase, September 5	7,000	4.30	30,100
Purchase, September 25	12,000	4.25	51,000
Totals	42,000		$175,350

Total cost $175,350 ÷ total units 42,000 = $4.175 weighted average cost per unit.

Assume that the ending inventory consisted of 14,000 units.

Value of ending inventory = 14,000 units × $4.175 per unit, or $58,450.

Moving Average Method

The moving average method can be used only with a perpetual inventory. The cost per unit is recomputed after every addition to the inventory.

	Total Units	Total Cost	Unit Cost
Beginning inventory	1,000	$ 5,000	$5.00
Sale of 200 units	800	4,000	5.00
Purchase of 1,200 @ $6	2,000	11,200	5.60
Sale of 1,000 units	1,000	5,600	5.60
Purchase of 1,000 @ $5	2,000	10,600	5.30

Note: Only purchases change the unit price as sales are taken out at the prior moving average unit cost.

Under the moving average method, the ending inventory is costed at the last moving average unit cost for the period.

Retail Inventory Method

Because of the great variety and quantity of inventory in some types of businesses, the reversed markup procedure of inventory pricing, such as the retail inventory method, may be both practical and appropriate.

It is necessary to maintain records of purchases at both cost and selling price and of sales at selling price in order to use the retail inventory method. With the information available, a ratio of cost to retail can be calculated and applied to the ending inventory at retail to compute the approximate cost.

	Cost	Retail
Inventory, at beginning of period	$ 100,000	$ 150,000
Purchases during the period	1,100,000	1,850,000
Totals	$1,200,000	$2,000,000
Sales during the period		1,800,000
Estimated ending inventory at retail		$ 200,000
Estimated ending inventory at cost (60% of retail)		$ 120,000

Computation of Ratio of Cost to Retail

$$\frac{\$1,200,000}{\$2,000,000} = 60\% \text{ of } \$200,000 = \$120,000$$

Physical inventories measured by the retail method should be taken periodically as a check on the accuracy of the estimated inventories.

The above illustration ignores the problem of changes made in selling prices after the original pricing of the goods.

Original selling prices are revised or modified, thus necessitating an understanding of the following terminology:

original retail: the first selling price at which goods are offered for sale

markup: the selling price raised above the original selling price

Inventory Pricing and Methods

markdown: the selling price lowered below the original selling price
markup cancellation: markup selling price decreased, but not below the original selling price
markdown cancellation: markdown selling price increased, but not above the original selling price
net markup: markup minus markup cancellation
net markdown: markdown minus markdown cancellation
markon: difference between the cost and the original selling price, plus any net markups

Original cost	$100
Original selling price ($50 markon)	$150
Markup	50
Original selling price plus markup	$200
Markup cancellation	25
Original selling price plus net markup	$175
Markdown (consists of $25 markup cancellation and a $25 markdown)	50
Original selling price minus markdown	$125
Markdown	25
Original selling price minus markdown	$100
Markdown cancellation	25
Original selling price minus net markdown	$125
Markup (consists of a $25 markdown cancellation and a $25 markup)	50
Original selling price plus net markup	$175

Theoretically speaking, the last selling price consisted of:

$50	markup
25	markup cancellation
25	markup cancellation
25	markdown
25	markdown
25	markdown cancellation
25	markdown cancellation
25	markup
$25	net plus change

and now the goods are priced at the original selling price plus a net markup of $25, or a total of $175.

The purpose of the conventional retail inventory method is to produce an inventory valuation (measurement) closely approximating what would be obtained by taking a physical inventory and pricing the goods at the lower of cost or market.

In order to approximate the lower of cost or market in the computations, *markdowns and markdown cancellations are excluded in calculating the ratio of cost to retail and are added to the retail inventory after the ratio is determined.*

In calculating the cost-to-retail ratio, any adjustment to the retail value will necessarily affect the ratio and hence the resultant cost figure. Adjustments that decrease the denominator of the ratio increase the ratio and the value for ending inventory at cost, thus increasing gross profit. In the interests of conservatism, as well as for other reasons, adjustments that decrease the retail figure should be avoided. Markups, which increase the dominator, however, are included *net* of cancellations.

Net markdowns (markdowns less markdown cancellations) are an example of adjustments that decrease the denominator. Including them in the retail figure violates the lower-of-cost-or-market rule. As shown below, net markdowns are not included in the calculation of the ratio, but *are* included in the determination of ending inventory after computing the ratio. The rationale for this is that the cost-to-retail ratio is presumed to be based on normal conditions, and a markdown is not a normal condition. When *applying* the ratio, however, to conform to the lower-of-cost-or-market rule, the retail value must be reduced by the amount of the markdowns.

Employee discounts obviously apply only to goods sold, not those remaining on hand. A sale at less than normal retail price to an employee does not represent a valid reduction to lower of cost or market, nor does it represent a valid adjustment of the cost-to-retail ratio or the value of the ending inventory. Hence, employee discounts should not enter into any of the calculations, but are deducted from retail, in the same way as markdowns, after the computation of the cost-to-retail ratio.

Inventory spoilage and shrinkage does affect the ending inventory figure, but should not enter into the cost-to-retail ratio calculation. It is an obvious distortion to make cost a higher percentage of retail merely because some items are missing from the retail inventory. When arriving at the final figure for inventory at cost, the amount of shrinkage is deducted either at cost or at retail depending upon whether shrinkage is stated at cost or at retail.

Inventory Pricing and Methods

Assume the following information:

	Cost	Retail
Inventory, beginning of the period	$200,000	$300,000
Purchases	550,000	800,000
Transportation-in	50,000	
Markups		100,000
Markup cancellations		20,000
Markdowns		70,000
Markdown cancellations		10,000

The calculations would be:

	Cost	Retail
Inventory, at beginning of period	$200,000	$ 300,000
Purchases	550,000	800,000
Transportation-in	50,000	
Markups		100,000
Markup cancellations		(20,000)
Totals (ratio of cost to retail 67.8%)	$800,000	$1,180,000
Markdowns		(70,000)
Markdown cancellations		10,000
Total goods at retail		$1,120,000
Less: Sales during the period		860,000
Inventory, ending (at retail)		$ 260,000
Inventory, ending (67.8% of $260,000)*		$ 176,280

*At estimated lower of cost or market

LIFO application The LIFO method of evaluating inventory can be applied to the retail inventory method by using procedures somewhat different from the conventional retail method. Basically two differences have to be taken into consideration:

1. Since the LIFO method produces a valuation approximating cost, and the conventional retail method produces a valuation approximating the lower of cost or market, to apply the LIFO concept to the conventional retail method it is necessary to include all markdowns as well as markups in determining the ratio of cost to retail.

2. With the LIFO method, the quantity of inventory on hand is from the earliest purchases during the year or from prior years' LIFO layers. The cost-to-retail ratio considers the

current relationship between cost and selling price. Therefore, the beginning inventory is omitted from the cost-to-retail ratio, because it may cause a distortion. In short, to apply the LIFO concept to the retail inventory method:
(a) All markdowns as well as markups are included in the cost to retail ratio.
(b) The beginning inventory data are not used to compute the cost to retail ratio.

	Cost	Retail
Inventory, beginning of period	omitted	omitted
Purchases	$550,000	$ 800,000
Transportation-in	50,000	
Markups		100,000
Markup cancellations		(20,000)
Markdowns		(70,000)
Markdown cancellations		10,000
Totals (ratio of cost to retail 73.2%)	$600,000	$ 820,000
Add: Inventory, beginning of period		300,000
Total goods at retail		$1,120,000
Less: Sales during period		860,000
Inventory, ending of period (at retail)		$ 260,000

Since the $260,000 ending LIFO inventory (at retail) is less than the $300,000 beginning LIFO inventory (at retail), it is obvious that a prior LIFO layer was partially depleted:

	Retail
Beginning inventory	$300,000
Ending inventory	260,000
LIFO layer depleted	$ 40,000

The $40,000 difference is multiplied by the beginning inventory cost-to-retail ratio (66.67%) and then subtracted from the beginning inventory at cost, as follows:

	Cost
Beginning inventory	$200,000
$40,000 × 66.67%	(26,668)
Ending inventory (at cost)	$173,332

Inventory Pricing and Methods

If the ending LIFO inventory (at retail) had been greater than the beginning LIFO inventory (at retail), a new LIFO layer would have been created which would have been costed at the new cost-to-retail ratio (73.2%).

The basic assumption of the retail inventory method is that there exists an equal distribution of goods (high-cost ratio and low-cost ratio) between sales, beginning inventory, and ending inventory. In instances where this basic premise does not prevail, cost ratios should be determined by departments or smaller units. This would require keeping (by departments) separate sales, purchases, markups, markdowns, and beginning and ending inventories.

Base Stock Method

The base stock method is similar to the LIFO method. It assumes a continuous permanent stock of inventory that is, in effect, a fixed asset. Excesses over this base stock are considered temporary inventory, and are priced at *current replacement cost.* Amounts below the base stock are similarly considered temporary, and are charged against revenue at replacement cost. The essential difference between the base stock method and LIFO is that the former uses replacement cost whereas LIFO relies on actual costs exclusively. Since the base stock method is not allowed for tax purposes, it is seldom encountered in practice.

Relative Sales Value Costing

This method is used when costs cannot be determined individually. Joint products, lump-sum purchase of assets (basket purchase), and large assets that are subdivided (real estate tracts) are examples of items that would be costed by their relative sales value.

ABC Company purchases four large pieces of machinery for $100,000. At the time of purchase an appraisal discloses the following fair values:

Machine #1	$ 12,000
Machine #2	28,000
Machine #3	40,000
Machine #4	30,000
Total	$110,000

The machines are priced at their relative fair values, as follows:

Machine #1	12/110 × $100,000	=	$ 10,909
Machine #2	28/110 × $100,000	=	25,455
Machine #3	40/110 × $100,000	=	36,364
Machine #4	30/110 × $100,000	=	27,272
Total cost allocated			$100,000

Firm Purchase Commitments

Losses on firm purchase commitments for inventory goods should be measured in the same manner as inventory losses and, if material, should be recognized in the accounts and disclosed separately in the income statement.

The recognition of losses, which are expected to arise from firm, noncancelable commitments and which arise from the decline in the utility of a cost expenditure, should be disclosed in the current period income statement.

In addition, all significant firm purchase commitments must be disclosed in the financial statements or in footnotes, whether or not any losses are recognized.

Disclosure

The general disclosure requirements for inventories are:

1. A description of accounting principles used and the methods of applying those principles (APB-22)
2. Any accounting principles or methods that are peculiar to a particular industry (APB-22)
3. Classification of inventories (ARB-43)
4. Basis of pricing inventories (ARB-43)
5. Method of determining inventories (LIFO, FIFO, average, etc.) (ARB-43)

All the above disclosures must be consistent from year to year, and if a significant change occurs, the following additional disclosures are necessary:

1. the nature of the change
2. if the change is significant, the effect on net income

Businesses dependent upon a limited number of sources for raw material or inventory or upon precarious sources (labor problems, foreign governments, etc.) should disclose the pertinent facts in their financial statements or footnotes thereto.

Inventory of Discontinued Segments

Inventories used in discontinued segments of a business should be written down to their net realizable value and the amount of write-down included as part of the gain or loss recognized on the disposal of the discontinued segment. However, such a write-down should not be attributable to any inventory adjustment that should have been recognized prior to the measurement date of the loss on disposal. In this event, the loss on the write-down should be included in the operating results of the discontinued segment (APB-30).

Inventory for Interim Financial Reporting

Generally, the same principles and methods are used to value inventories for interim financial statements as are used for annual reports. However, for practical purposes or otherwise there are some exceptions.

The use of estimated gross profit is frequently utilized to determine the cost of goods sold during an interim period. This procedure is acceptable for GAAP, as long as periodic physical inventories are taken to adjust the gross profit percentage used. Companies using the gross profit method for interim financial statements should disclose that fact and any significant adjustments that may occur in amounts determined by a physical count (APB-28).

When the LIFO method is used for interim financial statements and a LIFO layer is depleted, in part or in whole, that is expected to be replaced before the end of the fiscal period, it is acceptable to use the expected cost of replacement for the depleted LIFO inventory in determining cost of goods sold for the interim period (APB-28).

Inventory losses from market declines, other than those which are expected to be recouped before the end of the fiscal year, should be included in the results of operations of the interim period in which the loss occurs. Subsequent gains from market price recovery in later interim periods should be included in the results of operation in which the gain occurs, but only to the extent of the previously recognized losses (APB-28).

Standard costs are acceptable in determining inventory valuations for interim financial reporting. Unplanned or unanticipated purchase price, volume, or capacity variances should be included in the results of operations of the interim period in which they occur. Anticipated and planned purchase price, volume, or capacity variances that are expected to be recouped by the end of the fiscal year should be deferred at interim dates. In general, the same procedures for standard costs used at the end of the fiscal year should be used for interim financial reporting (APB-28).

Inventories in Business Combinations

Inventory acquired in a business combination accounted for by the purchase method is valued as follows:

Raw materials–current replacement cost
Finished goods–net realizable value less a reasonable profit
Work in process–net realizable value less a reasonable profit

Inventories acquired in a business combination accounted for as a pooling of interests are valued at the same cost as that to the acquired entity.

Inventory for Terminated Contracts

When inventory is acquired for a specific customer contract that is subsequently terminated for any purpose, the carrying value of such inventory should be adjusted to reflect any loss in value.

Inventories–Research and Development

Inventories of supplies used in research and development activities should be charged to expense unless they clearly have an alternative use or can be used in future research and development projects.

When research and development activities consume goods, supplies, or materials from other sources within an organization, the carrying value of such inventory should be charged to research and development expense. Goods produced by research and development activities that may be used in the regular inventory of the

Inventory Pricing and Methods

organization may be transferred physically to regular inventory, at which time a credit in the amount of the costs assigned to the goods should be made to the research and development department (FASB-2).

Inventories in Foreign Currency

Inventories carried at cost in a foreign currency are translated at historical exchange rates. Inventories carried at market in foreign currency are translated at the current exchange rate. An inventory carried at the lower of cost or market in a foreign currency is first translated into dollars (cost at historical rates, market at the current exchange rate) and then the lower of cost or market is determined, except that:

1. Translated market cannot exceed net realizable value in the foreign currency translated at the current exchange rate.
2. Translated market cannot be less than 1 above, reduced by an approximate normal profit translated at the current exchange rate.

All this really means is that the lower of cost or market is determined after everything has been translated into dollars (FASB-8).

Inventories–General Price-Level Changes

When preparing general price-level financial statements, the inventory method (FIFO, LIFO, average, etc.) will dictate the price index that must be used to restate inventory amounts (see General Price-Level Changes chapter).

Inventories–Intercompany Profits

Regardless of any minority interest, all (100%) of any intercompany profits in inventory must be eliminated for consolidated financial statements and investments in common stocks accounted for by the equity method (see Consolidated Financial Statements).

Inventories–Long-Term Construction-Type Contracts

The construction in progress account used in both the completed-contract and percentage-of-completion methods of accounting for long-term construction-type contracts is in fact an inventory account.

Inventories–Tax Allocation

Inventories accounted differently for financial accounting and tax purposes may create timing differences for which interperiod tax allocation may be necessary (APB-11).

Inventories–Accounting Change

An accounting change involving inventories in interim or annual reports necessitates accounting for the cumulative effect of the change and/or restatement of prior-period reports, including certain required *pro forma* information (APB-20).

Inventories–Nonmonetary Exchanges

A nonmonetary exchange of inventory held for sale in the ordinary course of business for similar property to be held for the same purpose does not complete the earning process and no gain or loss is recognized. The inventory received in the nonmonetary exchange should be recorded at the book value of the inventory surrendered, unless cash is also involved in the transaction (APB-29).

Inventory Profits

Profits from the sale of inventory, whose cost and selling price have increased significantly since acquisition, will probably include "ghost profits" or "inventory profits." These profits are considered fictitious, because the cost to replace the inventory has increased significantly and the normal gross profit on the inventory is considerably less than the gross profit containing the ghost or inventory profits.

During periods of rapid inflation, a significant portion of reported net income of a business may actually be ghost or inventory profits. The use of the LIFO method for pricing inventories may offset part or all of any ghost or inventory profits, because current purchases or production costs are matched against current revenue, leaving the earliest inventory on hand.

Inventory Pricing and Methods

Certain publicly held companies are required by the SEC to disclose in a supplemental statement the current replacement cost for cost of goods sold, inventories, and resulting ghost or inventory profits.

Conclusion

Inventory is tangible personal property held for sale in the ordinary course of business. Inventory may be raw materials, in various stages of being produced (work in process), or finished goods.

Matching of revenue and costs is an important objective in accounting for inventory to ensure the proper determination of income in accordance with GAAP.

Accounting for inventories is cost (basic principle), which has been defined as the price paid or consideration given to acquire an asset. In inventory accounting, cost is the sum of the expenditures and charges, directly or indirectly, in bringing goods to their existing condition or location. For inventory purposes, cost may be determined by specific identification or by the association of the flow of cost factors such as LIFO, FIFO, or average. In selecting an inventory cost method the primary objective is the selection of the method that under the circumstances most clearly reflects periodic income.

When the utility of the inventory, in the ordinary course of business, is no longer as great as its cost, a departure from the cost basis is required. This is accomplished by pricing the inventory at the lower of cost or market on an item-by-item basis or on the entire inventory.

Market is defined as current replacement cost, either by purchase or reproduction, except that a maximum and minimum limitation is imposed. The valuation of inventories at the lower of cost or market results in recording losses but not profits prior to the sale of the inventory. The reason that beginning and ending inventories are included in the computation of net income is to arrive at the cost of goods sold during the period of time covered by the statement.

FIFO and LIFO are inventory costing methods employed to measure the "flow of costs." FIFO matches the first cost incurred with the first revenue produced, whereas LIFO matches the last cost incurred with the first revenue produced. In periods of changing prices, different costs are matched with revenue for the same quantity sold, depending on whether LIFO or FIFO is used.

The LIFO method matches current costs and current revenue. When prices are rising, higher costs are matched to current revenue; when prices are falling, lower costs are matched to current revenue. This minimizes recognition of inventory profits or losses that arise from fluctuations in the value of the inventory.

If the base of a LIFO inventory is substantially depleted after a long period of price increases, the cumulative effect of the old costs being matched against current revenue may distort net income for the period.

Comprehensive Illustration

To illustrate the application of the FIFO, LIFO, and the weighted average methods of inventory valuation, assume the following facts:

Units Purchased During the Year

Date	Units	Cost per Unit	Total Cost
January 15	10,000	$5.10	$ 51,000
March 20	20,000	5.20	104,000
May 10	50,000	5.00	250,000
June 8	30,000	5.40	162,000
October 12	5,000	5.30	26,500
December 21	5,000	5.50	27,500
Totals	120,000		$621,000

Beginning inventory consisted of 10,000 units at $5.
Ending inventory consisted of 14,000 units.

Under *FIFO*, the first units in stock are the first units out, which means that the ending inventory is composed of the units purchased last. Since the ending inventory is 14,000 units and the December purchases were only 5,000 units, we must go back to October's purchases for another 5,000 units; and in order to make up the 14,000 units in the ending inventory, we need to take 4,000 units from the June purchases, as follows:

December purchases	5,000 units @ $5.50 = $27,500
October purchases	5,000 units @ 5.30 = 26,500
June purchases	4,000 units @ 5.40 = 21,600
Ending inventory using LIFO	14,000 units $75,600

Inventory Pricing and Methods

Under *LIFO,* the last units in stock are the first units out, which means that the ending inventory is composed of the units purchased first. Using LIFO, we must go back to the earliest inventory to start our calculations. The earliest inventory available is the *beginning inventory* of 10,000 units at $5, but the ending inventory is 14,000 units. Thus, we must go to the next earliest purchase, which is January, and use 4,000 units at the January price to complete the ending inventory valuation, as follows:

Beginning inventory	10,000 units @ $5.00 =	$50,000
From January's purchase	4,000 units @ 5.10 =	20,400
Ending inventory using LIFO	14,000	$70,400

Under the *weighted average* method we must find out what the weighted average cost per unit is and then multiply it by the 14,000 units in the ending inventory, thus:

	Units	Cost per Unit	Total Cost
Beginning inventory	10,000	$5.00	$ 50,000
Purchases:			
January 15	10,000	5.10	51,000
March 20	20,000	5.20	104,000
May 10	50,000	5.00	250,000
June 8	30,000	5.40	162.000
October 12	5,000	5.30	26,500
December 21	5,000	5.50	27,500
Totals	130,000		$671,000

Weighted average = total costs divided by total units

= $671,000 divided by 130,000

= $5.1615 per unit

Ending inventory = 14,000 × $5.1615 per unit = $72,261

Comparison of Three Methods	
Ending inventory, FIFO	$75,600
Ending inventory, LIFO	70,400
Ending inventory, weighted average	72,261

In periods of inflation, the FIFO method will always produce the highest ending inventory, resulting in the lowest cost of goods sold and the most gross profit. LIFO will produce the lowest ending inventory, resulting in the highest cost of goods sold and the least gross profit. The weighted average method will yield results that will fall between those of LIFO and FIFO.

INVESTMENT TAX CREDIT

Background

The present promulgated GAAP on Accounting for the Investment Credit are APB-2, which has been amended by APB-4 and FASB Interpretation-25, Accounting for an Unused Investment Tax Credit. Since APB-2 and APB-4 are silent on the extent of their coverage, apparently both regulated and unregulated companies must comply with the provisions herein, in accordance with the Addendum to APB-2. FASB Interpretation-25 specifically covers both regulated and unregulated companies.

Overview

The investment credit may be a significant factor in influencing the determination of net income. The problem remains as to *when* the investment credit should be reflected in an operating statement.

The three suggested methods are (1) a direct contribution to capital, (2) a deduction of taxes for the period in which the credit arises, and (3) amortization over the life of the property.

The preferred method is to amortize the investment credit to net income over the productive life of the acquired property (deferral method).

An alternative method, but probably not as acceptable, is to treat the credit as a reduction of taxes of the year in which the credit arises (flow-through method). In practice today, the flow-through method is used by most companies.

The argument to amortize the investment credit to net income (deferral method) is based on the basic principle of matching costs with revenue. The theoretical support for deducting the investment credit from the tax liability in the year the credit arises is based on the literal translation of the IRC in that the investment credit is a credit against taxes due.

Using an investment credit as a direct contribution to capital is irrational and unacceptable, because it bypasses the income statement entirely.

The SEC has issued a statement (ASR 96) to the effect that the only two acceptable methods are (1) amortization of the credit over the life of the acquired property and (2) a direct reduction of taxes in the year in which the credit arose.

Investment Tax Credit

Internal Revenue Code Provisions

The investment tax credit is available to all taxpayers who place into service any Section 38 property having a useful life of three years or more. Section 38 property consists of depreciable or amortizable: (1) tangible personal property, including that used as an integral part of manufacturing, extraction or production and (2) elevators and escalators.

Generally, real estate is not Section 38 property.

The maximum investment tax credit may not exceed the taxpayer's first $25,000 of tax liability, plus 50% of the tax liability over $25,000. For tax years ending in 1979 the 50% limit increases to 60%, 70% in 1980, 80% in 1981, and 90% thereafter.

For years beginning after December 31, 1975 on a first-in, first-out basis, investment tax credits may be carried back three years and carried forward seven years (Code Sec. 46). Prior to December 31, 1975 an investment tax credit of a current year had to be used first before any carryover to that year could be applied.

The tax credit is 10% of the qualified Section 38 property placed into service during the taxable year. There is no limit on new Section 38 property, but used property may not exceed $100,000 in a taxable year ($50,000 for married persons filing separately). However, to be included 100%, the qualified Section 38 property must have an estimated useful life of at least seven years. If the useful life is at least five years, then two-thirds of the cost of the qualified Section 38 property is included for the tax credit; if the useful life is at least three years, then only one-third of the cost is included in computing the 10% credit.

Mohamid Company purchased the following qualified Section 38 property during its taxable year:

Used property, 7-year life	$ 50,000
Used property, 3-year life	100,000
New property, 7-year life	200,000
New property, 3-year life	100,000

The company's tax liability before the investment tax credit was $30,000.

Computation of Investment Tax Credit

$50,000 Used property, 7-year life	100%	$ 50,000
$100,000 Used property, 3-year life ($^1/_3$ of 50,000)*		16,667
$200,000 New property, 7-year life	100%	200,000
$100,000 New property, 3-year life ($^1/_3$ of 100,000)		33,333
Total qualified Section 38 property		$300,000
Tentative investment tax credit		$ 30,000
Tax liability		$ 30,000
First $25,000 of tax liability		$ 25,000
50% of tax liability above $25,000		2,500
Allowable investment tax credit		$ 27,500

*Used property is limited to $100,000 cost.

The investment tax credit is allowed for the taxable year in which the qualified Section 38 property is placed into service.

Disposition of Section 38 property Special rules apply to Section 38 property on which an investment tax credit was taken if it is disposed of before the end of its estimated life. The computation of investment tax credit must be based on the early disposition of the Section 38 property, and any difference between the original investment tax credit taken and the recomputed credit must be added to the tax liability in the year of disposition.

A Section 38 asset, costing $10,000, with an estimated useful life of 10 years, is disposed of at the end of five years.

Original investment tax credit taken	$1,000
Recomputed investment tax credit based on five years ($^2/_3$ of $10,000 × 10%)	667
Additional tax liability in the year of disposition	$ 333

Accounting for Investment Tax Credits

The total amount of tax benefits which become available in a current period must be included in computing income tax expense

Investment Tax Credit

(books) for that current period (FASB Interpretation-25). The deferred method of tax allocation must be used. Investment tax credits are recognized for financial accounting purposes even though the same investment tax credits have not yet been realized for tax purposes. The theory that apparently justifies this treatment is that investment tax credits recognized in this manner will subsequently be realized as a reduction of an income tax liability of a future period.

> **OBSERVATION:** This promulgated GAAP (FASB Interpretation-25) requires that an investment tax credit be realized for financial accounting purposes before the same investment tax credit is realized for tax purposes. This is a violation of another existing promulgated GAAP (APB-2) which specifically prohibits the recognition of an investment tax credit before it is actually used as an offset against income tax liability.
>
> This conflict in GAAP can be apparently traced to the use of the "with and without" method used to compute deferred taxes. Under the "with and without" method, investment tax credits are recognized in computing deferred taxes. Thus, investment tax credits are recognized on timing differences for financial accounting purposes.

FASB Interpretation-25, further requires that any excess available investment tax credits not used in determining income tax expense for the current period must be used to reduce any existing net deferred tax credits which will reverse during the allowable carryforward periods of the related investment tax credits. Those investment tax credits which are used to offset existing net deferred tax credits will eventually be realized, as a reduction of income taxes payable, during the allowable carryforward period(s). When this occurs, a corresponding amount of net deferred tax credits must be reinstated and amortized over the period of its related timing difference.

As mentioned previously, unused investment tax credits can be carried back three years and carried forward seven years on a first-in, first-out, basis. When investment tax credits are carried forward they are included in computing income tax expense (books) for the current period (FASB Interpretation-25). Any excess investment tax credits not used in computing income tax expense for the current period are used to offset existing net deferred tax credits (FASB Interpretation-25).

Investment Tax Credit

Any investment tax credits not used in computing income tax expense for the current period, or used to offset existing net deferred tax credits, should be disclosed, if material, in the financial statements by footnote (APB-4).

When investment tax credits are carried back to prior years, income tax expense (per books) is reduced in the current period by the amount of refund of federal income taxes previously paid. In addition, the amount of investment tax credits which is carried back must be added to the total amount of investment tax credits recognized (per books) for the current period. The two preferable methods of accounting for the investment tax credit in the income statement when a carryback is involved are (APB-4):

1. The tax credit attributable to the carryback or carryforward is included in the total tax expense and is disclosed parenthetically or in a footnote.
2. The tax credit attributable to the carryback or carryforward is deducted as a separate item from the total tax expense.

Companies that defer and amortize investment tax credits over the productive life of the related asset (deferral method) should only include as a tax benefit for a current period the amount of amortization for the current year.

The following example will illustrate the major requirements of FASB Interpretation-25.

Assume the following facts for XYZ Corporation for its calendar year ended December 31, 19XX.

- $700,000 of available unused investment tax credits for the current period.
- $1,000,000 of pretax financial accounting income (per books).
- $200,000 of net timing differences which reduce taxable income.
- $800,000 of taxable income.
- 40% tax rate for current period.
- $900,000 of existing net deferred tax credits of which $600,000 will reverse (amortize) in the carryforward period of the unused investment tax credits.
- The maximum investment tax credit may not exceed the taxpayer's first $25,000 of tax liability, plus 50% of the tax liability over $25,000. For tax years ending in 1979 the 50%

Investment Tax Credit

limit increased to 60%, 70% in 1980, 80% in 1981, and 90% thereafter. For the purposes of this example the investment tax credit is limited to the taxpayer's first $25,000 of tax liability, plus 60% of the tax liability over $25,000.

Discussion

Income tax expense is computed on all taxable items included in pretax financial accounting income. In this example, all items included in financial accounting income are eventually taxable.

There are no permanent differences in this example. However, in any event, permanent differences do not affect subsequent periods (they do not reverse) and no interperiod tax allocation (deferred taxes) need be made to account for them. Therefore, if a permanent difference is taxable it is included in computing income tax expense (books) for the period. If a permanent difference is nontaxable it is excluded in computing income tax expense for financial accounting purposes.

The first computation in solving this example is to determine income tax expense on pretax financial accounting income (per books) and the current income tax liability on taxable income (tax return), as follows:

Income Tax Expense on Pretax Financial Accounting Income:

Pretax financial accounting income	$1,000,000
Rate of tax	40%
Income tax expense before allowable investment tax credit	$ 400,000
Allowable investment tax credit [($25,000 plus 60% of ($400,000 - $25,000)]	250,000
Income tax expense (per books)	$ 150,000

Current Income Tax Liability on Taxable Income:

Pretax financial accounting income	$1,000,000
Less: Timing difference	200,000
Taxable income	$ 800,000
Rate of tax	40%
Income tax liability before allowable investment tax credit	$ 320,000
Allowable investment tax credit [($25,000 plus 60% of ($320,000 - $25,000)]	202,000
Current income tax liability	$ 118,000

Investment Tax Credit

The $32,000 difference between income tax expense of $150,000 (books) and the current income tax liability of $118,000 (tax return) is the deferred tax expense on the net timing differences of $200,000, computed as follows:

Net timing differences	$200,000
Rate of tax	40%
Income tax expense before allowable investment tax credit	$ 80,000
Allowable investment tax credit (60% of $80,000)	48,000
Deferred tax expense on timing difference	$ 32,000

The allowable investment tax credit for financial accounting income purposes is $250,000. The promulgated GAAP (FASB Interpretation-25) requires that any excess available investment tax credit not used in the current period in determining income tax expense (books) must be used to reduce any net deferred tax credits which will reverse within the carryforward period of the available investment tax credit. From the information given, there are $900,000 of existing net deferred tax credits of which $600,000 will reverse (amortize) within the carryforward period. For financial accounting purposes, the maximum amount of existing net deferred tax credits which can be used to offset the excess available investment tax credit not used in the current period is $360,000 ($600,000 multiplied by the 60% limitation). Therefore, the maximum investment tax credit which can be recognized in this current period for financial accounting purposes in accordance with FASB Interpretation-25 is as follows:

Allowable investment tax credit on pretaxed financial accounting income (see first computation)	$250,000
Allowable investment tax credit on existing net deferred tax which will reverse within the carryforward period ($600,000 × 60% limitation)	360,000
Maximum investment tax credit which can be recognized for financial accounting purposes	$610,000
Available investment tax credits	$700,000

Investment Tax Credit

The journal entry to record the current income tax expense, deferred taxes for the current period and the offset of the excess available investment tax credits against the maximum amount of deferred tax credits is:

Income tax expense - deferred	$ 32,000	
Income tax expense - current	118,000	
Deferred tax credits	360,000	
Current tax liability		$118,000
Provision for deferred taxes		360,000
Deferred taxes		32,000

The credit to deferred taxes of $32,000 represents the deferred tax on the net timing difference which arose in the current period. The credit to the provision for deferred taxes is an income statement account and appears in the total provision for income taxes for the current period, as follows:

Provision for income taxes:	
Current	$ 118,000
Deferred	32,000
Provision for deferred taxes	(360,000)
Total provision for income taxes	$(210,000)

The balance in the net deferred tax credit account which will appear on the balance sheet is computed, as follows:

Balance, beginning of period	$900,000
Add: Deferred tax on net timing difference for current period	32,000
Less: Net deferred tax credit offset against excess available investment tax credit	(360,000)
Balance, end of period	$572,000

The computation of the ending balance and changes in investment tax credits for financial accounting and tax purposes is as follows:

	Financial	*Tax*
Beginning balance	$700,000	$700,000
Used in determining current income taxes	(250,000)	(202,000)
Used to offset existing net deferred tax credits	(360,000)	
Ending balance	$ 90,000	$498,000

Investment Tax Credit

In accordance with FASB Interpretation-25, the $90,000 of unused investment tax credits for financial accounting purposes may not be recorded on the books as an asset. However, if unused investment tax credits are material they should be disclosed by footnote in the financial statements (APB-4).

FASB Interpretation-25 also requires that deferred tax credits, which have been offset by investment tax credits, be reinstated in the subsequent period in which the investment tax credits are realized. In continuing the example of XYZ Corporation for its next succeeding calendar year, we will assume the following additional data to demonstrate the reinstatement of deferred taxes previously offset by investment tax credits:

- $90,000 of available unused investment tax credits for financial accounting purposes (balance from previous year)
- $498,000 of available unused investment tax credits for tax purposes (balance from previous year)
- $100,000 of available unused investment tax credits arising in current year
- $572,000 of existing net deferred tax credits (balance from previous year)
- $1,000,000 pretax financial accounting income
- $200,000 of net timing differences which reduce taxable income
- $800,000 of taxable income
- 40% tax rate
- Investment tax credit limited to $25,000 plus 60% over $25,000 (same as last year)

Income Tax Expense on Pretax Financial Accounting Income:

Pretax financial accounting income	$1,000,000
Rate of tax	40%
Income tax expense before allowable investment tax credit	$ 400,000
Allowable investment tax credit [$25,000 plus 60% of ($400,000 − $25,000) = $250,000. However, for book purposes there is only $190,000 available ($90,000 + $100,000)].	190,000
Income tax expense (per books)	$ 210,000

Investment Tax Credit

Current Income Tax Liability on Taxable Income:
Pretax financial accounting income	$1,000,000
Less: Timing difference	200,000
Taxable income	$ 800,000
Rate of tax	40%
Income tax liability before allowable investment tax credit	$ 320,000
Allowable investment tax credit [($25,000 plus 60% of ($320,000 − $25,000)]	202,000
Current income tax liability	$ 118,000

The $92,000 difference between income tax expense of $210,000 (books) and the current income tax liability of $118,000 (tax return) consists of $32,000 deferred tax expense on the current year's net timing difference of $200,000, and the balance of $60,000 represents net deferred tax credits that must be reinstated. The journal entry to record the current income tax expense, deferred taxes for the current period and to reinstate the deferred tax credits, is as follows:

Income tax expense - current	$118,000	
Provision for deferred taxes	60,000	
Income tax expense - deferred	32,000	
Current tax liability		$118,000
Deferred tax credits		92,000

The credit to deferred tax credits consists of $32,000 arising in the current period and $60,000 being reinstated. The debit to the provision for deferred taxes is an income statement account and appears in the total provision for income taxes, as follows:

Provision for income taxes:
Current	$118,000
Deferred	32,000
Provision for deferred taxes	60,000
Total provision for income taxes	$210,000

The balance in the net deferred tax credit account which will appear on the balance sheet is computed as follows:

Balance, beginning of period	$572,000
Add: Deferred tax on net timing difference for current period	32,000
Deferred taxes reinstated for investment tax credits realized	60,000
Balance, end of period	$664,000

The computation of the ending balance and changes in investment tax credits for financial accounting and tax purposes is as follows:

	Financial	Tax
Beginning balance	$ 90,000	$498,000
New investment tax credits for current year	100,000	100,000
Used for determining current income taxes	(190,000)	(202,000)
Ending balance	$ NONE	$396,000

The tax benefit of a net operating loss carryforward may be recognized when future realization is assured beyond any reasonable doubt (APB-11). This same treatment is not allowed for an investment tax credit carryforward which may not be recognized even though future realization is assured beyond any reasonable doubt (FASB Interpretation-25).

Business combinations When an unused investment tax credit is acquired in a business combination accounted for as a purchase transaction, no value is assigned to it (FASB Interpretation-25). This is because existing promulgated GAAP (APB-2) prohibits the recording of an unused investment tax credit as an asset under any circumstances. The treatment of unused investment tax credits acquired in a purchase transaction as promulgated by FASB Interpretation-25 is as follows:

1. At the date of the purchase transaction no value is assigned to any unused investment tax credits acquired in the transaction.

2. At the date that a tax benefit is realized from the acquired unused investment tax credit, any unamortized goodwill (positive or negative) which arose from the same purchase transaction is reduced or increased by the amount of the tax

Investment Tax Credit

benefit realized. The adjustment to goodwill is not made retroactively but is made prospectively. That is, there is no restatement of previously issued financial statements. The adjustment to goodwill is made in the period in which the tax benefit is realized and future periods. This means that the remaining amount of unamortized goodwill at the beginning of the period in which the tax benefit is realized is adjusted and the new balance is amortized over the current and remaining periods of amortization.

3. In the event that there is no unamortized goodwill at the beginning of the period in which the tax benefit is realized, then the noncurrent assets, if any, acquired in the same purchase transaction are reduced proportionately by the amount of the realized tax benefit. The adjustment is made prospectively in the same manner as goodwill (see 2. above).

4. If there is no unamortized goodwill or balances of noncurrent assets acquired in the same purchase transaction as the unused investment tax credit, or if the noncurrent assets are reduced to zero and realized tax benefits still exist, then any remaining realized tax benefits should be recorded as deferred credits and amortized to income over a period not to exceed forty years.

Other Considerations

Once a method of reporting the investment tax credit is selected, it should not be changed. A change may result in a consistency exception in the auditor's report (APB-4).

Only one method should be established for consolidated statements even though the members of the consolidating group may employ several different methods (APB-4).

In accounting for leverage leases the lessor must use the deferral method of accounting for the investment credit, or else the lease must be accounted for as a direct financing lease (FASB-13).

Disclosure

The two most acceptable forms of balance sheet presentation for the investment tax credit are (1) as a deduction from the corresponding asset and (2) as a deferred credit.

In the first case, the income statement will show a lower

depreciation expense for the year, because the depreciable base of the asset has been reduced by the credit and so the credit will not appear on the income statement. If, however, this year's amount of the credit is shown directly on the income statement, then the depreciation expense for the year should be higher by the same amount.

Whatever method is used to account for the investment tax credit, full disclosure of the method and amounts involved should be made, as should material amounts of unused investment credits.

Conflict in GAAP

APB-2 and APB-4 require that investment tax credits be disclosed parenthetically or by footnote unless they can actually be used as an offset against the current income tax liability, or carried back to prior years for a claim of refund. In other words, investment tax credits are not to be recorded on the books of an enterprise, or be used as an offset against the income tax liability unless they can be actually realized for tax purposes and represent an available tax benefit. The justification for this treatment is apparently based on the limited life of the investment tax credit as provided by federal tax regulations. Under current tax regulations, an investment tax credit can be carried back three years and carried forward seven years which is the same periods allowed for net operating losses.

The deferred tax method of interperiod tax allocation is required by APB-11 (Accounting for Income Taxes). APB-11 states that, "The tax effect of a timing difference should be measured by the differential between taxes computed with and without inclusion of the transaction creating the difference between taxable income and pretax accounting income." Thus, the "with and without" method of computing deferred taxes was established and investment tax credits are included in determining income tax expense (books) before the same investment tax credits are actually realized for tax purposes (see Deferred Tax Method in chapter on Income Taxes).

FASB Interpretation-25 condones the practice of recognizing investment tax credits for financial accounting purposes prior to their realization for tax purposes.

APB-11 permits the recognition, for financial accounting purposes, of a tax benefit resulting from an operating loss carryforward, providing that the realization of the tax benefit is assured beyond any reasonable doubt. Thus, income tax expense (books) can be reduced by the recognition of such an operating loss carryforward

Investment Tax Credit

before the tax benefit is actually realized for tax purposes. However, FASB Interpretation-25 prohibits the recognition of a tax benefit resulting from an investment tax credit, even if the realization of the tax benefit is assured beyond any reasonable doubt. Thus, the tax benefit of an operating loss carryforward can be recognized for financial accounting purposes before the same loss is realized for tax purposes, but the tax benefit of an investment tax credit cannot be recognized under any circumstances prior to its realization for tax purposes.

To add further confusion, FASB Interpretation-25 requires that any excess available investment tax credits, not used to determine the current income tax expense (books), must be used to reduce any existing net deferred tax credits which will reverse in the available carryforward period. The journal entry to record the use of the excess available investment tax credits to reduce existing net deferred tax credits is, as follows:

Deferred tax credits	$XX,XXX	
Provision for deferred taxes		$XX,XXX

The "provision for deferred taxes" appears in the income statement as part of the total current provision for income taxes. Thus, once again, current income tax expense is being reduced by the tax benefits of investment tax credits which have not yet been realized for tax purposes.

LEASES

Background

The main source of promulgated GAAP on Accounting for Leases is FASB-13, which has subsequently been amended or interpreted by the following:

    FASB-17—Accounting for Leases—Initial Direct Costs
    FASB-22—Changes in the Provisions of Lease Agreements Resulting from Refunding of Tax Exempt Debt
    FASB-23—Inception of the Lease
    FASB-26—Profit Recognition on Sales-Type Leases of Real Estate
    FASB-27—Classification of Renewals or Extensions of Existing Sales-Type or Direct Financing Leases
    FASB-28—Accounting for Sales with Leasebacks
    FASB-29—Determining Contingent Rentals
    FASB Interpretation-19—Lessee Guarantee of the Residual Value of Leased Property
    FASB Interpretation-23—Leases of Certain Property Owned by a Governmental Unit or Authority
    FASB Interpretation-24—Leases Involving Only Part of a Building
    FASB Interpretation-26—Accounting for Purchase of a Leased Asset by the Lessee during the Term of the Lease
    FASB Interpretation-27—Accounting for a Loss on a Sublease

The promulgated GAAP (FASB-13) defines a lease as an agreement that conveys the right to use assets (tangible or intangible) for a stated period. This broad definition includes certain transactions not generally considered leases and excludes leases of natural resources (oil, gas, minerals, and timber) and licensing agreements for manuscripts, patents, motion pictures, and copyrights.

Companies in regulated industries must comply with the promulgated GAAP in accordance with the Addendum to APB-2.

Substance over Form

Some lease agreements are such that an asset and a related liability should be reported on the balance sheet of an enterprise. The distinction is one of *substance over form* (basic principle) when the transaction actually *transfers substantially all the benefits and risks inherent in the ownership of the property.*

Established in GAAP are criteria to determine whether a lease transaction is in substance a transfer of the incidents of ownership. If at its inception a lease meets one or more of the following four criteria, the lease should be classified as a transfer of ownership:

1. By the end of the lease term, ownership of the leased property is transferred to the lessee.
2. The lease contains a bargain purchase option.
3. The lease term is substantially (75% or more) equal to the estimated useful life of the leased property.
4. At the inception of the lease the present value of the minimum lease payments, with certain adjustments, is 90% or more of the fair value of the leased property.

We shall examine the four criteria in more detail later.

A lease that transfers substantially all the benefits and risks inherent in the ownership of property is called a *capital lease*. Such a lease should be accounted for by the lessee as the acquisition of an asset and the incurrence of a liability. The lessor should account for such a lease as a sale or financing. These leases are referred to as *sales-type* or *direct financing leases.* All other leases, called *operating leases,* are accounted for as true leases.

Terminology

It is essential that the various terms used in accounting for leases be thoroughly understood.

Capital lease a lease that transfers substantially all the benefits and risks inherent in the ownership of the property to the lessee, who accounts for the lease as an acquisition of an asset and the incurrence of a liability.

Sales-type lease a lease that usually results in a manufacturer's or dealer's profit or loss to the lessor, transfers substantially all the benefits and risks inherent in the ownership of the leased property to the lessee; in addition, (1) the minimum lease payments are reasonably predictable of collection and (2) no important uncertainties exist regarding cost to be incurred by the lessor under the terms of the lease.

Direct financing lease a lease that does not result in a manufacturer's or dealer's profit or loss to the lessor, but does transfer substantially all the benefits and risks inherent in the ownership of the leased property to the lessee; in addition, (1) the minimum lease payments are reasonably predictable of collection and (2) no important uncertainties exist regarding costs to be incurred by the lessor under the terms of the lease.

Comparison of Sales-type and Direct Financing Leases

Both sales-type and direct financing leases transfer substantially all the benefits and risks inherent in the ownership of the leased property to the lessee, who records the transaction as a *capital lease*.

A sales-type lease usually gives rise to a manufacturer's or dealer's profit or loss, whereas a direct financing lease does not give rise to a manufacturer's or dealer's profit or loss.

In a sales-type lease, the *fair value* of the leased property at the inception of the lease differs from the cost or carrying amount; in a direct financing lease, the fair value of the leased property at the inception of the lease is the same as the cost or carrying amount. This is because a manufacturer's or dealer's profit or loss usually exists in a sales-type lease and fair value is usually the *normal selling price* of the property. In a direct financing lease fair value is usually cost.

It must be remembered that a lessor need not be a dealer or manufacturer to realize a profit or loss, if at the inception of the lease the fair value differs from the cost or carrying amount.

Fair value the price the leased property could be sold for between unrelated parties in an arm's-length transaction.

For the manufacturer or dealer, the fair value is usually the normal selling price less trade or volume discounts. However, fair value may be less than the normal selling price, and sometimes less than the cost of the property.

For others the fair value is usually cost less trade or volume discounts. However, fair value may be less than cost, especially in circumstances where a long period elapses between the acquisition of the property by the lessor and the inception of a lease.

Fair rental the rental rate for similar property under similar lease terms and conditions.

Related parties one or more entities subject to the significant influence over the operating and financial policies of another entity.

Executory costs usually insurance, maintenance, and taxes paid in connection with the leased property.

Bargain purchase option a lessee's option to purchase the leased property at a bargain price that makes the exercise of the option almost imminent.

Bargain renewal option a lessee's option to renew the lease at a bargain rental price that makes the exercise of the option almost imminent.

Estimated economic life the estimated remaining useful life of the property for the purpose for which it was intended, regardless of the term of the lease.

Estimated residual value the estimated fair value of the leased property at the end of the lease term. The estimated residual value shall not exceed the amount estimated at the inception of the lease except for the effect of any increases that result during construction or preacquisition period due to escalation provisions in the lease (see Leases with Escalation Clauses).

Unguaranteed residual value the estimated fair value of the leased property at the end of the lease term that is not guaranteed by the lessee or a third party unrelated to the lessor. A guarantee by a third party related to the lessee shall be considered a lessee guarantee.

Lessee's incremental borrowing rate the rate of interest that the lessee would have had to pay at the inception of the lease to borrow the funds, on similar terms, to purchase the leased property.

Inception of lease The date of the lease agreement or the date of a written commitment signed by the parties involved which sets forth the principal provisions of the lease transaction.
    A written commitment which does not contain all of the principal provisions of the lease transaction does not qualify under the promulgated GAAP (FASB-23).

Leases

> **OBSERVATION:** The first sentence of the definition of "inception of lease" in FASB-23 reads "The date of the lease agreement or commitment, if earlier." The last two words of the sentence ("if earlier") may be somewhat confusing to the reader. The commitment referred to is ostensibly an agreement to agree to enter into a lease. It is unlikely that such an agreement will ever be entered into after the lease agreement has been signed. Therefore, the words "if earlier" are confusing and completely unnecessary.

Interest rate implicit in the lease   the discount rate that, when applied to certain items (enumerated below), results in an aggregate present value equal to the fair value of the leased property at the beginning of the lease term, less any investment credit expected to be realized and retained by the lessor. The items that the discount rate is applied to are (1) the minimum lease payments, excluding executory costs such as insurance, maintenance, and taxes (including any profit thereon) that are paid by the lessor; and (2) the estimated fair value of the property at the end of the lease term, exclusive of any portion guaranteed by the lessee or third party unrelated to the lessor (unguaranteed residual value).

Initial direct costs (FASB-17)   Initial direct costs are those directly incurred by the lessor to negotiate and consummate a lease transaction. Initial direct costs include any portion of compensation paid to salespersons or others that is applicable to time spent in negotiating and successfully consummating a lease transaction. If the lease transaction is not successfully consummated, compensation paid to salespersons or others is not included in initial direct costs.

Other initial direct costs are:

1. legal fees
2. commissions
3. credit investigations
4. preparing and processing documents

Contingent rentals   are those which cannot be determined at the inception of the lease because they depend on future factors or events. Rental payments based on future sales volume, future machine hours, future interest rates and future price indexes are examples of contingent rentals. Contingent rentals can either increase or decrease lease payments (FASB-29).

Increases in minimum lease payments that occur during the preacquisition or construction period as a result of an escalation clause in the lease are not considered contingent rentals (see Leases with escalation clauses).

Lease Term

The term of a lease shall include the following time periods:

1. any fixed noncancelable term
2. any period(s) covered by a bargain renewal option
3. any period(s) in which penalties are imposed in an amount that reasonably assures the renewal of the lease by the lessee
4. any period(s) in which a guarantee by the lessee of the lessor's debt (related to the leased property) is expected to be in effect
5. any period(s) up to the exercisable date of a bargain purchase option
6. any period(s) in which the lessor has the option to renew or extend the lease term

Under no circumstances shall a lease term extend beyond the date a bargain purchase option becomes exercisable.

Noncancelable lease term a lease that is cancelable only (1) on some remote contingency, (2) with permission of the lessor, or (3) if the lessee enters into a new lease with the same lessor

Lessee's Minimum Lease Payments

Normal minimum lease payments include:

1. the minimum rent called for during the lease term
2. any payment(s) or guarantee(s) that the lessee must make or is required to make concerning the leased property at the end of the lease term (residual value), including:
   a. any amount stated to purchase the leased property
   b. any amount stated to make up any deficiency from a specified minimum

c. any amount payable for failure to renew or extend the lease at the expiration of the lease term

When a lease contains a *bargain purchase option,* the minimum lease payments include only (1) the *minimum rental payments over the lease term* and (2) *the payment required to exercise the bargain purchase option.*

Under any circumstances, the following should be excluded from any minimum lease payments:

1. a guarantee by the lessee to pay the lessor's debt on the leased property
2. the lessee's obligation (separate from the rental payments) to pay executory costs (insurance, taxes, etc.) in connection with the leased property
3. contingent rentals are never included in determining the minimum lease payments

> **OBSERVATION:** *FASB Interpretation-19 clarifies certain guarantees of the residual value of leased property made by a lessee, as follows:*
>
> 1. *A guarantee by a lessee to make up a residual value deficiency caused by damage, extraordinary wear and tear, or excessive usage is similar to a contingent rental, since the amount is not determinable at the inception of the lease. Therefore, this type of lessee guarantee does not constitute a lessee guarantee of residual value for purposes of computing the lessee's minimum lease payments.*
> 2. *A lessee's guarantee to make up a residual value deficiency at the end of a lease term is limited to the specified maximum deficiency called for by the lease.*
> 3. *Unless the lessor explicitly releases the lessee, a guarantee of residual value by an unrelated third party for the benefit of the lessor does not release the obligation of the lessee. Therefore, such a guarantee by an unrelated third party shall not be used to reduce the lessee's minimum lease payments. Costs incurred in connection with a guarantee by an unrelated third party are considered executory costs and are not included in computing the lessee's minimum lease payments.*

Leases

Lessor's Minimum Lease Payments

The minimum lease payments to a lessor is the sum of:

1. the minimum lease payments made by the lessee
2. any guarantee by a third party, unrelated to the lessee and lessor, of the residual value or rental payments beyond the lease term, providing such guarantor is financially capable of discharging the potential obligation

Classification of Leases by Lessees

If one or more of the following four criteria are present at the inception of a lease, it should be classified as a capital lease by the lessee.

I. Ownership of the property is transferred to the lessee by the end of the lease term.

II. The lease contains a bargain purchase option.

III. The lease term, at inception, is substantially (75% or more) equal to the estimated economic life of the leased property, including earlier years of use. [*Exception:* This particular criterion cannot be used for a lease that begins within the last 25% of the original estimated economic life of the leased property. For example: A jet aircraft that has an estimated economic life of 25 years is leased for five successive five-year leases. If the first four five-year leases were classified as operating leases, the last five-year lease could not be classified as a capital lease because the lease would commence within the last 25% of the estimated economic life of the property and would fall under this exception.]

IV. The present value of the minimum lease payments at the beginning of the lease term, excluding executory costs and profits thereon to be paid by the lessor, is 90% or more of the fair value of the property at the inception of the lease, less any investment tax credit retained by the lessor and expected to be realized by him. (*Exception:* This particular criterion cannot be used for a lease that begins within the last 25% of the original estimated economic life of the leased property.)

Lessee's discount rate   A lessee shall use the present value of the minimum lease payments, using his incremental borrowing rate unless he has knowledge of the implicit rate used by the lessor that is *lower* than his incremental borrowing rate.

Lessor's discount rate   A lessor shall compute the present value of the minimum lease payments, using the interest rate *implicit in the lease.*

Classification of Leases by Lessors

If at inception, a lease meets any one of the four criteria indicating that substantially all the benefits and risks of ownership have been transferred to the lessee, *and meets both the following conditions,* it shall be classified by the lessor as a sales-type or direct financing lease, whichever is appropriate.

1. *Collection of the minimum lease payments is reasonably predictable.* A receivable resulting from a lease subject to an estimate of uncollectibility based on experience shall not be precluded from being classified as either a sales-type or a direct financing lease.

2. *No important uncertainties exist for unreimbursable costs yet to be incurred by the lessor under the lease.* Important uncertainties include extensive warranties and material commitments beyond normal practice. The necessity of estimating *executory costs,* such as insurance maintenance and taxes, shall not be considered important uncertainties.

    NOTE: In the event the leased property is not acquired or constructed before the inception of the lease, this condition is not applied until such time as the leased property is acquired or constructed by the lessor (FASB-23) (see Leases with Escalation Clauses).

Changing a Provision of a Lease

If a change in a provision of a lease would have resulted in a different lease classification at the inception of the lease because of different criteria, a new lease agreement is created that must be reclassified according to its new criteria. Renewal, extension, or a new lease under which the lessee continues to use the same property is not considered a change in a lease provision.

Leases

Any action that extends the lease term, except to void a residual guarantee, or a penalty for failure to renew the lease at the end of the lease term, shall be considered a new lease agreement that must be classified according to this criteria.

Mere changes in estimates or circumstances do not cause a reclassification.

Refundings of tax-exempt debt If a change in a lease occurs as a result of a refunding by the lessor of tax-exempt debt and (1) the lessee receives the economic advantages of the refunding, (2) the revised lease qualifies and is classified either as a capital lease by the lessee or as a direct financing lease by the lessor, the change in the lease shall be accounted for on the basis of whether or not an extinguishment of debt has occurred, as follows:

1. Accounted for as an extinguishment of debt
   a. The lessee adjusts the lease obligation to the present value of the future minimum lease payments under the revised agreement, using the effective interest rate of the new lease agreement. Any gain or loss shall be treated as a gain or loss on an early extinguishment of debt.
   b. The lessor adjusts the balance of the minimum lease payments receivable and the gross investment in the lease (if affected) for the difference between the present values of the old and new or revised agreement. Any gain or loss shall be recognized in the current period.
2. Not accounted for as an extinguishment of debt
   a. The lessee accrues any costs connected with the refunding that it is obligated to reimburse to the lessor. The interest method is used to amortize the costs over the period from the date of the refunding to the call date of the debt to be refunded.
   b. The lessor recognizes as revenue any reimbursements to be received from the lessee for costs paid related to the debt to be refunded over the period from the date of the refunding to the call date of the debt to be refunded.

Accounting and Reporting by Lessees

Initial recording The lessee records a capital lease as an asset along with a corresponding liability. The initial recording value of a lease is the *lesser* of the fair value of the leased property or the present value of the minimum lease payments, excluding any portion representing executory costs and profit thereon to be paid by the lessor. Fair value is determined as at the inception of the lease and the present value of the minimum lease payments is computed as at the beginning of the lease term. The inception of the lease and the beginning of the lease term are not necessarily the same dates.

Since the definition of minimum lease payments (lessee's) *excludes* a lessee's obligation to pay executory costs (apart from the rental payments), any executory costs included in the minimum lease payments must be part of the rental payments, identified separately or not. Thus, there may be no executory costs at all to exclude from the minimum lease payments; or if such costs are included in the rental payments and are not separately identified (which is probably the most likely case), an estimate of the amount will be necessary.

The discount rate that the *lessee* uses to arrive at the present value of the minimum lease payments is his *incremental borrowing rate,* unless he has knowledge of the *interest rate implicit in the lease* used by the lessor, and it is lower. A *lessor* shall compute the present value of the minimum lease payments using the interest rate implicit in the lease that results in a present value equal to the fair value.

Leases with escalation clauses In lease agreements or written commitments in which the leased property is to be acquired or constructed by the lessor, there may be a provision for the escalation of the minimum lease payments during the construction or preacquisition period. Usually, the escalation is based on increased costs of acquisition or construction of the leased property. A provision to escalate the minimum lease payments during the construction or preacquisition period can also be based on other measures of cost or value, including general price-level changes, or changes in the consumer price index.

The relationship between the total amount of minimum lease payments and the fair value of a lease is such that when one increases so does the other. For example, assume that the total minimum lease payments of a particular lease are $100,000 payable in five equal annual installments, and the fair value of the same lease is $350,000. If the minimum lease payments are increased 20% to $120,000, it is quite likely that the fair value of the lease will increase correspondingly because the lease is just worth more money to an investor.

Leases

Promulgated GAAP (FASB-23) requires that increases in the minimum lease payments that occur during the preacquisition or construction period as a result of an escalation clause are to be considered in determining the fair value of the leased property at the inception of the lease for the purposes of the initial recording of the lease transaction by the lessee, or where fair value is used as a basis of allocation (see Leases involving land and buildings).

The initial recording value of a lease transaction by the lessee, which is required by FASB-13, is the lesser of the fair value of the leased property or the present value of the minimum lease payments. FASB-23 changes the lessee's determination of fair value for leases which contain escalation clauses from the fair value on the inception date to a fair value amount that includes the effect of any increases which have occurred as a result of the escalation clause. The changes embodied in FASB-23 are intended to create lease classifications that more closely reflect the substance of a lease transaction.

> **OBSERVATION:** *The question arises as to when leases of this type should be recorded on the books of the lessee. The promulgated GAAP appears to indicate that the initial recording should be made only after the effects of the escalation clause on the fair value of the leased property is determined. Otherwise, FASB-23 is silent in all respects as to when the lease transaction should be recorded. In the case of significant amounts of leases, it would appear to be illogical to wait several years to record the transaction. However, if this is the only viable alternative, full disclosure of all pertinent facts pertaining to the lease agreement or commitment should be made in a prominent footnote.*
>
> *The other alternative is to record these types of lease transactions immediately at the inception of the lease, utilizing whatever information is available and subsequently adjusting the recorded amounts when the effects of the escalation clauses are known. This alternative does not appear to be viable because of the difficulties mentioned in the following paragraphs.*
>
> *The last-enumerated criterion in FASB-13 for capitalizing a lease is when the present value of the minimum lease payments is 90% or more of the fair value of the leased property at the inception of the lease. When we consider this criterion for capitalizing a lease in conjunction with the alternative of recording lease transactions covered*

by FASB-23 at the inception of the lease and then subsequently adjusting the recorded amounts when the effects of the escalation clauses become known, the following problems arise, which are not addressed by either FASB-13 or FASB-23:

1. If we assume that FASB-23 requires that the fair value of leases with escalation clauses be determined at a future date, what fair value should be used to determine whether the lease is or is not a capital lease in accordance with the criterion of whether the present value of the minimum lease payments is 90% or more of the fair value of the leased property at the inception of the lease?

2. What if a lease of this type is capitalized in accordance with the criterion that the present value of the minimum lease payments is 90% or more of the fair value at inception of the lease, and subsequently as a result of the escalation clause the present value becomes less than 90% of the fair value, so that the lease should not have been capitalized?

3. Suppose a lease with an escalation clause is properly classified as an operating lease at inception of the lease and subsequently, as a result of the escalation clause, the lease qualifies as a capital lease?

The above are just a few of the complications that could arise in applying the provisions of FASB-23 to lease transactions. Some clarification must be forthcoming before this promulgated GAAP can be pragmatically applied.

FASB-23 also permits increases in the estimated residual value (see definition) that occur as a result of escalation provisions in leases in which the leased property is to be acquired or constructed by the lessor. For example, if the estimated residual value is 10% of the fair value at the inception of a lease and during the construction or preacquisition period of the leased property the effects of the escalation clause increase the fair value, then the estimated residual value is also allowed to increase above the amount which was estimated at the date of the inception of the lease.

Amortization The asset(s) recorded under a capital lease shall be amortized in a manner consistent with the lessee's normal depreciation policy for other owned assets. The period for amortization is

Leases

either (1) the estimated economic life or (2) the lease term, depending on which criterion was used to classify the lease. If the criterion used to classify the lease as a capital lease was either I (ownership of the property is transferred to the lessee by the end of the lease term) or II (lease contains a bargain purchase option), the asset is amortized over its estimated economic life. In all other cases, the asset is amortized over the lease term. Any *estimated residual value* is deducted from the asset to determine the amortizable base.

Interest expense: Interest method The interest method is used to produce a constant rate of interest on the remaining lease liability. A portion of each minimum lease payment is allocated to interest expense and/or amortization, and the balance is applied to reduce the lease liability. Any *residual guarantee(s)* by the lessee or penalty payments are automatically taken into consideration by using the interest method and will result in a balance at the end of the lease term equal the amount of the guarantee or penalty payments at that date.

Jones Company leases a tractor-trailer for $8,000 per year on a noncancelable five-year lease. Jones guarantees to the lessor that the tractor-trailer will have a residual value of at least $5,000 at the end of the lease term.

Assume that all other assumptions have been eliminated and that a 12% interest rate is used.

Present value of $8,000 payments × 5 years	12%	= $28,838
Present value of $5,000 one payment	12%	= 2,837
Total asset and lease obligation		$31,675

Note: The present value of the $8,000 series of annual rental payments is found in the present value of annuity tables, and the present value of the $5,000 residual guarantee (one payment) is found in the present value tables.

A schedule of interest expense, amortization, and reduction of the lease obligation of $31,675 to the $5,000 residual guarantee, using the interest method, follows:

Book Value Lease Obligations Beginning of Year	Rental Payments	12% Interest on Beginning Book Value	Amortization	Book Value Lease Obligations End of Year
$31,675	$ 8,000	$ 3,801	$ 4,199	$27,476
27,476	8,000	3,297	4,703	22,773
22,773	8,000	2,733	5,267	17,506
17,506	8,000	2,101	5,899	11,607
11,607	8,000	1,393	6,607	5,000
	$40,000	$13,325	$26,675	

Accounting for Lease Changes-Lessee

If a guarantee or penalty is rendered inoperative because of a renewal or other extension of the *lease term,* or if a new lease is consummated where the lessee continues to lease the same property, an adjustment must be made to the asset and lease obligation for the difference between the present values of the old and the revised agreements. In these cases, the present value of the future minimum lease payments under the new or revised agreement should be computed by using the original rate of interest on the initial lease.

Other lease changes should be accounted for as follows:

1. If a lease change results in revised minimum lease payments, but is also classified as a capital lease, an adjustment is made to the asset and lease obligation for the difference between the present values of the old and the new or revised agreement. The present value of the future minimum lease payments under the new or revised agreement should be computed by using the original rate of interest used on the initial lease.

2. If a new or revised agreement results from a lease change and is classified as an operating lease, gain or loss is recognized and the asset and lease obligation is eliminated from the books of account.

3. A renewal, extension, or new lease under which the lessee continues to use the same property, except when a guarantee or penalty is rendered inoperative (see above), is accounted for as follows:

a. *renewal or extension classified as a capital lease:* an adjustment is made for the difference between the original and revised present values, using the original discount rate
b. *renewal or extension classified as an operating lease:* the existing lease continues to be accounted for as a capital lease to the end of its lease term, and the renewal or extension is accounted for as an operating lease

When leased property under a capital lease is purchased by the lessee, it is accounted for as a renewal or extension of a capital lease (FASB Interpretation-26). Thus, any difference between the carrying amount and the purchase price on the date of purchase is treated as an adjustment of the carrying amount of the property.

Termination of a Capital Lease-Lessee

Gain or loss, if any, is recognized on the termination of a capital lease, and the asset and lease liability must be removed from the books of account.

Lessee's Operating Leases

A lessee records as rent expense, over the lease term, the rental payments on an operating lease. In all operating leases, rental payments shall be recognized on a straight line basis, unless some other systematic method is justified.

Lessee's Financial Statement Disclosure

Assets, accumulated amortization, and liabilities from capital leases should be reported separately in the balance sheet and classified as current or noncurrent in the same manner as other assets and liabilities.

Current amortization charges to income must be clearly disclosed, along with the additional information:

1. *gross assets:* as of each balance sheet date presented, in aggregate and by major property categories (this information may be combined with comparable owned assets)
2. *minimum future lease payments:* in total and for each of the next five years, showing deductions for executory costs, including any profit thereon, and the amount of imputed

interest to reduce the net minimum lease payments to present values

3. *minimum sublease income:* due in future periods under noncancelable subleases

Operating leases The following financial statement disclosure is required for all operating leases of lessees having noncancelable lease terms *in excess of one year.*

1. *minimum future rental payments:* in total and for each of the next five years
2. *minimum sublease income:* due in future periods under noncancelable subleases
3. *schedule of total rental expense:* showing the composition by minimum rentals, contingent rentals, and sublease income (excluding leases with terms of a month or less that were not renewed)

General disclosure A general description of the lessee's leasing arrangements, including (1) basis of contingent rental payments; (2) terms of renewals, purchase options, and escalation clauses; and (3) restrictions imposed by lease agreements, such as additional debt, dividends, and leasing limitations. Following is an illustration of a lessee's financial statement disclosure.

LESSEE'S FINANCIAL STATEMENT DISCLOSURE

Lessee's Balance Sheet

Assets	December 31 1978	1977
Leased property:		
Capital leases, less accumulated amortization (Note___)	$XXX,XXX	$XXX,XXX
Liabilities		
Current:		
Obligations under capital leases (Note___)	$XXX,XXX	$XXX,XXX
Noncurrent:		
Obligations under capital leases (Note___)	$ XX,XXX	$ XX,XXX

Capital Leases
Gross Assets and Accumulated Amortization

	December 31	
Type of Property	1978	1977
Manufacturing plants	$ XX,XXX	$XX,XXX
Retail stores	X,XXX	X,XXX
Other	XXX	XXX
Total	$XXX,XXX	$XX,XXX
Less: Accumulated amortization	XX,XXX	X,XXX
Capital leases, net	$XXX,XXX	$XX,XXX

Capital Leases
Minimum Future Lease Payments and Present Values of the Net Minimum Lease Payments

Year Ended December 31	
1979	$ XX,XXX
1980	X,XXX
1981	X,XXX
1982	X,XXX
1983	X,XXX
After 1983	XXX
Total minimum lease payments	$XXX,XXX
Less: Executory costs (estimated)	X,XXX
Net minimum lease payments	$XXX,XXX
Less: Imputed interest	XX,XXX
Present value of net minimum lease payments	$ XX,XXX

In addition to the foregoing statements and schedules, footnotes describing minimum sublease income and contingent rentals should be included, if required.

Operating Leases
Schedule of Minimum Future Rental Payments

Year Ended December 31	
1979	$ XX,XXX
1980	XXX,XXX
1981	XX,XXX
1982	XX,XXX
1983	XX,XXX
After 1983	XXX,XXX
Total future minimum rental payments	$XXX,XXX

In addition to the above information on operating leases, a footnote should be included describing minimum sublease income due in the future under noncancelable subleases.

Operating Leases
Composition of Total Rental Expense

	December 31	
	1978	1977
Minimum rentals	$XXX,XXX	$XXX,XXX
Contingent rentals	XX,XXX	XX,XXX
Less: Sublease rental income	(X,XXX)	(X,XXX)
Total rental expense, net	$XXX,XXX	$XXX,XXX

Note: The above schedule of total rental expense excludes leases with terms of one month or less that were not renewed.

In addition to the foregoing information on capital and operating leases, a footnote describing the general disclosure policy for the lessee's leases should be included containing (1) general leasing arrangements; (2) basis of contingent rental payments; (3) terms of renewals, purchase options, and escalation clauses; and (4) restrictions imposed by lease agreements, such as additional debt, dividends, and leasing limitations.

Accounting and Reporting by Lessors

Leases are classified for the lessor as either (1) sales-type, (2) direct financing, or (3) operating.

Sales-type leases are usually used by sellers of property to increase the marketability of expensive assets. The occurrence of a manufacturer's or dealer's profit or loss is generally present in a sales-type lease.

Direct financing leases do not give rise to a manufacturer's or dealer's profit or loss, and the fair value is usually the cost or the carrying amount of the property.

Recording Leases by Lessors

There are two steps in recording both sales-type and direct financing leases. Step 1 is to compute the gross investment in the lease, which is identical in each case. Step 2 will be explained for each kind of lease.

Step 1. Sales-type and direct financing leases The lessor's gross investment in a lease is the sum of the following:

1. the lessor's minimum lease payments
2. any unguaranteed residual value accruing to the benefit of the lessor (this is the estimated fair value of the lease property at the end of the lease term, which is not guaranteed) less any executory costs and profit thereon to be paid by the lessor. [*Note:* If the residual value is guaranteed, it would be included in the minimum lease payments.]

Step 2. Sales-type leases Using the interest rate implicit in the lease, the gross investment arrived at in step 1 is discounted to its present value, which becomes the sales price included in income for the period. [*Note:* When using the interest rate implicit in the lease, the present value will always be equal to fair value.]

The cost or carrying amount of the property sold, plus any *initial direct costs* (costs incurred by the lessor in negotiating and consummating the lease, such as legal fees and commissions) less the present value of the *unguaranteed residual value* accruing to the benefit of the lessor, is charged against income in the period of the sale. The difference between the gross investment computed in step 1 and the sales price computed above is recorded as unearned income, which is amortized to income over the lease term in proportion to the remaining balance (interest method). The unearned income is included in the balance sheet as a deduction from the related gross investment, which results in the net investment in the lease.

Step 2. Direct financing leases The difference between the gross investment computed in step 1 and the (a) cost or carrying amount of the property plus (b) any initial direct costs (legal fees, commissions, etc.) is recorded as unearned income, which is amortized to income over the lease term in proportion to the remaining balance (interest method). The unearned income is included in the balance sheet as a deduction from the related gross investment, which results in the net investment in the lease.

Other methods Other methods of recognizing income may be used for both sales-type and direct financing leases, provided the results are not materially different from those produced by the method prescribed.

Sales-type leases involving real estate FASB-26 covers a gain on a sales-type lease involving real estate. Losses on sales-type leases involving real estate are recognized and are not covered by FASB-26. A real estate lease that would otherwise be classified as a sales-type lease at the inception date shall be classified as an operating lease unless at the beginning of the lease term such a lease meets the criteria for full and immediate profit recognition as defined in the AICPA Industry Accounting Guide-Accounting for Profit Recognition on Sales of Real Estate (FASB-26). The criteria are as follows:

1. The buyer's initial investment in the real estate is large enough that there is a reasonable likelihood that the seller will collect the receivable from the buyer. The minimum down payment required, which depends on the type of property, ranges from 5% to 25% and is illustrated on the following schedule appearing in the AICPA Guide:

Leases

	Minimum Down Payment (% of Sales Value)
Land:	
Held for commercial, industrial, or residential development to commence within two years after sale	20%[1]
Held for commercial, industrial, or residential development after two years	25%[1]
Commercial and Industrial Property:	
Office and industrial buildings, shopping centers, etc.:	
Properties subject to lease on a long-term lease basis to parties having satisfactory credit rating; cash flow currently sufficient to service all indebtedness	10%
Single tenancy properties sold to a user having a satisfactory credit rating	15%
All other	20%
Other Income-Producing Properties (hotels, motels, marinas, mobile home parks, etc.):	
Cash flow currently sufficient to service all indebtedness	15%
Start-up situations or current deficiencies in cash flow	25%
Multi-Family Residential Property:	
Primary residence:	
Cash flow currently sufficient to service all indebtedness	10%
Start-up situations or current deficiencies in cash flow	15%
Secondary or recreational residence:	
Cash flow currently sufficient to service all indebtedness	15%
Start-up situations or current deficiencies in cash flow	25%
Single Family Residential Property (including condominium or cooperative housing):	
Primary residence of the buyer	5%[2]
Secondary or recreational residence	10%[2]

[1] Not intended to apply to volume retail lot sales by land development companies.

[2] If collectibility of the remaining portion of the sales price cannot be supported by reliable evidence of collection experience, a higher down payment is indicated and should not be less than 60% of the difference between the sales value and the financing available from loans guaranteed by regulatory bodies, such as FHA or VA, or from independent financial institutions.

2. The terms of the contract must require the buyer to increase his investment in the property each year after the appropriate down payment is made. The payments must be at least equal to an amount which will pay the total debt owed on the property, including any interest, over a maximum period, not to exceed twenty years.
3. If the seller continues to be involved with the property sold, his potential loss of profit as a result of continued involvement must be definitely limited by the contract in order to recognize profit at the time of sale. A seller's continued involvement after the sale may include arranging financing for the buyer, managing or constructing the property, or providing other services to the buyer in relation to the property after it is sold.

If the three conditions mentioned above are not met at the beginning of the lease term, then the lease must be classified as an operating lease by the lessor (FASB-26).

> **OBSERVATION:** It is important to distinguish between the inception of the lease and the beginning of the lease term. The inception of the lease is the date on which the lease agreement or commitment is executed (FASB-23). The beginning of the lease term is the date that the actual lease term commences (FASB-19). For example, ABC Company executes a lease agreement on September 1, 1979. The lease term is to begin on January 1, 1980, and run for five years to December 31, 1984. The inception of the lease is September 1, 1979, and the beginning of the lease term is January 1, 1980.

Balance Sheet Classification-Lessor

The resulting net investment in both sales-type and direct financing leases is subject to the same treatment as other assets in classifying as current or noncurrent.

Contingent Rentals-Lessor

Contingent rentals of sales-type and direct financing leases should be credited to income in the period earned.

Leases

Annual Review of Residual Values-Lessor

The unguaranteed residual values of both sales-type and direct financing leases should be reviewed at least annually to determine whether a decline, other than temporary, has occurred in their estimated values. If a decline is not temporary, the accounting for the transaction should be revised using the new estimate, and the resulting loss should be recognized in the period that the change is made. *Upward adjustments are not allowed.*

Accounting for Lease Changes-Lessor

The definition of lease term includes any periods in which penalties are imposed in an amount that reasonably assures the renewal of the lease by the lessee. The definition of minimum lease payments includes any payments or guarantees that the lessee is required to make concerning the leased property including any amount (1) to purchase the leased property, (2) to make up any deficiency from a specified minimum, and (3) for failure to renew or extend the lease at the expiration of the lease term. Guarantees and penalties, such as these, are usually canceled and become inoperative in the event the lease is renewed, is extended, or a new lease for the same property is consummated.

If a sales-type or direct financing lease contains a residual guarantee or a penalty for failure to renew and is rendered inoperative as a result of a lease renewal or other extension of the lease term, or if a new lease is consummated where the lessee continues to lease the same property, an adjustment must be made to the unearned income account for the difference between the present values of the old and the revised agreements. The present value of the future minimum lease payments under the new agreement should be computed by using the original rate of interest used for the initial lease. [*Note:* Care must be exercised in these circumstances to avoid an upward adjustment of any previously recorded residual values.]

In sales-type and direct financing leases which do not contain residual guarantees or penalties for failure to renew, an adjustment must be made to account for lease changes, renewals, or other extensions, including a new lease in which the lessee continues to lease the same property. If the classification of the lease remains unchanged or is classified as a direct financing lease and the amount of the remaining minimum lease payments is changed, an adjustment must be made to unearned income to account for the difference between the present values of the old and the new agreements. If a new classification results in a sales-type lease, it shall be classified and treated as a direct financing lease unless the transaction occurs within the last few months of the original lease, in which case it shall be classified as a sales-type lease (FASB-27).

If the classification of a lease is changed to an operating lease, the accounting treatment depends upon whether the operating lease starts immediately or at the end of the existing lease, as follows:

Starts immediately The remaining net investment is eliminated from the accounts and the leased property is recorded as an asset using the lower of (1) original cost, (2) present fair value, or (3) present carrying amount. The difference between the remaining net investment and the new recorded value of the asset is charged to income in the period of change.

Starts subsequently The existing lease continues to be accounted for as a sales-type or direct financing lease until the new operating lease commences, at which time the accounting treatment is the same as if the operating lease started immediately. Renewals and extensions usually commence at the end of the original sales-type or direct financing lease. Under these circumstances there should not be any remaining investment to eliminate from the books and the leased property is not recorded as an asset.

Termination of a Lease-Lessor

A termination of a lease is recognized in the income of the period by the following entries:

1. The remaining net investment is eliminated from the accounts.
2. The leased property is recorded as an asset using the lower of the (a) original cost, (b) present fair value, or (c) present carrying amount.

The resulting net adjustment from 1 and 2 is charged to income in the period of change.

Lessor's Operating Leases

Accounting for operating leases on the books of the lessor is handled in the usual manner. The cost of the property leased to the lessee is included in the lessor's property, plant, and equipment on the balance sheet and depreciated under the normal depreciation policy of the lessor.

Rental income received by the lessor should be reported and recognized on the straight line basis or some other systematic and rational method. The lessor's income statement will normally include the expenses of the leased property (unless it is a net lease), such as depreciation, maintenance, taxes, insurance, and other related items. However, if material, *initial direct costs* (those directly related to the negotiation and consummation of the lease) should be deferred and allocated to income over the lease term.

Lease Sale or Assignment to Third Parties

Sales or assignment of a sales-type or a direct financing lease does not negate the original accounting treatment. Profit or loss is recognized at the time of a sale or assignment, unless the seller assumes *substantial risks.*

Frequently, a sale of property *subject to an operating lease* is complicated by some type of indemnification agreement by the seller. The seller may guarantee that the property will remain leased or may agree to reacquire the property if the tenant does not pay the specified rent. These types of transactions cannot be accounted for as a sale because of the substantial risk assumed by the seller. The principle of *substance over form* must be applied to such situations and treated accordingly. Examples of *substantial risk* on the part of the seller are:

1. agreements to reacquire the property or lease
2. agreements to substitute another existing lease
3. agreements to use "best efforts" to secure a replacement buyer or lessee

Examples of *nonsubstantial risk* situations on the part of the seller are:

1. execution of a remarketing agreement that includes a fee for the seller
2. when the seller does not give priority to the releasing or other disposition of the property owned by a third party

If a sale to a third party purchaser is not recorded as a sale because of the substantial risk factor assumed by the seller, it should be accounted for as a *borrowing*. The proceeds from the "sale" are recorded as an obligation on the books of the seller. Rental payments made by the lessee under the operating lease are recorded as revenue to the seller, even if the rentals are paid to the third party. Each rental payment shall consist of imputed interest, and the balance as a reduction of the obligation. Any sale or assignment of lease payments under an operating lease, by the lessor, shall be accounted for as borrowings.

Lessor's Financial Statement Disclosure

The following financial statement disclosure is required by lessors whose *significant business activity is leasing* (not including "leveraged" leasing):

For sales-type and direct financing leases:

1. a schedule of the components of the *net investment* in leases, as of each balance sheet date, which shall include:
   a. future minimum lease payments
   b. executory costs
   c. allowance for uncollectibles
   d. unguaranteed residual values accruing to the benefit of the lessor
   e. unearned income
   f. contingent rentals
   g. amount of unearned income used to offset initial direct costs for direct financing leases
2. a schedule of the minimum lease payments, in total and for the next five years

For operating leases:

1. a schedule of the investment in property on operating leases, and property held for lease, by major categories, less accumulated depreciation, as at each balance sheet presented
2. a schedule of minimum future rentals on noncancelable operating leases, in total and for the next five years
3. the amount of contingent rentals included in each income statement presented

Leases

General disclosure for leases of lessors: a general description of the lessor's leasing arrangements.

LESSOR'S FINANCIAL STATEMENT DISCLOSURE

Lessor's Balance Sheet

	December 31	
Assets	1978	1977
Current assets:		
Net investment in sales-type and direct-financing leases (Note___)	$ XXX,XXX	$ XXX,XXX
Noncurrent assets:		
Net investment in sales-type and direct-financing leases (Note___)	$ XX,XXX	$ XX,XXX
Property on operating leases and property held for leases (net of accumulated depreciation of $X,XXX and $XX,XXX for 1978 and 1977, respectively) (Note___)	$ XX,XXX	$ XX,XXX

Schedule of Components—Net Investment in Leases
Sales-type and Direct Financing Leases

	1978	1977
Total minimum lease payments receivable	$X,XXX,XXX	$X,XXX,XXX
Less: Estimated executory costs, including profit thereon	XX,XXX	XX,XXX
Minimum lease payments	$X,XXX,XXX	$X,XXX,XXX
Less: Allowance for uncollectibles	XXX,XXX	XXX,XXX
Net minimum lease payments receivable	$X,XXX,XXX	$X,XXX,XXX
Add: Estimated unguaranteed residual values of leased properties	XXX,XXX	XXX,XXX
	$X,XXX,XXX	$X,XXX,XXX
Less: Unearned income	XXX,XXX	XXX,XXX
Net investment in sales-type and direct-financing leases	$X,XXX,XXX	$X,XXX,XXX

A footnote should be included for contingent rentals.

Lessor's Schedule of Minimum Lease Payments

Year Ended
December 31

1979	$ XXX,XXX
1980	XXX,XXX
1981	XXX,XXX
1982	X,XXX,XXX
1983	XXX,XXX
After 1983	X,XXX,XXX
Total minimum lease payments receivable	$X,XXX,XXX

Lessor's Schedule of Investment in Property on Operating Leases and Property Held for Lease (by Major Class Categories)

Data-processing equipment	$X,XXX,XXX
Transportation equipment	XXX,XXX
Construction equipment	XXX,XXX
Other	XX,XXX
Total	$X,XXX,XXX
Less: Accumulated depreciation	XXX,XXX
Net investment	$X,XXX,XXX

Lessor's Schedule of Minimum Future Rentals on Noncancelable Operating Leases

Year Ended
December 31

1979	$ XXX,XXX
1980	XXX,XXX
1981	XXX,XXX
1982	XXX,XXX
1983	XX,XXX
After 1983	XXX,XXX
Total minimum future rentals	$X,XXX,XXX

A footnote should be included for contingent rentals.

Leases Involving Real Estate

Leases involving real estate are divided into leases involving:

1. land only
2. land and building(s)
3. land, building(s), and equipment
4. only part of a building(s)

Review of classification of leases by lessees A review of the classifications of leases by lessees is necessary because accounting for leases involving real estate depends primarily on the criteria for classifying leases.

If one or more of the following four criteria are present at the inception of a lease, it should be classified as a capital lease by the lessee:

I. Ownership of the property is transferred to the lessee by the end of the lease term.

II. The lease contains a bargain purchase option.

III. The lease term, at inception, is substantially (75% or more) equal to the estimated economic life of the leased property, including earlier years of use. [*Exception:* This particular criterion cannot be used for a lease that begins within the last 25% of the original estimated economic life of the leased property]

IV. The present value of the minimum lease payments at the beginning of the lease term, excluding executory costs and profits thereon to be paid by the lessor, is 90% or more of the fair value of the property at the inception of the lease, less any investment tax credit retained by the lessor and expected to be realized by him. [*Exception:* This particular criterion cannot be used for a lease that begins within the last 25% of the original estimated economic life of the leased property.]

Leases involving land only A lessee shall account for a lease involving land only as a capital lease if either criterion I (ownership of property is transferred) or II (lease contains a bargain purchase option) is met. All other leases involving land only shall be classified as operating leases by the lessee.

A lessor shall account for a lease involving land only as a sales-type or a direct financing lease, whichever is appropriate, if either criterion I (ownership of property is transferred), or II (lease contains a bargain purchase option) is met; and (a) the collection of the minimum lease payments are reasonably predictable and (b) no important uncertainties exist regarding costs yet to be incurred by the lessor under the lease. All other leases involving land only shall be classified as operating leases by the lessor.

Leases involving land and building(s) Leases involving land and building(s) may be broken down into three categories, as follows:

1. leases that meet criterion I or II.
2. leases in which the fair value of the land is less than 25% of the total fair value
3. leases in which the fair value of the land is 25% or more of the total fair value

1. Leases that meet either criterion I (ownership of the property is transferred) or II (lease contains a bargain purchase option) are accounted for as follows:

Lessee The present value of the minimum lease payments, less executory costs and profits thereon (to be paid by the lessor), is allocated between the land and building(s) in proportion to their fair value at the inception of the lease. The present value assigned to the building(s) is amortized in accordance with the lessee's normal depreciation policy.

Lessor A lessor must additionally meet the criteria that (a) the collection of the minimum lease payments is reasonably predictable and (b) no important uncertainties exist regarding costs yet to be incurred by the lessor under the lease. If the additional criteria are met, a lessor shall account for a lease involving land and building(s) as a sales-type or a direct financing lease, whichever is appropriate. If the additional criteria are not met, the lessor shall account for the lease as an operating lease.

2. Fair value of the land is less than 25% of the total fair value at the inception of the lease.

(When applying criterion III (lease term substantially–75% or more–equal to the economic life) and IV (present value of the minimum lease payments–excluding executory costs–is 90% or

Leases

more of the fair value at inception), both the lessee and lessor shall consider the land and building(s) as a single unit, and the estimated economic life of the building(s) shall be the estimated economic life of the single unit.

Lessee The land and building(s) are accounted for as a single capitalized asset and amortized in accordance with the lessee's normal depreciation policy over the lease term if either criterion III (lease term is substantially–75% or more–equal to the economic life) or IV (present value of the minimum lease payments–excluding executory costs–is 90% or more of the fair value at inception) is met.

Lessor A lessor must additionally meet the criteria that (a) the collection of the minimum lease payments is reasonably predictable and (b) no important uncertainties exist regarding costs yet to be incurred by the lessor under the lease. If the additional criteria are met, the lessor accounts for the land and building(s) as a single capitalized asset, either as a sales-type or a direct financing lease, whichever is appropriate.

3. Fair value of the land is more than 25% of the total fair value at the inception of the lease.

When applying criteria III (*lease term* substantially–75% or more–equal to the economic life) and IV (present value of the minimum lease payments–excluding executory costs–is 90% or more of the fair value at inception), both the lessee and lessor shall consider the land and building(s) separately. To determine the separate values for the land and building(s), the lessee's incremental borrowing rate is applied to the fair value of the land to determine the annual minimum lease payments applicable to the land. The balance of the minimum lease payments remaining shall be attributed to the building(s).

Lessee The building(s) portion is accounted for as a capital lease and amortized in accordance with the lessee's normal depreciation policy over the lease term if the building(s) portion meets either criterion III (lease term substantially–75% or more–equal to the economic life) or IV (present value of the minimum lease payments–excluding executory costs–is 90% or more of the fair value at inception) is met.

The land portion shall be accounted for separately as an operating lease.

Lessor A lessor must additionally meet the criteria that (a) the collection of the *minimum lease payments* is reasonably predictable and (b) no important uncertainties exist regarding costs yet to be incurred by the lessor under the lease. If the additional criteria are met, the lessor accounts for the building(s) portion as a sales-type or a direct financing lease, whichever is appropriate.

The land portion shall be accounted for separately as an operating lease.

All other leases involving land and building(s) shall be accounted for as operating leases.

Leases involving land, building(s), and equipment Equipment values, if material, should not be commingled with real estate values in leases. The minimum lease payments attributed to the equipment shall, if necessary, be appropriately estimated and separately stated. The criteria for the classification of leases should be separately applied to the equipment to determine proper accountability.

Leases involving only part of a building(s) If the cost and fair value of a lease involving only part of a building(s) can be objectively determined, the lease classification and accountability shall be the same for any other land and building(s) lease. An independent appraisal of the leased property or replacement cost can be made as a basis for the objective determination of fair value (FASB Interpretation-24). In the event that cost and fair value cannot be objectively determined, leases involving only part of a building(s) should be classified and accounted for, as follows:

Lessee The lessee shall classify the lease only in accordance with criterion III, as follows: "The lease term, at inception, is substantially (75% or more) equal to the estimated economic life of the leased property, including earlier years of use." [*Exception:* This particular criterion cannot be used for a lease that begins within the last 25% of the original estimated economic life of the leased property.]

In applying the above criterion, the estimated economic life of the building(s) in which the leased premises are located shall be used.

In the event the above criterion is met, the leased property is capitalized as a single unit and amortized in accordance with the lessee's normal depreciation policy over the lease term. In all other cases, the lease shall be classified as an operating lease.

Leases

Lessor In all cases where the cost and fair value are indeterminable, the lessor shall account for the lease as an operating lease.

Leases Involving Government Units

Leases with government units usually lack fair values, have indeterminable economic lives, and cannot provide for transfer of ownership. These special provisions usually prevent their classification as any other than operating leases.

However, leases involving government units are subject to the same criteria as any other lease unless all of the following conditions exist and in that event they are classified as operating leases.

1. A government unit or authority owns the leased property.
2. The leased property is operated by or on behalf of a government unit or authority and is part of a larger facility such as an airport.
3. The leased property cannot be moved to another location because it is a permanent structure or part of a permanent structure.
4. Any government unit or authority can terminate the lease agreement at any time under the terms of the lease agreement, existing statutes, or regulations.
5. Ownership is not transferred to the lessee and the lessee cannot purchase the leased property.
6. Equivalent property in the same area as the leased property cannot be purchased or leased from anyone else.

Related Party Leases

Except in cases where the substance of a lease transaction clearly indicates that the terms and conditions have been significantly influenced by the related parties, these types of leases are classified and accounted for as if the parties were unrelated.

It is important to note that generally a subsidiary whose principal business activity is leasing property to its parent must be consolidated with the parent's financial statements.

Sale-Leaseback Transactions

With the promulgation of FASB-28, Accounting for Sales with Leasebacks, these types of transaction have become quite difficult to classify and record. The following terminology must be understood in order to comprehend the promulgated GAAP:

Sale-leaseback   an owner sells property and then leases back part or all of the same property. Such an owner is referred to as the seller-lessee.

Purchaser-lessor   the party who purchases the property and leases back the same property to the seller-lessee.

Profit or loss on the sale   is the amount which would have been recognized on the sale by the seller-lessee assuming there was no leaseback.

"Substantially all" or "minor"   Under the terms of the lease, the seller-lessee may have a "minor" portion or "substantially all" of the rights to the remaining use of the property. This is determined by the present value of a total "reasonable rental" for the rights to the remaining use of the property retained by the seller-lessee. The seller-lessee has transferred "substantially all" of the rights to the remaining use of the property to the purchaser-lessor if the present value of the total "reasonable rental" under the terms of the lease is 10% or less than the fair value of the property sold at the inception of the lease. The seller-lessee has transferred a "minor" portion of the remaining rights to the purchaser-lessor if the terms of the leaseback include the entire property sold and qualifies as a capital lease under FASB-13.

> ***OBSERVATION:*** *The promulgated GAAP (FASB-28) does not define "reasonable rental" or "fair value". However, FASB-13 defines "fair value" as the price the leased property could be sold for between unrelated parties in an arm's-length transaction. FASB-13 defines "fair rental" as the rental rate for similar property under similar lease terms and conditions.*

Accounting for Sale-Leasebacks

When an owner sells property and then leases the same property back again, the transaction is called a sale-leaseback. If the lease meets the criteria for capitalization, the purchaser-lessor records the acquisition of the property as a purchase and the lease as a direct financing lease. If the lease does not meet the criteria for capitalization, the acquisition of the property is recorded as a purchase and the lease as an operating lease.

Accounting for the sale-leaseback by the seller-lessee is determined by the degree of rights in the remaining use of the property the seller-lessee retains, as follows:

a. Substantially all
b. Minor
c. More than minor but less than substantially all

Substantially all If the entire property sold is leased back and the seller-lessee retains the rights to "substantially all" of the remaining use in the property, the seller-lessee records the lease as a capital lease provided it meets the criteria for capitalization under FASB-13. If the lease does not meet the criteria for capitalization, the seller-lessee records it as an operating lease. Whether the lease is recorded as a capital lease or an operating lease, any profit or loss (see definition) on the sale by the seller-lessee must be deferred and amortized as follows:

Capital lease The deferred profit or loss on the sale is amortized in proportion to the amortization of the leased property.

Operating lease The deferred profit or loss on the sale is amortized in proportion to the gross rental charged to expense over the lease term.

Whether a capital lease or an operating lease, if the leased asset is land only, the amortization of the deferred profit or loss on the sale must be on a straight-line basis over the lease term.

Minor If the seller-lessee retains the rights to a "minor" portion of the remaining use in the property, the seller-lessee shall account for the sale and leaseback as two independent transactions based on their separate terms. However, the lease must provide for a reasonable amount of rent, considering prevailing market conditions at the inception of the lease. The seller-lessee must increase or decrease the profit or loss on the sale by an amount, if any, which brings the total rental for the leased property to a reasonable amount. Any amount created by this adjustment shall be amortized, as follows:

Capital lease the deferred or accrued amount is amortized in proportion to the amortization of the leased property.

Operating lease the deferred or accrued amount is amortized in proportion to the gross rental charged to expense over the lease term.

Whether a capital lease or an operating lease, if the lease asset is land only, the amortization of the deferred or accrued amount must be on a straight-line basis over the lease term.

> ***OBSERVATION:*** *If the total rental on the lease is less than a reasonable amount compared to prevailing market conditions at the inception of the lease, a profit on the sale would have to be increased and a loss on the sale would have to be decreased.*
>
> *In the case of an operating lease, the journal entry would be a debit to prepaid rent and a credit to profit or loss. The prepaid rent is amortized in an amount which increases the periodic rental expense over the lease term to a reasonable amount. Conversely, if the total rental on the lease is more than a reasonable amount compared to prevailing market conditions at the inception of the lease, a profit on the sale would have to be decreased and a loss on the sale would have to be increased. The journal entry would be a debit to profit or loss and a credit to deferred rent. The deferred rent is amortized in an amount which decreases the periodic rental expense over the lease term to a reasonable amount.*
>
> *In the case of a capital lease, the debit to prepaid rent or the credit to deferred rent is not made. Instead, the debit or credit increases or decreases the amount which is recorded for the leased property. The leased property is then amortized in the usual manner.*

More than minor but less than substantially all If the seller-lessee retains the rights to more than a minor but less than substantially all of the remaining use in the property, the seller-lessee shall recognize any excess profit (not losses) determined at the date of sale, as follows:

Capital lease The excess profit is any amount which exceeds the recorded amount of the leased asset as determined under FASB-13 (the lesser of the fair value of the leased property or the present value of the minimum lease payments).

Operating lease The excess profit is any amount which exceeds the present value of the minimum lease payments over the term of the lease. The seller-lessee shall use its incremental borrowing rate or, if known and lower, the implicit rate of interest in the lease to compute the present value of the minimum lease payments.

> **OBSERVATION:** There is an apparent mistake in the promulgated GAAP (FASB-28). Section 3b. provides that "The seller-lessee . . . and realizes a profit on the sale in excess of (i) the present value of the minimum lease payments over the lease term, if the leaseback is classified as an operating lease, or (ii) the recorded amount of the leased asset, if the leaseback is classified as a capital lease." This does not mean that the profit must be more than (i) or (ii), but rather the profit is, in fact, that amount which exceeds (i) or (ii), which is the interpretation used in the restatement herein.

Accounting for Certain Losses on Sale-Leasebacks

Under any circumstances, if the fair value of the property at the time of the sale-leaseback is less than its undepreciated cost, the seller-lessee shall recognize immediately a loss in an amount not to exceed the difference between the fair value and the undepreciated cost of the property sold.

Subleases and Similar Transactions

Unless the original lease agreement is replaced by a new agreement, the original lessor shall continue to account for the lease as before.

A termination of a lease is recognized by a lessor in the income of the period in which termination occurs, by the following entries:

1. The remaining net investment is eliminated from the accounts.
2. The leased property is recorded as an asset using the lower of the (a) original cost, (b) present value at termination, or (c) present carrying amount at termination.

If an original lessee is relieved of the primary obligation under an original lease, the transaction should be accounted for by the lessee, as follows:

Capital leases Termination of the lease occurs and gain or loss is recognized in income of the period. A loss contingency should also be provided for if the original lessee remains secondarily liable on the lease.

Operating leases A loss contingency should be provided for if the original lessee remains secondarily liable on the lease.

When a lessee subleases leased property, the original lease continues and a simultaneous new lease is created in which the lessee becomes a sublessor. The results are that the original lessee is both a lessee in the original lease and at the same time, a sublessor in the new lease. In situations like this the original lease continues to be accounted for as if nothing happened, but the new lease must be classified and accounted for separately.

If an original lessee is not relieved of the primary obligation under an original lease, the transaction should be accounted for by the original lessee-sublessor, as follows:

1. If the criterion for the original lease was I (ownership of the property is transferred before the end of the lease term) or II (lease contains a bargain purchase option), the new lease shall be classified based on its own new criteria. If the new lease qualifies for capitalization, it shall be accounted for as a sales-type or a direct financing lease, whichever is appropriate, and the unamortized balance of the asset under the original lease shall be treated as the cost of the leased property to the sublessor (original lessee).

    In the event that the new lease does not qualify for capitalization, it shall be treated as an operating lease. [*Note:* As stated earlier, the original lease continues to be accounted for in the usual manner.]

2. If the criterion for the original lease was III (lease term is substantially—75% or more—equal to the estimated economic life of the leased property at the inception of the lease) or IV (present value of the minimum lease payments— excluding executory costs—is 90% or more of the fair value at inception), the new lease shall be capitalized only if it meets criterion III and (a) the collection of the minimum lease payments is reasonably predictable and (b) no important uncertainties exist regarding costs yet to be incurred by the lessor under the lease. If the new lease meets the criteria above, it is accounted for as a direct financing lease, with the

unamortized balance of the asset under the original lease as the cost of the leased property.

If the new lease does not meet the specific conditions above, it is accounted for as an operating lease. [*Note:* As stated earlier, the original lease continues to be accounted for in the usual manner.]

In any event, if the original lease is an operating lease, the sublease is accounted for as an operating lease also.

Even though the sublessor (original lessee) remains primarily obligated under an original lease, a loss may be recognized on a sublease (FASB Interpretation-27). The loss is measured as the difference between the unamortized cost of the leased property (net carrying amount) and the present value of the minimum lease payments which will be received under the terms of the sublease.

> **OBSERVATION:** *FASB Interpretation-27 is silent as to recognition of any gain on subleases in which the sublessor (original lessee) remains primarily obligated under the original lease. However, FASB-13, paragraph 39, implies that both gain or loss may be recognized on sales-type and direct financing leases.*

FASB Interpretation-27 also reaffirms that estimated costs and expenses directly associated with a decision to dispose of a business segment should include future rental payments on long-term leases less any future rentals to be received from subleases of the same properties (ARB-30). The gain or loss is measured as the difference between the unamortized cost of the leased property (net carrying amount) and the present value of the minimum lease payments which will be received under the terms of the sublease. The gain or loss is included in the overall gain or loss on the disposal of the business segment.

> **OBSERVATION:** *FASB Interpretation-27 is not clear on its coverage of subleases which are classified as operating leases. There is a strong argument that gain or loss on an operating sublease be included as part of the overall gain or loss on disposal of a business segment. APB-30 specifically states that all costs and expenses which are directly associated to the decision to dispose of a business segment be*

included in the overall gain or loss on the disposal. If a business segment has a long-term operating lease which is subleased and classified as an operating lease as part of the overall disposal of the segment, then any gain or loss would obviously be directly associated with management's decision to dispose of the segment. The gain or loss would be measured as the difference between the present value of the future rental payments which must be paid on the original lease and the present value of the future rental receipts which will be collected on the operating sublease. The journal entry to record a loss would be a debit to the gain or loss account for disposal of the business segment and a credit to a deferred account. The deferred credit account would be amortized each year in an amount which would make up the difference between the payment made on the original lease and the rental collected on the operating sublease.

Accounting and Reporting for Leverage Leases

A lessee shall classify and account for "leveraged" leases in the same manner as "nonleveraged" leases. *Only a lessor* must classify and account for leveraged leases in the specific manner prescribed herein.

GAAP define a leveraged lease as a lease having all the following characteristics:

1. A leveraged lease meets the definition of a direct financing lease, as follows:
   A direct financing lease is a lease that does not result in a manufacturer's or dealer's profit or loss (this is because the fair value of the leased property at the inception of the lease is the same as the cost or carrying amount), but does transfer substantially all the benefits and risks inherent in the ownership of the lease property to the lessee; in addition:
   a. The minimum lease payments are reasonably predictable of collecting.
   b. No important uncertainties exist regarding costs to be incurred by the lessor under the terms of the lease.
2. It involves at least three parties: (a) a lessee, (b) a lessor, and (c) a long-term creditor. [*Note:* The lessor is sometimes referred to as the "equity participant."]

3. The financing is sufficient to provide the lessor with substantial leverage in the transaction and is nonrecourse as to the general credit of the lessor.
4. Once the lessor's net investment is completed, it declines in the early years and rises in later years before being liquidated. These fluctuations in the lessor's net investment can occur more than once in the lease term.

If the investment tax credit is accounted for as provided herein and a lease meets the preceding definition, it shall be classified and accounted for as a leverage lease.

The initial and continuing investment of the lessor in a leveraged lease shall be recorded "net" of the nonrecourse debt, as follows:

1. rentals receivable, net of that portion applicable to principal and interest on the nonrecourse debt
2. a receivable for the amount of the investment tax credit to be realized on the transaction
3. the estimated residual value of the leased property
4. unearned and deferred income consisting of (a) the estimated pretax lease income or loss, after deducting initial direct costs of negotiating and consummating the lease transaction, that remains to be allocated to income over the lease term, and (b) the investment tax credit that remains to be allocated to income over the lease term

The investment in a leveraged lease, less applicable deferred taxes, shall represent the lessor's net investment for purposes of computing periodic net income from the leveraged lease. The following method is used to compute periodic net income:

1. A projected cash flow analysis is prepared for the lease term.
2. The rate of return on net investment in the years it is positive is computed (usually by trial and error).
3. Every year the net investment is increased or decreased by the difference between the net cash flow and the amount of income recognized, if any.

The amount of net income that is recognized each year consists of:

1. pretax lease income or loss (allocated from the unearned income portion of the net investment)
2. investment tax credit (allocated from the deferred income portion of the net investment)
3. the tax effect of the pretax lease income or loss recognized (which is reflected in tax expense for the year)

Any tax effect on the difference between pretax accounting income or loss and taxable income or loss is charged or credited to deferred taxes.

All the important assumptions affecting the estimated net income from the leveraged lease, including any estimated residual values, should be reviewed at least annually.

If at the inception or at any time during the lease, the projected net cash receipts over the initial or remaining lease term are less than the lessor's initial or current investment, the resulting loss shall be immediately recognized.

Upward adjustments of the estimated residual value are not permitted.

The lessor's financial statement disclosure for leveraged leases shall include the amount of deferred taxes separately stated.

When leveraged leasing is a significant part of the lessor's business activity, a schedule of the components of the net investment in leveraged leases shall be fully disclosed in the footnotes to the financial statements.

Business Combinations

A business combination, in itself, does not affect the classification of a lease. However, if as a result of a business combination, a lease is revised or modified to the extent that under the promulgated GAAP (FASB-13) it is considered a new agreement, it should be reclassified on the basis of its revision or modification.

Ordinarily, under the purchase method or pooling-of-interests method of effecting a business combination, a lease retains its previous classification under FASB-13 and is accounted for in the same manner as it was prior to the combination.

The acquiring company in a business combination accounted for by the purchase method shall account for a leverage lease by assigning a fair value (present value, net of tax) to the net investment in a leveraged lease based on the remaining future cash flows with appropriate recognition for any future estimated tax effects. After the fair value (present value, net of tax) of the net investment is determined, it should be allocated to net rentals receivable, estimated residual value, and unearned income. Thereafter, a company should account for the leveraged lease by allocating the periodic cash flow between the net investment and the lease income.

In a business combination where an acquired lease has not been conformed to FASB-13, the acquiring company should classify such a lease to conform retroactively to FASB-13.

Comprehensive Illustration–Capital Lease

Paine Corporation leases a computer under a noncancelable five-year lease for annual rental payments of $10,000. The fair value of the computer at the inception of the lease is $36,048, and the incremental borrowing rate of Paine is 10%. There are no executory costs and no investment tax credit available. The annual rent of $10,000 is considered a fair rental as opposed to a bargain rental. The estimated economic life of the computer is 10 years.

Classification of Lease by Paine as Lessee

A review is made of the criteria involved in the provisions of the lease to determine its classification.

1. Criterion I is not met, because there is no transfer of the ownership of the lease property before the end of the lease term.
2. Criterion II is not met, because the lease does not contain a bargain purchase option.
3. Criterion III is not met, because the lease term (five years) is not equal to 75% or more of the estimated economic life (10 years) of the leased property. [*Note:* There are no other provisions affecting the lease term other than the five-year noncancelable term.]
4. Criterion IV is met, because the present value ($37,908) of the minimum lease payments, excluding executory costs and profits thereon paid by the lessor, is 90% or more of the fair value ($36,048) of the leased property. [*Note:* The present value computations are given below.]

Paine Corporation should record the transaction as a capital lease.

Accounting for the Lease by Paine

The initial recording value of the leased property, at the inception of the lease, is the lesser of the fair value of the leased property or the present value of the minimum lease payments, excluding any portion that represents executory costs and profit thereon to be paid by the lessor.

The discount rate used by the lessee to find the present value of the minimum lease payments is his incremental borrowing rate of 10%, unless the lessee has knowledge of the interest rate implicit in the lease, used by the lessor, which is lower.

The interest rate implicit in the lease is 12%, which is the discount rate that, when applied to the minimum lease payments of $10,000 per year for five years, results in a present value equal to the fair value of the leased property at the inception of the lease.

This means that Paine must use its incremental borrowing rate of 10% to discount the minimum lease payments to their present value, which is $37,908.

The initial recording value of the leased property is the lesser of the fair value of the leased property at inception or the present value of the minimum lease payments using the lower interest rate. Therefore, the $36,048 fair value is less than the minimum lease payments of $37,908 (computed by using the lower incremental borrowing rate) and is used to initially record the lease, as follows:

Lease property, capital leases	$36,048	
Obligations, capital leases		$36,048

[*Note:* The present value of the minimum lease payments using the interest rate implicit in the lease will always be the same as the fair value of the property at the inception of the lease.)

Amortization by Lessee

The asset(s) recorded under a capital lease shall be amortized in a manner consistent with the lessee's normal depreciation policy for other owned assets. The period for amortization is either (1) the estimated economic life or (2) the lease term, depending on which criterion was used to classify the lease. If the criterion used to classify the lease as a capital lease was either criterion I (ownership of the property is transferred to the lessee by the end of the lease term) or criterion II (lease contains a bargain purchase option), the asset is amortized over its economic life. In all other cases, the asset is amortized over the lease term. Any residual value is deducted from the asset to determine the amortizable base.

Since the Paine Corporation's lease qualified under criterion IV (present value of the minimum lease payments, excluding executory costs and profit thereon paid by the lessor, is 90% or more of the fair value of the leased property), the amortization period must be over the lease term.

A schedule of amortization, interest expense, and lease obligation payments for Paine Corporation's computer lease, using the interest method, follows:

Book Value Lease Obligations Beginning of Year	Rental Payments	12% Interest on Beginning Book Value	Amortization	Book Value Lease Obligations End of Year
$36,048	$10,000	$ 4,326	$ 5,674	$30,374
30,374	10,000	3,645	6,355	24,019
24,019	10,000	2,882	7,118	16,901
16,901	10,000	2,028	7,972	8,929
8,929	10,000	1,071	8,929	—
	$50,000	$13,952	$36,048	

[*Note:* The interest rate used is 12%, which is the interest rate implicit in the lease.]

LONG-TERM CONTRACTS

Background

ARB-45 is the main source of promulgated GAAP on Long-Term Construction-type Contracts. Governmental contracts are specifically excluded from the promulgated GAAP and are discussed elsewhere in the chapter on Government Contracts.

Since the promulgated GAAP is silent on the extent of its coverage, companies in regulated industries should comply in accordance with Addendum to APB-2.

Overview

Because of the length of time involved in long-term construction contracts, the problem exists as to when income should be recognized. Two methods are generally followed to account for these long-term contracts: the completed-contract method and the percentage-of-completion method.

Completed-Contract Method

The completed-contract method recognizes income only on completion or substantial completion of the contract.

A contract is regarded as substantially complete if the remaining costs are insignificant.

Excess of accumulated costs over related billings should be reflected in the balance sheet as a current asset, and excess of accumulated billings over related costs should usually be reflected as a current liability. In the case of more than one contract, the accumulated costs or liabilities should be separately stated on the balance sheet. The preferred terminology for the balance sheet presentation should be "(Costs) (Billings) of uncompleted contracts in excess of related (billings) (costs)."

In some cases, it is preferable to allocate general and administrative expenses to contract costs as opposed to period income. In years when no contracts are completed, a better matching of costs and revenues is achieved by carrying general expense as a charge to the contract. If a contractor has many jobs, however, it is more appropriate to charge these expenses to current periods.

In all cases, although income is not recognized until completion of the contract, a provision for an expected loss should be recognized when it becomes evident that a loss on the contract is apparent.

The primary advantage of the completed-contract method is that it is based on final results rather than on estimates. The primary disadvantage of the completed-contract method is that it does not reflect current performances when the period of the contract extends over more than one accounting period.

Accounting for the Completed-Contract Method

The following are important points to remember in accounting for contracts under the completed-contract method:

1. Charge applicable overhead and direct costs to a construction in progress account (an asset).
2. Credit billing and/or cash received to advances on construction in progress account (a liability).
3. At completion of the contract, gross profit or loss is recognized as follows:

    Contract price − total costs = gross profit or loss

4. At interim balance sheet dates, the excess of either the construction in progress account or the advances account over the other is classified as a current asset or a current liability. It is a *current* asset or a *current* liability because of the *normal operating cycle concept.*
5. An expected loss on the total contract is discovered by:
    a. adding estimated costs to complete to the recorded costs to date to arrive at total contract costs.
    b. adding to advances any additional revenue expected to arrive at total contract revenue.
    c. subtracting b from a to arrive at total estimated loss on contract.

Losses should be recognized in full in the year they are discovered.

Percentage-of-Completion Method

Revenues are generally recognized when (1) the earning process is complete or virtually complete and (2) an exchange has taken place.

Accounting for long-term construction contracts on the

percentage-of-completion method is an exception to the basic realization principle. This exception is based on the evidence that the ultimate proceeds are available and the consensus that a better measure of periodic income results (matching-of-revenue-and-cost principle).

The principal advantages of the percentage-of-completion method are the reflection of the status of the uncompleted contracts and the periodic recognition of income currently rather than irregularly as contracts are completed.

The principal disadvantage of the percentage-of-completion method is the necessity of relying on estimates of the ultimate costs.

The percentage-of-completion method recognizes income as work progresses on the contract.

The recommended method for recognizing income is to determine the percentage of estimated total income either (1) that incurred costs to date bear to total estimated costs based on the most recent costs information or (2) that may be indicated by such other measure of progress toward completion appropriate to the work performed.

During the early stages of a contract, all or a portion of items such as material and subcontract costs may be excluded if it appears that the results would produce a more meaningful allocation of periodic income.

When current estimates of the total contract costs indicate a loss, a provision for the loss on the entire contract should be made. However, when a loss is indicated on a total contract that is part of a related group of contracts, the group may be treated as a unit in determining the necessity of providing for losses.

Income to be recognized under the percentage-of-completion method at various stages should not ordinarily be measured by interim billings.

Accounting for the Percentage-of-Completion Method

The following are important points to remember in accounting for contracts under the percentage-of-completion method:

1. Journal entries and interim balance sheet treatment are the same as the completed-contract method *except* that the amount of estimated gross profit earned in each period is recorded by charging the construction in progress account and crediting realized gross profit.

Long-Term Contracts

2. Gross profit or loss is recognized in each period by the following formula:

$$\frac{\text{Total cost to date}}{\text{estimated total cost}} \times \text{total estimated gross profit or loss} - \text{gross profit recognized to date} = \text{realized gross profit}$$

3. An estimated loss on the total contract is recognized immediately in the year it is discovered. However, any previous gross profit or loss reported in prior years must be deducted from the total estimated loss.

Choice of Method

The percentage-of-completion method is preferred when the estimated cost to complete and the extent of construction progress are reasonably determinable. When estimates are unreliable, the completed-contract method should be used.

Disclosure

Generally, long-term construction-type contracts require no special disclosure, since they are, in fact, the nature of the contractor's business. However, unusual extraordinary commitments should be fully disclosed in the financial statements or footnotes thereto.

Comprehensive Illustration

The following example demonstrates the accounting involved in both the completed-contract and percentage-of-completion methods:

The following data pertain to a $2,000,000 long-term construction contract:

	1975	1976	1977
Costs incurred during the year	$ 500,000	$700,000	$ 300,000
Year-end estimated costs to complete	$1,000,000	$300,000	—
Billing during the year	$ 400,000	$700,000	$ 900,000
Collections during the year	$ 200,000	$500,000	$1,200,000

Long-Term Contracts

The journal entries for both the completed-contract method and the percentage-of-completion method for the three years are as follows:

1975	Completed Contract		% of Completion	
Construction in progress	$ 500,000		$ 500,000	
Cash or liability		$ 500,000		$ 500,000
Accounts receivable	$ 400,000		$ 400,000	
Advance billings		$ 400,000		$ 400,000
Cash	$ 200,000		$ 200,000	
Accounts receivable		$ 200,000		$ 200,000
Construction in progress	no entry		$ 166,667	
Realized gross profit (P&L)				$ 166,667

1976				
Construction in progress	$ 700,000		$ 700,000	
Cash or liability		$ 700,000		$ 700,000
Accounts receivable	$ 700,000		$ 700,000	
Advance billings		$ 700,000		$ 700,000
Cash	$ 500,000		$ 500,000	
Accounts receivable		$ 500,000		$ 500,000
Construction in progress	no entry		$ 233,333	
Realized gross profit (P&L)				$ 233,333

1977				
Construction in progress	$ 300,000		$ 300,000	
Cash or liability		$ 300,000		$ 300,000
Accounts receivable	$ 900,000		$ 900,000	
Advance billings		$ 900,000		$ 900,000
Cash	$1,200,000		$1,200,000	
Accounts receivable		$1,200,000		$1,200,000
Construction in progress	no entry		$ 100,000	
Realized gross profit (P&L)				$ 100,000
Advance billings	$2,000,000		$2,000,000	
Cost of construction		$1,500,000		$2,000,000
Realized gross profit (P&L)		$ 500,000		—

Long-Term Contracts

Computation of Realized Gross Profit

1975

$$\frac{\$\ 500{,}000}{\$1{,}500{,}000} \times \$500{,}000 - 0 = \$166{,}667$$

1976

$$\frac{\$1{,}200{,}000}{\$1{,}500{,}000} \times \$500{,}000 - \$166{,}667 = \$233{,}333$$

1977

$$\frac{\$1{,}500{,}000}{\$1{,}500{,}000} \times \$500{,}000 - \$400{,}000 = \$100{,}000$$

Total gross profit $\underline{\$500{,}000}$

MARKETABLE SECURITIES

Background

Accounting for certain marketable securities is covered by FASB-12 and five subsequent FASB Interpretations, as follows:

    10–Personal Financial Statements
    11–Changes in Market Value After Balance Sheet Date
    12–Accounting for Previously Established Allowance Accounts
    13–Consolidations Involving Different Balance Sheet Dates
    16–Clarification of Definitions and Accounting for Marketable Equity Securities That Become Nonmarketable

The procedures enumerated herein apply to all companies, including mutual savings banks, that do not have specialized accounting practices in accounting for marketable securities. In addition, some of the promulgated GAAP apply to those companies in industries that do have specialized accounting practices in accounting for marketable securities.

Nonprofit organizations, mutual life insurance companies, and employee benefit plans are specifically excluded from complying with the promulgated GAAP. Nonmarketable securities are not covered and are completely excluded.

Investments accounted for by the equity method are generally not covered by FASB-12.

Personal financial statements prepared in conformity with GAAP must comply with FASB-12 (FASB Interpretation-10).

Overview

The promulgated GAAP (FASB-12) differentiates between those industries having specialized accounting practices with respect to marketable equity securities and those which have no specialized practices.

An equity security is defined as any instrument that represents an ownership share or the right to acquire or sell an ownership share at a determinable price. This includes stock options, warrants, rights, puts, calls, and common, preferred, and other forms of capital stock. Preferred stock that is redeemable at the option of the owner or must be redeemed by the issuer is specifically excluded from the definition of an equity security for purposes of the promulgated GAAP, as are treasury stock and convertible bonds.

Realized gain or loss-the difference between the net proceeds from the sale of a marketable security and its cost.

Net unrealized gain or loss-the difference between market value and the cost of a marketable security, which may be computed for one or more securities, or the aggregate of an entire securities portfolio.

Marketability

In order for a security to be classified as a marketable security, it must be marketable. Marketability is evidenced by whether a security can be readily bought or sold. A current *bid* and *ask* price is evidence of marketability for both over-the-counter stocks and stocks traded on a national exchange, except that over-the-counter quotations issued by the National Quotations Bureau, Inc., may not be used unless three quotations are available.

The determination of marketability is made as of the balance sheet date.

Marketability of equity securities traded on foreign markets is determined in the same way, provided the foreign market's trading volume and scope of activities are comparable to a U.S. counterpart.

Restricted or legend stock is not considered marketable unless it can qualify for sale within one year and is marketable as defined herein. Market prices for unrestricted shares of the same class of stock that is restricted can be used in determining marketability.

A temporary lack of a market (no trades or quotations) at the balance sheet date does not render an equity security nonmarketable, if a market closely precedes the balance sheet date. Moreover, if the balance sheet date falls on a day when markets are closed, the first trading day afterward should be used. Where the lack of quotations by NASDAQ or the lack of three quotations from the National Quotations Bureau, Inc., for the over-the-counter securities is temporary, a market price may be determined by:

1. the first quotation by NASDAQ preceding the balance sheet date
2. one quotation from the National Quotations Bureau, Inc., on the balance sheet date or on the first day preceding the balance sheet date that quotations are available

Industries Not Having Specialized Practices

Any company that does not account for marketable securities by a specialized industry practice should follow these procedures for accounting for them:

Marketable Securities

1. Marketable securities should be classified into two groups: current group and noncurrent group. *In the case of unclassified balance sheets, all marketable securities are to be classified as noncurrent.*
2. The total cost and the total market for each group should be determined.
3. The carrying amount of each group is the lower of cost or market for each group.
4. Unrealized losses on the group classified as current are deducted on the income statement in determining net income for the period. The credit side of the entry is to a valuation account, as follows:

   Loss on marketable securities $X,XXX
       Allowances for losses,
       marketable securities $X,XXX

5. Unrealized losses on the group classified as noncurrent are reported separately as a reduction of stockholders' equity. The credit side of the entry is to a valuation account, as follows:

   Stockholders' equity $X,XXX
       Allowances for losses,
       noncurrent marketable
       securities $X,XXX

6. Subsequent unrealized gains or losses are reported in the same manner (the current group through the income statement and the noncurrent group through the equity section of the balance sheet). *However, under no circumstances can either the current group or the noncurrent group be valued in excess of the original cost of the group.*

   Unrealized losses on the noncurrent group of marketable securities are reported as a reduction of stockholders' equity, whereas unrealized losses on the current group are reported as a reduction of net income.

   Allowance for losses account for both groups are *contra accounts* and are deducted from the related groups for balance sheet purposes.

Reclassification Any change of a particular security from one group (current or noncurrent) to the other group (current or noncurrent) must be made at the lower of cost or market on the date of transfer. The lower of cost or market on the date of transfer becomes the new cost basis, and any gain (to the extent of prior realized or unrealized losses) or loss is accounted for as if realized, and is included in the determination of net income for the period.

Subsequent unrealized gains or losses are recorded by adjusting the allowance for losses account, except that under no circumstances can either group be valued in excess of its original cost.

Sale of a security A sale of a security from either the current or the noncurrent group results in a realized gain or loss and is reported in the income statement for the period. The cost of the security sold will usually be its original cost unless it was transferred from one group to another or a security in the noncurrent group was written down as a result of a decline in market value that was not temporary.

> ***OBSERVATION:*** *Since unrealized losses in both the current and noncurrent portfolios are based on the aggregate cost or market of the entire portfolio, the original cost of each security in each portfolio is not changed. Therefore, when a security is sold, its original cost is deducted from the portfolio and the aggregate cost, market, and related valuation account are recomputed. The only time an original cost of a security is changed is when it is transferred from one group to another or if a security in the noncurrent group is written down as a result of a decline in its market price that is other than temporary.*

An entity that is consolidated with a parent shall first determine its total cost and market for its current group and its noncurrent group before combining those aggregate totals with the parent's aggregate totals.

In the consolidation of a parent's statements with a subsidiary's statements of a different balance sheet date, the following applies (FASB Interpretation-13):

1. The parent and each subsidiary comply with the promulgated GAAP as at the date of their own balance sheet, and then the aggregate totals are combined for consolidation purposes.

2. Intervening events occurring between the balance sheet date of the subsidiary and that of the parent which materially affect the financial position or the results of operations should be adequately recognized or disclosed in the consolidated financial statements (ARB-51).

The marketable securities of an investment accounted for by the equity method shall not be combined with those of the investor. Obviously, such an entity could, itself, be subject to the provisions of the promulgated GAAP (FASB-12).

Disclosure The following disclosures for marketable securities shall be made in the financial statements or footnotes thereto by a company which does not follow specialized industry accounting practices for marketable equity securities.

1. As at the date of each balance sheet presented, the total cost and market value of marketable equity securities indicating which is the carrying value for:
   a. total marketable securities
   b. total current marketable securities
   c. total noncurrent marketable securities
2. As at the date of the most recent balance sheet presented, the total gross unrealized gains and the total gross unrealized losses for:
   a. total marketable securities
   b. total current marketable securities
   c. total noncurrent marketable securities
3. For each income statement presented:
   a. the net realized gain or loss included in net income
   b. the cost basis that was used in computing realized gain or loss
   c. the change in any valuation account that has been included in the equity section of the balance sheet, and the amount of any change that was included in the determination of net income.
   In unclassified balance sheets, the above disclosures for the current portfolio are omitted.
4. In consolidated balance sheets that contain both specialized and nonspecialized practices for accounting for marketable securities, the disclosure requirements for both should be made.

Marketable Securities

5. Significant net realized and net unrealized gains and losses on marketable securities arising after the date of the balance sheet and prior to their issuance should be disclosed.

Financial statements should not be adjusted for realized gains and losses or for changes in market values of marketable securities that occur subsequent to the balance sheet date. A special procedure is discussed later for permanent declines in the noncurrent portfolio of marketable securities.

Industries Having Specialized Practices

Investment companies, brokers, and dealers in securities, stock life and casualty insurance companies, and other industries that follow specialized practices in accounting for marketable securities must comply with the promulgated GAAP (FASB-12) to a limited extent, as follows:

1. Marketable equity securities must be carried at the lower of cost or market, except market has a broader definition in those industries which do have specialized practices for marketable securities.
2. Market value may be whatever is permitted in a specific specialized industry, such as appraised value or fair value.

   OBSERVATION: *In industries in which either the cost basis or the market basis is accepted practice, an election to use the market basis does not require justification as an accounting change (APB-20) or compliance with the related disclosure requirements (FASB-12).*

3. Marketable securities should be classified into a current group and a noncurrent group. In unclassified balance sheets, all marketable securities are to be classified as noncurrent. This provision is exactly the same as that for industries which do not have specialized practices.
4. The aggregate carrying amount of a portfolio of marketable securities is the lower of cost or market (as defined herein) at the balance sheet date. A valuation account shall be used to record any excess of aggregate cost of a portfolio over aggregate market value. This provision is exactly the same as for industries which do not have specialized practices in

Marketable Securities

accounting for marketable securities, except for the broader definition of market value.

5. Marketable securities portfolios of investments accounted for by the equity method should not be combined with portfolios of the investors.

6. Portfolios of entities that use the same specialized industry accounting practices for marketable securities should be combined into a single portfolio to determine the aggregate lower of cost or market value.

7. Specialized industry practices for reporting realized or unrealized gains or losses on marketable securities are not changed by the promulgated GAAP.

8. If a parent company recognizes realized gains or losses on marketable securities in determining net income, all subsidiaries and investments accounted for by the equity method must conform to this practice, for the purposes of consolidation. Otherwise, accepted accounting practices for marketable securities followed by a subsidiary or an investment accounted for by the equity method shall be retained in consolidating, even if such practices differ from those of the parent.

> **OBSERVATION:** *Since realized gains and losses are almost always recognized (GAAP), the only subsidiary or investment accounted for by the equity method that could logically be subject to conforming is one which follows a specialized industry practice that does not recognize realized gains or losses.*

9. When two or more subsidiaries do not follow specialized industry practices and are consolidated with a parent which does follow specialized industry practices, the current and noncurrent portfolios of such subsidiaries are kept separate from those of the parent in consolidating, for the purpose of determining carrying amounts.

Disclosures The following disclosures for marketable securities shall be made in the financial statements or footnotes thereto by a company which follows specialized industry accounting practices for marketable equity securities.

Marketable Securities

1. For companies that include unrealized gains and losses on marketable securities in the equity section of the balance sheet and not in the determination of net income:
   a. as at the most recent balance sheet the gross unrealized gains and the gross unrealized losses
   b. for each income statement presented, the changes in net unrealized gains or losses
2. In consolidated balance sheets that contain both specialized and nonspecialized practices for accounting for marketable securities, the disclosure requirements for both should be made.
3. Significant net realized and net unrealized gains and losses on marketable securities arising after the balance sheet date and prior to their issuance should be disclosed.

Financial statements should not be adjusted for realized gains and losses or changes in market values of marketable securities that occur subsequent to the balance sheet date. A special procedure is discussed later for permanent declines in the noncurrent portfolio of marketable securities.

For the purposes of companies that follow specialized accounting practices, unrealized gains and losses are those which constitute the present accepted practice in a particular industry (FASB-12).

Permanent Declines—Noncurrent Group

These provisions pertain to all companies, whether or not they follow specialized industry practices in accounting for marketable equity securities.

Adjustments to the noncurrent group are handled as a reduction of the equity section of the balance sheet and do not enter into the determination of net income for any period. Therefore, if a decline in one or more securities of the noncurrent group is other than temporary in nature, it will never be recorded as a loss on the income statement. *Thus, if a decline in one or more securities of the noncurrent group is other than temporary, the loss is recognized in the income statement for that period and not as a reduction of the equity section of the balance sheet.* The journal entry is:

Marketable Securities

Realized loss on marketable securities	$XX,XXX	
Investment in marketable securities		$XX,XXX

If a noncurrent marketable security is written down because of a loss that is other than temporary, and the security remains a part of the noncurrent group, any subsequent increase in value is not recognized in the income statement, but is used in the computation of the total unrealized gain or loss on the noncurrent group and is applied as a reduction or increase of the equity section of the balance sheet.

To determine whether a decline at the balance sheet date is permanent or temporary, reference to changes in market price or a realized gain or loss that occurs subsequent to the balance sheet date but prior to the issuance of the financial statements should be taken into consideration. However, the amount of permanent decline for an individual marketable security cannot exceed the amount that existed at the date of the balance sheet. Recoveries of a permanent decline in a marketable security after the balance sheet date and prior to the issuance of the financial statements should be taken into consideration, because such a recovery tends to indicate that all or part of the decline was, in fact, not permanent (FASB Interpretation-11).

Income Tax Effects

Tax effects of unrealized gains or losses entering into the determination of net income must be reflected in the computation of deferred income taxes. *However, the tax effects of unrealized capital losses should only be recognized when it is absolutely certain that the benefit will be realized by the offset of the capital losses against capital gains.*

Comprehensive Illustration

The following schedule of marketable securities was prepared for the LKM Corporation:

Marketable Securities

Schedule 1
MARKETABLE SECURITIES PORTFOLIO

	First Year			Second Year		
	Cost	Market	Unrealized Gain or (Loss)	Cost	Market	Unrealized Gain or (Loss)
Current Group:						
Security A	$1,000	$1,500	$ 500	$1,000	$1,500	$ 500
Security B	4,000	3,500	(500)	4,000	4,500	500
Security C	3,000	2,000	(1,000)	3,000	3,500	500
Totals	$8,000	$7,000	$(1,000)	$8,000	$9,500	$1,500
Noncurrent Group:						
Security X	$2,000	$2,500	$ 500	$2,000	$2,000	—
Security Y	1,500	1,000	(500)	1,500	2,000	500
Security Z	6,000	5,500	(500)	6,000	5,200	(800)
Totals	$9,500	$9,000	$ (500)	$9,500	$9,200	$ (300)

At the end of the first year, the carrying amount of the current group is the total market value of $7,000. Since the original cost was $8,000, the $1,000 unrealized loss must be recorded, as follows:

Loss on marketable securities	$1,000	
Allowance for losses,		
current marketable securities		$1,000

The carrying value of the noncurrent group at the end of the first year is the market value of $9,000. Since the original cost was $9,500, the unrealized loss of $500 must be recorded, as follows:

Stockholders' equity	$500	
Allowance for losses,		
noncurrent marketable securities		$500

The unrealized loss of $500 on the noncurrent marketable securities is deducted from the equity section of the balance sheet and does not enter into the determination of net income for the period.

At the end of the second year, the carrying value of the current group is $8,000 (the original cost), even though the market value is $9,500, because *the valuation may never exceed the original cost*. The journal entry to adjust the valuation account is:

Marketable Securities

    Allowance for losses,
       current marketable securities $1,000
          Gain on marketable securities $1,000

The gain on marketable securities appears in the income statement for the period.

The carrying value of the noncurrent group at the end of the second year is the market value of $9,200, which is $300 less than the original cost of $9,500. However, the net book value is $9,000 ($9,500 original cost, less allowance for losses account of $500), so the allowance for losses account must be reduced from $500 to $300, as follows:

    Allowance for losses,
       noncurrent marketable securities $200
          Stockholders' equity $200

The unrealized gain of $200 on the noncurrent group is not reported in the income statement, but reduces the allowance for losses account set up the previous year.

Reversals of previous year's writedowns are not considered as unrealized gains, but as a change in an accounting estimate of a prior realized loss. Actually, the original writedown represented a reduction in the net realizable value of the marketable securities, and any subsequent recovery reduces or eliminates the need for an allowance for losses account.

NONMONETARY TRANSACTIONS

Background

The promulgated GAAP on Nonmonetary Transactions is APB-29 and FASB Interpretation-30, Accounting for Involuntary Conversions of Nonmonetary Assets. The following types of transactions are specifically excluded from the promulgated GAAP:

1. accounting for business combinations (purchase and pooling-of-interests methods)
2. a nonmonetary transfer of assets between companies or persons under common ownership control
3. issuance of capital stock for the acquisition of nonmonetary assets or services
4. stock dividends and stock splits, issued or received

Companies in regulated industries are covered by the promulgated GAAP on Nonmonetary Transactions (see Addendum to APB-2).

Monetary Assets or Liabilities

Business transactions usually involve cash or monetary assets or liabilities that are exchanged for goods or services.

Monetary assets or liabilities are fixed in terms of currency and are usually contractual claims to fixed amounts of money. Examples of monetary assets and liabilities are cash, accounts and notes receivable, and accounts and notes payable.

Nonmonetary Assets or Liabilities

Some business transactions involve the exchange or transfer of nonmonetary assets or liabilities which are not fixed in terms of currency.

Nonmonetary assets or liabilities are those other than monetary assets or liabilities. Examples of nonmonetary assets and liabilities are inventory, investments in common stock, property, plant and equipment, liability for advance rent collected, and common stock.

Under certain circumstances, a monetary asset or liability may become nonmonetary. For example, a marketable bond being held to maturity would qualify as a monetary asset because its face amount is fixed in terms of currency. However, if the same bond was being held for speculation, it would properly be classified as a nonmonetary asset because the amount that will be received when it is sold is not determinable and therefore not fixed in terms of currency.

Exchange (Reciprocal Transfer)

An exchange is a reciprocal transfer, in which each party to the transaction receives and/or gives up assets, liabilities, or services. Exchanges can be either monetary or nonmonetary, or a combination of both. Nonmonetary exchanges are usually for the mutual convenience of two businesses. Examples include an exchange of inventory for trucking services or a trade of a starting quarterback for three linemen and a future draft choice.

Nonreciprocal Transfer

A nonreciprocal transfer is a transaction in one direction, in which one party to the transaction usually acquires either an intangible asset or nothing. Examples of nonreciprocal transfers are:

1. declaration and distribution of a dividend
2. acquisition of treasury stock
3. sale of capital stock
4. conversion of convertible debt
5. charitable contributions

Nonreciprocal Transfers to Owners

If the fair value of a nonmonetary asset is realizable by an outright sale and can be reasonably measured, prior to a nonreciprocal transfer of such nonmonetary assets to the owners, then the distribution to the owners should be accounted for at the fair value.

Fair Value

Accounting for nonmonetary assets or liabilities should be based on the fair value of the assets (or services) received or surrendered, whichever is more clearly evident. The only exceptions to this rule are (1) when fair value is undeterminable and (2) when the earning process is not completed. Fair value of nonmonetary transfers should be determined by reference to the estimated realizable value of similar assets sold for cash, quoted market prices, independent appraisals, and other available evidence. If cash could have been received in lieu of the nonmonetary asset, then the amount of cash may be a basis for the valuation of the nonmonetary asset.

Fair Value Not Determinable

Because of uncertainties, there may be situations where the fair value of a nonmonetary transfer cannot be determined with reasonable accuracy. In these cases, the only valuation available may be the recorded book value of the nonmonetary asset.

Earning Process Not Complete

A basic principle states that "When the earning process is complete and an exchange has taken place, only then is the realization of revenue recognized." There are two types of nonmonetary exchanges that do not result in completion of the earning process:

1. an exchange of property held for sale in the ordinary course of business for similar property to be held for the same purpose
2. an exchange of productive assets used in business but not held for sale for similar property to be held for the same purpose.

In these two cases the nonmonetary exchange should be based on the recorded amount (book value) of the nonmonetary asset surrendered, unless the exchange includes an amount of monetary consideration. The amount of the monetary consideration included in the nonmonetary exchange should be accounted for, as follows:

Recipient of the monetary consideration The recipient of the monetary consideration should recognize realized gain on the exchange to the extent that the monetary amount exceeds a proportionate share of the recorded amount of the asset relinquished.

If the transaction results in a loss, the entire loss on the exchange should be recognized.

Nonmonetary Transactions

Payor of the monetary consideration The payor of the monetary consideration should not recognize any gain on the exchange and should record the cost of the nonmonetary asset received at the amount of the nonmonetary asset surrendered, plus the amount of the monetary consideration paid.

If the transaction results in a loss, the entire loss on the exchange should be recognized. The formula for the recognition of gain when cash is received in a nonmonetary exchange that would not otherwise result in the completion of the earning process is as follows:

$$\frac{\text{Cash received}}{\text{cash received + fair market value of asset received}} \times \text{gain} = \text{recognized amount of gain}$$

An asset with a $6,000 cost is exchanged for $4,000 in cash and an asset with a fair value of $8,000. Both assets were held for sale in the ordinary course of business, and except for the cash the earning process would not have been completed and no gain would be recognized. Using the formula for recognition of gain the computation is:

$$\frac{\$4,000}{\$4,000 + \$8,000} \times \$6,000 = \$2,000$$

Basis of acquired asset:

Original cost	$6,000
Less: Cash received	4,000
	$2,000
Add: Recognized gain	2,000
Basis of acquired asset	$4,000

Losses are recognized in full (conservatism).

Gain or Loss

Gain or loss, when applicable, should be recognized in nonmonetary transactions. A difference in the gain or loss for tax purposes and that recognized for accounting purposes may constitute a timing difference in income tax provision.

Involuntary Conversion of Nonmonetary Assets to Monetary Assets

When a nonmonetary asset is involuntarily converted to a monetary asset, a monetary transaction results, and gain or loss must be recognized in the period of conversion (FASB Interpretation-30). The gain or loss is the difference between the carrying amount of the nonmonetary asset and the proceeds from the conversion.

Gain or loss from an involuntary conversion of a nonmonetary asset to a monetary asset should be classified as from continuing operations, extraordinary items, disposal of a segment, etc., according to the particular circumstances (APB-30). In addition, a gain or loss recognized for tax purposes in a period different from that for financial accounting purposes (books) creates a timing difference, for which interperiod tax allocation may be necessary (APB-11).

If the amount of proceeds that will be received, from the involuntary conversion of the nonmonetary asset, cannot be determined, the gain or loss shall be recognized and classified as a contingency (see chapter on Contingencies).

The involuntary conversion of a LIFO inventory layer, at an interim reporting date, does not have to be recognized if the proceeds are reinvested in replacement inventory by the end of the fiscal year (FASB Interpretation-30).

> **OBSERVATION:** *This is the same treatment afforded a temporary liquidation of a LIFO inventory layer at interim dates which is expected to be corrected by the end of the annual period (see Interim Financial Reporting).*

In the event the proceeds from an involuntary conversion of a LIFO inventory layer are not reinvested in replacement inventory by the end of the fiscal year, gain for financial accounting purposes need not be recognized providing the taxpayer does not recognize such gains for income tax reporting purposes (FASB Interpretation-30).

Examples of involuntary conversion are the total or partial destruction of property through fire or other catastrophe, theft of property, or condemnation of property by a governmental authority (eminent domain proceedings).

Disclosure

Adequate disclosure of the nature of the nonmonetary transaction, the basis of accounting for assets transferred, and gains or losses recognized should be disclosed in the financial statements for the period.

Conclusion

All nonmonetary transactions except those for which fair value is undeterminable or for which the earning process is not complete are based on the fair value of the asset surrendered or received, whichever is more clearly evident. Gain or loss is recognized on nonmonetary transactions. In the event that fair value cannot be reasonably determined, the recorded book value may be used. In exchanges where the earning process is not complete, gain is recognized to the extent "boot" is received, and losses are recognized in full.

A gain or a loss recognized for tax purposes in a period different from that for financial accounting purposes creates a timing difference, for which interperiod income tax allocation may apply (APB-11).

OIL AND GAS PRODUCING COMPANIES

Background

The promulgated GAAP on Accounting and Reporting by Oil and Gas Producing Companies is FASB-19, which superseded FASB-9, and was to be effective for fiscal years beginning after December 15, 1978. Because the SEC rejected the successful efforts accounting method embodied in FASB-19 for a current value method, FASB-19 was subsequently amended in February 1979 by FASB-25 (see Effects of FASB-25, below). Nonpromulgated GAAP, in the form of industry practices, exists for alternative methods (full-costing, current-value, and discovery-value accounting methods).

The promulgated GAAP (FASB-19) covers only producing activities and specifically excludes the transporting, refining, and marketing of oil and/or gas. In addition, the promulgated GAAP does not cover the following:

1. production of other wasting (nonregenerative) natural resources
2. production of geothermal steam
3. extraction of hydrocarbons as a by-product of the production of geothermal steam (Geothermal Steam Act of 1970)
4. extraction of hydrocarbons from shale, tar sands, or coal
5. accounting for interest on funds borrowed to finance oil and/or gas producing activities.

Moreover, the promulgated GAAP generally applies to oil and gas producing companies that are regulated for rate-making purposes.

Effects of FASB-25

The effective date of the promulgated GAAP on Oil and Gas Producing Companies (FASB-19) has been suspended indefinitely insofar as it requires the use of the successful efforts method of accounting (FASB-25). In other respects, the effective date of FASB-19 has been changed to fiscal years ending after December 25, 1979, although earlier application is encouraged.

Other changes made by FASB-25 which are included in this chapter in their appropriate place are:

Oil and Gas Producing Companies

1. Disclosure of net reserve quantities may be shown, as outside supplementary information, accompanying but not necessarily an integral part of the financial statements.
2. Disclosure must be made of the method used for accounting for costs incurred in gas and oil producing activities and the manner of disposing of related capitalized costs.
3. The definitions of reserves used in FASB-19 are completely rescinded. The definitions that shall be used are those adopted by the SEC for its reporting purposes and which are in effect on the date reserve disclosures are made. Revision of previously reported reserves do not have to be made in the event the SEC changes its definitions of reserves.

Furthermore, FASB-25 specifically states that for the purposes of the promulgated GAAP on Accounting Changes (APB-20) the provisions of FASB-19 pertaining to the successful efforts method remain in effect. Since FASB-19 expresses a preference for the successful efforts method of accounting and rejects other methods, an enterprise that changes to any method other than the successful efforts will have the burden of justifying such change (APB-20).

The income tax allocation requirements of FASB-19 were not changed by FASB-25 and therefore remain in effect.

Overview

The promulgated GAAP supports and advocates the traditional historical cost accounting approach. The major problem is in understanding the activities and related terminology pertaining to the oil and gas producing industry.

Properties includes any ownership in, or an interest representing the right to, or the participation in, the extraction of oil and/or gas. Includes also nonoperating interests, such as a royalty interest, or production interest payable in oil and/or gas. Properties exclude contracts representing the right to purchase oil and/or gas (supply contracts).

Reservoir refers to a separate confined underground formation containing a natural accumulation of producible oil and/or gas.

Field refers to one or more reservoirs related to the same individual geological structual feature and/or stratigraphic condition.

Proved area is that part of the property in which proved reserves have been specifically attributed.

Proved reserves The following definitions of proved reserves are those adopted by the SEC on December 19, 1978 (ASR-257) and were current at the date of publication. These definitions were developed by the Department of Energy for its financial reporting purposes.

Proved oil and gas reserves. Proved oil and gas reserves are the estimated quantities of crude oil, natural gas, and natural gas liquids which geological and engineering data demonstrate with reasonable certainty to be recoverable in future years from known reservoirs under existing economic and operating conditions, i.e., prices and costs as of the date the estimate is made. Prices include consideration of changes in existing prices provided only by contractual arrangements, but not on escalations based upon future conditions.

1. Reservoirs are considered proved if economic producibility is supported by either actual production or conclusive formation test. The area of a reservoir considered proved includes (a) that portion delineated by drilling and defined by gas-oil and/or oil-water contacts, if any, and (b) the immediately adjoining portions not yet drilled, but which can be reasonably judged as economically productive on the basis of available geological and engineering data. In the absence of information on fluid contacts, the lowest known structural occurrence of hydrocarbons controls the lower proved limit of the reservoir.
2. Reserves which can be produced economically through application of improved recovery techniques (such as fluid injection) are included in the "proved" classification when successful testing by a pilot project, or the operation of an installed program in the reservoir, provides support for the engineering analysis on which the project or program was based.
3. Estimates of proved reserves do not include the following: (a) oil that may become available from known reservoirs but is classified separately as "indicated additional reserves"; (b) crude oil, natural gas, and natural gas liquids, the recovery of which is subject to reasonable doubt because of uncertainty as

to geology, reservoir characteristics, or economic factors; (c) crude oil, natural gas, and natural gas liquids, that may occur in undrilled prospects; and (d) crude oil, natural gas, and natural gas liquids, that may be recovered from oil shales, coal, gilsonite and other such sources.

Proved developed oil and gas reserves. Proved developed oil and gas reserves are reserves that can be expected to be recovered through existing wells with existing equipment and operating methods. Additional oil and gas expected to be obtained through the application of fluid injection or other improved recovery techniques for supplementing the natural forces and mechanisms of primary recovery should be included as "proved developed reserves" only after testing by a pilot project or after the operation of an installed program has confirmed through production response that increased recovery will be achieved.

Proved undeveloped reserves. Proved undeveloped oil and gas reserves are reserves that are expected to be recovered from new wells on undrilled acreage, or from existing wells where a relatively major expenditure is required for recompletion. Reserves on undrilled acreage shall be limited to those drilling units offsetting productive units that are reasonably certain of production when drilled. Proved reserves for other undrilled units can be claimed only where it can be demonstrated with certainty that there is continuity of production from the existing productive formation. Under no circumstances should estimates for proved undeveloped reserves be attributable to any acreage for which an application of fluid injection or other improved recovery technique is contemplated, unless such techniques have been proved effective by actual tests in the area and in the same reservoir.

Wells, related equipment and facilities includes the cost of drilling and equipping *completed* wells, access to proved reserves, and facilities for extracting, treating, gathering, and storing the oil and/or gas.

Uncompleted wells, equipment and facilities includes the costs of all uncompleted wells, equipment and facilities.

Support equipment and facilities includes the cost of support equipment and facilities used in producing oil and/or gas. Examples are construction and grading equipment, seismic equipment, vehicles, repair shops, warehouses, camps, and division, district, or field offices.

Stratigraphic test wells (expendable wells) are generally drilled without the intention of being completed for production, and are a geological drilling effort to gather information about specific geologic conditions. Core tests and other expendable holes are classified as stratigraphic test wells.

A stratigraphic test well drilled in a proved area is called a *development-type stratigraphic test well.* When drilled on an unproved area, these wells are called exploratory-type stratigraphic test wells.

Service wells are wells drilled to service or support production in an existing field. Examples are injection wells (gas, water, steam, air, etc.) and observation wells.

Development wells are wells drilled for producing oil and/or gas in a proved area known to be productive.

Exploratory wells are wells drilled for exploration or discovery, usually on unproved areas. If a well is classified as a development, service, or stratigraphic test well, it cannot be an exploratory well.

Supply agreements are long-term contracts or similar agreements that represent the right to purchase oil and/or gas, including those with foreign governments.

Discovery-value accounting refers to estimated methods used to determine the value of oil and/or gas reserves, either when discovered or at a later date when developed. The most common estimated valuation methods are:

1. Current cost—the amount of cash that currently would have to be paid to acquire the same asset. Similar to current reproduction cost or current replacement cost.

2. Current exit value in orderly liquidation—the net amount of cash that would be received in the current orderly liquidation of the asset.

3. Expected exit value in due course of business—the nondiscounted amount of cash the asset is expected to bring in the due course of business, less any direct costs incurred in its

disposal (net realizable value). Under this method the oil and/or gas reserves would be valued at an amount equal to the estimated net cash flow from the reserves.
4. Present value of expected cash flow—the present value of the expected cash inflows from the reserves, less the present value of the expected related cash outflows to produce the cash inflows. Various different discount rates have been recommended, such as the prime rate, company's cost of capital, and the rate on long-term government bonds.

Under the discovery-value accounting method, property acquisition and other prediscovery expenditures would be deferred and written off when the areas to which the costs apply have been explored and the reserves, if any, determined and valued.

Under the promulgated GAAP (FASB-19), the discovery-value accounting method is unacceptable.

Current-value accounting One of the four valuation methods mentioned above in discovery-value accounting is applied on a continuous basis, and oil and/or gas reserves are revalued at each financial statement date using the most current information available. Property acquisition and other prediscovery expenditures are deferred and written off when the areas to which the costs apply have been explored and the oil and/or gas reserves, if any, determined and valued.

The uncertainties and inherent unreliability in using estimates to value oil and/or gas reserves renders the discovery value and current value methods as undesirable.

Under the promulgated GAAP (FASB-19), both the discovery-value and current-value methods are unacceptable.

Full-costing accounting considers all costs of unsuccessful and successful property acquisition and exploration activities as a cost of discovering reserves. Thus, all costs are considered an integral part of the acquisition, discovery, and development of oil and/or gas reserves, and costs that cannot be directly related to the discovery of specific reserves are nonetheless capitalized.

In full costing, a country is usually selected as a cost center, and all costs incurred within the cost center are capitalized and subsequently amortized against the oil and/or gas reserves produced within the cost center. There is a limitation that capitalized costs of a cost center should not exceed the value of the oil and/or gas reserves of the same cost center.

Under the promulgated GAAP (FASB-19), the full-costing accounting method is unacceptable.

Successful-efforts costing a cause-and-effect relationship between costs incurred and the discovery of specific reserves is required. The incurrence of a cost with no identifiable future benefit is usually expensed under the successful-efforts methods. The two major variations in the successful-efforts costing method are (1) the use of a small "area of interest" cost center, or (2) the accounting treatment of an item is determined by its nature. When a small "area of interest" cost center, such as a field, lease, or reservoir, is used, costs relating to the cost center are capitalized and subsequently amortized against the oil and/or gas reserves discovered within the cost center. When the nature of the expenditure is used as the method for capitalizing or expensing an expenditure, the nature of the expenditure determines its treatment. As a result, geological and geophysical costs and unsuccessful exploratory wells (dry holes) are immediately charged to expense. In addition, some companies use a combination of both variations to determine whether an expenditure is capitalized or expensed.

Under successful-efforts costing, all property acquisition costs are capitalized when incurred, though different methods may subsequently be used to dispose of these costs.

Under present tax law, intangible drilling costs are generally deductible as an expense in the year incurred.

The promulgated GAAP (FASB-19) is generally based on the successful-efforts costing method.

Background Information

In 1975, the Energy Policy and Conservation Act, public law 94-163, was enacted by Congress. Title V, Section 503, of the act grants the following powers to the Securities and Exchange Commission:

> to prescribe rules applicable to persons engaged in the production of crude oil or natural gas, or make effective by recognition, or by other appropriate means indicating a determination to rely on, accounting practices developed by the Financial Accounting Standards Board, if the Securities and Exchange Commission is assured that such practice will be observed by persons engaged in the production of crude oil or natural gas to the same extent as would result if the

Securities and Exchange Commission had prescribed such practices by rule.

In addition, the Energy Policy and Conservation Act of 1975 requires that certain information about national energy be compiled for both domestic and foreign operations, and consist of the following data:

(1.) The separate calculation of capital, revenue, and operating cost information pertaining to–
(a) prospecting,
(b) acquisition,
(c) exploration,
(d) development, and
(e) production,
including geological and geophysical costs, carrying costs, unsuccessful exploratory drilling costs, intangible drilling and development costs on productive wells, the cost of unsuccessful development wells, and the cost of acquiring oil and gas reserves by means other than development. Any such calculation shall take into account disposition of capitalized costs, contractual arrangements involving special conveyance of rights and joint operations, differences between book and tax income, and prices used in the transfer of products or other assets from one person to any other person, including a person controlled by, controlling, or under common control with such person.

(2) The full presentation of the financial information of persons engaged in the production of crude oil or natural gas, including–
(A) disclosure of reserves and operating activities, both domestic and foreign, to facilitate evaluation of financial effort and result; and
(B) classification of financial information by function to facilitate correlation with reserve and operating statistics, both domestic and foreign.

(3) Such other information, projections, and relationships of collected data as shall be necessary to facilitate the compilation of such data base.

Securities Act Release No. 5706, issued on May 12, 1976, requires that certain information relating to oil and/or gas properties, reserves, and production be disclosed in registration statements, proxy statements, and reports filed with the Commission.

Securities Act Release No. 5801, issued on January 31, 1977, states that the Commission, consistent with its policy established in Accounting Series Release No. 150, will look to the FASB to provide leadership in setting forth accounting standards and principles for the producers of oil and/or gas.

Securities Act Release No. 5837, issued on June 30, 1977, solicits comments from interested parties with respect to the Commission's responsibility under the Energy Policy and Conservation Act of 1975. The release also states that the Commission will attempt to coordinate the reporting requirements promulgated by the FASB in its own disclosure and reporting requirements.

Securities Release No. 5861 and Securities Release 5877, issued on August 31, 1977, and October 26, 1977, respectively, generally adopt as a Commission regulation the accounting standards and disclosures that are contained in FASB-19. These releases apply to filings with the SEC and to reports filed with the Department of Energy.

Securities Release No. 5878, also issued on October 26, 1977, deals with replacement cost information (ASR 190) for certain registrants. In lieu of replacement cost information the release requires the disclosure of the present value of future net revenues estimated to be received in the future from the production of proved oil and/or gas reserves. This release becomes effective for filings covering fiscal years ending after December 24, 1978.

On August 31, 1978 the SEC issued ASR-253 which included the following:

1. Adopted the successful efforts accounting method and disclosure requirements of FASB-19.

2. Indicated that a form of full cost accounting for oil and gas producing companies will be developed by the SEC as an acceptable reportable alternative for the SEC.

3. Concluded that the full cost and successful efforts method based upon historical costs fails to provide sufficient information for gas and oil producing companies and that the SEC would take steps to develop an accounting method based on current valuation of proved oil and gas reserves.

4. Adopted disclosure rules for certain information regardless of the accounting method used.

5. Adopted the definition of proved reserves which differed from those prescribed by FASB-19.

Oil and Gas Producing Companies

On December 19, 1978 the SEC issued ASR-257 and ASR-258 which included the following:

1. Reaffirmed the conclusions the SEC prescribed in ASR-253 (enumerated above).
2. Adopted definitions of proved reserves developed by the Department of Energy for its reporting purposes.
3. Described the form of full cost accounting for gas and oil producing companies that would be acceptable as an alternative to the successful efforts method for reporting to the SEC.

Accounting Principles—Basic Concepts

The promulgated GAAP (FASB-19) does not address itself to the transporting, refining, and marketing aspects of oil and/or gas production. The functions covered by the promulgated GAAP are (1) acquisition of properties, (2) exploration, (3) development, and (4) production.

Generally, the incurrence of a cost that results in the acquisition of an asset is capitalized and subsequently amortized, unless the asset becomes impaired or worthless, in which case it is reduced in value or written off. Costs that do not result in the acquisition of an asset, such as carrying costs of undeveloped properties, geological and geophysical (G&G) costs, and the costs of drilling exploratory wells that do not find proved reserves, are charged to expense when incurred.

Costs incurred to operate and maintain producing wells, related equipment and facilities, become part of the total production costs (also known as lifting costs). The other part of production costs comprise depreciation, depletion, and amortization of the costs capitalized as property acquisition, exploration, and development costs.

Before the accounting treatment of a cost can be determined, it must be first classified as a cost of acquiring properties, exploring, developing, or producing. For example, support equipment and labor can be classified as any of the functional activities in the oil and gas industry. Labor used in developing a producing well is capitalized and subsequently amortized, whereas labor costs incurred in operating producing wells become part of production costs.

The following is a brief discussion of the accounting principles and basic concepts involved in each function of the oil and gas industry:

Acquisition of properties includes all costs to purchase, lease, or otherwise acquire a proved or unproved property, including broker's, legal, and recording fees, and other costs incurred in acquiring properties. The acquisition of properties may include the transfer of all or part of the rights and responsibilities of operating the properties (operating interest) or none of the rights or responsibilities of operating (nonoperating interest).

If the interest in the property acquired is of substance a borrowing repayable in cash or its equivalent, it should be treated as a borrowing and not as the acquisition of an interest in the property.

If part or all of an interest in a property is sold and substantial uncertainty exists in the recovery of the applicable costs involved, or if the seller has a substantial future performance obligation to drill a well or to operate the property without reimbursement, no gain should be recognized on these types of conveyances.

As in all nonmonetary exchanges of like property gain or loss is recognized only to the extent of any "boot" received, as follows:

1. exchange of assets used in oil and gas producing activities for other assets used in oil and gas producing activities
2. a joint pooling of assets to find, develop, or produce oil and/or gas from a particular property

Unproved properties should be reclassified to proved properties when proved reserves are attributed to the property. Periodic assessment of unproved properties should be made to determine whether they have been impaired. Impairment is likely if a dry hole has been drilled and there are no future plans to continue drilling, or if the end of a lease approaches and drilling has not commenced on the property. Losses for impairment of unproved properties are made by a charge to income and a credit to a valuation account in the year the impairment occurs.

If an unproved property is abandoned or becomes worthless, all related capitalized costs should be charged first against any related allowance for impairment account, and any excess charged to income of the period that the unproved property is abandoned or becomes worthless. If only a small portion of an amortization base is abandoned or becomes worthless, then that portion should be considered fully amortized and its cost charged to the accumulated depreciation, depletion, or amortization account, and no gain or loss is recognized.

The unit-of-production method is used to amortize (deplete) all capitalized property acquisition costs of proved properties. As stated previously, this amortization (depletion) becomes part of the production costs (lifting costs). Amortization rates should be reviewed at least annually and revisions should be accounted for prospectively as changes in accounting estimates (APB-20).

In proved properties that contain both oil and gas reserves, a common unit of measure based on the approximate relative energy content of the oil and gas should be used as the unit of production in the current period. Amortization is then based on the converted common unit of measure. In the event that either oil or gas dominates the content of both reserves and current production, unit-of-production amortization may be computed on the dominant mineral only.

Exploration includes all costs relating to the search for oil and/or gas reserves, including depreciation and applicable costs of support equipment and facilities, drilling exploratory wells, and exploratory-type stratigraphic test wells. Exploration costs may be incurred before the actual acquisition of the property, and in this sense they are sometimes referred to as prospecting costs.

Some exploration costs do not represent the acquisition of an identifiable asset, and are therefore charged directly to expense when incurred. The cost of carrying and maintaining undeveloped properties is an expense, because such costs do not increase the potential that the properties will contain proved reserves. Examples of these types of expenses are delay rentals, taxes on properties, legal costs, and land maintenance.

Geological, topographical, and geophysical studies (G&G costs) and related salary and other expenses are also expensed, because they do not represent the acquisition of an identifiable asset. The studies are frequently made before the acquisition of the property and represent research or information costs. More frequently than not G&G costs are incurred and the properties are never acquired.

Pending the determination of whether a well has proved reserves, all costs of drilling exploratory wells are capitalized and are classified as uncompleted wells, equipment and facilities. The disposition of exploratory wells and their related costs is usually made shortly after completion, and if the well has proved reserves, the costs are capitalized and reclassified as wells, related equipment and facilities. However, if no proved reserves are found, the capitalized costs of drilling the well, less any salvage value, is charged to expense.

Sometimes an exploratory well cannot be classified as having found proved reserves on completion of drilling, because justification for major capital expenditures, such as a trunk pipeline, must be made, which may depend on the success of additional exploratory wells in the same area. In this event, the exploratory well and its related costs may be carried on the books as an asset for a period not exceeding one year, providing both of the following conditions are met:

1. A sufficient quantity of reserves was found to justify the completion as a producing well if the required capital expenditures are made.
2. Drilling of other exploratory wells has commenced or is firmly planned for the near future.

If the above conditions are not met, the exploratory well and all its related costs are charged to expense.

The unit-of-production method is used to amortize all capitalized exploration costs, including support equipment and facilities. As stated previously, this amortization becomes part of the cost of production (lifting costs).

Development includes all costs incurred in creating a production system of wells, related equipment and facilities, on proved reserves so that the oil and/or gas can be lifted (produced). Development costs are associated with specific proved reserves; exploration costs are associated with unproved reserves. The cost of building a road to gain access to proved reserves is a development cost, as is the cost of providing facilities for extracting, treating, gathering, and storing the oil and/or gas. Development costs also include depreciation and operating costs of support equipment and facilities used in development activities.

Development costs are associated with previously discovered proved reserves with known future benefits. Therefore, under the promulgated GAAP, unsuccessful development wells (dry holes) are capitalized as a cost of creating the overall production system for proved reserves.

The unit-of-production method is used to amortize (deplete) all capitalized development costs. As stated previously, this amortization (depletion) becomes part of the production costs (lifting costs). Amortization rates should be reviewed at least annually, and revisions should be accounted for prospectively as changes in accounting estimates (APB-20).

In proved properties that contain both oil and gas, a common unit of measure based on the approximate relative energy content of the

Oil and Gas Producing Companies

oil and gas should be used as the unit of production for the purpose of determining the number of units produced in the current period. Amortization is then based on the converted common unit of measure. In the event that either oil or gas dominates the content of both reserves and current production, unit-of-production amortization may be computed on the dominant mineral only.

Production includes all costs incurred in lifting the oil and/or gas to the surface, and gathering, treating, field processing, and field storage. The promulgated GAAP provides that the production function terminate at the outlet valve on the leased property or the field production storage tank, or under unusual circumstances, at the first point at which the oil and/or gas is delivered to a main pipeline, refinery, marine terminal, or a common carrier.

Production costs include labor, fuel, and supplies needed to operate the developed wells and related equipment, repairs, property taxes, and insurance on proved properties, and wells, related equipment and facilities.

Costs incurred to operate and maintain the production system become part of the total production costs (lifting costs). The other part of the production costs consists of the depreciation, depletion, and amortization of the costs capitalized as acquisition of properties, exploration, and development costs.

Support Equipment and Facilities

Costs for support equipment and facilities may be incurred for exploration, development, or production activities. Generally, these costs are capitalized and depreciated over their estimated useful lives or the life of the lease, whichever is appropriate. The depreciation expense and related costs of operating the support equipment and facilities is charged to the related activity (exploration, development, or production). When support equipment and facilites are utilized for more than one activity, the depreciation expense and operating costs should be allocated between the activities on a reasonable basis.

Residual salvage values and estimated costs of dismantlement, restoration, and abandonment should be considered in determining depreciation and amortization rates.

Balance Sheet–Subsequent Information

The promulgated GAAP requires that information that becomes available subsequent to the balance sheet date and prior to the

Oil and Gas Producing Companies

issuance of the financial statements should be taken into consideration in determining conditions that existed at the balance sheet date. The determination at the balance sheet date of whether an exploratory well has found proved reserves, the impairment of unproved properties, and similar conditions may be based on information that becomes available subsequent to the balance sheet date and prior to the issuance of the financial statements.

Income Tax Considerations

Comprehensive interperiod income tax allocation (APB-11) should be applied for items that enter into the determination of pretax accounting income and taxable income in different periods (timing differences). However, a future tax benefit arising from an excess of statutory depletion over cost depletion is not treated as a timing difference but is accounted for as a permanent difference in the period in which it is allowed as a deduction for income tax purposes.

Disclosure

Considerable disclosure is required by the promulgated GAAP for an oil and gas producing company issuing a full set of financial statements. A lesser amount of disclosure is necessary for interim financial statements, discussed later in this chapter. Disclosures may be incorporated in the body of the financial statements. However, disclosure of reserve quantities can be made as supplementary information not an integral part of the financial statements but accompanying them (FASB-25).

The method of accounting for costs incurred in oil and gas producing activities and the manner of disposing of capitalized costs must be fully disclosed (FASB-25).

The net quantities of crude oil which includes condensate and natural gas liquids should be stated in barrels. The net quantities of natural gas should be stated in cubic feet. Net quantities of crude oil and gas, if significant, should be reported for the company's home country and each foreign geographic area (country or group of countries) in which significant reserves are located.

In determining net quantities the following rules shall apply:

1. Net quantities shall exclude oil and gas subject to purchase under long-term supply, purchase, or similar agreements, including those with foreign governments. However, if the

company participates in the operation of the oil and/or gas producing properties or otherwise acts as a producer, this information is reported separately (see below).
2. Companies issuing consolidated financial statements shall include all the net quantities attributable to the parent company and all the net quantities attributable to the consolidated subsidiaries whether or not wholly owned.
3. Net quantities of investments that are proportionately consolidated shall include the proportionate share of the investee's net quantities of oil and gas reserves.
4. Net quantities of investments that are accounted for by the equity method shall be excluded. (This information is separately reported; see below).
5. Net quantities shall include any from royalty interests owned if the information is available. If the information is not available, a statement of that fact must be made and net quantities *produced* attributable to the royalty interest must be disclosed for each period presented.
6. Net quantities include operating and nonoperating interest in properties.
7. Net quantities shall not include interests of others in properties.

Beginning, ending, and changes in, net quantities in proved reserves and proved developed reserves of crude oil (including condensate and natural gas liquids) and natural gas must be reported at the end of each year in which a complete set of financial statements is presented.

The following chart illustrates the method of disclosing net quantities recommended in the promulgated GAAP:

Oil and Gas Producing Companies

	Total Worldwide		United States		Foreign Geographic Area A		Foreign Geographic Area B		Other Foreign Geographic Areas	
	Oil	Gas	Oil	Gas	Oil	Gas	Oil	Gas	Oil	Gas
Proved developed and undeveloped reserves:										
1. Beginning of year	X	X	X	X	X	X	X	X	X	X
2. Revisions of previous estimates	X	X	X	X	X	X	X	X	X	X
3. Improved recovery	X	X	X	X	X	X	X	X	X	X
4. Purchases of minerals-in-place	X	X	X	X	X	X	X	X	X	X
5. Extensions, discoveries and other additions	X	X	X	X	X	X	X	X	X	X
6. Production	(X)	(X)	(X)	(X)	(X)	(X)	(X)	(X)	(X)	(X)
7. Sales of minerals-in-place	(X)	(X)	(X)	(X)	(X)	(X)	(X)	(X)	(X)	(X)
8. End of year	X	X	X	X	X	X	X	X	X	X
9. Proved developed reserves:										
Beginning of year	X	X	X	X	X	X	X	X	X	X
End of year	X	X	X	X	X	X	X	X	X	X
Oil and gas applicable to long-term supply agreements with foreign governments or authorities in which the company acts as producer:										
10. Proved reserves at end of year	X	X	X	X	X	X	X	X	X	X
11. Received during the year	X	X	X	X	X	X	X	X	X	X
12. Company's proportional interest in reserves of investees accounted for by the equity method, end of year	X	X	X	X	X	X	X	X	X	X

An explanation of each item in the chart follows:

1. *Beginning of year*–the total net quantities at the beginning of the year

Oil and Gas Producing Companies

2. *Revisions of previous estimates*–upward or downward revision of proved reserves resulting from new information or changes in economic factors
3. *Improved recovery*–changes during the year resulting from new recovery techniques
4. *Purchases of minerals-in-place*–purchases during the year of proved developed and undeveloped reserves
5. *Extensions, discoveries, and other additions*–proved reserves resulting from the extension of previously discovered reservoirs, discovery of new fields or new reservoirs in old fields, and other additions
6. *Production*–the total amount of net quantities produced for the year
7. *Sales of minerals-in-place*–sales during the year of proved developed and undeveloped reserves
8. *End of year*–the total net quantities at the end of the year (All items above this item should add up to this item.)
9. *Proved developed reserves*–net quantities of proved developed reserves only for the beginning and ending of the year. Proved developed reserves includes oil and/or gas expected to be recovered through existing wells using existing equipment and operation methods. Proved undeveloped reserves are those where oil and/or gas is expected to be recovered from new wells on undrilled acreage or from existing wells that require major expenditures for completion.

Net quantities subject to purchase under long-term supply agreements with foreign governments or authorities and net quantities received during the year under such agreements must be separately disclosed as indicated in items 10 and 11.

An investor's share of net quantities of an investment accounted for by the equity method shall be separately disclosed at the end of the year (as indicated in item 12).

In addition to the information required on net quantities of oil and/or gas reserves, the promulgated GAAP requires the following disclosures:

Capitalized costs   the total amount of capitalized costs and related accumulated depreciation, depletion, amortization, and valuation allowances for:

1. mineral interests in properties
2. wells, related equipment and facilities
3. support equipment and facilities used in oil and/or gas producing activities
4. uncompleted wells, equipment and facilities

> **OBSERVATION:** This complies with the disclosure of balances of major classes of depreciable assets by nature and function required by promulgated GAAP (APB-12).

Function costs the total costs, whether capitalized or expensed, for each functional activity of oil and gas producing companies, as follows:

1. property acquisition costs
2. exploration costs
3. development costs
4. production costs

These functional costs should include the depreciation expense of support equipment and facilities, but exclude the expenditure to acquire such equipment and facilities.

For the purpose of this disclosure, production costs do not include depreciation, depletion, and amortization of capitalized property acquisition costs, exploration costs, and development costs.

These functional costs which are incurred in a foreign country should be separately disclosed by geographic areas in the same way that net quantities of oil and gas are disclosed.

Economic factors and significant uncertainties that affect any portion of a company's proved reserves shall be fully disclosed. The following are examples of these types of factors:

1. contractual obligations to sell a significant amount of reserves at prices substantially less than market
2. major expenditures, such as a pipeline or a facility, that are required before production can start
3. unusually high development or production costs

The only specific disclosure for interim financial statements required by the promulgated GAAP is the total amount of capitalized costs and related accumulated depreciation, depletion, amortization, and valuation allowances for:

1. mineral interests in properties
2. wells, related equipment and facilities
3. support equipment and facilities used in oil and/or gas producing activities
4. uncompleted wells, equipment and facilities

In both annual and interim reports, disclosure of a favorable or an unfavorable event, or a major discovery, any of which causes a significant change in reserve data should be fully explained.

Segmental Reporting

Segmental reporting (FASB-14) is not necessary for oil and/or gas producing companies, because the functional activities of property acquisition, exploration, development, and production are not considered industry segments. However, the promulgated GAAP does require some disclosure information based on geographic areas.

PENSION PLANS

Background

The present promulgated GAAP for pension plans is APB-8, Accounting for the Cost of a Pension Plan, and FASB Interpretation-3, which covers Accounting for the Cost of a Pension Plan Subject to the Employee Retirement Income Security Act of 1974.

The promulgated GAAP (APB-8) is silent on its coverage of regulated industries. Therefore, in accordance with the Addendum to APB-2, companies in regulated industries should comply.

Overview

Retirement plans fall into two groups—tax qualified and unqualified. Since employers can deduct contributions made to qualified trusts, and the income from the trust is usually exempt from taxes, qualified plans are most often found in practice. There are three general types of tax-qualified plans:

Pension plans The employer provides actuarially determined contributions based on determinable benefits that will be paid to employees.

Profit-sharing plans The employer provides contributions based on profits, and hence the benefits are not determinable in advance.

Stock bonus plans The employer provides contributions based on profits or some other designated base, and benefits are distributed in stock of the employer. Usually, this type of arrangement is called an ESOP (Employee Stock Ownership Plan).

A pension plan may be contributory or noncontributory; that is, the employees may be required to contribute to the plan, or the employer may shoulder the entire cost. The plan may be funded or unfunded; that is, the employer may make cash contributions to a trustee, or it may make only credit entries on its books reflecting the pension liability under the plan. In any event, the amount funded in any given period is unrelated to the pension plan expense for the period, although coincidentally, they may be the same. Pension plans are accounted for on the accrual basis, and any difference between the amount charged against income for a period and the amount actually funded is recorded as accrued or prepaid pension costs.

A company may limit its legal obligation for a pension plan by providing that benefits are payable only to the extent of the net assets in the pension fund. Any *legal liability* in excess of amounts funded or accrued must be recorded on the books as a deferred pension charge and a pension liability.

Regardless of whether or not a company limits its pension liability, pension plans are accounted for on the assumption that the company will continue in business (going-concern principle) and benefits will continue to be paid.

> **OBSERVATION:** Many pension plans provide that a company may, at its discretion, discontinue contributions and/or the plan itself. The resulting legal position is that the company has no legal liability for future pension fund contributions, and employees have no rights to any benefits beyond those already provided for in the pension fund. However, the position of promulgated GAAP is one of substance over form and that a business is viewed as an entity which will continue to exist (going-concern concept). Therefore, GAAP require that the "no future legal liability clauses" of a pension plan be ignored for the purposes of determining annual pension costs.

Defined benefit plan defines the method of determining employee benefits that are expected to be paid on retirement. Based on the benefits that are expected to be paid, the employer's contributions can be actuarily computed.

Defined contribution plan defines the method of determining the employer's contributions to the plan, while benefits will be predicated on the amounts accumulated by the contributions. If no mention is made about defined benefits, the pension cost to charge against income is the amount of the employer contribution.

Frequently, defined contribution plans provide for some method of determining benefits for employees. In these cases, if in substance the plan does provide defined benefits, the annual pension cost should be determined by an acceptable actuary method, and not the employer's contribution.

Deferred compensation plan is a contractual agreement that specifies that a portion of the employee's compensation will be set aside and paid in future periods as retirement benefits. GAAP cover only those deferred compensation plans that in substance are pension plans.

Deferred profit sharing plan usually provides for future retirement benefits out of accumulated profit sharing deposits made by the employer for each employee. Generally, the amount of deposit made each year by the employer is the pension cost. However, if in substance the arrangement is a pension plan, it is covered by the promulgated GAAP (APB-8).

All employees who are reasonably expected to receive benefits from a pension plan must be included in the calculation of pension costs.

If in substance all or part of an arrangement is a pension plan, it must be accounted for in accordance with the promulgated GAAP. Different actuarial cost methods may be used where a company has more than one plan. If a company has two or more plans, they may be treated as one for determining pension costs, if substantially the same class of employees is covered and the assets of each plan can be used to pay benefits to the covered employees.

Actuarial Cost Methods

Actuarial cost methods are techniques developed by actuaries to determine the funding of a pension plan. For the purposes of GAAP an actuarial cost method must be systematic and rational and must be consistently applied from year to year.

An actuarial cost method is based on *actuarial assumptions,* which are factors that determine the estimated cost of benefits each employee will receive from the pension plan. Mortality tables, employee turnover, retirement age, administrative expenses, interest earned on pension funds, and the date an employee receives vested benefits are some of the more important actuarial assumptions. *Vested benefits* are payments that an employee has an irrevocable right to receive at a predetermined date provided that sufficient funds are available in the pension fund. Vested benefits accrue to an employee whether or not he or she continues to work for the employer.

Actuaries use actuarial assumptions to estimate the overall cost of a pension plan. Actuarial assumptions may change from time to time, necessitating an amendment to the pension plan.

Actuarial valuation is a process used to calculate the amount of periodic contributions an employer must make in order to meet the actuarial assumptions of the pension plan. Actuarial valuation includes the determination of present values of the estimated benefits to be paid in accordance with the actuarial cost method used in the plan.

Three important factors that an actuarial cost method must take into consideration are (1) past-service costs, (2) normal costs, and (3) prior-service costs. *Past-service costs* arise from future benefits granted to employees, at the inception of the plan, based on prior employment.

> **OBSERVATION:** The justification for charging past-service costs to present and future periods is that benefits derived from past-service costs granted at the inception of a plan are based on continued employment, present employment and future employment.

After the inception of the pension plan, the annual cost for any year is called *normal cost*.

Prior-service costs are any pension cost relating to a prior period as determined at any time. Prior costs almost always arise from an amendment to the pension plan, but include unamortized past service costs.

> **OBSERVATION:** All actuarial cost methods do not treat past-service, normal, and prior-service costs in the same manner. For instance, in the individual level premium and aggregate methods, past-service costs are not determined separately but are included in the computation of normal cost for the year. In the accrued benefit cost method and in most other commonly used methods, past-service cost is computed separately from normal costs.

The following are the more important actuarial cost methods:

Accrued Benefit (Unit Credit Method) The pension cost incurred in each year after the inception of the plan (normal cost) is equal to the present value of the future benefits credited to each employee for his or her own employment during the year.

Pension cost arising from future benefits granted to employees, at the inception of the plan, based on prior employment (past-service cost) is the present value of such benefits at the inception of the plan.

Under the accrued benefit cost method (unit-credit method), the employer's annual contribution usually consists of the normal cost for the year and an amount for the amortization of past-service costs, or an amount equal to the interest that would have been earned on the unfunded balance of the past-service costs.

Prior-service costs are usually handled in the same way as past service costs.

The accrued benefit (unit-credit) method is primarily based on employment that has already been rendered.

Projected Benefit This actuarial cost method is based on past, present, and future services of an employee and assigns the entire projected cost of benefits to the past, present, and future periods. The result is that the employer's annual contributions are a predetermined amount which, when accumulated on the basis of the actuarial assumptions, would yield a pension fund equal to the benefits for all employees who live to collect pensions.

The more common projected benefit cost methods are:

Entry age normal Each employee is assumed to have entered the plan when hired, or at the earliest time eligible if the plan was in existence at the time of employment and that employer contributions are assumed to have been made on this basis to the date of the actuarial valuation. This results in a level annual employer's contribution (normal cost). It also means that the normal cost, under this method, includes an amount for past, present, and future benefits. Therefore, the accumulated normal cost prior to the inception of the plan is equal to the total past-service costs.

The entry-age-normal-cost method may be used on an individual employee basis or an aggregate of a group of employees.

Individual level premium Pension cost is computed individually from the date an employee enters the plan to the date of his or her retirement. An annual level premium is determined that will provide each employee's benefits at retirement date. If an employee enters the plan at inception, past-service costs will be included in computing the annual level premiums. The annual level premium is the normal cost, which includes an amount for past-service costs. Under this method, past-service cost is not determined separately.

In cases where benefits are based on compensation, a level percentage of an employee's compensation is used to determine the individual level premium.

Because past-service cost for employees nearing retirement is amortized over a short period, this method usually results in high initial costs.

The *terminal funding method,* which provides for funding of benefits at the end of the active employment of an employee, and the *pay-as-you-go method,* which recognizes pension costs when benefits are paid to retired employees, are not considered rational and systematic, and are therefore not acceptable methods under GAAP.

Application of GAAP

For the purposes of GAAP, a pension plan is an agreement, express or implied, between an employer and its employees, that provides for retirement benefits which are defined or can be estimated. The agreement need not be in writing if the existence of a pension plan is implied by company policy.

Other provisions of the promulgated GAAP are:

1. Death and disability payments are not considered a pension plan, unless they are an integral part of the pension plan and are included in the periodic pension payment to employees.
2. Deferred compensation plans, deferred profit-sharing plans, separate death and disability plans are excluded from the promulgated GAAP, unless in substance they qualify as a pension plan.
3. A pension plan may be written or implied and may be funded or unfunded.

> ***OBSERVATION:*** *Those plans which are not covered in the promulgated GAAP for pension plans (APB-8) should be accounted for under existing nonpromulgated GAAP.*

Actuarial Gains and Losses

Actuarial gains and losses are the difference between actuarial estimates and actual results. Actuarial assumptions such as mortality rates, employee turnover, administrative costs, and gain or loss on pension fund assets almost always vary from the estimate to the actual. These differences are actuarial gains or losses which may be realized or unrealized.

Under promulgated GAAP, both realized and unrealized actuarial gains and losses should be recognized in pension costs on the basis of a systematic and rational method. This can be accomplished by

Pension Plans

including in the actuarial assumptions an annual percentage for the expected gain or loss. This is called the *interest assumption method*. Alternatively, the realized or unrealized actuarial gain or loss is separately computed and spread prospectively over the current and future periods. This spreading application is a separate adjustment of the normal cost for the year, and should be done over a period of from 10 to 20 years. Furthermore, net actuarial gains may be used to reduce the amount of amortization of prior-service costs and interest on unfunded unamortized prior-service costs, as long as the period of amortization is not changed. Actuarial gains and losses on debt securities that are being held to maturity need not be recognized.

> **OBSERVATION:** One of the major reasons for the promulgation of GAAP in accounting for pension plans was to eliminate unusual fluctuations in pension cost from year to year. Promulgated GAAP resolved this problem by requiring that the timing of the recognition of actuarial gains and losses be accomplished in a consistent systematic and rational manner over a period of from 10 to 20 years. Obviously, immediate recognition does not achieve the requirements of the promulgated GAAP and is usually considered unacceptable.
>
> All actuarial gains or losses that are spread or averaged over the required 10 to 20 years are considered to be adjustments of the normal cost for each year.

Three present methods of recognizing actuarial gains and losses are:

1. immediate recognition
2. spreading (applies gains and losses to current and future costs)
3. averaging (an average of net gains and net losses of past performances is applied to normal costs)

For GAAP, actuarial gains and losses should be spread over current and future years (10 to 20 years) or the averaging method should be used.

If an actuarial gain or loss arises from a *single* event, unrelated to normal business, the actuarial gain or loss is recognized immediately or is spread over current and future years (10 to 20). Examples of actuarial gains or losses arising from single transactions unrelated to normal business operations are the closing of a plant and a merger or acquisition accounted for as a purchase. In each example, the actuarial gain or loss arising from the transaction would be included in computing the total gain or loss of the entire transaction, which is recognized immediately. Because of the nature of a pooling of interests, the actuarial gain or loss would be spread over current and future years.

Other Considerations

The difference in a change from one acceptable accounting method for pension costs to another acceptable method should be made prospectively to the pension costs of the current and future years. No retroactive adjustment should be made to retained earnings.

If a pension plan becomes overfunded (fund assets exceed all prior-service costs), the provision for pension costs should include the effects of the overfunding over current and future years.

> *OBSERVATION: For the purposes of promulgated GAAP, overfunding means that the net assets of the fund plus any net unfunded balance sheet items (accruals less prepayments and deferrals) exceed all actuarial computed pension costs that should have been made to the fund as at a specific valuation date. Any overfunded amount is treated as an actuarial gain and is spread prospectively over 10 to 20 years. Alternatively, the annual pension cost may be decreased by the equivalent interest amount on prior years' excess funding over the required provisions.*

Under no circumstances should the cost of a pension plan be made directly to retained earnings.

When recognition of pension cost for tax purposes is different from that for financial accounting purposes, income tax allocation should be made (APB-11).

Pension cost is recognized for unfunded plans in the same manner as for funded plans. However, because no interest is earned on fund assets (since there is no fund), the current year's normal costs should be increased by an interest amount equal to what would have been earned if the prior years' pension costs had been funded. Interest on any unfunded pension costs, whether the plan is partially funded or completely unfunded, must always be added to the normal pension costs for the year. Interest is computed, at

Pension Plans

the rate the fund is earning or could earn, on the difference between the amount that should have been funded and the amount that was actually funded.

Amount of Annual Pension Cost

The annual provision for pension cost should be based on an acceptable actuarial cost method and should result in a provision between the following minimum and maximum amounts:

Minimum should not be less than

1. normal cost
2. interest on any unfunded prior-service cost
3. if necessary, a provision for vested benefits

A provision for vested benefits is necessary when the total present value of vested benefits exceeds by 5% or more the sum of the pension fund, increased by any balance sheet pension plan accruals, and when such amount is more than 95% of the comparable excess at the beginning of the year. A provision for vested benefits is not necessary if the actuarial cost method employed does not develop a separate amount for past-service cost or if the total annual pension costs equal or exceed (1) the normal cost, (2) the interest on unfunded pension plan costs, and (3) an amount equivalent to amortization, over 40 years or less, of all past-service costs (unless fully amortized) and any increases or decreases in prior-service costs arising from plan amendments (unless fully amortized).

For the sake of further clarification, an excess of the total present value of vested benefits must exist at both the beginning and the end of the year before a provision may be necessary. The provision for vested benefits may be equal to the lesser of:

1. 5% of the excess at the beginning of the year
2. an amount required to reduce the beginning excess by 5%
3. an amount that would make the total annual pension cost equal to (a) the normal cost, (b) the interest on unfunded costs, and (c) an amount equivalent to amortization, over 40 years or less, of all past-service costs (unless fully amortized) and any increases or decreases arising from plan amendments (unless fully amortized)

Pension Plans

OBSERVATION: The promulgated GAAP, Accounting for Pension Plans (APB-8), does not specify how a pension fund should be valued to comply, if necessary, with the provision for vested benefits. For example, the fund could be valued (1) at the book value of its net assets, (2) at the market value of its net assets, or (3) at the total amount of all prior employer contributions actually paid into the fund. Obviously, each method would produce significantly different results.

OBSERVATION: The promulgated GAAP (APB-8) requires that the pension fund and any balance sheet accruals for the pension fund be added together and compared to the present value of all vested benefits to determine whether a provision for vested benefits is necessary. This requirement apparently assumes that all pension funds are accounted for on a cash basis and do not record the related accrual as a receivable on their books. This is obviously unrealistic.

OBSERVATION: The minimum annual pension cost defined in the promulgated GAAP contemplates that an accrued benefit cost method will be used. As a result, the actuarial value of vested benefits can usually be determined. However, if a projected benefit cost method is used the actuarial value of vested benefits will more than likely have to be estimated.

Maximum cost should not be more than

1. normal cost
2. 10% of past-service costs (until fully amortized)
3. 10% of any increase or decrease in prior-service costs arising from plan amendments
4. interest on the difference between the provision and the amount funded

The 10% limitation on amortization of past- and prior-service costs is considered necessary to prevent the distortion of pension cost in the early years of a plan.

Pension Plans

OBSERVATION: *The maximum annual pension cost defined in the promulgated GAAP is approximately equal to the maximum deduction allowable for federal income tax purposes. The deduction is generally limited to the normal cost for the year plus 10% amortization of past-service costs.*

Employee Retirement Income Security Act of 1974 (ERISA)

ERISA is primarily concerned with the funding of pension plans, the provisions relating to employee participation and vesting benefits, and the safeguarding of employees' pension rights. ERISA became law on September 2, 1974, for pension plans adopted after January 1, 1974. Pension plans existing prior to January 1, 1974, were subject to ERISA for years commencing after December 31, 1975, unless earlier compliance was elected.

Any change in pension costs resulting from compliance with ERISA should be included in annual pension expense subsequent to the adoption of ERISA, and shall fall within the minimum and maximum limitations set forth in the promulgated GAAP (APB-8).

If prior to the adoption of ERISA it appears likely that compliance will have a significant effect on future pension plan expense, funding of pension costs, or unfunded vested benefits, a disclosure of such effects with approximate estimates should be made in the financial statements or in footnotes thereto.

One of the provisions of ERISA requires the funding of a minimum annual amount unless a waiver is obtained from the Secretary of the Treasury. This minimum annual amount should be recognized as a liability in accordance with the provisions of the promulgated GAAP and may necessitate a charge to pension expense for the period, a deferred charge, or a combination of both.

Another provision of ERISA imposes a liability on the employer in the event the pension plan is terminated. If it is clearly evident that the plan will be terminated and if the liability imposed exceeds the pension fund's assets and balance sheet accruals, the liability should be recorded. In those instances where a liability is imposed and is not reasonably determinable, full disclosure shall be made in the financial statements or in footnotes thereto, including an estimate of the range of the liability (FASB Interpretation-3).

Pension Plans

Disclosure

The following disclosure pertaining to pension plans should be made in the financial statements or in footnotes thereto:

1. full description of the plan, including the employees covered
2. full description of the accounting and funding policies
3. the pension plan expense for the current period
4. excess of the total present value of vested benefits over amounts that have been provided for them (the pension fund plus balance sheet accruals minus balance sheet prepayments and deferrals)
5. nature and effect of all items affecting comparability for all periods presented

An example of the appropriate disclosure for a pension plan is:

> The company and its subsidiaries have several pension plans covering substantially all of their employees, including certain employees in foreign countries. The total pension expense for the year was $_____, which includes, as to certain of the plans, amortization of prior service cost over periods ranging from 25 to 40 years. The company's policy is to fund pension cost accrued. The actuarially computed value of vested benefits for all plans as of December 31, 19___, exceeded the total of the pension fund and balance-sheet accruals less pension prepayments and deferred charges by approximately $_____. A change during the year in the actuarial cost method used in computing pension cost had the effect of reducing net income for the year by approximately $_____.
>
> > **OBSERVATION:** *Unamortized prior-service cost which by definition includes unamortized past-service cost, should not appear on the balance sheet, unless, as at the balance sheet date, a legal liability exists for payment of these costs. Any legal liability for pension costs at the balance sheet date should be reflected on the balance sheet.*
> >
> > *The disclosure of unamortized prior-service cost which has not become a legal liability is common in present accounting practice. This may very well be influenced by the present requirements that these amounts be disclosed by companies under the jurisdiction of the SEC.*

Pension Plans

Comprehensive Illustration

A company adopts a pension plan with the following provisions:
1. Plan is noncontributary
2. Trustee–First National Bank
3. Vested benefits accrue at retirement
4. Retirement age–65 years
5. Mortality table–1970 group

Additional information:
1. The trustee expects to earn 8% on funds deposited.
2. The company elects to use the accrued-benefit cost method for computing all costs.
3. Each employee will receive a $500 annuity for each year of service.

With the above information we shall compute the past-service cost and normal cost of Employee #1, based upon the following facts:

Employee #1, is 55 years old and according to the mortality table is expected to live to 77. He started to work for the company at age 40.

Past-service cost The employee has worked for the company for 15 years and is entitled to $7,500 per year on retirement (15 years × $500 per year). The mortality table indicates that he will receive 12 payments of $7,500. We must compute how much money must be in the trust fund at age 65 to make the 12 annual payments of $7,500.

The present value of an annuity of 12 payments of $7,500, using the expected earnings of the trust fund of 8%, is

$$\$7,500 \times 7.536 = \$56,520$$

In order to make the 12 payments of $7,500, the trust fund, earning 8%, will need $56,520 when this employee retires. However, because the $56,520 is needed at age 65 and the employee is now 55, the $56,520 must be discounted for 10 years. The present value of $56,520 discounted 10 years at 8% (trust fund estimated earning rate) is:

$$\$56,520 \times 0.463 = \$26,169$$

GAAP GUIDE / 31.13

Pension Plans

This $26,169 will earn 8% compounded annually for 10 years and will grow to $56,520, which will also earn 8% and from which the 12 annuity payments of $7,500 each will be made. The $26,169 is this employee's past-service costs at the inception of the plan.

Normal costs The company's plan has now been in effect for one year, and the employee has earned another $500 annuity as provided for in the plan. The present value of a $500 annuity for 12 years at 8% is

$$\$500 \times 7.536 = \$3,768$$

In order to make the 12 payments of $500, the trust fund will require $3,768 earning 8% when the employee reaches age 65.
Again, we must discount the $3,768 back to one year after the plan, or nine years, to obtain the present value.

$$\$3,768 \times 0.500 = \$1,884$$

The $1,884 is the normal cost for the year for this employee.

The following table shows this employee's normal costs for the 10 years, between the inception of the plan and age 65.

Year			Normal Cost
1	Inception of Plan		
2	$ 3,768 × 0.500	=	$1,884.00
3	3,768 × 0.540	=	2,034.72
4	3,768 × 0.583	=	2,196.74
5	3,768 × 0.630	=	2,373.84
6	3,768 × 0.681	=	2,566.00
7	3,768 × 0.735	=	2,769.48
8	3,768 × 0.794	=	2,991.79
9	3,768 × 0.857	=	3,236.71
10	3,768 × 0.926	=	3,489.17

This table depicts a feature of the accrued-benefit cost method in that normal costs increase each year. Obviously, this is due to the fact that there is less and less time for the funded amount to earn interest.

Let us assume that the company funds the above employee's pension costs by delivering the trustee a check for:

1. $26,169 for all past-service costs
2. $1,884 for the normal cost for the year

The *maximum* pension plan expense is:

1. Normal cost	$1,884.00
2. 10% of past-service costs	2,616.90
3. 10% of prior-service costs	—
4. Interest on unfunded costs	None
Maximum pension plan expense	$4,500.90

The *minimum* pension plan expense is:

1. Normal cost	$1,884.00
2. Interest on unfunded costs	None
3. Provision for vested benefits	—
Minimum pension plan expense	$1,884.00

No provision for vested benefits need be made, because there are none in the illustration.

Had the company funded only $10,000 of the past-service costs and $1,000 of the normal costs, the computations would be:

The *maximum* pension plan expense is:

1. Normal cost	$1,884.00
2. 10% of past-service costs	2,616.90
3. 10% of prior-service costs	—
4. Interest on unfunded costs**	1,364.24
Maximum pension plan expense	$5,865.14

$$** \ 884 \times 0.08 = \$ \ \ \ 70.72$$
$$16{,}169 \times 0.08 = \underline{1{,}293.52}$$
$$\underline{\$1{,}364.24}$$

The *minimum* pension plan expense is:

1. Normal cost	$1,884.00
2. Interest on unfunded costs	1,364.24
3. Provision for vested benefits	—
Minimum pension plan costs	$3,248.24

Pension Plans

The journal entry for the maximum pension plan expense where the company funded all costs is:

Pension plan expense	$ 4,500.90	
Prepaid pension plan expense	23,552.10	
Cash		$28,053.00

The journal entry for the minimum pension plan expense where the company funded all costs is:

Pension plan expense	$ 1,884.00	
Prepaid pension plan expense	26,169.00	
Cash		$28,053.00

The journal entry for the maximum pension plan expense where the company funded $10,000 for past-service costs and $1,000 for normal costs is:

Pension plan expense	$ 5,865.14	
Deferred pension plan expense	884.00	
Prepaid pension plan expense	5,134.86	
Cash		$11,000.00
Pension plan liability		884.00

In this illustration the company has no legal liability for the unfunded past-service costs, and under promulgated GAAP the $16,169.00 ($26,169.00 − $10,000) difference that is not funded need not be recorded. The difference of $884 ($1,884 − $1,000) of normal cost that is not funded is, however, recorded under promulgated GAAP, even though contractually it is not a legal liability.

The journal entry for the minimum pension plan expense where the company funded $10,000 for past-service costs and $1,000 for normal costs is:

Pension plan expense	$ 3,248.24	
Deferred pension plan expense	884.00	
Prepaid pension plan expense	7,751.76	
Cash		$11,000.00
Pension plan liability		884.00

QUASI-REORGANIZATIONS

Background

Current promulgated GAAP on quasi-reorganizations appears in ARB-43, Chapter 7A. This promulgated GAAP is silent on the extent of its coverage. Apparently all unregulated businesses should comply with the promulgated GAAP and, in accordance with the Addendum to APB-2, companies in regulated industries must also comply.

A quasi-reorganization is frequently referred to as a corporate readjustment.

Overview

When a business reaches a turnaround point and profitable operations seem likely, a quasi-reorganization may be appropriate to eliminate the accumulated deficit from past unprofitable operations. The resulting financial statements will have more credibility, making it easier for the company to borrow money for its profitable operations. In addition, by eliminating the deficit in retained earnings, the possibility of paying dividends in the future becomes more likely.

Although the corporate entity remains unchanged in a quasi-reorganization, a new basis of accountability is established. Assets are usually restated downward to their fair values, and stockholders' equity is adjusted so that retained earnings has a zero balance. Retained earnings is adjusted to a zero balance by charging the deficit either (1) to capital contributed in excess of par or (2) to capital contributed other than for capital stock (usually donated capital). Obviously, this means that capital accounts (other than for capital stock) must be available to absorb the deficit in retained earnings (after all quasi-reorganization adjustments are made).

Although the capital stock account may not be used to absorb a deficit in retained earnings, it is certainly permissible for a corporation to reduce the par value of its existing capital stock and to transfer the resulting excess to a capital contributed in excess of par account (paid-in capital). As a matter of fact, this procedure is frequently accomplished in a quasi-reorganization.

The following types of situations justify a quasi-reorganization, providing that capital accounts (other than for capital stock) are available to absorb the resulting retained earnings deficit after all adjustments:

1. Historical cost of assets clearly requiring adjustment so that realistic financial reporting is possible.
2. An acceptable alternative to legal proceedings resulting in a reorganization
3. A large deficit from past operations exists

In financial accounting, stockholders' equity is usually made up of:

1. capital contributed for stock, to the extent of the par or stated value of each class of stock presently outstanding
2. a. capital contributed in excess of par or stated value of each class of stock whether as a result of original issues, any subsequent reductions of par or stated value, or transactions by the corporation in its own shares
   b. capital received other than for stock whether from shareholders or others (such as donated capital)
3. retained earnings (or deficit), which represents the accumulated income or loss of the corporation

Generally, items properly chargeable to current or future years' income accounts may not be charged to capital accounts. An exception to this rule occurs in accounting for quasi-reorganizations.

Accounting and Reporting

If a corporation elects to restate its assets and stockholders' equity through a quasi-reorganization, it must make a clear report of the proposed restatements to its shareholders and obtain their formal consent.

Assets should be written down to their fair values; and if fair values are not readily determinable, conservative estimates may be used. Estimates may also be used to provide for known possible losses prior to the date of the quasi-reorganization, when amounts are indeterminable.

If estimates are used and the amounts are subsequently found to be excessive or insufficient, the difference should be charged or credited to the capital account previously charged or credited, and not to retained earnings.

The steps in the accounting procedure follow:

1. All amounts to be written off should be charged to retained earnings, irrespective of whether retained earnings has or will have a deficit.
2. After all amounts to be written off are recognized and charged to retained earnings, any debit balance in retained earnings may be transferred by journal entry to either (a) capital contributed in excess of par or (b) capital contributed other than for capital stock.

   It makes no difference whether the two capital accounts above were previously existing or were created as a result of the quasi-reorganization.

   It is important to remember that it is improper to increase a credit balance in retained earnings by an accounting or quasi reorganization, but it is acceptable to eliminate a deficit.
3. If a deficit in retained earnings is transferred to an allowable capital account, any subsequent balance sheet must disclose, by dating the retained earnings, that the balance in the retained earnings account has increased since the date of reorganization. For example:

   Retained earnings, since July 1, 19XX $1,234,567

   The dating of retained earnings following a quasi-reorganization would rarely if ever be of significance after a period of 10 years. There may be exceptional circumstances that could justify a period of less than 10 years (ARB-46).
4. New or additional shares of stock may be issued or exchanged for other shares or existing indebtedness. For example, stockholders may agree to subscribe to additional shares, or bondholders may agree to accept capital stock in lieu of interest in arrears, in order to provide new cash for future operations. Accounting entries for these types of transactions are handled in accordance with GAAP.
5. Corporations with subsidiaries should follow the same procedures, so that no credit balance remains in consolidated retained earnings after a quasi-reorganization where losses have been charged to allowable capital accounts.

   In those cases, where losses have been charged to the allowable capital accounts, instead of a credit balance in consolidated retained earnings, the parent company's interest in such retained earnings should be regarded as capitalized by the quasi-reorganization in the same way retained

GAAP GUIDE / 32.03

earnings of a subsidiary are capitalized on the date of its acquisition.

6. The effective date of the quasi-reorganization from which income of the corporation is thereafter determined should be as close as possible to the date of formal stockholders' consent and preferably at the start of a new fiscal year.

Under no circumstances should adjustments made pursuant to a quasi-reorganization be included in the determination of net income for any period (APB-9).

If not previously recognized, a tax benefit arising prior to a quasi-reorganization, which is realizable beyond a reasonable doubt, should be recorded as an asset at the date of the reorganization. Such tax benefits may result from the amount of deficit in retained earnings that was applied to paid-in capital as a result of a quasi-reorganization, or from loss carryforwards that arose prior to the quasi-reorganization (APB-11). However, the tax benefit of an unused investment tax credit may never be recorded as an asset (APB-2 and APB-4).

Disclosure

Adequate disclosure of all pertinent information should be made in the financial statements. A new retained earnings account dated as at the effective date of the quasi-reorganization should be established and reflected in subsequent financial statements. Usually, the dating of the new retained earnings account can be eliminated after 10 years and in unusual circumstances earlier than 10 years (ARB-46).

Comprehensive Illustration

The following example demonstrates the procedures which must be used in accounting for a quasi-reorganization.

The Centrex Company, founded in 1970, has experienced losses in each of its first six years of operation. In May 1976, however, the company acquired two patents on an advanced solar-heating unit, which in several months has become the standard for the industry. The quarter ended September 30, 1976, was extremely profitable, and the patent and accompanying licensing agreements indicate that continuing profitability is quite likely.

The company is closely held, and the stockholders have agreed in principle to a quasi-reorganization. Negotiations have been held with various creditors regarding capitalizing debts.

The balance sheet of the company at December 31, 1976, appeared as follows:

Assets

Cash	$ 25,000
Accounts receivable (net)	410,000
Plant and equipment (net)	1,670,000
Other assets	80,000
Total assets	$2,185,000

Liabilities and Equity

Accounts payable	$ 840,000
Notes payable–other	300,000
Equipment notes payable	240,000
Common stock	500,000
Paid-in capital–common stock	1,017,000
Retained earnings	(712,000)
Total liabilities and equity	$2,185,000

The stockholders and creditors have approved the following plan of informal reorganization effective January 1, 1977:

1. The current shareholders will exchange their 100,000 shares of $5 par stock for 100,000 shares of $1 par stock.
2. The creditors have agreed to accept $300,000 in a 5% preferred stock for $300,000 of accounts payable.
3. The plant and equipment will be written down to its fair value of $1,100,000.
4. $70,000 of accounts receivable will be written off as uncollectible.
5. Other assets will be written down to their fair value of $50,000.

The first step in a quasi-reorganization is to write down all assets to their fair values. In the example the journal entry would be:

Retained earnings	$ 670,000		
Plant and equipment		$	570,000
Accounts receivable			70,000
Other assets			30,000

Quasi-Reorganizations

Next, the change in the par value of the common stock is recorded:

Common stock	$ 400,000	
Paid-in capital–common stock		$ 400,000

The following journal entry records the new preferred stock issued for $300,000 of accounts payable:

Accounts payable	$ 300,000	
5% preferred stock		$ 300,000

After all the quasi-reorganization adjustments are made, the deficit in retained earnings ($1,382,000) is eliminated against the paid-in capital–common stock, leaving a zero balance in retained earnings:

Paid-in capital–common stock	$1,382,000	
Retained earnings		$1,382,000

The Centrex Company balance sheet after giving effect to the reorganization appears as:

Centrex Company
Assets

Cash	$ 25,000
Accounts receivable (net)	340,000
Plant and equipment (net)	1,100,000
Other assets	50,000
Total assets	$1,515,000

Liabilities and Equity

Accounts payable	$ 540,000
Notes payable–other	300,000
Equipment notes payable	240,000
Common stock ($1 par)	100,000
5% Preferred stock	300,000
Paid-in capital–common stock	35,000
Retained earnings since January 1, 1977	-0-
Total liabilities and equity	$1,515,000

Retained earnings must be dated on the balance sheet after a reorganization.

REAL AND PERSONAL PROPERTY TAXES

Background

ARB-43, Chapter 10A (as amended), provides the existing promulgated GAAP for accounting for real and personal property taxes. Since the promulgated GAAP is silent as to its coverage, it is assumed that companies in regulated industries must comply in accordance with the Addendum to APB-2.

Accounting and Reporting

Although many states have different laws or precedents as to when the legal liability accrues for real and personal property taxes, the general rule is that they accrue on the date they are assessed. However, the exact amount of tax may not be known on the assessment date, and a reasonable estimate must be made. The inability to determine the exact amount of real and personal property taxes is not an acceptable excuse for failure to recognize the existing tax liability. In those cases where the accrued amount is subject to a great deal of uncertainty, the liability should be appropriately described as estimated.

Whether the amount of the accrued tax liability for real and personal property taxes is known or estimated, it should be reported as a current liability in the balance sheet.

A monthly accrual over the fiscal period of the taxing authority is considered the most acceptable basis for recording real and personal property taxes. This will result in the appropriate accrual or prepayment at any closing date.

An adjustment to the estimated tax liability of a prior year will have to be made when the exact amount has been determined. This adjustment is made in the income statement of the period in which the exact amount has been determined, either as an adjustment to the current year's provision or as a separate item on the income statement.

It is sometimes proper to capitalize real estate taxes on property being developed for internal use or sale to customers. However, in most circumstances real and personal property taxes are considered an expense of doing business and are reported in the appropriate income statement (1) as an operating expense, (2) as a deduction from income, or (3) allocated to several expense accounts, such as manufacturing overhead and general and administrative expenses.

Real and Personal Property Taxes

As a general rule, real and personal property taxes should not be combined with income taxes.

> **OBSERVATION:** *The promulgated GAAP does not describe the criteria for capitalizing or not capitalizing real estate taxes.*

The most important consideration in accounting for real and personal property taxes is consistency. The accounting treatment, and reporting, must be consistently applied from year to year.

REGULATED INDUSTRIES

Accounting Principles

The extent that GAAP must be applied to regulated industries is contained in an Addendum to APB-2.

The financial statements of a regulated business, intended for public use, should be based on existing GAAP with appropriate recognition given to the rate-making process. An auditor must comply with the first standard of reporting, which requires that financial statements be presented in accordance with GAAP.

Unless specifically excluded, all promulgated GAAP applies to companies in regulated industries.

RESEARCH AND DEVELOPMENT COSTS

Background

The promulgated GAAP on accounting for research and development costs (R&D) is FASB-2. In addition, FASB Interpretation-4 covers R&D acquired in a business combination accounted for by the purchase method, and FASB Interpretation-6 covers the applicability of R&D in respect to computer software. All three of the above promulgated GAAP are silent as to the extent of their coverage. Therefore, it is assumed that companies in both unregulated and regulated industries must comply with the provisions of these promulgated GAAP. Regulated companies are included in accordance with the Addendum to APB-2.

Specifically excluded from these promulgated GAAP are the following:

1. Activities that are unique to the extractive industries, such as prospecting, exploration, drilling, mining, and similar items. However, R&D which is comparable in nature to other companies not in the extractive industry, such as the development or improvement of techniques and processes is covered by the promulgated GAAP.

2. R&D performed under contract for others, including indirect costs which are specifically reimbursable under a contract.

Overview

Research is the planned efforts of a company to discover new information that will help create a new product, service, process, or technique, or vastly improve one in current use. Development takes the findings generated by research and formulates a plan to create the desired item or to improve the existing one. Development in the context of this area of GAAP does not include normal improvements in existing operations. The promulgated GAAP does not include market research and testing, because these items specifically relate to the selling and marketing operations of a company. In addition, general and administrative expenses not *directly* related to the R&D activities are also not included in the promulgated GAAP.

The underlying basic principle in accounting for R&D is conservatism, because the high degree of uncertainty of any resulting future benefit. Since at the time of performing the R&D, there is no possible method of determining any future success, the most conservative approach is to expense the item in the period incurred.

Accounting and Reporting R&D

All R&D costs covered by the promulgated GAAP are expensed when incurred except R&D machinery, equipment, and facilities which have alternative future uses either in R&D activities or otherwise. Machinery, equipment, and facilities, which have alternative future uses, should be capitalized. However, depreciation or amortization on such capitalized R&D machinery, equipment, and facilities is charged to expense. All expenditures in conjunction with an R&D project including personnel costs, materials, equipment, facilities, and intangibles, for which the company has no alternative future use beyond the specific project for which the items were purchased, are expensed. Indirect costs, including general and administrative expenses, which are *directly* related to the R&D are also expensed when incurred.

As mentioned previously, it is important to remember that R&D costs related to market research or testing, and general and administrative expenses that are not directly related to R&D activity, are costs not covered by the promulgated GAAP.

Research and development costs acquired by the purchase method in a business combination shall be assigned their fair values, if any, in accordance with existing promulgated GAAP (APB-16). The subsequent accounting by the acquirer of these R&D costs shall be made in compliance with the promulgated GAAP enumerated herein. Those R&D costs with future alternative use shall be capitalized, and all others expensed (FASB Interpretation-4).

R&D activities associated with computer software are not excepted from the promulgated GAAP, and are accounted for in the same manner as other R&D discussed herein. However, because of the diverse uses of computer software, a brief discussion of different R&D related to software applications, and how they should be accounted for under the promulgated GAAP, are elaborated on at the end of this chapter.

Disclosure

The amount of R&D charged to expense for the period must be disclosed in the financial statements for each period presented.

A company in a regulated industry which defers R&D costs in

Research and Development Costs

compliance with the Addendum to APB-2 must disclose the following additional information:

1. Accounting policies in regard to R&D, including the basis for amortization
2. The total amount of R&D that has been expensed, capitalized, or deferred for each period that an income statement is presented

R&D and Computer Software

The following specific circumstances involving R&D and computer software are discussed in detail in the promulgated GAAP:

1. The development of a computer system to improve an administrative or a selling procedure would *not* be considered R&D. An example of such a system is the computerized reservation system developed by a hotel chain.
2. The cost of leasing a computer software system is not part of R&D unless it is specifically for R&D uses. If so, it should be treated as any R&D item and be expensed, unless it has an alternative future use.
3. Developing a software system for an outsider under a contractual agreement is excluded from the promulgated GAAP. However, speculative internal development of a software system, for which there is no outside commitment, would be accounted for as R&D and any costs incurred in researching the conceptual framework of the system or translating the framework into a design would be R&D. If development of a software system is only part of a product or process, the same criteria apply. An example of when the software is only part of the process would be the development of a computer system to generate audiovisual presentations.
4. Ongoing costs related to improving existing software systems are not R&D items.
5. Costs incurred in the internal development of a computer software system for use in a company's own R&D activities should be charged to expense when incurred. The alternative future test does not apply in this area.

RESULTS OF OPERATIONS

Background

There are three separate promulgated GAAP in the area of reporting the results of operations, as follows:

APB-9 (as amended), Reporting the Results of Operations
APB-30 (as amended), Reporting the Results of Operations–Reporting the Effects of Disposal of a Segment of a Business, and Extraordinary, Unusual, and Infrequently Occurring Events and Transactions
FASB-16, Prior Period Adjustments
FASB Interpretation-27, Accounting for a Loss on a Sublease

APB-9 clearly indicates that it applies to general-purpose statements prepared in conformity with GAAP that present the results of operations. Investment companies, insurance companies, and certain nonprofit organizations which have developed special formats for income statements that differ from the typical commercial formats need not comply with the provision of APB-9, which requires that net income be presented as one amount. Otherwise these entities are covered by APB-9. Both APB-30 and FASB-16 are silent in respect to these particular companies, so it is assumed that they must fully comply with these promulgated GAAP.

FASB-16 specifically covers companies in regulated industries in accordance with the Addendum to APB-2. APB-9 and APB-30 are silent on their coverage of companies in regulated industries. However, in accordance with the Addendum to APB-2, the assumption is that all three of these promulgated GAAP cover both unregulated and regulated companies.

Overview

Prior to the issuance of APB-9 there were differences in the accounting profession as to what should, or should not, be included in net income. Proponents of the *all-inclusive concept* believe that all items affecting net increases in owners' equity, except dividends and capital transactions, should be included in computing net income. These proponents support their position with the following reasons:

1. Extraordinary items are part of income, and annual income

statements over the life of an entity when added together should represent total net income as reported.
2. Omission of extraordinary items will distort the total financial position of an enterprise.
3. Extraordinary items may be manipulated, or possibly overlooked, if they are not included on a regular basis.
4. An income statement that includes all charges or credits arising during the year is simple to prepare, easy to understand, and not subject to variations based on judgment.

Proponents of the *current operating performance concept,* who advocate excluding extraordinary items from net income, maintain the following position:

1. Net income should place emphasis on the normal operations of an enterprise and exclude nonrecurring extraordinary items.
2. The annual income statement's primary purpose is to inform those interested in what an entity was able to earn under the current year's operating conditions.
3. Net income for the year should reflect as clearly as possible what happened under that year's conditions, in order that comparability may be made with prior years and with the performance of other enterprises in the same industry.
4. Readers of financial statements are frequently unable to determine net income from normal operations, when extraordinary items are included in the computation of net income.
5. A material extraordinary item included in net income may be so distorting in its effect as to lead to unsound judgment about the current operating performance of the company.

Although the two schools of thought still exist, present-day GAAP support the all-inclusive concept. Net income should include all items of income and loss during a reporting period, except prior-period adjustments, dividends, and capital transactions. All extraordinary items should be segregated and shown separately in the income statement.

APB-9 further describes capital transactions as those:

1. charges or credits arising from transactions in a company's own capital stock
2. transfers to and from appropriated retained earnings
3. adjustments made pursuant to a quasi-reorganization

Extraordinary Items

Extraordinary items are transactions and other events that are (1) material in nature, (2) of a character significantly different from the typical or customary business activities, (3) not expected to recur frequently, and (4) not normally considered in evaluating the ordinary operating results of an enterprise. Extraordinary items must be separately disclosed in the income statement, net of any related income tax effect.

Extraordinary items are usually determined by informed professional judgment, taking into consideration all the facts involved in a particular situation. However, some areas of promulgated GAAP require that an item be treated as extraordinary. The following are the more common items which, if material, should be reported as an extraordinary item:

1. the tax benefit of an operating loss carryforward when recognized in periods subsequent to the year of loss (APB-11)
2. the tax benefit of a loss carryforward when recognized in periods subsequent to the year of loss (APB-11)
3. the profit or loss on disposal of a significant part of the assets, or a separate segment, of the previously separate companies of a business combination, when disposed of within two years after the date of the combination (APB-16)
4. a significant write-off of an intangible asset (APB-17)
5. gains on restructuring payables (FASB-15)
6. most gains or losses on the extinguishment of debt (FASB-4)
7. most expropriations of property (APB-30)

The cumulative effect of an accounting change is reflected in the income statement, net of related tax effects, between extraordinary items and net income. On the other hand, a gain or loss on discontinued operations is reflected in the income statement, net of

Results of Operations

related income tax effects, between income from continuing operations and extraordinary items.

For reporting purposes extraordinary items arising as part of the net income from an investment accounted for by the equity method are combined with extraordinary items of the investor.

If professional judgment dictates individual treatment of a material event or transaction that does not qualify as an extraordinary item, it may be separately reported as a component of income from continuing operations with appropriate footnote disclosure. However, in this event, the separately identified item should not be reported net of its related tax effects.

Prior-Period Adjustments

An SEC staff interpretation of GAAP recently questioned the use of prior-period adjustments to account for certain negotiated settlements of litigation. One criterion for a prior-period adjustment had been that the event which caused the adjustment depended primarily on the determination of persons other than management.

The two most common types of prior-period adjustments had been settlements of litigation and settlements of income taxes. The SEC concluded that management plays a significant role in any negotiated settlement and that these settlements do not meet the criteria for a prior-period adjustment.

Consequently the definition of a prior-period adjustment has been narrowly redefined by FASB-16 as either:

1. a correction of an error in a prior-period statement, or
2. an adjustment for the realization of the tax benefits of the preacquisition operating-loss carryforwards of purchased subsidiaries

All other items of profit and loss (including accruals for loss contingencies) shall be included in the determination of net income for the period. Items which previously had qualified for treatment as prior-period adjustments will now be included in net income and will require disclosure as necessary for conformity with other requirements of GAAP.

Interim-period adjustments An adjustment of prior interim periods of a current fiscal year can include any of the following settlements:

1. litigation or similar claims
2. income taxes
3. renegotiation
4. utility revenues governed by rate-making processes

In adjusting interim periods of the current year, any adjustment of prior periods is made to the first interim period of the current year. Adjustments to the other interim periods of the current year are related to the interim period affected.

The effects (1) on income from continuous operations, (2) on net income, and (3) on earnings per share of an adjustment to a current interim period must be fully disclosed.

Accounting changes Present promulgated GAAP is unaffected by the new narrow definition of prior-period adjustments.

Accounting changes that will necessitate adjustments of prior periods for reporting purposes are:

1. reporting a change in an entity
2. an accounting change from the LIFO method to any other method
3. an accounting change in reporting long-term construction contracts
4. a change to or from the full-cost method used in the extractive industries

In addition, a change in accounting methods of constituents of a pooling of interest to conform with the parent company is still applied retroactively, and financial statements presented for prior periods should be restated.

In those rare material cases when prior-period adjustments are recorded, the resulting effects should be disclosed in the period in which the adjustments are made by *restating the balance of retained earnings at the beginning of such period.*

Both the gross and net effect (of related income taxes) of prior-period adjustments on net income should be disclosed in the year of adjustment and all years presented (APB-9).

Discontinued Operations

Discontinued operations are identifiable segments of a business that have been or will be disposed of.

Results of Operations

Identifiable entity Segments of a business are components that represent a major class of a firm's business, usually taking the form of a subsidiary, division, department, or other identifiable entity.

Segments of a business have separate assets and results of operations and activities that can be clearly distinguished for financial reporting purposes.

Facts that indicate there is no separate identity suggest that the form of business should not be classified as a segment of a business.

Measurement date The measurement date of a disposal of a segment of business is the date management commits itself to a formal plan for action to sell or otherwise dispose of the segment.

> ***OBSERVATION:*** *The plan of disposal should be carried out within one year from the measurement date. If a plan of disposal is estimated to be completed within one year, and subsequently is not, any revision of the net realizable value of the segment should be treated as a change in an accounting estimate and should therefore be made prospectively.*

Disposal date The disposal date is the date of closing, in the case of a sale, or the date operations cease, in the case of abandonment.

Determination of gain or loss The estimated loss on disposal of a segment of business should be provided for as of the *measurement date.*

In the case of a gain, it should not be recognized until it is realized (realization principle), which is usually the *disposal date.*

Determination of gain or loss on disposal of a segment of business should be made as of the measurement date, based on estimates of the net realizable value.

Results of Operations

Net losses from operations between the measurement date and the expected disposal date should be provided for in the determination of gain or loss.

Estimates should be based on the amounts that can be projected with reasonable accuracy.

> ***OBSERVATION:*** *Cost, expenses, and other adjustments associated with normal business activities which should have been recognized prior to the measurement date should not be included in the gain or loss on disposal of a segment, but should be included in income (loss) from discontinued operations. Severance pay, additional pension costs, and employee relocation expenses are costs directly associated with the decision to dispose of the segment and are properly includable in the gain or loss on disposal.*

Long-term leases FASB Interpretation-27 reaffirms that estimated costs and expenses directly associated with a decision to dispose of a business segment should include future rental payments on long-term leases less any future rentals to be received from subleases of the same properties (ARB-30). The gain or loss is measured as the difference between the unamortized cost of the leased property (net carrying amount) and the present value of the minimum lease payments which will be received under the terms of the sublease. The gain or loss is included in the overall gain or loss on the disposal of the business segment.

> ***OBSERVATION:*** *FASB Interpretation-27 is not clear on its coverage of subleases which are classified as operating leases. There is a strong argument that gain or loss on an operating sublease be included as part of the overall gain or loss on disposal of a business segment. APB-30 specifically states that all costs and expenses which are directly associated to the decision to dispose of a business segment be included in the overall gain or loss on the disposal. If a business segment has a long-term operating lease which is subleased and classified as an operating lease as part of the overall disposal of the segment, then any gain or loss would obviously be directly associated with management's decision to dispose of the segment. The gain or loss would be measured as the difference between the present value of the future rental payments which must be paid on the original*

Results of Operations

lease and the present value of the future rental receipts which will be collected on the operating sublease. The journal entry to record a loss would be a debit to the gain or loss account for disposal of the business segment and a credit to a deferred account. The deferred credit account would be amortized each year in an amount which would make up the difference between the payment made on the original lease and the rental collected on the operating sublease.

Disclosure Notes to the financial statements for the period encompassing the measurement date should include:

1. identity of the segment of business
2. expected date of disposal
3. manner of disposal
4. description of the remaining assets and liabilities of the segment of business
5. income and loss from operations and other proceeds from disposal of the segment of business, from the measurement date to the date of the balance sheet

Presentation of Net Income

The following is the preferred method of financial statement presentation of net income:

Results of Operations

Income (loss) from continuing operations, before provision for income taxes	$XXXXX	
Provision for income taxes	XXX	
Income (loss) from continuing operations		$XXXXX
Discontinued operations (note ___)		
Income (loss) from operations of discontinued division A (less applicable income taxes $XX)	$ XXXX	
Loss (gain) on disposal of division A, including provision of $XX for operating losses during phase-out period (less applicable income taxes of $XX)	XXX	
Net income (loss) from discontinued operations		XXXX
Net income (loss) before extraordinary items		$XXXXX
Extraordinary items (note ___) (less applicable income taxes of $XX)		XX
Cumulative effect on prior years (to December 31, 19XX) of a change in an accounting principle (less applicable income taxes of $XX).		XXX
Net income		$XXXXX

Results of Operations

Earnings per share (EPS) for extraordinary items is not required but is strongly recommended by APB-15 and APB-30. EPS for discontinued operations and the resulting gain or loss on the disposal of the segment may or may not be presented (APB-30).

When common stock equivalents or other dilutive securities cause a dilution in one of the EPS data presented on the face of the income statement, and at the same time cause an antidilution in another EPS data presented on the same income statement, all the EPS data presented should be computed using the common stock equivalents or other dilutive securities (APB-30).

Whenever prior-period adjustments have been recorded during any period included in a five- or ten-year historical financial summary, the reported amounts of net income and components thereof should be appropriately restated.

SEGMENTAL REPORTING

Background

The promulgated GAAP on segmental reporting are:

FASB-14, Financial Reporting for Segments of a Business Enterprise

FASB-18, Financial Reporting for Segments of a Business Enterprise–Interim Financial Statements

FASB-24, Reporting Segment Information in Financial Statements that are Presented in Another Enterprise's Financial Report

Companies that are subject to government regulations for setting rates are not specifically referred to in the promulgated GAAP. Therefore, in accordance with the Addendum to APB-2, regulated companies should comply with the provisions of the promulgated GAAP (FASB-14) for reporting segmental information.

Segmental information for each fiscal year presented is required of all enterprises that issue a complete set of financial statements in conformity with GAAP. However, segmental information is not required (FASB-24) in the following circumstances:

1. If a complete set of financial statements are consolidated or combined in the financial report of another enterprise, then the segmental information does not have to be disclosed in the accompanying separate complete set of financial statements when presented in the same financial report containing the consolidated or combined statements. However, segmental information would have to be disclosed for the consolidated or combined statements.

2. A complete set of financial statements for a foreign investee that is not a subsidiary need not disclose segmental information when presented in the same financial report of a primary reporting enterprise unless the foreign investee's separately issued financial statements already disclose the required segmental data. In other words, if the non-subsidiary foreign investee's financial statements already contain the required segmental information then it must be disclosed when such financial statements are presented in the same financial report of a primary reporting entity.

Segmental Reporting

3. A complete set of financial statements of any enterprise which is presented in the financial report of a nonpublic enterprise need not disclose segmental information. A nonpublic enterprise is not required to disclose segmental information (FASB-21–see below).

> **OBSERVATION:** FASB-24 differentiates between a complete set of financial statements being "presented" and a set which is "consolidated" or "combined". Although the distinction is not clear, it is assumed that being "presented" means that the complete set of financial statements is included in the financial report but not "consolidated" or "combined".

Disclosure of segmental information is required in a complete set of financial statements of an investment accounted for by the cost or equity method when such statements are presented in the financial report of another enterprise. However, all of the percentage tests required by FASB-14 are computed by excluding the amounts attributable to the investment accounted for by the cost or equity method. For example, the 10% revenue test to determine a reportable segment under FASB-14 must be computed on the total of all the enterprise's industry segments. When determining the same test for an investment accounted for by the cost or equity method, all revenue from such an investment is excluded and the 10% is computed only on the other industry segments of the primary reporting entity. All other percentage tests required by FASB-14 are determined in the same manner (e.g., by excluding the amounts attributable to the investment accounted for by the cost or equity method).

The following definitions are used in segmental reporting (FASB-24):

Segmental information is the information which is required to be disclosed by FASB-14, namely, an enterprise's (1) operations in different industries, (2) foreign operations and export sales, and (3) major customers.

Complete set of financial statements include financial position, changes in financial position, results of operations, all necessary footnotes and prepared in conformity with GAAP.

Financial report includes one or more complete sets of financial statements and other information (annual reports, SEC filings, etc).

Foreign investee not a subsidiary of the primary reporting enterprise is an entity organized and domiciled in a foreign country of which fifty percent (50%) or more of its voting stock is owned by foreign residents.

Nonpublic Enterprise (FASB-21)

A nonpublic enterprise is an enterprise other than one

1. whose debt or equity securities are traded in a public market
2. that is required to file financial statements with the SEC

An enterprise loses its status as nonpublic when it issues financial statements in preparation for the sale of any class of securities in a public market.

A public market is a foreign or domestic stock exchange or an over-the-counter market.

A nonpublic enterprise is not required to disclose earnings per share (APB-15) or segment information (FASB-14) in a complete set of separately issued financial statements. The nonpublic enterprise may be a subsidiary, joint venture, or any other investee.

If the nonpublic enterprise elects to disclose earnings per share or segment information, it must comply with the disclosure requirements of GAAP. It may not disclose this information on an arbitrary basis.

Overview

Promulgated GAAP (FASB-14) requires that annual financial statements contain segmental information about a company's operations in (1) different industries, (2) foreign operations and export sales, and (3) major customers.

Financial reporting of segmental information of a business is not required in interim financial statements (FASB-18).

The required financial statement information is basically a disaggregation of the entity's regular financial statements. The accounting principles used in preparing the financial statements should be used for the segment information, *except* that many intercompany transactions that are eliminated in consolidation are included in segmental reporting.

It is not necessary to present segment data regarding unconsolidated subsidiaries or investees. However, identification must be made about the specific industry and geographic area in which these companies operate.

It is important to remember that transactions between the segments of an enterprise are not eliminated, as in consolidation; rather they are reported on a gross basis.

Terminology

The following terminology is used in segmental reporting:

Industry segment A part of a company that sells primarily to outsiders for a profit. Vertically integrated operations of a company are not considered industry segments.

Reportable segment Any part of a company for which segment reporting is required by the criteria explained herein.

Revenue Sales either to outsiders or to other segments of the company. Intersegmental sales should be based on sales or transfer prices used by the company. However, intersegmental sales should not include the cost of shared facilities or other joint costs.

Interest earned on intersegmental trade receivables is included in intersegmental sales, if the receivable or other asset is included in the industry segment's identifiable assets (see below). However, interest on advances or loans between industry segments is not included in intersegmental revenues.

Operating income or loss of an industry segment should include interest on loans or advances between industry segments, if the industry segment's principal operations are financial (banking, insurance, leasing, etc.).

Industry segment's operating profit or loss Revenue less operating expenses, as defined herein. Operating expenses include those related to intersegmental sales as well as those to unaffiliated customers. Corporate overhead which cannot be identified with any specific revenue production should be allocated in a reasonable manner among the segments benefited. Intersegmental purchases are accounted for on the basis of transfer and sales prices used by the company. The operating profit or loss of an industry segment shall not include the following:

1. revenue not derived from the operation of any industry segment
2. revenue earned at the corporate level
3. general corporate expenses

Segmental Reporting

4. interest expense, except for an industry segment whose principal operation is financial
5. foreign or domestic income taxes
6. equity in the income or loss from an unconsolidated subsidiary or investee
7. gain or loss on discontinued operations
8. extraordinary items
9. minority interests
10. cumulative effect of a change in an accounting principle

Operating expenses of industry segments should be determined by their nature and not by the fact that they are recorded as general corporate expenses. If an expense would ordinarily be deducted in computing the operating profit or loss of an industry segment, then it should be so included, regardless of how it was entered on the records. In other words, the nature of the expense should determine its deductibility as an operating expense of an industry segment.

Identifiable assets are either the tangible and intangible assets used exclusively by a segment, or the allocated portion of assets used jointly by more than one segment. General corporate assets are not allocated to segments, and loan and investment accounts are not considered assets unless income from them is included in segment profit or loss.

Goodwill, less any amortization, is included in an industry segment's identifiable assets. An industry segment's identifiable assets should be net of any valuation accounts, such as allowance for doubtful accounts, accumulated depreciation, etc.

Loans and advances between industry segments whose principal operations are financial (banking, leasing, insurance, etc.) and whose income is derived from such loans and advances should be included as an identifiable industry segment asset.

Determining Reportable Segments

There are three steps in determining the reportable segments of an enterprise:

1. identifying the enterprise's products and services
2. grouping the products and services into industry segments

Segmental Reporting

3. selecting the significant industry segments

Grouping Products and Services

Although several systems exist for classifying business activities, the determination of industry segments depends primarily on the judgment of management. Existing profit centers are useful in collecting segment data, unless they cross industry lines.

Industry segmentation of foreign operations should also be performed. However, those foreign operations for which segmentation is impractical should be reported as a single segment, and appropriately disclosed.

Selecting Reportable Segments

10% tests A test is made each fiscal year to determine an enterprise's reportable segments. A reportable segment must satisfy one or more of the following tests:

1. Its revenue (as defined herein to mean revenue both from intercompany and from outsiders) is at least 10% of all the enterprise's industry segments.
2. Its operating profit or loss is 10% or more of the greater of a or b below.
    a. the total of all the enterprise's industry segments that had operating profits
    b. the total of all the enterprise's industry segments that had operating losses
3. Its identifiable assets (as defined herein) are 10% or more of the enterprise's combined industry segments' identifiable assets.

> *OBSERVATION:* To determine criterion 2 above, all losses of industry segments which had operating losses are totaled, and all profits of industry segments which had operating profits are totaled. The greater of the two totals (losses or profits) is then used to apply the 10% test, as follows:

Segment	Losses	Profits
A	$ 1,000	
B		$2,000
C		1,000
D	3,000	
E	7,000	
Totals	$11,000	$3,000

Under the 10% rule, the $11,000 is used and the reportable segments are those which have losses or profits in excess of $1,100 (10% of $11,000). Therefore, industry segments B, D, and E qualify as reportable segments for this particular criterion.

In the event that it is impractical to disaggregate part or all of a foreign operation, it should be treated as a single industry segment and should be included in the combined revenue, combined operating profit or loss, and combined identifiable assets of the company's industry segments.

Comparability test Since the determination of a reportable segment is made each fiscal year, a reportable segment of the immediate prior years may fail to meet the 10% test in the current year. However, if the reportable segment that fails to meet the current year's test is expected to satisfy the 10% test in future years, in order to satisfy the criterion of comparability it would have to be included in the current year, even though it failed to meet the test. On the other hand, if an industry segment that usually never qualifies as a reportable segment happens to qualify because of an unusual event, it may be necessary to exclude the segment on the basis of distorting comparability.

75% test Combined revenue from sales to outsiders, by all reportable segments, must be at least 75% of the total revenue of all the industry segments of an enterprise. If the 75% test is not met by the reportable segments which passed the 10% and comparability tests, additional industry segments must be added to meet the 75% test. These additional industry segments do not have to pass the 10% or comparability test. Within the framework described above, it is desirable to combine segments as necessary to keep the total number of segments at ten or less.

Dominant Segments

If the revenue, operating profit or loss, and identifiable assets of a segment all exceed 90% of the respective totals for the enterprise, and no other segment meets any 10% test, that segment is considered *dominant*. A dominant segment must be identified, but none of the detailed disclosures applying to multisegment enterprises need be reported.

Information to Be Reported

The enterprise must report revenue, profitability, and identifiable assets for each business segment, total unsegmented foreign operations, and the aggregate of other business which is not by itself significant.

As to revenue, the enterprise should report separately sales to outsiders and intercompany transfers. Transfers should be costed at the rate used by the company for operating purposes, and that basis should be disclosed.

Operating profit or loss of each reportable segment and the amount of expenses allocated to that segment should be disclosed. The methods used to allocate expenses should be consistently applied. In addition to operating profit or loss, the company is free to present some other measure of profitability as long as the methods used in determining the amounts are disclosed.

The aggregate amount of identifiable assets must be disclosed for each segment and in total.

The company must also disclose the types of products and any significant segmental accounting policies not already disclosed in the regular financial statements.

Other disclosures required for each reportable segment include:

1. depreciation, depletion, and amortization
2. capital expenditures
3. equity in unconsolidated but vertically integrated subsidiaries, and the geographic area in which they operate
4. the effect on operating profit of segments due to a change in accounting principle

OBSERVATION: *The pro forma effects of the retroactive application of a change in an accounting principle, and the pro forma supplemental information relating to a business combination accounted for by the purchase method (APB-16), need not be presented for individual reportable segments.*

Reportable segment information may be presented in footnotes to the statements or in separate schedules.

The information presented for revenue, operating profit or loss, and identifiable assets must be reconciled to the related financial statements' amounts for revenue, pretax income, and total assets.

Foreign Operations and Export Sales

Information regarding operations outside the enterprise's home country or which generate revenue from sales or transfers between geographic areas should be included in the financial statements.

An enterprise should report segment information for each significant geographic area. A geographic area is a country or a group of countries that is treated as a homogeneous unit for segmental reporting purposes. A geographic area is significant if it meets either of the following tests:

1. Revenue from unaffiliated customers is 10% or more of consolidated revenue.
2. Identifiable assets are 10% or more of consolidated total assets.

The enterprise should disclose revenue, operating profit or loss (or net income or some measure of profitability), and identifiable assets.

When an enterprise has export sales to outsiders which are 10% or more of total sales to outsiders, these amounts should be disclosed.

The enterprise should identify the geographic areas for which it is presenting segment information, and may disclose the information in the statements, footnotes, or a separate schedule.

The amounts shown as revenue, operating profit or loss (or other measure of profitability), and identifiable assets must be reconciled to the related amounts shown in the financial statements for revenue, pretax income, and total assets.

Segmental Reporting

Information about Major Customers

An enterprise that makes 10% or more of its revenue from sales to a single customer or government must disclose such facts. The disclosures required include the identity of the segment, and the amount of revenue involved. Even if the enterprise is not otherwise required to present segment information, it must conform to this requirement.

Restatement of Previously Reported Segment Information

Since the reporting of segment information is required on a comparative basis, previously reported information must be restated when:

1. The statements of the company have been restated for a change in accounting principle or entity.
2. The company has changed the segment or geographic grouping of its operation, which results in changes in the information presented.

Comprehensive Illustration

The following segmental disclosure appeared in the December 31, 1977, financial statements of Harcourt Brace Jovanovich, Inc.

The principal sources of the company's business are the following:

Segment	*Principal Activities*
School instructional materials	Publishing textbooks and related learning materials, and distributing supplies to elementary and secondary schools.
University and professional publishing and instruction	Publishing scientific and medical books and journals, college textbooks, reprint editions of scholarly works, books and other materials for use in conducting bar review courses

Segmental Reporting

Segment	Principal Activities
	and CPA accreditation courses; distributing professional books; publishing books and journals and conducting seminars for lawyers and other practitioners, including continuing education.
Popular enterprises	Providing instructional entertainment at three marine parks, operating several restaurants and a number of fast-food outlets.
Periodical subscriptions and advertising	Publishing business and professional periodicals and directories, farm magazines and rural-county directories, a magazine for elementary schoolteachers, and magazines that have paid mail subscription or newsstand sales or both.
General books	Publishing books of general interest (including children's books) in hardcover, in trade paperback editions, and in mass-market paperback editions; operating book clubs; operating a general bookstore; publishing high-priced illustrated books sold mainly by mail.
Tests and testing services	Publishing tests, and providing scoring services, to assess learning aptitudes and achievements of students and others, and to furnish assessment skills to an executive management service.
Insurance	Selling accident and health and life insurance to individuals, primarily through a farm-magazine subscription sales force, and underwriting and servicing life insurance also generated thereby; acting as general insurance brokers and agents in New York City and its suburbs.

Segmental Reporting

Sales and revenues and income from operations for each of these segments are shown on pages 00 and 00. Segment sales and revenues consist of sales and services provided to unaffiliated customers; intersegment sales are not material. Segment income from operations includes segment sales and other publishing income, less operating expenses directly traceable to the segment. General corporate expenses benefiting more than one segment, which include compensation of general corporate officers, certain occupancy costs, stockholder reporting expenses, general insurance, and legal and other corporate consulting fees and expenses, are not allocated to segments.

Consolidated Sales and Revenues By Sources, 1973-1977

	1977		1976		1975		1974		1973	
	Amount	%	Amount	%	Amount	%	Amount	%	Amount	%
School instructional materials	$109,344,034	29.5	$ 96,746,532	35.8	$ 90,097,760	37.3	$ 77,325,681	37.8	$ 68,831,039	38.9
University and professional publishing and instruction	83,376,749	22.5	73,237,322	27.1	69,630,791	28.9	59,191,248	28.9	48,443,365	27.4
Popular enterprises	60,015,015	16.2	—	—	—	—	—	—	—	—
Periodical subscriptions and advertising	52,137,971	14.0	36,201,794	13.3	30,382,168	12.6	26,702,713	13.1	24,607,403	13.9
General books	31,015,468	8.3	31,584,892	11.7	21,832,971	9.0	13,528,937	6.6	11,571,782	6.5
Tests and testing services	24,925,939	6.7	23,746,824	8.8	21,303,087	8.8	20,814,978	10.2	17,321,338	9.8
Insurance	10,273,504	2.8	8,858,476	3.3	8,099,969	3.4	7,006,332	3.4	6,111,257	3.5
	$371,088,680	100.0%	$270,375,840	100.0%	$241,346,746	100.0%	$204,569,889	100.0%	$176,886,184	100.0%

Segmental Reporting

Consolidated Income from Operations By Sources, 1973–1977

	1977 Amount	1977 %	1976 Amount	1976 %	1975 Amount	1975 %	1974 Amount	1974 %	1973 Amount	1973 %
School instructional materials	$16,202,661	38.6	$15,891,954	47.0	$16,916,880	54.7	$11,998,025	47.2	$10,601,534	47.9
University and professional publishing and instruction	11,161,632	26.6	10,355,444	30.6	11,105,255	35.9	8,374,741	33.0	5,282,409	23.9
Popular enterprises	10,409,911	24.8	—	—	—	—	—	—	—	—
Periodical subscriptions and advertising	4,593,876	10.9	3,679,302	10.9	2,731,988	8.8	2,576,287	10.1	2,800,010	12.7
General books	(603,577)	(1.4)	2,199,783	6.5	(1,575,778)	(5.1)	(419,354)	(1.6)	812,751	3.7
Tests and testing services	3,207,615	7.6	4,194,694	12.4	3,673,852	11.9	3,985,873	15.7	3,623,025	16.4
Insurance	2,899,595	6.9	2,626,616	7.8	2,474,197	8.0	2,645,864	10.4	2,413,003	10.9
Unallocated corporate overhead	(5,869,976)	(14.0)	(5,141,580)	(15.2)	(4,415,607)	(14.2)	(3,757,620)	(14.8)	(3,417,347)	(15.5)
	$42,001,737	100.0%	$33,806,213	100.0%	$30,910,787	100.0%	$25,403,816	100.0%	$22,115,385	100.0%

Note: Income from operations for 1973–1976 has been restated to exclude net interest expense.

Segmental Reporting

Identifiable assets, capital expenditures, and depreciation and amortization by segment for the year ended December 31, 1977, were as follows:

	Assets	Capital Expenditures	Depreciation and Amortization
School instructional materials	$ 74,809,678	$ 4,333,265	$ 2,153,768
University and professional publishing and instruction	59,664,933	7,159,186	3,757,840
Popular enterprises	73,921,849	10,425,400	3,836,850
Periodical subscriptions and advertising	25,361,552	1,282,076	528,510
General books	22,473,489	669,298	578,438
Tests and testing services	8,820,970	457,633	405,675
Insurance	8,923,162	70,740	33,346
General corporate	24,765,184	4,515,250	95,793
	$298,740,817	$28,912,848	$11,390,220

The company's export and foreign subsidiary sales are less than 10% of total revenues, and no single customer, including governmental agencies, accounts for 10% or more of total revenues.

STOCKHOLDERS' EQUITY

Background

This chapter contains promulgated and nonpromulgated GAAP pertaining to items properly included or related to stockholders' equity. The specific promulgated GAAP included herein is:

   ARB-43, Chapter 1A–Capital Surplus
   ARB-43, Chapter 1A–Donated Stock
   ARB-43, Chapter 1A–Treasury Stock
   ARB-43, Chapter 1B–Profits or Losses on Treasury Stock
   ARB-43, Chapter 7B–Stock Dividends and Split-ups
   APB-10, Paragraphs 10 and 11–Liquidation Preference of Preferred Stock
   APB-12, Paragraphs 9 and 10–Capital Changes

Companies in regulated industries should comply with promulgated GAAP in accordance with the Addendum to APB-2.

Considerable nonpromulgated GAAP exist in the area of stockholders' equity, some of which is covered in this chapter.

Overview

The various elements constituting stockholders' equity must be clearly classified according to source. Stockholders' equity may be broadly classified into (1) legal capital, (2) paid-in capital, (3) minority interests, and (4) retained earnings.

Legal Capital

Legal capital may consist of common or preferred shares. Preferred shares may be participating or nonparticipating as to the earnings of the corporation, may be cumulative or noncumulative as to the payment of dividends, may have a claim as to assets on liquidation of the business, and may be callable for redemption at a specified price. Usually, preferred stock does not have voting rights.

Common stock usually has the right to vote, the right to share in earnings, a preemptive right to a proportionate share of any additional common stock issued, and the right to share in assets on liquidation.

Generally, preferred stock is issued at a par value, but common stock may have a par or a no-par value. When no-par common stock is recorded at a particular amount it is called the "stated value."

Any difference between the par value or stated value of stock and the actual price paid is either a discount if issued for less, or a premium if issued for more, than par or stated value.

A corporation's charter contains the types and amounts of stock that it can legally issue, which is called the "authorized capital stock." When part or all of the authorized capital stock is issued, it is called "issued capital stock." Since a corporation may own issued capital stock in the form of "treasury stock," the amount of issued capital stock in the hands of stockholders is called "outstanding capital stock." In summary, capital stock may be (1) authorized, (2) authorized and issued, and (3) authorized, issued, and outstanding.

Frequently, a corporation sells its capital stock by subscriptions. An individual subscriber becomes a stockholder on subscribing to the capital stock, and on full payment of the subscription a stock certificate evidencing ownership in the corporation is issued. When the subscription method is used to sell capital stock a subscription receivable account is debited, and a capital stock subscribed account is credited. On payment of the subscription the subscription receivable account is credited and cash or other assets are debited. On the actual issuance of the stock certificates the capital stock subscribed account is debited and the regular capital stock account is credited. Obviously, if any discount or premium is involved (the difference between the par or stated value and the price received), a separate account must be set up that is usually designated as "premium (discount) on common (preferred) stock." A premium is classified as paid-in capital and a discount is deducted from the capital stock.

Legal Capital—Disclosures

When financial statements are prepared in conformity with GAAP, capital changes must be disclosed in a separate statement(s), or footnote(s) to the financial statement. This requirement is in addition to disclosure of the changes in retained earnings, although all capital changes may be included in one statement. Capital accounts that may have to be disclosed because of changes during the year are capital stock, paid-in capital, retained earnings, treasury stock, and other capital accounts in the particular circumstances (APB-12, paragraphs 9 and 10).

Numerous different types of disclosures pertaining to the components of stockholders' equity are required by GAAP. The more usual disclosures are:

Capital stock By each different class, the total number of shares authorized, issued, and outstanding; also, the number of shares reserved for stock options outstanding for future grants and the changes during the year. Any unusual voting rights should also be disclosed.

Paid-in capital The total amount of paid-in capital (capital in excess of par) for each class of security should be disclosed.

Retained earnings The total appropriated and unappropriated retained earnings.

Restrictions on dividends, participation rights, and liquidation preferences should be fully disclosed, as should the pertinent rights and privileges of the various classes of stockholders.

In the case of options, warrants, and convertible securities, the conversion rates and exercise prices must be disclosed.

Preferred or other senior securities that have preference in involuntary liquidation in excess of their par or stated value must be disclosed as follows (APB-10):

a. call price per share or in the aggregate at which the security may be called or redeemed through a sinking fund
b. the amount per share and total of all cumulative preferred dividends in the arrear

Paid-In Capital

All stockholders' equity that is not classified as legal capital, minority interests, or retained earnings is usually designated as paid-in capital. The common sources of paid-in capital result from:

1. excess of par or stated value paid for capital stock
2. sale of treasury stock
3. the issuance of detachable stock purchase warrants (APB-14)
4. donated assets
5. that created by a corporate readjustment or quasi-reorganization

ARB-43, Chapter 1A, paragraph 6 states the following in reference to donated stock:

> "If capital stock is issued nominally for the acquisition of property and it appears that at about the same time, and pursuant to a previous agreement or understanding, some portion of the stock so issued is donated to the corporation, it is not permissible to treat the par value of the stock nominally issued for the property as the cost of that property. If stock so donated is subsequently sold, it is not permissible to treat the proceeds as a credit to surplus of the corporation."

Charges should not be made to paid-in capital, however created, that are properly chargeable to income accounts of the current or future years (ARB-43, Chapter 1A, paragraph 2).

Minority Interests

Minority interests in consolidated financial statements should be separately disclosed in the stockholders' equity section of the balance sheet.

Retained Earnings

Appropriated retained earnings should be clearly distinguished from unappropriated retained earnings.

Treasury Stock

Treasury stock is not generally considered an asset, because it is widely held that a corporation cannot own part of itself. Under no circumstances should a corporation account for a dividend on its own treasury stock as income. However, under some circumstances, if adequately disclosed, treasury stock may be shown as an asset (ARB-43, Chapter 1A, paragraph 4; the circumstances are not described).

Accounting and reporting When treasury stock is acquired with the intent of retiring the stock (whether or not retirement is actually accomplished) and the price paid is in excess of the par or stated value, the excess may be charged against either (1) any paid-in capital arising from past transactions in the same class of stock or (2) retained earnings.

Stockholders' Equity

When the price paid for the acquired treasury stock is less than par or stated value, the difference must be credited to paid-in capital.

When treasury stock is acquired for purposes other than retirement, it should be shown separately in the balance sheet as a deduction from stockholders' equity; or, as mentioned previously, under certain circumstances it may be shown as an asset, provided that it is adequately disclosed.

A gain on the sale of treasury stock should be credited to paid-in capital from the sale of treasury stock. Losses on the sale of treasury stock should first be applied to (1) any paid-in capital arising from past transactions in the same class of stock and then to (2) retained earnings.

If treasury stock is donated to a corporation and then subsequently sold, the entire proceeds should be credited to paid-in capital from the sale of donated treasury stock.

Treasury stock may be reacquired for two broad reasons (intent governs):

1. for retirement (whether it is or not)
2. other than for retirement (ARB–43, Chapter 1B)

To be retired The amount of reacquired treasury stock is deducted from outstanding stock, and the price paid in excess of par or stated value is charged against either (1) any previously recorded paid-in-capital from the same issue or (2) retained earnings.

---

100 shares of $50 par value common stock are purchased for $60 per share with the intent of retiring the stock.

Common stock	$5,000	
Paid-in capital or retained earnings	1,000	
Cash		$6,000

If the price paid was $40 per share:

Common stock	$5,000	
Cash		$4,000
Paid-in capital		1,000

For other than retirement purposes In our previous example ($60 per share), the journal entry would be:

Stockholders' Equity

    Common stock–treasury $6,000
      Cash $6,000

The cost of treasury stock would be shown as a reduction of stockholders' equity.

Gain or loss on disposal In our previous example, assume the stock was not acquired with the intent of retirement and was subsequently sold for $70 per share:

    Cash $7,000
      Common stock–treasury $6,000
      Paid-in capital   1,000

Gains on treasury stock must be credited to paid in capital–gain on sale of treasury stock.

If the same stock was sold for $50 per share:

    Cash $5,000
    (See Note)   1,000
      Common stock–treasury $6,000

Note: Any loss should be charged first against any previously recorded paid-in capital from the same stock and then to retained earnings.

Dividends

A dividend is a pro rata distribution by a corporation, based on shares of a particular class and usually represents a distribution of earnings.

Cash dividends Cash dividends are the most common type of dividend distribution. Preferred stock usually pays a fixed dividend, expressed in dollars or a percentage.

Three dates are usually involved in a dividend distribution:

1. *date of declaration:* The date the board of directors formally declares the dividend to the stockholders
2. *date of record:* The date the board of directors specifies that stockholders of record on a certain date are entitled to the dividend payment

3. *date of payment:* The date the dividend is actually disbursed by the corporation or its paying agent.

Dividends are recorded on the books of the corporation as a liability (dividends payable) on the date of declaration. Dividends are paid only on authorized, issued, and outstanding shares, thereby eliminating any dividend payment on treasury stock.

Stock dividends A stock dividend is accounted for the same way as a cash dividend, except that since there is no tangible distribution, an amount equal to the fair market value of the stock dividend is transferred from retained earnings to capital stock and, if appropriate, to paid-in capital.

LPS Corporation declares a 5% stock dividend on its 1,000,000 shares of outstanding $10 par common stock (5,000,000 authorized). On the date of declaration, LPS stock is selling for $20 per share.

Total stock dividend (5% of 1,000,000)   50,000 shares
Value of 50,000 shares @ $20 per share (market) $1,000,000

Journal entry:

Retained earnings	$1,000,000	
Capital stock, $10 par common		$500,000
Paid-in capital, $10 par common		500,000

To record declaration by the board of directors of a 5% stock dividend on the $10 par common capital stock.

Stock split It is important to differentiate between a stock dividend and a stock split, because the accounting treatment is radically different.

When a stock distribution is more than 20% to 25% of the previously outstanding shares, it is classified as a stock split and *no part of retained earnings should be capitalized,* except that required by the laws of the state of incorporation of the corporation.

Stock splits should not be referred to as dividends, and related corporate resolutions, notices, and announcements should use "split effected in the form of a dividend" or avoid the use of the word dividend at all.

GAAP GUIDE / **38.07**

Stockholders' Equity

A stock split of 3 for 1 is made by ABC Company. (Prior to the split, there are 100,000 shares $1 stated value outstanding which are selling for $20 per share). What is the journal entry to record the split?

$$100{,}000 \times 2 = 200{,}000 \text{ to be issued}$$
$$\text{Stated value} \times \$1$$
$$\text{Legal requirement to capitalize} = \$200{,}000$$

Retained earnings	$200,000	
Common stock ($1)		$200,000

Stock Rights

A shareholder's interest in a corporation does not change on account of a stock dividend or a stock split except as to the total number of shares representing his stock interest. The cost of a stockholder's original shares should be reallocated among the new number of shares after a stock dividend or split. Gain or loss is then recognized on the basis of the adjusted cost per share (ARB-43, Chapter 7B). Stock rights should be recorded by the recipient by allocating the original cost of the stock between the stock right, using the following formula:

$$\frac{\text{Market value of stock right}}{\text{market value of stock right} + \text{market value of stock}} \times \text{cost of stock} = \text{value of right}$$

Original cost of stock is $100. Market value of stock is $90 and the market value of the stock right is $6. At what price should the stock right be recorded?

$$\frac{\$6}{\$6 + \$90} \times \$100 = \$6.25$$

The journal entry to record the stock right is:

Investment in stock right	$6.25	
Investment in stock		$6.25

No accounting entry is necessary for the entity issuing the stock right or warrant, except for detachable stock purchase warrants or similar rights which are accounted for separately and assigned a value (see chapter on Convertible Debt).

When a stock right or warrant is used to purchase the specified security, the cost of the right or warrant is treated as part of the investment in the new security.

STOCK ISSUED TO EMPLOYEES

Background

APB No. 25 (generally applicable to most stock option plans initiated after December 31, 1972) and ARB No. 43, Chapter 13B (issued June 1953) establish the current promulgated GAAP for Accounting for Stock Issued to Employees. FASB Interpretation-28, Accounting for Stock Appreciation Rights and Other Variable Stock Option or Award Plans, is an interpretation of APB-15 (Earnings per Share) and APB-25 (Stock Issued to Employees). ARB 43 originally established principles and procedures for accounting for "traditional" stock options. APB 25 applies these principles to the various types of stock options and plans that have been developed since the issuance of ARB 43. For instance, it specifies accounting principles for stock options and plans where future events determine the number of shares to be granted the employee and/or the exercise price. APB 25 specifically supersedes ARB 43 in establishing new criteria for measuring a company's compensation cost. APB 25 deliniates the income tax treatment originating from any options, purchases, or award plans.

Similarly to many other areas of accounting, GAAP applies to the substance of an option plan rather than its form. In accounting for an option plan, a company must comply with the GAAP applicable to the option's underlying substance.

The promulgated GAAP on accounting for stock issued to an employee is silent as to its coverage of companies in regulated industries. Therefore, in accordance with the Addendum to APB-2, companies in regulated industries should comply with the provisions of the promulgated GAAP.

A description of the more common types of plans follows:

Typical fixed plan Terms are fixed at the date of grant to determine the number of shares of stock involved and the option price to the employee. Transferability of the stock acquired by the employee is usually restricted and the plan generally provides that the employee must perform current and/or future services.

Stock option and purchase plan An employee is granted the right to purchase a fixed number of shares at a certain price during a specified period.

Stock bonus and award plan An employee is granted a bonus or award in a fixed number of shares or a specified dollar amount which is payable in shares. The employee usually makes no payment to receive the bonus or award of stock.

Shadow or phantom stock plan The employee receives cash, stock, or a combination of both, in an amount equal to a specified increase in the market price of the employer corporation's stock or an amount equal to a specified increase in the dividend distributions of the employer corporation.

Combination and elective plan The employee is granted rights to more than one plan, or the right to select alternatives under one plan. The separate rights may be granted at different intervals or simultaneously and may run concurrently or for different periods. These plans are sometimes referred to as tandem or alternate stock plans.

Overview

A stock option can be compensatory or noncompensatory. A compensatory stock option involves services rendered to the employer corporation and a noncompensatory stock option does not. Accounting for noncompensatory stock options presents few problems. However, when a stock option is compensatory, the compensation costs must be measured, and this may involve some problems.

Noncompensatory Plans

Certain stock options and stock purchase plans are not intended to compensate employees. For example, a corporation's intent may be to raise additional capital or to diversify its ownership to include employees and officers. Usually, the terms of the option will clearly indicate the nature and purpose of the plan.

A plan is noncompensatory if the cash received per share is very close to the amount of cash that would be received if the same deal was offered to all shareholders. In these types of transactions, a company does not generally recognize any compensation costs.

The essential characteristics of noncompensatory stock options or stock purchase plans are:

1. Substantially all full-time employees meeting limited employment qualifications may participate. Excluded are officers and employees who own more than a specific amount of the outstanding stock in the corporation.

2. Stock is offered equally to eligible employees, but the plan may limit the total amount of shares that can be purchased.
3. The time permitted to exercise the rights is limited to a reasonable period.
4. Any discount from the market price is no greater than would be a reasonable offer of stock to shareholders or others.

Plans that do not contain these characteristics are usually classified as compensatory plans. In a compensatory plan, the company receives cash or another asset in addition to an employee's services for the stock it issues.

Compensatory Plans

Stock options may give rise to compensation, usually out of an offer or agreement by a corporation to issue shares to one or more officers or employees (grantees) at a stated price less than the prevailing market. In some instances the grantees' options are exercisable under certain conditions, such as the length of employment of an employee. In other cases, the grantees may agree to take the shares only for investment purposes and not for resale.

Under traditional stock option and stock purchase plans, an employer corporation grants options to purchase shares of its stock, often at a price lower than the prevailing market, making it possible for the individual exercising the option to have at least a potential profit at the moment of acquisition. Most option agreements provide that the purchaser must retain the stock for a minimum period, thus eliminating the possibility of speculation.

Options that give rise to compensation result in compensation expense on the books of the corporation and in compensation income to the recipient. The cost of compensation is measured by the excess of the quoted market price of the stock over the option price on the measurement date.

Measurement Date

The quoted market price of the shares granted under an option may vary considerably over the period of the option. This creates a problem in determining a date that may be used to measure the cost of compensation if the shares are offered at less than market. At least six dates can be considered:

1. date of adoption of the option plan
2. date on which the option is granted to an employee
3. date on which the grantee has performed any conditions precedent to the exercise of the option
4. date on which the grantee may first exercise the option
5. date on which the option is exercised by the grantee
6. date on which the grantee disposes of the stock acquired

The measurement date for determining compensation costs in stock options is the first date on which the following is known, which is usually the date the option is granted:

1. number of shares an employee is entitled to receive
2. option or purchase price

Plans that have variable terms which are dependent on events that will occur after the grant date will have a measurement date different from the grant date.

In a stock option for current services, the measurement date may be the end of the fiscal period if the following conditions are met:

1. An established formal plan provides the terms of the award.
2. The plan details how to determine the total dollar amount due to an employee. It is possible that the *actual* amount will be indeterminable at the end of the period because it is dependent on an item, such as net income, which will not be known at that time.
3. The employee is being compensated for services rendered in the current period.

If a company transfers stock to a trustee, agent, or other third party, the measurement date becomes the date of transfer to the trustee if the following items are irrevocable:

1. transfer of the stock to the trust
2. terms of the trust agreement
3. specified employee(s) who will receive the stock

In essence, if all three of the above are met, the company has given up any alternative use of the shares except for the ones specifically stipulated in the stock option agreement.

If treasury stock is distributed in a stock option plan, it is unacceptable to measure compensation costs by the amount paid to reacquire such treasury stock. The only exception to this rule is when a company meets all the conditions in an irrevocable transfer to a trustee (above). In this event, the company may elect to measure its compensation costs by the amount paid to reacquire treasury stock, provided the treasury stock is reacquired during the current period in which the award is made and distribution to the employee occurs shortly after the close of the period.

The measurement date for stock options consisting of convertible securities can be determined only after the conversion ratio is known. Compensation is measured on the measurement date by the market price of the convertible security or the security into which it is convertible, *whichever is higher*.

If a company renews a stock option or extends the period during which the recipient can exercise the option, then a new measurement date is established as if a new option had just been granted.

The measurement date does not change merely because the agreement stipulates that termination of employment alters the number of shares an employee will receive.

Variable awards Under "variable plan awards" the number of shares of stock which an employee can acquire or the exercise price, or both are not determinable until after the date of grant (FASB Interpretation-28). "Variable plan awards" include stock appreciation rights and other variable plans in which the number of shares, exercise price, or both are contingent on a future event.

The vesting period in "variable plan awards" usually runs from the date of grant to the exercise date. For the purposes of GAAP, "variable plan awards" become vested on the date that the employee's right to receive the benefits under the plan are not contingent on any additional services to be performed by the employee (FASB Interpretation-28).

Compensation expense is charged to the "service period" which is the period(s) in which the related services are performed by the employee (FASB Interpretation-28). If the service period cannot be determined by the terms of the plan or otherwise then the service period is presumed to be the same as the vesting period (FASB Interpretation-28). If the variable plan award is for past services, compensation costs are charged as an expense of the period in which the plan was granted.

When the service period of a variable plan award covers more than one fiscal period, compensation costs between the date of grant and the measurement date must be estimated, as follows:

1. In the year of grant or first fiscal period compensation costs must be measured with whatever information is available. If the number of shares are known but not the exercise price, then an exercise price must be estimated. If the exercise price is known but not the number of shares, then the number of shares must be estimated. If both the number of shares and the exercise price are unknown, then reasonable estimates must be made based upon all information available.
2. Compensation costs are initially measured as the difference between the quoted market price and the option price multiplied by the number of shares involved.
3. In subsequent periods, compensation costs are adjusted, but not below zero, for any increase or decrease in the quoted market price. The adjustment is made to compensation expense of the period in which the change in the quoted market price occurs.
4. The accrued compensation costs for a right which is cancelled or forfeited shall be adjusted by decreasing compensation expense in the period of cancellation or forfeiture. Such adjustments are considered as changes in accounting estimates and are made in the period of change and/or future periods.
5. Accrued compensation costs should be charged to expense over the periods (service period) in which the employee performs the related services.

Measuring Compensation Costs

The amount of compensation, or the value of the stock option, is the excess of the unadjusted quoted market price of the stock at the measurement date over the amount the employee must pay in cash or other assets. Often, closely held or nonpublic corporation's market quotations are not available and other methods of valuation must be used. No compensation would be recorded if the employee purchases the stock for an amount equal to or greater than the market price.

OBSERVATION: The value of a stock option may be affected by many factors, such as transferability, and other restrictions. In spite of the recognition of these factors the promulgated GAAP requires (as a practical solution) the use of a quoted market price to measure compensation costs relating to both restricted or unrestricted stock. Only if a quoted market price is not available can an estimate be used.

Compensation costs related to options for convertible stock are based on the higher market price of either the convertible stock awarded or the underlying security for which the convertible stock can be exchanged.

Cash paid to settle an earlier option right with an employee is the measure of compensation, and the earlier measure of compensation (date the option was granted) should be adjusted.

If a company uses cash to reacquire stock shortly after the stock was issued to an employee through a stock option plan, then the cash paid is used to measure the compensation cost.

If a principal stockholder (one with an interest greater than 10%) establishes a stock option for an employee, the company should recognize compensation costs in accordance with the plan, as long as it derives benefits from the transaction. Stated differently, if the principal stockholder's actions benefit the company by keeping a valuable employee or attempting to improve employee service to the firm, then compensation costs should be recognized in accordance with GAAP. However, if the plan is granted because of a special relationship between an employee and the principal, a prior obligation unrelated to the company, or the company obviously does not benefit, then no compensation costs should be recognized. Obviously, the donated compensation costs by the principal stockholder should be credited to a capital account.

If compensation costs are to be measured at a date in the future, a company must make a reasonable estimate of what the compensation costs will be. Since the measurement date is unknown, the price of the stock at the end of each period should be used. If the number of shares is also unknown, a reasonable estimate, given the known facts, must be made.

OBSERVATION: Adjustments to estimates in future periods should be made as a change in an accounting estimate. A change in an accounting estimate is made in the period of change and/or in future periods. No restatement of prior financial statements is made.

When a stock option plan combines two or more plans, compensation cost for each subplan may be measured separately. If the plan gives the employee a choice as to which section of the plan is to be exercised, the measurement at the end of each period should be based on an estimate of which part of the plan the employee is most likely to elect at that point in time.

Related Tax Effects

A company usually realizes a tax deduction for any amount the employee declares as ordinary income. The tax deduction is taken in the year in which the employee includes the benefits from the stock option in his or her gross income. This corporate tax reduction results in a timing difference, because on the company's books the compensation cost is reflected as an expense during the period of related employee service, but is recognized on the tax return in the year the employee includes the benefit in gross income. In such cases deferred taxes should be recorded.

If a tax reduction exists above and beyond that which is recognized as a deferred tax, it should be added to paid-in capital in excess of par in the period of the tax deduction.

It is also possible that recorded compensation cost will be greater than the allowable tax reduction. In such cases a company may deduct the difference from paid-in capital in the period of the tax reduction. This reduction is limited to the amount that the tax reduction for the same plan previously increased paid-in capital.

A company can incur additional compensation costs by reimbursing an employee for the tax benefit derived from the stock option plan. This reimbursement should be recognized as an additional expense against income.

Recognition of Compensation Costs

Compensation costs should be recognized as an expense over the period of employment attributable to the option. If this period is not stated, a reasonable estimate must be made taking into account the circumstances implied by the terms of the agreement.

Stock issued in accordance with a plan for past and future services of an employee must be allocated between expired costs and future costs. Future costs should be charged to the periods in which the employee performs services. In the event stock options are exercised before the related compensation costs are actually incurred, a deferred or prepaid compensation account is set up. Unearned compensation costs should be written off to the period(s) in which they were actually earned, and any balances at a reporting date should be deducted from stockholders' equity.

Recognition of a stock option is made in accordance with the substance of the transaction. Therefore, if an employee gives an employer a nonrecourse note as consideration for stock issued with the stock as collateral, in substance the transaction may be the grant of a stock option. In this event, compensation costs should be measured and the nonrecourse note should be reported as a reduction of stockholders' equity and not as an asset.

Common Stock Equivalents

To the extent that they are payable in common stock, stock options, rights, and other award plans are common stock equivalents for the purposes of determining earnings per share (APB-15). Stock options, rights and other awards which are payable solely in cash are not common stock equivalents.

In applying the treasury stock method to determine the dilutive effect, the accrued compensation costs for the stock options, rights or other award plans, are considered additional proceeds.

Disclosure

When a company issues financial statements, it must adequately disclose the status of all option plans at the end of the period being reported. This disclosure should include:

1. number of shares covered by each option
2. exercise price
3. number of shares that could be exercised
4. number of shares exercised
5. option price of exercised shares

Companies filing with the SEC must meet additional disclosure requirements (Regulation SX).

Comprehensive Illustrations

The following examples demonstrate the accounting treatment for stock options.

Stock Issued to Employees

An officer of a corporation is granted an option to purchase 100 shares of $20 par value stock for $30 when the market price is $40.

Compensation–officers	$1,000	
Outstanding stock options		$1,000

Subsequently, when the stock option is exercised, the journal entry is:

Cash	$3,000	
Outstanding stock options	1,000	
Common stock		$2,000
Paid-in capital		2,000

Outstanding stock options are part of stockholders' equity and are usually classified as paid-in capital until they are exercised.

In more complex situations (such as those where stock options are granted on the basis of performance over a number of years) it becomes necessary to estimate compensation costs for reporting purposes between the date of grant and the measurement date.

Moreover, deferred taxes must be recognized when the corporation expenses the compensation costs for reporting purposes but not for tax purposes. This is because the compensation costs based on a stock option are not usually deductible until the employee exercises the option.

An example of a more complex situation follows

An officer of a corporation is granted an option to purchase up to 1,000 shares of stock ($50 par value) at the end of two years at 80% of the then market price. The amount of the option will be determined by the total net income of the corporation for the two years in accordance with the following schedule:

Number of Shares	Net Income
200	0 to $500,000
500	$500,001 to $1,000,000
700	$1,000,001 to $1,500,000
1,000	above $1,500,000

At the end of the first year assume the following facts:

   Market price of stock $ 100
   Corporate net income $700,000
   Corporate tax rate   50%

What is the accrual for compensation costs at the end of the first year?
Compensation costs at the end of the first year are:

   500 shares × 20% × market price
   or
   500 × $20 = $10,000

The journal entry at the end of the first year is:

Deferred taxes	$ 5,000	
Compensation costs	10,000	
Outstanding stock options		$10,000
Income tax expense		5,000

At the end of the second year, corporate net income is $400,000 and the market price of the stock is $110.
The journal entry at the end of the second year to record the stock option is:

Deferred taxes	$2,700	
Compensation costs	5,400	
Outstanding stock options		$5,400
Income tax expense		2,700

The compensation costs and deferred taxes were found by valuing the entire option at the end of two years and subtracting the previous year's compensation costs and related deferred taxes.
The journal entry when the officer exercises the stock option is:

Cash ($110 × 0.80 × 700 shares)	$61,600	
Outstanding stock options	15,400	
Common stock ($50 par × 700 shares)		$35,000
Paid-in capital		42,000

TROUBLED DEBT RESTRUCTURING

Background

FASB-15, Accounting by Debtors and Creditors for Troubled Debt Restructuring contains the promulgated GAAP on this subject and supersedes FASB Interpretation-2, Imputing Interest on Debt Arrangements Made under the Federal Bankruptcy Act.

The promulgated GAAP (FASB-15) specifically covers companies in regulated industries in accordance with the Addendum to APB-2. In addition, Early Extinguishment of Debt (APB-26) arising from a troubled debt restructuring is now covered by FASB-15 and excluded from APB-26.

For the purposes of the promulgated GAAP (FASB-15), troubled debt restructuring does not include the following:

1. changes in lease agreements (FASB-13)
2. employment-related agreements, such as deferred compensation contracts or pension plans
3. A debtor's failure to pay trade accounts that do not involve a restructure agreement
4. A creditor's legal action to collect accounts that do not involve a restructure agreement

Troubled debt restructuring arranged under any provision of the Federal Bankruptcy Act is covered by the promulgated GAAP unless the debtor generally restates its liabilities, as in the case of a corporate readjustment or quasi-reorganization.

The promulgated GAAP generally establishes standards for accounting and reporting, by both the debtor and creditor, for a troubled debt restructuring.

Overview

A "troubled" debt restructuring is one in which the creditor allows the debtor certain concessions that he would not normally consider. The concessions *must be* made in light of the debtor's financial difficulty, and the objective of the creditor *must be* to maximize recovery of his investment. Troubled debt restructurings are often the result of legal proceedings or of negotiation between the parties.

Troubled debt restructures include situations in which:

1. The creditor accepts a third-party receivable, or other asset(s) of the debtor, in lieu of his receivable from the debtor.
2. The creditor accepts an equity interest in the debtor in lieu of his receivable. (This is not to be confused with convertible securities, which are *not* troubled debt restructings.)
3. The creditor accepts modification of the terms of the debt including but not limited to:
   a. reduction in stated interest rate
   b. extension of maturity at a favorable interest rate
   c. reduction in face amount of the debt
   d. reduction in accrued interest

The reductions mentioned in a, c, and d can be either absolute or contingent.

Definition of Terms

A *receivable (or payable)* is defined as a contractual right to receive or pay money that is already recorded on the debtor's or creditor's balance sheet, and includes accrued interest, premiums, discounts, issue costs, and any related valuation allowances. Although transactions affecting these accounts take on a variety of forms, it is the *substance,* not the form, that should govern the accounting.

The *time of restructuring* is defined as the date an agreement to restructure is consummated.

Not all debt restructurings can be considered troubled, even though the debtor is in financial difficulty. Circumstances in which the restructuring is not troubled include:

1. The debtor satisfies the debt by giving fair value of assets or equity that at least equals either
   a. the creditor's recorded receivable, or
   b. the debtor's carrying amount of the payable.
2. The creditor reduces the interest rate primarily in response to changes in market rates.
3. The debtor issues at or near the current market new marketable securities in exchange for the old securities (the fact that the debtor can obtain at similar rates and conditions funds from other sources, is evidence that the restructuring is not troubled).

Accounting and Reporting by Debtors

A debtor accounts for a troubled debt restructuring by the type of restructuring. Types of restructuring include:

1. transfer of asset(s) in full settlement
2. granting an equity interest in full settlement
3. modification of terms of the debt
4. combinations of the above three types

Transfer of asset(s) The debtor will recognize a gain in the amount of the excess of the carrying amount of the payable (and accrued interest, premiums, etc.) over the fair value of the asset(s) given up. Fair value is, of course, an arm's-length purchase or sale price. The gain, or loss, is reported in net income of the period.

> *OBSERVATION:* Fair value may be determined either by the assets given up or the amount of payable, whichever is more clearly evident. However, in the case of a partial settlement, the value of the asset(s) given up must be used. This eliminates the need to allocate the fair value of the payable between the settled portion and the remaining outstanding balance.

The excess of the carrying amount of the debt over the fair value of the asset(s) given up is the gain on debt restructuring. However, the difference between the fair value and the carrying amount of the asset(s) given up is the gain or loss on the transfer of asset(s), which is included in net income in the period the transfer occurs.

Transfer of equity interest The difference between the fair value of the equity interest and the carrying amount of the payable is recognized as gain or loss. As a practical matter the difference will always be a gain, since it is unlikely the debtor would exchange fair value in *excess* of his obligation to satisfy his creditors.

The difference between the fair value and the carrying amount of the equity interest given up is the gain or loss on the transfer of asset(s), which is included in net income in the period the transfer occurs.

Modification of terms A restructuring that does not involve the transfer of assets or equity will often involve the modification of the

Troubled Debt Restructuring

terms of the debt. In a modification the debtor accounts for the effects of the restructuring prospectively, and does not change the carrying amount unless the carrying amount exceeds the total future cash payments specified by the new terms. The *total future cash payments* are the principal and any accrued interest at the time of the restructuring which continues to be payable by the new terms. *Interest expense* is computed by a method which causes a constant effective rate (such as the interest method). The new effective rate of interest is the discount rate at which the carrying amount of the debt is equal to the present value of the future cash payments.

When the total future cash payments are less than the carrying amount, the debtor should reduce the carrying amount accordingly and recognize the difference as a gain. When there are several related accounts (discount, premium, etc.), the reduction may need to be allocated among them. All cash payments after the restructuring go to reduce the carrying amount, and *no* interest expense is recognized after the date of restructure.

When there are indeterminate future payments or anytime the future payments might exceed the carrying amount, the debtor recognizes no gain. The debtor should assume that the future contingent payments will have to be made at least to the extent necessary to obviate any gain.

In estimating future cash payments for any purpose *in this area,* it is assumed that the maximum amount of periods (and interest) is going to occur.

Combination of types When a restructuring involves a combination of asset or equity transfer and modification of terms, the fair value of any asset or equity is used first to reduce the carrying amount of the payable. The difference between the fair value and the carrying amount of any asset(s) transferred is recognized as gain or loss. No gain on restructuring can be recognized unless the carrying amount exceeds the total future cash payments.

Repossessions and foreclosures shall be accounted for in the same manner as satisfaction by surrender of assets.

All gains on debt restructure are aggregated and included in net income for the period. If substantial, the gains are reported as an extraordinary item (net of tax effects).

Contingently payable amounts Amounts contingently payable in future periods are recognized as payable and as interest expense in accordance with the treatment of other contingencies. The criteria for contingencies are:

1. probability that the liability has been incurred
2. the amount must be reasonably estimatable

If any contingently payable amounts were included in the total future cash payments, they must now be deducted from the carrying amount of the restructured payable to the extent they originally prevented recognition of a gain at the time of the restructuring.

In estimating future payments subject to fluctuation, estimates should be based on the interest rate in effect at the time of restructure. A change in future rates is treated as a change in an estimate. The accounting for these fluctuations cannot result in an immediate gain. Rather, the future payments will reduce the carrying amount and any residual value shall be considered gain.

Incidental cost of restructure In an issuance of equity the incidental costs are charged against the equity issued. All other direct costs are either deducted from recognized gains, or, if no gain exists, they are expensed in the period.

Disclosure by debtors The debtor must disclose the following regarding any debt restructurings during a period:

1. description of the terms of each restructuring
2. aggregate gain on restructure and related tax effect
3. aggregate net gain or loss on asset transfer
4. per share amount of aggregate gain on restructure, and related tax effect

The debtor should also disclose contingently payable amounts included in the carrying amount of restructured payables, and the total of contingently payable amounts and the conditions under which the amounts become payable or are forgiven.

Accounting by Creditors

The creditor accounts for restructure by the same categories as the debtor. The treatment of each type of restructure is explained below.

Receipt of assets or equity When the creditor receives either assets or equity as full settlement of a receivable, he should account for these at their fair value at the time of the restructuring. The fair value of the receivable satisfied can be used if it is more clearly determinable than the fair value of the asset or equity acquired. In partial payments the creditor *must* use the fair value of the asset or equity received.

The excess of the recorded receivable over the fair value of the assets received is recognized as a loss. The creditor accounts for these assets as if they were acquired for cash.

Modification of terms When the creditor accepts a modification of terms, he accounts for the restructuring prospectively and does not change the recorded investment *unless* it exceeds the total future cash payments (as defined in the terms of the new agreement).

The creditor recognizes interest income at a constant rate of effective interest. For the effective rate the creditor uses the discount rate at which the present value of the future cash receipts is equal to the recorded investment.

If the total future cash receipts are less than the recorded investment, the investment should be reduced and a loss is recognized. All subsequent cash received is applied to reduce the balance of the recorded investment, and none is considered interest.

When the restructured receivable involves indeterminate future cash receipts, the creditor recognizes a loss to the extent that the minimum future cash receipts are less than the recorded investment. As for contingently receivable amounts, the creditor excludes them from the total future cash receipts unless they are *probable* and can be *reasonably estimated.* If exclusion results in a deficiency, it is recognized as a loss. Flexible payments should be estimated on the basis of the minimum allowable length of time.

Naturally, contingently receivable interest should not be recognized until it is earned *and* the contingency has been resolved. However, before these amounts can be recognized as income, they must first be used to reduce the recorded investment *to the extent* that contingent receipts (which were considered receivable) avoided recognition of a loss on restructuring.

Combination of types The creditor shall reduce his recorded investment by the fair value of assets received. Any loss recognized is limited to the excess of the remaining recorded investment over the total future cash receipts. Any future interest income is recognized at a constant effective rate of interest (interest method) or other accepted specialized industry practice that is used for receivables.

Related matters Foreclosures are accounted for in the same manner as the receipt of assets or equity. Losses, to the extent that they were not previously recognized by valuation allowances, enter into net income for the period.

If a loss from a troubled debt restructuring has been previously provided in a valuation allowance account, such a loss shall be deducted from its related valuation allowance and not charged directly to net income.

Fluctuation in interest rates after a restructuring are accounted for as changes in an accounting estimate in the period they occur. A creditor shall recognize a loss and reduce its restructured receivable when fluctuations in interest rates cause the minimum future cash receipts to fall below the recorded investment in the restructured receivable.

Legal fees and other direct costs resulting from a troubled debt restructuring shall be expensed by the creditor when incurred.

Creditor disclosure The creditor shall disclose the following regarding troubled debt restructurings:

1. restructured receivables, by major category,
    a. aggregate recorded investment
    b. gross interest income that would have been earned if there had been no restructuring
    c. gross interest income on restructured receivables that is included in net income for the period (Modified receivables with a rate of interest greater than or equal to the rate the creditor would require for similar risk receivables need not be included in the disclosures above.)
2. amount(s) of any commitment(s) to lend additional funds to any debtor who is a party to a restructuring

These disclosures may be made in aggregate by major category.

Substitution of debtors When a restructuring involves the addition of or substitution of a new debtor for the old debtor, the substance of the transaction determines the correct treatment.

Disclosure Index

This Disclosure Index contains both required and recommended disclosures that are currently in use. Although the utmost care has been exercised in the preparation of this Index, it is not meant to be a substitute for professional judgment. There are circumstances in which disclosure is not required or recommended, but because of special factors, professional judgment may dictate that disclosure is necessary for a fair presentation.

This Disclosure Index has been designed to assist the preparer or reviewer of financial statements in determining whether necessary disclosures have been made. Its proper use can expedite the preparation or review of financial statements.

BALANCE SHEET

Cash

1. Withdrawal restrictions on funds
2. Segregation of funds to be used for specific purposes

Marketable Securities

1. Specialized industry practices
2. Method of valuation
3. Aggregate cost and market for current portfolio and noncurrent portfolio
4. Carrying value of each portfolio
5. Gross unrealized gains and losses for each portfolio
6. Net realized gain or loss included in determining net income of the period
7. Amount of change in valuation allowances
8. Significant net realized and unrealized gains and losses subsequent to the balance sheet date
9. Significant net realized and unrealized gains and losses occurring between a parent company and a subsidiary with different balance sheet dates
10. Investments accounted for by the equity method should not be

Disclosure Index

           combined with current or noncurrent portfolios of marketable securities
11. Financial statements that contain entities which have specialized industry practices and which do not have specialized industry practices must include the necessary disclosure of FASB-12 for both circumstances
12. Investments accounted for by the equity method may not be combined with current or noncurrent portfolios of marketable securities
13. Investments in affiliated companies should be separately identified
14. It may be desirable to identify government securities separately

Notes Receivable

1. Trade notes receivable
2. Nontrade segregated by type:
   a. from subsidiaries or affiliates
   b. from officers or employees
3. Installment notes receivable
4. Equity in accounts sold
5. Due from factors
6. Pledged as collateral
7. Face amount of notes
8. Effective interest rates
9. Notes discounted–contingent liability
10. Repayment terms and dates
11. Amounts of unearned income, discounts, premiums, finance charges, and interest deducted from related notes receivable
12. Allowance for possible losses
13. Noncurrent portions properly classified
14. Significant balances with one customer
15. Government contracts (CPFF) properly disclosed

Imputed Interest on Notes Receivable (Payable)

1. Description of note
2. Effective interest rate
3. Face amount of note
4. Value of any rights or privileges exchanged

5. Fair value of nonmonetary transaction except in those cases in which the earning process is not culminated
6. Unearned interest and finance charges deducted from related notes

Accounts Receivable

1. Trade accounts receivable
2. Nontrade segregated by type:
    a. from subsidiaries or affiliates
    b. from officers or employees
    c. tax refunds
    d. claims against government contracts (CPFF)
3. Allowance for uncollectible accounts
4. Accounts sold (contingent liability)
5. Equity retained in accounts sold
6. Accounts receivable–discounted
7. Accounts receivable–pledged
8. Accounts receivable–factored
9. Significantly large balances
10. Unbilled receivables shown separately from billed receivables
11. Possible provision for sales returns, allowances, or discounts
12. Amounts from affiliates or subsidiaries properly classified as current or noncurrent

Inventories

1. Basis of valuation and method of costing
2. Significant changes and effect on net income
3. Amounts by major categories
4. Amounts pledged as collateral
5. Amounts valued in excess of cost, such as precious metals, minerals, etc.
6. Substantial or unusual losses separately disclosed
7. Losses on firm purchase commitments
8. Principles particular to a given industry
9. Replacement cost and effect on net income of depleted LIFO layer
10. SEC filings–current replacement costs
11. Oil and gas producing companies must comply with special disclosure requirements
12. Consignments

Disclosure Index

Prepaid Items

1. Segregated into types
2. Properly classified as current or noncurrent

Depreciable Assets and Depreciation

1. Basis for valuation
2. Balances of major classes of depreciable assets by nature or function
3. Accumulated depreciation, either by major classes or in total
4. Description of depreciation methods used by major classes
5. Depreciation expense for the period
6. Significant commitments for depreciable assets
7. Significant sale-and-leasebacks
8. Segregation of depreciable assets not used in trade or business (idle facilities, investments, etc.)
9. Pledged as collateral
10. Estimated costs of completion for depreciable assets being constructed
11. Regulated companies subject to the rate-making process must disclose the nonrecognition of deferred income taxes resulting from the use of the declining-balance method of depreciation

Unconsolidated Investments

1. Name of each investment
2. Percentage of ownership
3. Accounting policies with respect to each investment
4. Differences between the carrying value and underlying equity in net assets and the treatment of such difference
5. Quoted market value of each investment (not required for subsidiaries)
6. Summary of assets, liabilities, and results of operation for each significant investment
7. Effect on the investor of any outstanding conversions or dilutive securities of the investee
8. If investment is 20% or more and the equity method is not used, the reason(s) must be disclosed
9. If investment is less than 20% and the cost method is not used, the reason(s) must be disclosed

Disclosure Index

10. Changes in the status of an investment
11. Declaration of intent to reinvest the undistributed earnings of a subsidiary (nonaccrual of income taxes)
12. Declaration of intent that undistributed earnings will be in the form of a tax-free liquidation (nonaccrual of income taxes)
13. The cumulative amount of undistributed earnings on which a parent company or investor has not recognized income taxes
14. Significant tax credits and deductions resulting from investments

Intangible Assets

1. Method of amortization and estimated useful life
2. Carrying basis of intangibles
3. Explanation of the nonamortization of pre-11/1/70 intangibles

Deferred Income Taxes

1. Segregated between net current amount and net noncurrent amount
2. Operating-loss carryforwards not used, including expiration dates
3. Significant other unused tax credits or deductions including expiration dates
4. Reason(s) for significant differences in the customary relationship between income tax expense and pretax accounting income
5. Nature of significant differences between pretax accounting income and taxable income
6. Components of income tax expense for the period (intraperiod tax allocation)
7. Tax effects of adjustments to prior periods
8. Amount of operating-loss carryback applied during the period

Leases—Lessee

1. Description of lessee's leasing arrangements:
    a. basis of contingent payments
    b. renewal or purchase options
    c. escalation clauses
    d. restrictions on dividends, further leasing, additional debt, etc.
2. Capital leases:
    a. Gross amount of assets by major classes under capital leases in accordance with their nature and/or function

Disclosure Index

      b. Aggregate future minimum lease payments for the period and for each of the five succeeding fiscal years, less executory costs (including profit thereon) included in the minimum lease payments
      c. Amount of imputed interest necessary to reduce the net minimum lease payments to its present value
      d. Total minimum sublease rentals to be received under noncancelable subleases
      e. Total amount of contingent rentals actually incurred during each period presented
3. Operating leases:
      a. Aggregate future minimum rental payments for the period and for the next succeeding five fiscal years
      b. Total minimum rentals to be received under noncancelable subleases
      c. Total rental expense for each period presented

Leases–Lessor

Where leasing, excluding leveraged leases, is a significant portion of a lessor's business in terms of net assets, revenue, or net income, the following is required for both sales-type and direct-financing leases:

1. The components of the net investment in leases, including:
      a. future minimum lease payments less executory costs (and profits thereon) included in the minimum lease payments
      b. accumulated allowance for uncollectible minimum lease payments
      c. unguaranteed residual values accruing to the lessor
      d. unearned income
2. Future minimum lease payments to be received for each of the five succeeding fiscal years
3. Total contingent rentals included in income for each period presented
4. For direct-financing leases only: the amount of unearned income used to offset initial direct costs charged to income for each period presented
5. For operating leases:
      a. by major classes of property on lease or held for lease and according to nature or function; (1) cost, (2) carrying amount, and (3) accumulated depreciation in total

b. minimum future rentals on noncancelable leases in the aggregate and for each of the five succeeding fiscal years
c. Total contingent rentals included in income for each period presented
6. General description of the lessor's usual leasing arrangements

Leveraged Leases

1. Deferred taxes related to leveraged leases should be separately disclosed
2. A separate presentation of pretax income from leveraged leases should be made in the income statement or footnote thereto to include (1) pretax income, (2) the tax effect on pretax income, and (3) the amount of investment tax credit recognized during the period
3. When leveraged leasing constitutes a significant portion of a lessor's business activity in terms of assets, revenue, or net income, the following components of the net investment balance in leveraged leases should be disclosed by footnote:
   a. rentals receivable, net of rentals applicable to principal and interest on nonrecourse debt
   b. estimated residual value of the leased property
   c. unearned or deferred income, including (1) estimated pretax lease income less initial direct costs and (2) investment tax credit remaining to be allocated to income over the lease term
   d. the amount, if any, remaining to be collected for the investment tax credit realized on the transaction

Unbilled Costs

1. Expenditures billable to customers
2. Unreimbursed costs and fees (CPFF contracts)
3. Costs and estimated earnings in excess of billings on uncompleted contracts

Notes Payable

1. Description of note
2. Amount of note
3. Effective interest rate

Disclosure Index

4. Segregation of type of notes:
    a. trade
    b. banks
    c. items collateralized
    d. related parties—stockholders, directors, officers, or employees
    e. intercompany
5. Nonmonetary transaction:
    a. imputed interest
    b. premium or discount
    c. face amount
    d. effective interest rate
    e. valuation of rights or privileges

Accounts Payable

1. Segregation by types:
    a. trade
    b. nontrade
    c. related parties
    d. intercompany
2. Accounts collateralized

Income Taxes Payable

1. Segregated between current and deferred
2. Amounts in dispute

Other Current Liabilities

1. Current accruals
2. Current portion of long-term obligations
3. Customer's advances or deposits
4. Guarantees, warranties, etc.
5. Billings in excess of costs and estimated earnings on uncompleted contracts

Long-Term Obligations

1. Description of terms and interest rates
2. Assets pledged, restrictions on dividends or retained earnings, sinking fund requirements, etc.
3. Current portions shown as current
4. Capitalized lease obligations
5. Convertibility
6. Nonmonetary transactions:
    a. imputed interest
    b. premium or discount
    c. face amount
    d. effective interest rates
    e. valuation of rights and privileges

Unrealized Gross Profits on Installment Sales

Stockholders' Equity

1. Common stock:
    a. title of each class
    b. par or stated value
    c. number of shares authorized, issued and outstanding
    d. reserved shares and purpose
2. Preferred stock:
    a. title of each class
    b. par or stated value
    c. number of shares authorized, issued, and outstanding
    d. reserved shares and purpose
    e. convertibility
    f. call price
    g. cumulative or noncumulative
    h. dividends in arrears
    i. participating or nonparticipating
    j. preference in liquidation
3. Stock subscriptions:
    a. description
    b. details of amounts

Disclosure Index

4. Additional capital:
   a. segregated by source
   b. restrictions
5. Retained earnings:
   a. appropriated and unappropriated
   b. dividend restrictions
   c. stock dividends
   d. treasury stock restrictions where required by charter or state law
   e. dated, in case of a quasi-reorganization
6. Treasury stock:
   a. number of shares
   b. basis of valuation
   c. reserved shares and purpose

STATEMENT OF CAPITAL CHANGES

A statement of changes in the separate accounts of stockholders' equity, including retained earnings, is necessary when financial position, changes in financial position, and results of operations are presented in conformity with GAAP. This disclosure may be presented as a separate statement, as part of the basic financial statements, or in footnotes thereto.

STATEMENT OF CHANGES IN FINANCIAL POSITION

A statement of changes in financial position is required for presentations that purport to present both financial position and results of operations in conformity with GAAP.

1. Prepared on a broad concept that discloses all significant financing and investing activities of the enterprise
2. Working capital provided from or used in operations
3. Total increase (decrease) in working capital
4. Schedule of changes in each element of working capital
5. Prepared on a gross basis except for normal trade-ins to replace equipment
6. Isolated statistics of working capital should not be shown

Disclosure Index

INCOME STATEMENT

1. Substantial sales to one customer or a few customers
2. Method of recognizing long-term construction-type contracts
3. Method of reporting revenues for cost reimbursement contracts
4. Method of reporting income from leases
5. Proportionate share of income from investees
6. Depreciation expense separately shown
7. Significant interest income or expense
8. Amount of investment tax credit, accounting method, and carryovers
9. Method of foreign exchange conversion
10. Gain or loss on foreign exchange
11. Significant losses on firm purchase commitments
12. Unusual or infrequently occurring items other than extraordinary should be separately shown
13. Research and development costs
14. Bad debt reserves of savings and loan associations
15. Policyholders' surplus of stock life insurance companies
16. Pension plan expense
17. Discontinued operations
18. Gain or loss from extinguishment of debt
19. Cumulative effect of an accounting change
20. Extraordinary items
21. Intraperiod income tax allocation
22. Reasons for significant variations between income tax expense and pretax accounting income
23. Material differences between pretax accounting income and taxable income
24. Earnings per share (primary and fully diluted for complex capital structures)

GENERAL

Accounting Policies

1. Description of all significant accounting policies (Summary of Significant Accounting Policies)
2. Methods of applying accounting principles:
    a. selection from acceptable alternatives

Disclosure Index

    b. peculiar to a particular industry
    c. unusual application of GAAP

Accounting Changes

1. Description of change
2. Nature and justification
3. Effect of change:
   a. cumulative effect
   b. restatement of financials
4. Reason for omitting cumulative effect and *pro forma* information
5. Change in method of amortizing new assets:
   a. nature of change and method
   b. effect on net income in period of change
   c. related per share data
6. Change in reporting entity (restatement):
7. Correction of error in previous financial statements
   a. nature of error
   b. effect on components of net income
   c. related per share data

Business Combinations

1. Purchase method:
   a. name, description, and total cost of acquisition
   b. method of accounting (purchase)
   c. period in which results of operations are included
   d. amortization of goodwill
   e. other pertinent information
   f. contingent payments
   g. *pro forma* results for current period as if acquisition had been combined from the beginning of fiscal year, and comparative year, if presented
2. Pooling of interests:
   a. name and brief description of companies combined
   b. basis of presentation in current period and restatements of prior periods
   c. method of accounting (pooling)
   d. description and amount of shares issued
   e. separate results of operation for each combining company

Disclosure Index

    f. nature of adjustments to net assets of each combining company in order to adopt the same accounting policies
    g. change in fiscal year
    h. reconciliation of revenue and earnings previously reported by acquiring company with combined amounts presented in the financial statements
    i. *pro forma* information of proposed pooling to stockholders
    j. gain or loss on disposal of significant portions of the assets or segments of combining companies
    k. pooling consummated after balance sheet date but before issuance of financial statements
    l. earnings of separate companies where new corporation is formed to effectuate combination

Commitments and Contingencies

1. Probable and reasonably possible losses where liability can be ascertained
2. Nature and range of loss
3. Remote losses on guarantees and similar items
4. Pending litigation
5. Guarantees of subsidiaries or affiliates
6. Tax contingencies
7. Accounts sold with recourse
8. Renegotiation of government contracts
9. Losses after balance sheet date but before issuance of financial statements
10. All material commitments
11. Gain contingencies that are not misleading as to likelihood of realization
12. Unused letters of credit
13. Information on noncancelable leases which are not capitalized

Development Stage Enterprises

1. Cumulative net losses
2. Cumulative income statement
3. Cumulative statement of changes in financial position
4. Date and number of shares of stock issued for cash or other consideration

Disclosure Index

    4. Nature and valuation of noncash consideration received for stock issued
    6. Description of development stage enterprises

Foreign Currency Exchange

1. Aggregate exchange gain or loss included in the determination of net income
2. Significant foreign rate changes
3. Foreign operations excluded
4. Method of foreign exchange conversion
5. Description and quantification of effects of rate changes

Extraordinary Items

1. Nature and amount of each item with related tax effects
2. Unamortized cost of intangible assets included as extraordinary charge
3. Tax benefit of any operating-loss carryforward reported as an extraordinary item in the period realized
4. Investor's share of investee's extraordinary items
5. Extinguishment of debt

Extinguishment of Debt

1. Description of extinguishment
2. Gain or loss
3. Related tax effects

Government Contracts

1. Advance payments as offsets
2. Inability to provide for renegotiation
3. Significant portion of a company's business
4. Basis of provision for renegotiations
5. Reasonable estimate of termination not possible
6. Material termination claims
7. Controversial items
8. Claims against government segregated

Disclosure Index

Interim Financial Reporting

1. Interim inventory cost method
2. Material contingencies
3. Significant seasonable variations in revenue
4. Disposal of a segment
5. Changes in accounting principle or estimate
6. Significant variations between income tax expense and pretax accounting income

Oil and Gas Producing Companies

1. Reserves and operating activities—domestic and foreign
2. Oil and gas properties, reserves, and production
3. Present value of future net revenues from production of proved oil and gas reserves
4. Quantities of crude oil and natural gas
5. Proportionate share of investee's quantities
6. Quantities from royalties
7. Long-term supply agreements with foreign governments
8. Capitalized costs, related depreciation, depletion, amortization, and valuation allowances:
    a. mineral interests in property
    b. wells, related equipment and facilities
    c. support equipment and facilities
    d. uncompleted wells, equipment and facilities
9. Functional costs:
    a. property acquisitions
    b. exploration
    c. development
    d. production
10. Economic factors and significant uncertainties for proved reserves

Pension Plans

1. Effects of compliance with ERISA
2. Full description of plan:
    a. employees covered
    b. accounting policies
    c. funding policies
3. Pension plan expense for current period

Disclosure Index

4. Present value of vested benefits over amounts provided
5. Nature and effect of items affecting amounts provided
6. Unamortized prior-service costs which have not become a legal liability

Quasi-Reorganizations

1. Disclose all pertinent information
2. Date retained earnings account

Segmental Reporting

1. Nonpublic companies are not required to disclose EPS data and segmental information
2. Industry segments and foreign operations
3. Sales and revenue:
   a. to unaffiliated customers
   b. to intercompany segments
   c. types of products
   d. revenue of each reportable segment
   e. accounting policies
4. Operating profit or loss:
   a. allocation of common operating costs and expenses
   b. exclude revenue not derived from operations
   c. exclude general corporate overhead, interest expense, income taxes, earnings from unconsolidated subsidiaries, discontinued operations, minority interests, extraordinary items, and cumulative effect of a change in an accounting principle
5. Other measures of profitability may be used
6. Tangible and intangible identifiable assets:
   a. by industry segments or foreign operations
   b. exclude assets for general corporate use which are not used in any reportable segment
7. Other reportable segment information (by industry segments):
   a. depreciation, depletion, or amortization
   b. capital expenditures
   c. net income from unconsolidated subsidiaries and investees whose operations are vertically integrated
   d. nature and amount of unusual or infrequently occurring items included in the operating profit or loss of a reportable segment

Disclosure Index

    e. effect on a reportable segment's operating profit or loss of a change in an accounting principle
    f. method(s) used to allocate common costs between reportable segments
8. Export sales
9. Significant sales to one customer
10. Significant sales to governments if they exceed 10% of consolidated sales
11. All segmental information reconciled to financial statements

Stock Options

1. Status of all option plans:
    a. number of shares covered by each option and date of grant
    b. exercise price
    c. number of shares that can be exercised
    d. number of shares exercised
    e. option price of exercised shares
    f. expiration dates
2. All pertinent information about stock option plan, etc.

Short-Term Obligations Expected to Be Refinanced

1. General description of irrevocable financing agreement
2. Terms of new obligation or details of equity securities to be issued
3. Amount excluded from current liabilities as a result of refinancing

Supplementary Information on Changing Prices

1. Income from continuing operations, on a constant dollar and current cost basis
2. Purchasing power gain or loss on net monetary items
3. Current cost amounts of inventory and property, plant and equipment
4. Increases or decreases in current cost amounts of inventory and property, plant, and equipment, net of inflation
5. Five year summary of financial data, including:
    a. income

Disclosure Index

    b. sales and other operating revenues
    c. net assets
    d. dividends per common share
    e. market price per share

Tax Examinations

1. Examination or litigation in progress
2. All pertinent information
3. Settlement of examination or litigation

Troubled Debt Restructuring

1. Debtors troubled debt restructuring:
   a. description of terms of restructuring
   b. aggregate gain and related tax effect
   c. aggregate gain or loss on transfer of assets
   d. per share data on aggregate gain on restructure (net of related tax)
   e. contingent payable amounts with description of terms
2. Creditors troubled debt restructuring:
   a. restructured receivables by major categories
   b. aggregate recorded investment
   c. gross interest income not earned as a result of debt restructuring
   d. gross interest income on restructured receivables included in current net income
   e. commitments to lend additional funds to debtor

AUDITOR'S REPORT

Scope Limitation

1. Time constraints
2. Insufficient competent evidence:
   a. inability to observe inventory
   b. inability to confirm receivables

Disclosure Index

      c. client restrictions
      d. restrictions on the use of audit procedures
3. Inadequate records

Other Auditor's Report

1. Report being based in part on another auditor's report
2. Sharing of responsibility

Departure from GAAP

1. Lack of conformity to GAAP
2. Material departure
3. Inadequate disclosure

Consistency

1. Exception to change in accounting principle
2. Inconsistency of accounting principles

Uncertainties

1. Recurring losses (going concern principle)
2. Deficiency in working capital
3. Inability to obtain financing
4. Failure to comply with loan agreement

Topical Index

Topical Index

ACCOUNTING CHANGES
Background **1.01**
  Coverage of GAAP **1.01**
Changes in an accounting estimate **1.09**
  Causes of change in estimate **1.09**
Changes in accounting principles **1.02**
  Change in composition of inventory costs **1.03**
  Change in estimate as a result of change in principle **1.02**
  Examples of changes in principles **1.03**
  Exceptions **1.04**
  Newly promulgated GAAP **1.02**
  Rule of preferability **1.02**
Comprehensive illustration **1.11**
Financial summaries **1.11**
  Presentation of accounting changes **1.04**
Nondiscretionary effects **1.05**
  Calculation of effect impossible **1.05**
  Pro forma presentation **1.06**
Oil and gas producing companies **1.01**
Reporting accounting changes—interim periods **1.08**
  Cumulative effect **1.07**
  Cumulative effect cannot be calculated **1.08**
  Disclosures **1.08**
  Nature and justification **1.08**
  Pro forma effects **1.08**
  Publicly traded companies **1.08**
Reporting a change in accounting estimate **1.09**
  Disclosures **1.09**
  Procedures **1.09**
Reporting a change in accounting principle **1.03**
  Changes requiring restatement **1.04**
  Cumulative effect **1.03**
    Presentation in income statement **1.04**
  Direct effects **1.04**
  Earnings per share data **1.04**
Reporting a change in an entity **1.10**
  Disclosures **1.10**
  Procedures **1.10**
Reporting corrections of errors **1.10**
  Definition of prior period adjustment **1.10**
  Disclosures **1.10**
Types of accounting **1.01**
ACCOUNTING POLICIES
Background **2.01**
  Coverage of GAAP **2.01**
  Unaudited reports **2.01**
Comprehensive illustration **2.02**
Disclosure **2.02**
Overview **2.01**
  Compliance with GAAP **2.01**
  Preferable presentation of disclosure **2.01**

ACCOUNTING POLICIES: Overview (continued)
  Method of applying such principles **2.02**
  Significant accounting policies **2.01**
ACCOUNTS RECEIVABLE
  Allowance for uncollectibles **8.05**
  Current—assets and liabilities **8.05**
  Factoring **8.06**
  Installment sales **20.04**
  Officers or employees **8.07**
  Pledging **8.06**
ACID-TEST RATIO
  Current—assets and liabilities **8.04**
ACTUARIAL ASSUMPTIONS
  Pension plans **31.03**
ACTUARIAL COST METHOD
  Pension plans **31.03**
    Accrued benefit (unit credit) **31.04**
    Projected benefit **31.05**
ACTUARIAL GAINS OR LOSSES
  Pension plans **31.06**
ACTUARIAL VALUATION
  Pension plans **31.03**
ALL-INCLUSIVE CONCEPT
  Results of operations **36.01**
ALLOWANCE FOR BAD DEBTS
  Allowance method **8.05**
  Current—assets and liabilities **8.05**
  Direct write-off method **8.05**
AMORTIZATION
  Goodwill **21.02**
  Intangible assets **21.02**
  Interest on receivables and payables **22.03**
  Investment tax credit **25.01**
  Leases **26.13**
  Negative goodwill **21.04**
  Past-service costs **31.07**
ANTIDILUTION
  Earnings per share **13.07**
APPRAISAL VALUES
  Business combinations **3.02**
  Depreciable assets and depreciation **11.04**
  Depreciation of appraisal values **11.04**

BAD DEBTS
  Current—assets and liabilities **8.05**
BARGAIN PURCHASE OPTION
  Leases **26.04**
BARGAIN RENEWAL OPTION
  Leases **26.04**
BASE STOCK METHOD
  Inventory pricing and methods **24.14**

Topical Index

BUSINESS COMBINATIONS
  Acquisition of stock directly from subsidiary **3.13**
    Determining acquirer's stock interest **3.13**
  Application of pooling-of-interests method **3.21**
    Accounting prior to consummation date **3.21**
    Accounts combined at cost **3.21**
    Disposal of significant portion of assets **3.21**
    Expenses of combination **3.21**
    Foreign currency translation **16.06**
    Intercorporate investments **3.21**
    Reporting in period of combination **3.21**
    Restatement of prior years' statements **3.21**
    Treasury stock **3.21**
  Background **3.01**
    Coverage of GAAP **3.01**
    Regulated industries **3.01**
  Conditions for pooling of interests **3.15**
    Acquisition of 90% or more of voting stock **3.17**
      Determining independence **3.17**
      Equivalent number of shares **3.18**
      Transfer of net assets **3.19**
    Acquisition of voting common stock **3.17**
    Autonomy of combining interests **3.16**
    Completion of plan **3.16**
    Effective date of consummation of plan **3.17**
    Inconsistent transactions **3.21**
    Independence of combining companies **3.16**
    No change in equity **3.20**
    Proportionate shares for stockholders **3.20**
    Same rights to stockholders **3.20**
  Different classes of capital stock **3.11**
    Computing parent's investment **3.12**
    Guidelines for preferred stock issues **3.11**
  Disclosure for pooling of interests **3.22**
    Adjustments to net assets **3.22**
    Amount of shares issued **3.22**
    Change in fiscal year **3.22**
    Description of companies **3.22**
    Method of accounting **3.22**
    Reconciliation of revenue and earnings **3.22**
    Results for each separate company **3.22**
    Unconsummated plans **3.22**
  Disclosure for purchase method **3.05**
    Basic disclosures **3.06**
    Supplemental disclosures **3.06**
  Earnings per share **13.22**
  Inventory in business combinations **24.17**
  Investment tax credit **25.11**
  Overview **3.01**
    Definition of business combination **3.01**
    Pooling **3.01**
    Purchase **3.01**
    Pooling-of-interests method **3.15**

BUSINESS COMBINATIONS (continued)
  Purchase method **3.02**
    Determination of cost **3.02**
    Fair value **3.02**
  Purchase versus pooling of interests **3.06**
    Goodwill **3.06**
    Negative goodwill **3.06**
    Purchase of assets **3.07**
    Purchase of stock interest **3.08**
  Step-by-step acquisition **3.14**

CAPITAL CHANGES
  Equity method **14.03**
  Stockholders' equity **38.01**
CAPITAL LEASE
  Leases **26.02**
CAPITAL STRUCTURE
  Complex capital structures **13.09**
    Fully diluted EPS **13.09**
    Presentation of EPS **13.09**
    Primary EPS **13.09**
  Earnings per share **13.08**
  Simple capital structures **13.08**
    Presentation of EPS **13.08**
CARRYBACK LOSSES
  Income taxes **19.04**
CARRYFORWARD LOSSES
  Income taxes **19.05**
CASH SURRENDER VALUE OF LIFE INSURANCE
  Current—assets and liabilities **8.06**
CHANGES IN FINANCIAL POSITION
  Background **4.01**
    Existing GAAP **4.01**
    Regulated industries **4.01**
    Statements issued for internal use only **4.01**
    Unclassified balance sheets **4.01**
  Cash format **4.05**
    Cash provided (used) in operations **4.05**
    Changes in current accounts **4.05**
    Increase (decrease) in cash **4.05**
    No separate schedule of changes **4.05**
  Comprehensive illustration **4.05**
  Concept of funds **4.02**
    All financial resources **4.02**
    Cash **4.02**
    Cash and marketable securities **4.02**
    Cash basis **4.02**
    Changes in working capital **4.04**
      Each element **4.04**
      Increase (decrease) in working capital **4.04**
    Funds provided (used) in operations **4.03**
    Net quick assets **4.02**

Topical Index

CHANGES IN FINANCIAL POSITIONS: Concept of funds (continued)
Net working capital **4.04**
Statement format **4.03**
Unclassified balance sheets **4.03**
Gross basis **4.02**
 Conflict with FASB-12 **4.02**
 Normal trade-ins **4.02**
Overview **4.01**
 All changes in financial position **4.01**
 Broad concept **4.01**
 Exception–book entries **4.01**
 Financing and investing activities **4.01**
 Working capital–operations **4.01**
  Net changes in **4.01**
Per share amounts **4.05**
 Isolated statistics **4.05**
 Per share information **4.05**

COMBINED FINANCIAL STATEMENTS
Consolidated financial statements **5.04**

COMMON STOCK
Marketable securities **28.01**
Stockholders' equity **38.02**
 Authorized **38.02**
 Issued **38.02**
 Legal capital **38.01**
 Outstanding **38.02**
 Par value **38.02**
 Stated value **38.02**
 Subscriptions **38.02**
 Treasury stock **38.02**

COMMON STOCK EQUIVALENTS (CSE)
Convertible debt **13.04**
Definition **13.03**
Determination of CSE **13.03**
Dilution **13.03**
Earnings per share **13.03**
Materiality (3% rule) **13.07**
Security becoming a CSE after issuance **13.03**
Substance over form **13.03**
Types of CSE **13.04**
 Contingent shares **13.04**
 Convertible debt **13.04**
 Convertible stock **13.04**
 Participating securities **13.04**
 Stock options, warrants, etc. **13.04**

COMPARABILITY
Comparative financial statements **5.04**
Consistency **5.04**

COMPENSATORY PLANS
Stock issued to employees **39.02**

COMPLETED-CONTRACT METHOD
Long-term contracts **27.01**

COMPREHENSIVE ILLUSTRATIONS
Accounting changes **1.11**
Accounting policies **2.02**
Changes in financial position **4.05**
Completed-contract method **27.04**
Cost method **14.06**
Cost to equity method **14.08**
Current value accounting **9.04**
Deferred compensation contracts **10.01**
Earnings per share **13.23**
Equity method **14.07**
Extinguishment of debt **15.02**
Financial reporting and changing prices **15.64**
General price-level changes **17.08**
Intangible assets **21.06**
Interest on receivables and payables **22.03**
 Interest method **22.03**
Inventory pricing and methods **24.21**
 Average method **24.22**
 FIFO method **24.21**
 LIFO method **24.22**
Leases **26.44**
Marketable securities **28.09**
Pension plans **31.13**
Percentage-of-completion method **27.04**
Presentation of net income **36.08**
Purchase method **3.02**
Quasi-reorganization **32.04**
Segmental reporting **37.10**
Stock issued to employees **39.09**

CONSISTENCY
Comparability **5.04**
Comparative financial statements **5.04**

CONSOLIDATED FINANCIAL STATEMENTS
Accounting and reporting **5.01**
 Disclosures when cost method is used **5.03**
 Disposal of a subsidiary **5.03**
 Exclusion of a subsidiary **5.02**
 Minority interest **5.03**
 Purchase of net assets **5.02**
 Retained earnings of a subsidiary **5.01**
 Step-by-step acquisition **5.02**
 Subsidiary with different fiscal years **5.01**
 Use of cost method **5.03**
 Use of equity method **5.03**
Background **5.01**
 Coverage of GAAP **5.01**
 Regulated industries **5.01**
Combined financial statements **5.04**
 Justification–consolidated statements **5.04**
Comparative financial statements **5.04**
 Comparability **5.04**
 Consistency **5.04**

GAAP GUIDE / **42.05**

Topical Index

CONSOLIDATED FINANCIAL STATEMENTS (continued)
  Consolidated work papers **5.05**
    Compared with regular work papers **5.05**
  Consolidation versus equity method **5.05**
    One-line consolidation **5.05**
  Disclosure **5.16**
    Consolidation policy **5.16**
  Entity theory **5.13**
  Income tax considerations **5.14**
    Deferred income taxes **5.14**
  Intercompany transactions **5.05**
    Intercompany bond holdings **5.10**
    Intercompany dividends **5.13**
    Intercompany stock holdings **5.13**
    Receivables and payables **5.05**
    Unrealized profits in inventory **5.06**
    Unrealized profits in long-lived assets **5.08**
  Minority interests **5.14**
    Father-son-grandson affiliation **5.14**
    In net income **5.14**
    Presentation on balance sheet **5.14**
  Overview **5.01**
    When consolidated statements should be prepared **5.01**

CONSTANT DOLLAR DISCLOSURES
  Financial reporting and changing prices **15.51**

CONTINGENCIES
  Accrual of loss contingency **6.02**
    Requirements **6.02**
  Background **6.01**
    Coverage of GAAP **6.01**
    Regulated industries **6.01**
  Classification of contingencies **6.02**
    How a loss contingency may arise **6.02**
    Types **6.02**
  Contingency reserves **6.04**
    Establishment of reserve **6.04**
    Types **6.04**
    Use of reserves **6.04**
  Disclosure of noninsurance **6.05**
  Disclosure of reasonably possible losses **6.03**
  Disclosure of remote losses **6.03**
  Gain contingencies **6.04**
    Disclosure requirements **6.04**
  No accrual of loss contingency **6.03**
    Accrual of loss—range of losses **6.02**
    Disclosure requirements **6.02**
  Overview **6.01**
    Definition of contingency **6.01**
  Regulated industries **6.03**
    Disclosure requirements **6.03**

CONTINGENCIES (continued)
  Unasserted claims **6.03**
    Disclosure not required **6.03**

CONTINGENT RENTALS
  Leases **26.23**

CONVERTIBLE DEBT
  Accounting and reporting **7.01**
    Conversion feature attached **7.01**
    Conversion feature not attached **7.01**
    Par or face value **7.02**
    Relative fair value **7.02**
    Resulting premium or discount **7.02**
  Background **7.01**
    Regulated industries **7.01**
    Substance of transaction **7.01**
    Time of issuance **7.01**
  Other considerations **7.02**
    Common stock equivalents **7.02**
  Overview **7.01**
    Convertible debt—characteristics **7.01**
      Callable **7.01**
      Conversion price **7.01**
      Interest rate **7.01**
      Issue price **7.01**
      Subordination **7.01**

CORPORATE READJUSTMENT
  Quasi-reorganization **32.01**

COST METHOD
  Equity method **14.02**

COST-PLUS-FIXED-FEE CONTRACTS
  Disclosure **18.01**
  Government contracts **18.01**
  Renegotiation **18.02**
  Termination claims **18.02**
  Typical provisions **18.01**

COST RECOVERY METHOD
  Depreciable assets and depreciation **11.09**
  Installment method of accounting **20.01**

CUMULATIVE EFFECT
  Accounting change **1.03**
  Calculation not possible **1.05**
  Reporting in interim periods **1.08**

CURRENT ASSETS AND CURRENT LIABILITIES
  Background **8.01**
    Coverage of GAAP **8.01**
  Cash surrender value of life insurance **8.06**
  Computing life insurance expense **8.07**
  Current assets **8.02**
    Categories **8.02**
    Definition **8.02**
  Current liabilities **8.02**
    Definition **8.02**

Topical Index

CURRENT ASSETS AND CURRENT LIABILITIES:
Current liabilities (continued)
  Recorded at present values **8.03**
  Types **8.03**
Current obligations expected to be refinanced **8.07**
  Alternative financing sources **8.09**
    Revolving credit agreements **8.09**
  Amount which can be excluded **8.08**
  Conditions for exclusion **8.08**
  Coverage of GAAP **8.07**
  Disclosure **8.09**
  Prerequisites for reclassification **8.08**
  Source of GAAP **8.07**
Disclosures **8.07**
Factoring **8.06**
Operating Cycle **8.01**
  Definition **8.01**
  Determination of current–assets and liabilities **8.01**
  Natural business year **8.01**
Pledging **8.06**
Working capital **8.03**
  Acid-test ratio (quick ratio) **8.04**
  Changes in elements of working capital **8.03**
  Current ratio (working capital ratio) **8.04**
  Definition **8.03**
  Statement of changes in financial position **8.03**
CURRENT COST DISCLOSURES
Financial reporting and changing prices **15.51**
CURRENT OBLIGATIONS EXPECTED TO BE REFINANCED
Current assets and current liabilities **8.07**
CURRENT OPERATING INCOME
Current value accounting **9.03**
CURRENT OPERATING PERFORMANCE CONCEPT
Results of operations **36.02**
CURRENT RATIO
Current assets and current liabilities **8.04**
CURRENT VALUE ACCOUNTING
Background **9.01**
Comprehensive illustration **9.03**
Current value income **9.02**
  Current operating income **9.03**
  Current value income **9.03**
  Realized income **9.03**
Current value methods **9.01**
  Entry value system **9.01**
  Exit value system **9.01**
Financial reporting and changing prices **15.51**
Holding gains **9.02**
  Realized **9.02**
  Unrealized **9.02**

CURRENT VALUE ACCOUNTING (continued)
Monetary and nonmonetary items **9.02**
  Monetary items **9.02**
  Nonmonetary items **9.02**
Oil and gas producing companies **30.04**
Overview **9.01**
CURRENT VALUE INCOME
Current value accounting **9.02**

DEBT ISSUED WITH STOCK PURCHASE WARRANTS
Convertible debt **7.01**
DEFERRAL METHOD
Investment tax credit **25.01**
DEFERRED COMPENSATION CONTRACTS
Background **10.01**
Compensation contracts treated like pension plans **10.01**
  Coverage of GAAP **10.01**
Comprehensive illustration **10.01**
Overview **10.01**
  Basis of accounting **10.01**
  Determination of total liability **10.01**
Pension plans **10.01**
DEFERRED INCOME TAXES
Consolidated financial statements **5.14**
Deferred tax method **19.10**
Income taxes **19.10**
Installment method of accounting **20.04**
DEFERRED TAX METHOD
Computation **19.11**
Consistent application **19.11**
Definition of taxable income **19.10**
Gross change method **19.14**
Income taxes **19.10**
Individual method **19.14**
Net amount on balance sheet **19.15**
Net change method **19.14**
Permanent differences **19.11**
Short-cut approach **19.14**
Tax expense **19.11**
Tax liability **19.11**
DEFINED BENEFIT PLAN
Pension plans **31.01**
DEFINED CONTRIBUTION PLAN
Pension plans **31.02**
DEFINED PROFIT-SHARING PLAN
Pension plans **31.02**
DEPARTURE FROM COST BASIS
Inventory pricing and methods **24.03**
DEPLETION
Annual depletion expense **11.11**

Topical Index

DEPLETION (continued)
  Cost depletion **11.10**
  Depletion rate per unit **11.11**
  Depreciable assets and depreciation **11.11**
  Disclosure **11.11**
  Recoverable units **11.11**
DEPRECIABLE ASSETS AND DEPRECIATION
  Asset cost **11.01**
    Capitalized **11.01**
    Normal expenditures **11.01**
    Razing and removal costs **11.01**
    Unnecessary expenditures **11.01**
  Background **11.01**
    Coverage of GAAP **11.01**
    Regulated industries **11.01**
  Depletion **11.10**
    Annual depletion expense **11.11**
    Cost depletion **11.10**
    Depletion rate per unit **11.11**
    Recoverable units **11.11**
  Depreciation methods **11.06**
    Cost recovery **11.09**
    Declining balance **11.08**
    Inflation and depreciation **11.10**
    Matching concept **11.06**
    Other types of depreciation **11.10**
      Present value **11.10**
      Replacement **11.10**
      Retirement **11.10**
    Straight line **11.06**
    Sum-of-the-years'-digits **11.07**
    Systematic and rational allocation **11.06**
    Timing differences **11.10**
    Units of production **11.06**
  Disclosure **11.11**
    Accumulated allowances **11.11**
    Deducted from related asset **11.11**
    Depreciation and depletion **11.11**
    Depreciation expense for period **11.11**
    Major classes of assets **11.11**
    Method used **11.11**
  Estimated useful life **11.02**
    Longevity **11.02**
    Maintenance policy **11.02**
    Physical life **11.02**
    Service life **11.02**
  Improvement of depreciable assets **11.04**
  Write-up of assets **11.04**
    Depreciation of appraisal values **11.04**
    GAAP prohibits **11.04**
DEPRECIATION
  Cost recovery **11.09**
  Declining balance **11.08**

DEPRECIATION (continued)
  Deducted from related assets **11.11**
  Depreciable assets and depreciation **11.05**
  Disclosure **11.11**
  Functional depreciation **11.05**
  Matching concept **11.06**
  Physical depreciation **11.06**
  Present value **11.10**
  Replacement depreciation **11.10**
  Retirement depreciation **11.10**
  Straight line **11.06**
  Sum-of-the-years'-digits **11.07**
  Units of production **11.06**
DEVELOPMENT STAGE ENTERPRISES
  Accounting and reporting **12.01**
    Basic financial statements **12.01**
      Conformity with GAAP **12.01**
  Background **12.01**
    Current promulgated GAAP **12.01**
    Established operating companies **12.01**
    Extractive industries **12.01**
    Real estate properties **12.01**
    Regulated industries **12.01**
  Disclosure **12.02**
    Accumulated losses **12.02**
    Cumulative changes in financial position **12.02**
    New accounting principle **12.02**
    No longer in development stage **12.03**
    Statement of stockholders' equity **12.02**
      Noncash consideration **12.02**
      Number of shares **12.02**
  Overview **12.01**
    Development stage **12.01**
      Establishing a new business **12.01**
      Principal operations **12.01**
DIRECT EFFECTS
  Accounting change **1.04**
DIRECT FINANCING LEASES
  Leases **26.16**
DISCLOSURES
  Accounting changes in interim periods **1.08**
  Accounting estimates **1.09**
  Accounting policies **2.02**
  Business combinations—pooling of interests **3.22**
  Business combinations—purchase method **3.05**
  Change in an entity **1.10**
  Consolidation policy **5.16**
  Correction of prior-period errors **1.10**
  Current assets and current liabilities **8.07**
  Current obligations expected to be refinanced **8.09**
  Depletion **11.11**
  Depreciation methods **11.11**
  Development stage enterprises **12.02**

Topical Index

DISCLOSURES (continued)
  Earnings per share **13.22**
  Equity method **14.05**
  Extinguishment of debt **15.02**
  Financial reporting and changing prices **15.51**
    Constant dollar disclosure **15.57**
    Current cost disclosure **15.59**
  Foreign operations and exchanges **16.11**
  Gain contingency **6.04**
  Government contracts **18.02**
  Income taxes **19.23**
    Claims for refund **19.24**
    Components of tax expense **19.24**
    Deferred charges and credits **19.24**
    Indefinite reversal criteria **19.24**
    Operating loss carryforward **19.24**
    Prior-period adjustments **19.24**
    Significant unused credits and deductions **19.24**
  Installment method of accounting **20.04**
  Intangible assets **21.05**
    Amortization **21.05**
    Estimated useful life **21.05**
    Goodwill **21.05**
    Negative goodwill **21.05**
  Interest on receivables and payables **22.03**
  Interim financial reporting **22.03**
  Inventory pricing and method **24.15**
  Investment tax credit **25.13**
  Lessee's disclosures **26.16**
  Lessor's disclosures **26.27**
  Long-term contracts **27.04**
  Loss contingencies **6.02**
  Marketable securities **28.05**
    Nonspecialized industries **28.05**
    Specialized industries **28.07**
  Noninsurance **6.05**
  Nonmonetary transactions **29.05**
  Oil and gas producing companies **30.15**
  Pension plans **31.12**
  Quasi-reorganization **32.04**
  Reasonably possible losses **6.03**
  Remote losses **6.03**
  Research and development costs **35.02**
  Results of operations **36.08**
  Segmental reporting **37.08**
  Stockholders' equity **38.02**
    Call prices **38.03**
    Capital changes **38.03**
    Conversion rates **38.03**
    Dividends in arrears **38.03**
    Exercise prices **38.03**
    Legal capital **38.03**
    Liquidation preference **38.03**

DISCLOSURES: Stockholders' equity (continued)
    Minority interests **38.04**
    Participation rights **38.03**
    Restriction on dividends **38.03**
    Retained earnings **38.03**
    Stock dividend **38.03**
    Stock split **38.03**
    Treasury stock **38.03**
  Stock issued to employees **39.08**
  Troubled debt restructuring **40.05**
    Debtors **40.05**
    Creditors **40.07**
DISCONTINUED OPERATIONS
  Income taxes **19.20**
  Inventory pricing and methods **24.16**
    Loss on write-down **24.16**
  Results of operations **36.05**
    Disposal date **36.06**
    Gain or loss **36.06**
    Identifiable entity **36.06**
    Measurement date **36.06**
DISCOUNTED NOTES RECEIVABLE
  Current assets and current liabilities **8.05**
DISCOUNTED TAX ALLOCATION
  Income taxes **19.16**
DISCOVERY VALUE ACCOUNTING
  Oil and gas producing companies **30.05**
DISPOSAL OF A SEGMENT
  Results of operations **36.05**
  Segmental reporting **37.05**
DIVIDENDS
  Stockholders' equity **38.06**
    Cash dividend **38.06**
    Pro rata distribution **38.06**
    Stock dividend **38.07**
    Stock split **38.07**
DOLLAR-VALUE LIFO
  Inventory pricing and methods **24.07**
DOMINANT SEGMENTS
  Segmental reporting **37.08**
DONATED STOCK
  Stockholders' equity **38.01**

EARNINGS PER SHARE
  Antidilution **13.07**
  Definition **13.07**
  Background **13.01**
    Coverage of GAAP **13.01**
    Regulated industries **13.01**
    Special purpose statements **13.01**
  Business combinations **13.21**
    Pooling method **13.22**
    Purchase method **13.22**

GAAP GUIDE / **42.09**

Topical Index

EARNINGS PER SHARE: (continued)
  Common stock equivalents **13.03**
    Contingent shares **13.04**
      Certain level of earnings **13.05**
      Contingent on future market price **13.05**
      Future earnings and future market price **13.05**
    Definition **13.03**
    Determination of CSE **13.03**
    Dilution **13.03**
    EPS computation for subsidiary–parent **13.06**
    Future conversion of CSE **13.04**
    Materiality **13.07**
    Presentation of stock dividend **13.06**
    Security becoming a CSE after issuance **13.03**
    Shares in escrow accounts **13.05**
    Stock issued to employees **39.01**
    Substance over form **13.03**
    Types of CSE **13.04**
      Convertible debt and convertible preferred stock **13.04**
      Participating securities **13.04**
      Stock options, warrants, and similar instruments **13.04**
  Complex capital structures **13.09**
    Exclusion of antidilutive securities **13.09**
    Fully diluted earnings **13.09**
    Primary earnings **13.09**
    Primary EPS vs. fully diluted EPS **13.09**
    Securities in fully diluted EPS **13.09**
  Comprehensive illustration **13.23**
  Disclosures **13.22**
    All rights and privileges of the various security holders **13.22**
    Basis on which primary and fully diluted EPS have been calculated **13.22**
    Effects of recapitalization **13.22**
    Other specific disclosures **13.23**
  Dual presentation of net income **13.09**
    Definition **13.09**
  If-converted method **13.18**
    Adjustments to net income **13.18**
    Assumptions **13.18**
    Objectives **13.20**
    Summary of steps necessary **13.20**
    When used **13.18**
  Loss per share **13.21**
  Modified treasury stock method **13.15**
    Adjustments to net income **13.15**
    Procedures **13.15**
    Summary of steps necessary **13.17**
    When used **13.15**
  Nonpublic enterprise **13.01**
    Definition **13.01**

EARNINGS PER SHARE: Nonpublic enterprises (continued)
    Suspension of disclosure requirement **13.01**
  Overview **13.02**
    Accounting changes **13.02**
    Dilution effect ignored **13.02**
    Dual presentation **13.03**
    Prior period adjustments **13.02**
    Prominent presentation of EPS **13.02**
    Subsequent events affecting EPS **13.03**
  Simple capital structures **13.08**
    Definition **13.08**
    Presentation of EPS **13.08**
  Treasury stock method **13.12**
    Procedures **13.14**
    Theory behind treasury stock method **13.15**
    When used **13.12**
  Two-class method **13.21**
    Procedures **13.21**
    When used **13.21**
  Weighted average shares **13.10**
EMPLOYEE RETIREMENT INCOME SECURITY ACT (ERISA)
  Pension plans **31.11**
ENTITY THEORY
  Consolidated financial statements **5.13**
ENTRY VALUE SYSTEMS
  Current value accounting **9.02**
EQUITY METHOD
  Adjustments **14.02**
    Capital transactions **14.03**
    Definition of outstanding shares **14.04**
    Discontinuance of equity method **14.03**
    Dissimilar investments **14.03**
    Intercompany profits and losses **14.03**
    Investment account **14.03**
    Ownership decreases below 20% **14.04**
    Ownership increases above 20% **14.04**
    Permanent declines in investment **14.03**
    Preferred stock dividends **14.04**
    Restricted foreign investments **14.04**
    Sale of investment **14.03**
    Temporary investments **14.04**
    Underlying equity **14.03**
    Untimely financial reports **14.03**
  Background **14.01**
    Corporate joint ventures **14.01**
    Exclusions **14.01**
    Leasing subsidiaries **14.01**
    Regulated industries **14.01**
  Comprehensive illustrations **14.06**
    Cost method **14.06**
    Cost to equity method **14.08**

Topical Index

EQUITY METHOD: Comprehensive illustrations (continued)
    Equity method **14.07**
    Conclusion **14.05**
    Cost method **14.02**
        Continuing operating losses **14.02**
        Dividends are income **14.02**
        Original investment **14.02**
        Ownership to less than 20% **14.02**
    Disclosure **14.05**
        Accounting policies **14.05**
        Carrying value **14.05**
        Convertible securities **14.05**
        Description of investment **14.05**
        Equity method not used **14.05**
        Extent of disclosure **14.05**
        Percentage of ownership **14.05**
        Quoted market prices **14.05**
        Summary **14.05**
            Assets **14.05**
            Liabilities **14.05**
            Results of operations **14.05**
    Equity method **14.02**
        Dividends not income **14.02**
        Investor's share of earnings **14.03**
        One-line consolidation **14.03**
        Original investment **14.02**
    Overview **14.01**
        Consolidation more meaningful **14.01**
        Control less than majority **14.01**
        Dividends received **14.01**
        Effect of equity method **14.01**
        Less than 20% **14.02**
        Proportionate share of net income **14.02**
        Significant influence **14.02**
        More than 20% **14.02**
ESTIMATED RESIDUAL VALUE
    Leases **26.04**
ESTIMATED USEFUL LIFE
    Depreciable assets and depreciation **11.02**
    Intangible assets **21.03**
    Physical life **11.02**
    Service life **11.02**
EXCHANGE RATE
    Average exchange rate **16.03**
    Current exchange rate **16.02**
    Foreign operations and exchanges **16.02**
    Historical exchange rate **16.02**
    Spot rate **16.08**
EXECUTORY COSTS
    Leases **26.04**
EXIT VALUE SYSTEMS
    Current value accounting **9.02**

EXPORT SALES
    Segmental reporting **37.07**
EXTINGUISHMENT OF DEBT
    Accounting for extinguishments of debt **15.01**
        Method of accounting **15.01**
        Net carrying amount **15.01**
        Reacquisition price **15.02**
        Treatment for other extinguishments **15.02**
    Background **15.01**
        Coverage of GAAP **15.01**
    Comprehensive illustration **15.02**
    Disclosure **15.02**
        Description of transaction **15.02**
        Gain or loss **15.02**
        Gain or loss per share **15.02**
        Tax effect **15.02**
    Gain or loss **15.02**
        Computation **15.02**
        Reasons for refunding **15.02**
        Reported as extraordinary item **15.02**
    Overview **15.01**
        Definition **15.01**
        Main problem **15.01**
EXTRACTIVE INDUSTRIES
    Development stage enterprises **12.01**
EXTRAORDINARY ITEMS
    Carryforwards **36.03**
    Changes in financial position **4.03**
    Criteria **36.03**
    Extinguishment of debt **15.02**
    Income taxes **19.19**
    Interim period **23.02**
    Results of operations **36.03**

FACTORING
    Current assets and current liabilities **8.06**
FINANCIAL ACCOUNTING INCOME
    Income taxes **19.01**
FINANCIAL REPORTING AND CHANGING PRICES
    Background **15.51**
    Comprehensive illustrations **15.64**
    Constant dollar disclosures **15.57**
        Five-year summary **15.58**
        Income from continuing operations **15.59**
        Items to be restated **15.58**
        Net operating revenue **15.58**
        Purchasing power gain or loss on net monetary items **15.59**
    Current cost disclosure **15.59**
        Current cost **15.60**
        Evidence for current costs **15.63**
        Explanatory statements **15.62**
        Five-year summary **15.60**

Topical Index

FINANCIAL REPORTING AND CHANGING PRICES: Current cost disclosure (continued)
    Income from continuing operations **15.61**
    Increase or decrease in property, plant and equipment **15.61**
    Inventory, property, plant and equipment at end of year **15.61**
    Measurement of assets and expenses **15.62**
    Net realizable value **15.62**
    Value in use **15.63**
  Minimum supplementary information **15.56**
    Depreciation **15.56**
    Effective date **15.56**
    Recoverable amounts **15.57**
    Regulated industries **15.56**
  Monetary assets and liabilities **15.53**
  Net monetary position **15.54**
    Table of monetary-nonmonetary classification **15.55**
  Nonmonetary assets and liabilities **15.54**
  Overview **15.53**
    Current value accounting **15.53**
    General price-level accounting **15.53**
  Table of consumer price index **15.68**
  Terminology **15.52**
    Constant dollar accounting **15.52**
    Current cost accounting **15.52**
    Current cost/constant dollar accounting **15.52**
    Current cost/nominal dollar accounting **15.52**
    Historical cost/constant dollar accounting **15.52**
    Historical cost/nominal dollar accounting **15.52**
    Income from continuing operations **15.52**
    Public enterprise **15.52**

FIRM PURCHASE COMMITMENTS
  Inventory pricing and methods **24.15**

FIRST-IN, FIRST-OUT (FIFO)
  Inventory pricing and methods **24.06**

FLOW OF COST FACTORS
  Inventory pricing and methods **24.05**

FLOW-THROUGH METHOD
  Investment tax credit **25.01**

FOREIGN EXCHANGE CONTRACTS
  Definition **16.06**
  Discount or premium **16.08**
  Foreign operations and exchange **16.06**
  Gain or loss **16.07**

FOREIGN OPERATIONS AND EXCHANGE
  Background **16.01**
    Coverage of GAAP **16.01**
    Regulated industries **16.01**
  Conclusion **16.11**
  Disclosure **16.11**
  Exclusion of foreign operations **16.11**
    Circumstances **16.11**

FOREIGN OPERATIONS AND EXCHANGE: Exclusion of foreign operations (continued)
    Disclosure of excluded foreign operations **16.11**
  Foreign exchange contracts **16.06**
    Criterion for recognizing gain or loss **16.06**
    Deferred gain or loss **16.07**
    Definition **16.06**
    Discount or premium **16.08**
    Gain or loss on hedging contract **16.07**
    Methods to determine gain or loss **16.07**
      Deferred **16.07**
      Not deferred **16.08**
    Reasons for entering into **16.06**
    Use of averages **16.08**
  Income taxes **16.08**
    Creation of timing difference **16.08**
    Difference in effective tax rates **16.09**
    Inclusion of tax effect of gain or loss **16.10**
    Objective of translation **16.09**
    Rules for translating deferred taxes **16.09**
  Overview **16.01**
    Conformity with GAAP **16.01**
    Regulated industries **16.01**
  Restating financial statements **16.02**
    Conformity with GAAP **16.02**
    Current exchange rate **16.02**
    Historical exchange rate **16.02**
    Inventories in foreign currency **24.18**
    List of assets, liabilities, and stockholders' equity items with corresponding translation rate **16.04**
    Monetary assets and liabilities **16.02**
  Translating **16.02**
    Business combination—pooling **16.06**
    Different balance sheet dates **16.06**
    Lower of cost or market **16.05**
    Monetary items **16.02**
    Revenue and expense **16.03**
    Unamortized policy acquisition costs **16.05**
  Segmental reporting **37.07**
  Single or several transactions **16.01**
    Computation of gain or loss **16.02**

FULL-COSTING ACCOUNTING
  Oil and gas producing companies **30.06**

FULLY DILUTED EARNINGS
  Earnings per share **13.09**

GAIN CONTINGENCIES
  Contingencies **6.04**

GENERAL PRICE-LEVEL CHANGES
  Advantages of restatement **17.06**
  Background **17.01**
    Coverage of GAAP **17.01**

Topical Index

GENERAL PRICE-LEVEL CHANGES (continued)
  Comprehensive illustration **17.08**
  Disadvantage of restatement **17.06**
  Financial reporting and changing prices **15.51**
  General **17.01**
    Basis of price-level statements **17.01**
    General price-level financial statements **17.07**
    Rules for preparation **17.07**
  General price-level gain or loss **17.04**
    Individual items **17.04**
    Percentage change in price index **17.05**
    Restating net monetary position **17.05**
  Inventories—general price level **24.18**
  Monetary assets and liabilities **17.02**
    Changes in purchasing power **17.02**
    Definition **17.02**
  Net monetary position **17.03**
    Definition **17.03**
    Determination of monetary or nonmonetary **17.03**
    Negative **17.03**
    Positive **17.03**
  Nonmonetary assets and liabilities **17.02**
    Definition **17.02**
    Restatement **17.02**
  Overview **17.01**
    What price-level statements represent **17.01**
  Price indexes **17.03**
    Formula for restatement **17.04**
  Schedule of price-level gain or loss **17.06**
    Procedures **17.06**
    When loss or gain occurs **17.06**
GOLD
  Inventory pricing and methods **24.05**
GOODWILL
  Amortization **21.02**
  Intangible assets **21.02**
  Purchase method **3.06**
  Recording **21.02**
  Step-by-step acquisition **3.14**
GOVERNMENT CONTRACTS
  Background **18.01**
    Coverage of GAAP **18.01**
  CPFF contracts **18.01**
    Advance payments **18.02**
    Recognition of profits **18.01**
    Typical provisions **18.01**
  Overview **18.01**
    Cost-plus-fixed-fee arrangement **18.01**
  Renegotiation **18.02**
    Adjustment of original selling price **18.02**
    Collection not reasonably assured **18.02**
    Disclosure **18.02**
    Provision for renegotiation **18.02**

GOVERNMENT CONTRACTS (continued)
  Terminated war and defense contracts **18.02**
    Determination of profit or loss **18.03**
    Disclosure **18.03**
    Disposal credits **18.03**
    Termination claims **18.03**
GROSS PROFIT METHOD
  Inventory pricing and methods **24.16**

HOLDING GAINS
  Current value accounting **9.02**
  Realized **9.02**
  Unrealized **9.02**

IF-CONVERTED METHOD
  Earnings per share **13.18**
INCOME TAXES
  Background **19.01**
    Coverage of GAAP **19.01**
    Regulated industries **19.01**
  Changes in investment **19.08**
    Deferred taxes resulting from **19.08**
    Investment becomes a subsidiary **19.08**
    Investment falls below 20% **19.09**
    Subsidiary relationship **19.08**
  Deferred tax method **19.10**
    Computation of deferred tax **19.11**
    Consistent application **19.11**
    Definition of taxable income **19.10**
    Gross change method **19.14**
    Individual method **19.14**
    Net amount on balance sheet **19.15**
    Net change method **19.14**
    Permanent differences **19.11**
    Short-cut approach **19.14**
    Tax expense **19.11**
    Tax liability **19.11**
    With and without method **19.10**
  Disclosure **19.23**
    Claims for refunds and offsets **19.24**
    Components of tax expense **19.24**
    Deferred charges and credits **19.24**
    Differences between taxable income and pretax accounting income **19.24**
    Indefinite reversal criteria **19.24**
    Operating-loss carryforward **19.24**
    Prior-period adjustments **19.24**
    Significant unused credits or deductions **19.24**
  Discounting tax allocation accounts **19.16**
  Glossary **19.25**
    Deferred taxes **19.25**
    Income taxes **19.25**
    Income tax expense **19.25**

Topical Index

INCOME TAXES: Glossary (continued)
   Income tax liability **19.25**
   Indefinite reversal criteria **19.25**
   Interperiod tax allocation **19.25**
   Intraperiod tax allocation **19.25**
   Net of tax presentation **19.25**
   Permanent differences **19.25**
   Pretax accounting income **19.25**
   Taxable income **19.26**
   Tax carrybacks and carryforwards **19.25**
   Tax effects **19.25**
   Timing differences **19.26**
  Income taxes—interim periods **19.17**
   Adjustment to net deferred credits **19.17**
   Determination of interim period tax **19.17**
   Discontinued operations **19.20**
   Effect of change—accounting principle **19.22**
   Estimated annual effective tax rate **19.17**
   Extraordinary items **19.19**
    Realization of tax benefit **19.19**
   Recognition of tax benefit of prior years' operating loss **19.22**
   Required by GAAP **19.17**
   Tax in more than one jurisdiction **19.23**
    Exceptions **19.23**
   Use of actual effective tax rate **19.19**
  Indefinite reversal criteria **19.07**
   Controlling interests **19.08**
   Specific plan **19.07**
  Intraperiod tax allocation **19.16**
   Relationship between income tax expense and other items **19.16**
  Matching concept **19.15**
   Interperiod tax allocation—principles **19.16**
   Undistributed earnings of investees **19.16**
  Measuring timing differences **19.09**
   Determining if undistributed earnings will be realized in dividends **19.09**
   Use of estimates and assumptions **19.09**
  Offsetting—taxes payable **19.17**
  Operating losses **19.04**
   Carrybacks **19.04**
   Carryforwards **19.05**
    Extraordinary items **19.05**
   Tax benefits **19.05**
    Purchased subsidiary **19.05**
    Quasi-reorganization **19.05**
    Realizable beyond any reasonable doubt **19.05**
  Overview **19.01**
   Financial accounting income **19.01**
   Going concern concept **19.01**
   Taxable income **19.01**

INCOME TAXES: Overview (continued)
   Timing differences **19.02**
  Permanent differences **19.03**
   Bad debt allowances—S&L associations **19.04**
   Policyholders' surplus—stock life insurance **19.04**
   Types **19.03**
  Railroad gradings and tunnel bores **19.09**
   Tax allocation must be made **19.09**
  Timing differences **19.02**
  Timing differences—special areas **19.06**
   Investment in common stock—equity method **19.06**
   Losses of a subsidiary **19.07**
   Undistributed earnings of a subsidiary **19.06**
  Transactions that cause timing differences **19.02**
   Four basic causes **19.02**
  United Kingdom Tax Benefits **19.25**
  U.S. steamship companies **19.09**
INDEFINITE REVERSAL CRITERIA
  Income taxes **19.07**
INDUSTRY SEGMENT
  Segmental reporting **37.04**
INFLATION ACCOUNTING
  Financial reporting and changing prices **15.51**
INITIAL DIRECT COSTS
  Leases **26.26**
INSTALLMENT METHOD OF ACCOUNTING
  Background **20.01**
   Existing GAAP **20.01**
   Regulated industries **20.01**
  Cost recovery method **20.01**
   Expenses of collection **20.01**
   Recover cost first **20.01**
   Recovery of cost doubtful **20.01**
   Revenue recognition **20.01**
   Sunk-cost theory **20.01**
  Deferred income taxes **20.04**
   Installment sales for tax purposes **20.04**
   Normal accrual accounting **20.04**
   Timing difference **20.04**
  Disclosure **20.04**
   Balance sheet presentation **20.04**
   Classification as current asset **20.04**
   Percentage relationship **20.04**
   Unrealized gross profit **20.04**
  Overview **20.01**
   Collectibility **20.01**
   Extended collection period **20.01**
  Recording installment sales **20.02**
   Different products and departments **20.03**
   Gross profit ratio **20.02**
   Part recovery cost **20.02**

Topical Index

INSTALLMENT METHOD OF ACCOUNTING: Recording installment methods (continued)
    Part recovery profit **20.02**
    Realized gross profit **20.02**
    Repossessed goods **20.03**
    Selling and administrative costs **20.03**
    Separate records **20.03**
    Title to goods **20.03**
    Unrealized gross profit **20.03**
    Value of repossessed goods **20.03**
INTANGIBLE ASSETS
  Amortization **21.02**
    Amortization period **21.03**
    Income tax effect **21.03**
    Method **21.03**
  Background **21.01**
    Coverage of GAAP **21.01**
  Comprehensive illustrations **21.06**
  Cost of intangibles **21.02**
    Measurement of cost **21.02**
  Disclosure **21.05**
  Disposal of goodwill **21.04**
  Negative goodwill **21.03**
    Amortization **21.04**
    Reduction of noncurrent assets **21.03**
  Overview **21.01**
    Definition of intangible asset **21.01**
    Identifiability **21.01**
    Life **21.01**
    Manner of acquisition **21.01**
    Transferability **21.01**
  Savings and loan associations **21.05**
    Net-spread method **21.05**
    Separate-valuation method **21.06**
  Step-by-step acquisitions **21.04**
INTERCOMPANY BOND HOLDINGS
  Consolidated financial statements **5.10**
INTERCOMPANY DIVIDENDS
  Consolidated financial statements **5.13**
INTERCOMPANY STOCK HOLDINGS
  Consolidated financial statements **5.13**
INTERCOMPANY TRANSACTIONS
  Bonds **5.10**
  Dividends **5.13**
  Receivables and payables **5.05**
  Sales and purchases **5.05**
  Stock **5.13**
  Unrealized profits in inventory **5.06**
  Unrealized profits—long-lived assets **5.08**
INTEREST METHOD
  Leases **26.14**
  Receivables and payables **22.03**

INTEREST ON RECEIVABLES AND PAYABLES
  Amortization of discount or premium **22.03**
    Conditions for discount or premium **22.03**
    Interest method **22.03**
  Background **22.01**
    Coverage of GAAP **22.01**
    Exclusion **22.01**
  Comprehensive illustrations **22.03**
  Determining present value **22.02**
    Guidelines **22.02**
    Objectives **22.02**
  Disclosure **22.03**
  Overview **22.01**
    Recorded at present value **22.01**
    Rights and privileges attached **22.02**
    Valuation in noncash transactions **22.02**
    Statement presentation—discount or premium **22.03**
INTEREST RATE IMPLICIT
  Leases **26.04**
INTERIM FINANCIAL REPORTING
  Accounting and reporting **23.01**
    Disclosure of material contingencies **23.03**
    Income taxes **23.03**
    Product costs **23.02**
    Recognition of revenues **23.01**
    Rules for other costs and expenses **23.02**
  Background **23.01**
    Coverage of GAAP **23.01**
  Inventory for interim financial reporting **23.02**
    Inventory losses **23.02**
    LIFO method **23.02**
    Standard costs **23.02**
    Use of estimated gross profit **23.02**
  Oil and gas producing companies **30.15**
  Overview **23.01**
    Discussion of interim reports **23.01**
  Summarized interim financial statements **23.03**
    Disclosures—fourth quarter results **23.03**
    Information to be included **23.03**
INTERPERIOD TAX ALLOCATION
  Income taxes **19.16**
  Oil and gas producing companies **30.15**
INTRAPERIOD TAX ALLOCATION
  Income taxes **19.16**
INVENTORY PRICING AND METHODS
  Background **24.01**
    Coverage of GAAP **24.01**
  Base stock method **24.14**
  Comprehensive illustrations **24.21**
  Conclusion **24.20**
  Cost methods **24.05**
    Assumptions **24.05**

Topical Index

INVENTORY PRICING AND METHODS
Cost methods (continued)
  Flow of cost factors **24.05**
  Inventory identification **24.05**
    Objectives **24.05**
Costs **24.03**
Departure from cost basis **24.03**
Disclosure **24.15**
Dollar-value LIFO **24.07**
Firm purchase commitment **24.15**
First-in, first-out method (FIFO) **24.06**
Inventories—accounting change **24.19**
Inventories—construction-type contracts **24.18**
Inventories-general price-level changes **24.18**
Inventories in business combinations **24.17**
  Valuation **24.17**
Inventories in foreign currency **24.18**
Inventories—intercompany profits **24.18**
Inventories—interim reporting **24.16**
  Inventory losses **24.16**
  LIFO method **24.16**
  Standard costs **24.17**
  Use of estimated gross profit **24.16**
Inventories—nonmonetary exchanges **24.19**
Inventories—research and development **24.17**
Inventories—tax allocation **24.19**
Inventory for terminated contracts **24.17**
Inventory of discontinued segments **24.16**
  Loss on write-down **24.16**
Inventory profits **24.19**
Inventory systems **24.01**
  Periodic **24.01**
  Perpetual **24.01**
Last-in, first-out method (LIFO) **24.06**
  Disclosures **24.06**
  LIFO layers **24.06**
Lower of cost or market **24.03**
  Exceptions **24.05**
  Market **24.03**
  Maximum **24.03**
  Minimum **24.03**
    Reasons for maximum and minimum **24.04**
Moving average method **24.08**
Overview **24.01**
  Classification of inventories **24.01**
  What inventories include **24.01**
Relative sales value costing **24.14**
Retail inventory method **24.09**
  Assumptions **24.09**
  Computing cost-to-retail ratio **24.09**
  Cost-to-retail ratio **24.09**
  LIFO application **24.12**
    Computing cost-to-retail ratio **24.13**

INVENTORY PRICING AND METHODS: Retail inventory method (continued)
    Differences from conventional method **24.13**
    Purpose **24.09**
  Standard costs **24.06**
    Use of standards **24.06**
    Variations from standards **24.06**
  Title of goods **24.02**
    Terminology **24.02**
    When title to goods passes to buyer **24.02**
  Weighted average method **24.08**
INVESTMENT TAX CREDIT
  Accounting for investment tax credit **25.03**
    Business combinations **25.11**
    Carryback and carryfoward **25.04**
    Example **25.05**
    Offset of deferred tax credits **25.04**
    Unused investment tax credit **25.04**
  Background **25.01**
    Coverage of GAAP **25.01**
  Disclosure **25.13**
  IRC provisions **25.02**
    Carryback or carryforward **25.02**
    Disposition of Section 38 property **25.03**
    Estimated useful life **25.02**
    Maximum investment tax credit **25.02**
    Section 38 property **25.02**
  Other considerations **25.13**
  Overview **25.01**
    Deferral method **25.01**
    Flow-through method **25.01**
    Methods of recognition **25.01**
    SEC statement ASR 96 **25.01**

LAST-IN, FIRST-OUT METHOD (LIFO)
  Inventory pricing and methods **24.06**
  LIFO layers **24.06**
LEASES
  Accounting and reporting by lessees **26.10**
    Amortization **26.13**
    Initial recording **26.10**
    Interest expense: interest method **26.14**
    Leases with escalation clauses **26.11**
  Accounting and reporting by lessors **26.20**
  Accounting and reporting for leveraged leases **26.41**
    Amount of net income recognized **26.42**
    Characteristics of leveraged leases **26.41**
    Computation of periodic net income **26.42**
    Initial and continuing investment **26.42**
  Accounting for lease changes—lessee **26.15**
    Change in classification **26.15**
    Change in lease term **26.16**
    Change in minimum lease payments **26.15**

Topical Index

LEASES: Accounting for lease changes—lessee (continued)
    Inoperative guarantee or penalty **26.15**
  Accounting for lease changes—lessor **26.24**
    Change to direct financing lease **26.24**
    Change to operating lease **26.25**
    Change to sales-type lease **26.25**
    No change in classification **26.24**
  Annual review of residual values—lessor **26.24**
  Background **26.01**
    Coverage of GAAP **26.01**
  Balance sheet classifications—lessor **26.23**
  Business combinations **26.43**
    Change in lease classification **26.43**
  Changing a provision of a lease **26.09**
    Reclassification of lease agreement **26.08**
    Refundings of tax-exempt debt **26.10**
  Classification of leases by lessees **26.08**
    Four criteria for classification **26.08**
    Lessee's discount rate **26.09**
    Lessor's discount rate **26.08**
  Classification of leases by lessors **26.09**
    Additional criteria for classification **26.09**
  Comprehensive illustration **26.44**
  Contingent rentals—lessor **26.23**
  Leases involving government units **26.34**
  Leases involving real estate **26.30**
    Fair value of land is more than 25% **26.32**
      Lessee **26.32**
      Lessor **26.33**
    Leases involving land and building **26.31**
      Transfer of ownership **26.31**
        Lessee **26.31**
        Lessor **26.31**
    Leases involving land, building(s) and equipment **26.33**
    Leases involving land only **26.30**
    Leases involving only part of building(s) **26.33**
      Lessee **26.33**
      Lessor **26.34**
  Review of leases by lessees **26.30**
  Leases term **26.06**
    Duration of lease term **26.06**
    Noncancelable lease term **26.06**
  Lessee's minimum lease payment **26.06**
    Bargain purchase option **26.07**
    Normal minimum lease payments **26.07**
  Lessee's operating leases **26.16**
  Lessee's statement disclosure **26.16**
    Capital leases **26.16**
    General disclosure **26.17**
    Illustrations **26.17**
    Operating leases **26.17**

LEASES (continued)
  Lessor's minimum lease payments **26.08**
  Lessor's operating leases **26.25**
    Initial direct costs **26.26**
  Fair rental **26.04**
  Fair value **26.04**
  Initial direct costs **26.05**
  Interest rate implicit in the lease **26.05**
  Lessee's incremental borrowing rate **26.04**
  Related parties **26.04**
  Lessor's statement disclosure **26.27**
    General disclosure **26.28**
    Illustration **26.28**
    Operating leases **26.27**
    Sales-type and direct financing leases **26.27**
  Recording leases by lessors **26.20**
    Direct financing leases **26.21**
    Lessor's gross investment **26.20**
    Other methods **26.21**
    Sales-type leases **26.20**
    Sales-type leases involving real estate **26.21**
  Related party leases **26.34**
  Sale-leaseback transactions **26.35**
    Accounting for certain losses on sale-leasebacks **26.35**
    Accounting for sale-leasebacks **26.35**
      Minor **26.35**
      More than minor but less than substantially all **26.35**
      Substantially all **26.35**
    Terminoloy **26.35**
      Profit or loss on the sale **26.35**
      Purchaser-lessor **26.35**
      Sale-leaseback **26.35**
      Substantially all or minor **26.35**
  Sale or assignment to third parties **26.26**
    Nonsubstantial risk of the seller **26.26**
    Recognition of profit or loss **26.26**
    Sale recorded as a borrowing **26.27**
    Substantial risk of the seller **26.26**
  Sales-type vs. direct financing leases **26.03**
    Bargain purchase option **26.04**
    Bargain renewal option **26.04**
    Dealer's profit or loss **26.03**
    Estimated residual value **26.04**
    Executory costs **26.04**
  Subleases and similar transactions **26.38**
    Capital leases **26.39**
    Operating leases **26.39**
      Original lessee is obligated **26.39**
    Recognition of loss **26.39**
  Substance over form **26.01**
    Criteria for transfer of ownership **26.02**

Topical Index

LEASES (continued)
  Termination of a capital lease—lessee **26.16**
  Termination of a lease—lessor **26.25**
  Terminology **26.02**
    Capital lease **26.02**
    Direct financing lease **26.03**
    Sales-type lease **26.02**
LESSEE'S INCREMENTAL BORROWING RATE
  Leases **26.04**
LESSOR'S IMPLICIT INTEREST RATE
  Leases **26.05**
LEVERAGED LEASES
  Leases **26.41**
LONG-TERM CONTRACTS
  Accounting—completed-contracts **27.02**
    Important points **27.02**
  Accounting—percentage-of-completion **27.03**
    Important points **27.03**
  Background **27.01**
    Coverage of GAAP **27.01**
  Choice of method **27.04**
  Completed-contract method **27.01**
    Advantages and disadvantages **27.02**
    Allocation of G&A expenses **27.01**
    Balance sheet classifications **27.01**
    Provision for expected loss **27.01**
    Recognition of income **27.01**
  Comprehensive illustration **27.04**
  Disclosure **27.04**
  Overview **27.01**
    Methods for long-term contracts **27.01**
  Percentage-of-completion method **27.02**
    Advantages and disadvantages **27.03**
    Provision for expected loss **27.03**
    Recognition of income **27.03**
LOSS CONTINGENCIES
  Contingencies **6.03**
LOWER OF COST OR MARKET
  Foreign operations and exchange **16.05**
    Translation **16.05**
  Inventory pricing and methods **24.03**
  Marketable securities **28.06**

MARKETABLE SECURITIES
  Background **28.01**
    Coverage of promulgated GAAP **28.01**
    Employee benefit plans **28.01**
    Investments—equity method **28.01**
    Mutual life insurance companies **28.01**
    Nonmarketable securities **28.01**
    Nonprofit organizations **28.01**

MARKETABLE SECURITIES: Background (continued)
    Nonspecialized industry practices **28.01**
    Personal financial statements **28.01**
    Specialized industry practices **28.01**
  Definition of a marketable security **28.01**
    Common stock **28.01**
    Convertible bonds **28.01**
    Preferred stock **28.01**
    Puts and calls **28.01**
    Stock options **28.01**
    Stock rights **28.01**
    Stock warrants **28.01**
    Treasury stock **28.01**
  Realized gain or loss **28.02**
  Unrealized gain or loss **28.02**
  Comprehensive illustration **28.09**
  Income Taxes **28.09**
  Industries having specialized practices **28.06**
    Brokers and dealers **28.06**
    Casualty insurance companies **28.06**
    Compliance with promulgated GAAP **28.06**
      Accounting change **28.06**
      Aggregate cost or market **28.06**
      Appraised value **28.06**
      Broader definition for market **28.06**
      Conforming to a parent's practices **28.07**
      Current group **28.06**
      Fair value **28.06**
      Investments—equity method **28.07**
      Lower of cost or market **28.06**
      Noncurrent group **28.06**
      Unclassified balance sheets **28.06**
      Valuation accounts **28.06**
    Disclosure—specialized industry practices **28.07**
      Changes in net unrealized gains or losses **28.08**
      Consolidated balance sheets **28.08**
        Nonspecialized industry practices **28.08**
        Specialized industry practices **28.08**
      Gross unrealized gains and losses **28.08**
      Inclusion of unrealized gains and losses **28.08**
      Stockholders' equity **28.08**
      Subsequent events **28.08**
  Industries not having specialized practices **28.02**
    Accounting procedure **28.02**
      Current group **28.03**
      Lower of cost or market **28.03**
      Noncurrent group **28.03**
      Total cost and total market **28.03**
      Unclassified balance sheet **28.03**
    Consolidation **28.04**
      Aggregate cost or market **28.04**
      Different balance sheet dates **28.04**

Topical Index

MARKETABLE SECURITIES: Industries not having specialized practices(continued)
   Investment–equity method **28.05**
   Disclosure **28.05**
      Change in valuation account **28.05**
      Consolidated balance sheets **28.05**
      Cost basis **28.05**
      Gross unrealized gains **28.05**
      Gross unrealized losses **28.05**
      Net realized gains or losses **28.06**
      Subsequent events **28.06**
      Total cost and market **28.05**
      Unclassified balance sheets **28.05**
   Reclassification **28.03**
      Date of transfer **28.04**
      Lower of cost or market **28.04**
      New cost basis **28.04**
   Sale of a security **28.04**
      Basis–original cost **28.04**
      Realized gain or loss **28.04**
      Reported in net income **28.04**
   Subsequent gains or losses **28.04**
      Adjustment of allowance account **28.04**
      Not to exceed original cost **28.04**
   Unrealized losses **28.03**
      Allowance account **28.03**
      Current group **28.03**
      Noncurrent group **28.03**
   Marketability **28.02**
      Determination of marketability **28.02**
      Balance sheet date **28.02**
      Foreign stock markets **28.02**
      Lack of market **28.02**
      Restricted or legend stock **28.02**
   Evidence of marketability **28.02**
      Current "bid" and "ask" **28.02**
      Over–the–counter securities **28.02**
   Overview **28.01**
   Permanent declines–noncurrent group **28.08**
      Decline in market–other than temporary **28.08**
      Determination of permanent decline **28.09**
         Subsequent recoveries **28.09**
      New cost basis **28.09**
      Recognize a realized loss **28.08**
      Subsequent increases **28.09**
MATCHING CONCEPT
   Depreciable assets and depreciation **11.06**
   Depreciation method **11.06**
   Income taxes **19.15**
   Percentage–of–completion method **27.01**
MINORITY INTERESTS
   Consolidated financial statements **5.14**

MINORITY INTERESTS (continued)
   Equity method **14.01**
   Father–son–grandson affiliation **5.14**
   In net income **5.14**
   Presentation on balance sheet **5.14**
   Stockholders' equity **38.04**
MODIFIED TREASURY STOCK METHOD
   Earnings per share **13.15**
MONETARY AND NONMONETARY ITEMS
   Current value accounting **9.02**
   Financial reporting and changing prices **15.51**
   Foreign operations and exchange **16.02**
      Monetary assets and liabilities **16.02**
   General price–level changes **17.02**
      Changes in purchasing power **17.02**
      Definition **17.02**
      Net monetary position **17.03**
   Nonmonetary transactions **29.01**
MOVING AVERAGE METHOD
   Inventory pricing and methods **24.08**

NATURAL BUSINESS YEAR
   Current assets and current liabilities **8.01**
NEGATIVE GOODWILL
   Intangible assets **21.03**
   Purchase method **3.6**
NET CARRYING AMOUNT
   Extinguishment of debt **15.01**
NET REALIZABLE VALUE
   Current assets **8.02**
   Financial reporting and changing prices **15.51**
   Inventory pricing and methods **24.03**
NONCOMPENSATORY PLANS
   Stock issued to employees **39.02**
      Characteristics **39.02**
      Definition **39.02**
NONDISCRETIONARY EFFECTS
   Accounting change **1.05**
NONMONETARY TRANSACTIONS
   Background **29.01**
      Coverage of GAAP **29.01**
   Conclusion **29.06**
      Interperiod tax allocation **29.06**
   Disclosure **29.05**
   Earnings process not complete **29.03**
      Basis of monetary consideration **29.03**
      Formula for recognition of gain **29.04**
      Payor of monetary consideration **29.04**
      Recipient of monetary consideration **29.03**
   Exchange (reciprocal transfer) **29.02**
   Fair value **29.02**
   Fair value not determinable **29.03**

Topical Index

NONMONETARY TRANSACTIONS (continued)
  Gain or loss **29.04**
  Involuntary Conversion **29.05**
  Monetary assets or liabilities **29.01**
  Nonmonetary assets or liabilities **29.01**
  Nonreciprocal transfer **29.02**
  Nonreciprocal transfers to owners **29.02**
NONPUBLIC ENTERPRISES
  Definition **13.01**
  Earnings per share **13.01**
  Segmental reporting **37.03**
  Suspension of disclosure requirements **13.01**
NONRECIPROCAL TRANSFER
  Nonmonetary transactions **29.02**
NORMAL COST
  Pension plans **31.04**

OFFSETTING–TAXES PAYABLE
  Income taxes **19.17**
OIL AND GAS PRODUCING COMPANIES
  Accounting principles–basic concepts **30.10**
    Acquisition of properties **30.11**
      Amortization **30.11**
      Costs **30.10**
      Nonmonetary exchange **30.11**
      Sale of an interest in property **30.11**
    Development **30.13**
      Amortization **30.13**
      Costs **30.13**
    Exploration **30.12**
      Amortization **30.12**
      Conditions for carrying exploratory well as an asset **30.13**
      Costs **30.12**
      Exploratory wells **30.12**
    Production **30.14**
      Costs **30.14**
      Lifting costs **30.14**
  Background **30.01**
    Coverage of GAAP **30.01**
  Background information **30.07**
    Accounting Series Release 253 **30.09**
    Accounting Series Release 257 **30.10**
    Accounting Series Release 258 **30.10**
    Energy Policy and Conservation Act of 1975 **30.07**
    Securities Act Release No. 5706 **30.08**
    Securities Act Release No. 5801 **30.09**
    Securities Act Release No. 5837 **30.09**
    Securities Act Release No. 5861 **30.09**
    Securities Act Release No. 5877 **30.09**
    Securities Act Release No. 5878 **30.09**
  Balance sheet–subsequent information **30.14**

OIL AND GAS PRODUCING COMPANIES
(continued)
  Disclosure **30.15**
    Capitalized costs **30.18**
    Function costs **30.19**
    Illustration of net quantities **30.17**
    Interim financial statement **30.15**
    Net quantities of crude oil and gas **30.15**
    Rules for determining net quantities **30.15**
  Effects of FASB-25 **30.01**
    Accounting changes **1.01**
    Definition of reserves **30.02**
    Disclosure **30.02**
  Income tax considerations **30.15**
    Interperiod tax allocation **30.15**
  Overview **30.02**
    Current value accounting **30.06**
    Development well **30.05**
    Discovery value accounting **30.05**
      Current costs **30.05**
      Current exit value in liquidation **30.05**
      Expected exit value **30.05**
      Present value of expected cash flow **30.06**
    Exploratory well **30.05**
    Field **30.02**
    Full-costing acounting **30.06**
    Properties **30.02**
    Proved area **30.03**
    Proved reserves **30.03**
      Proved developed reserves **30.04**
      Proved undeveloped reserves **30.04**
    Reservoir **30.02**
    Service well **30.05**
    Stratigraphic test well **30.05**
      Development–type test well **30.05**
    Successful efforts costing **30.07**
    Supply agreements **30.05**
    Support equipment and facilities **30.04**
    Uncompleted wells, equipment and facilities **30.04**
    Wells, related equipment and facilities **30.04**
  Segment reporting **30.20**
  Support equipment and facilities **30.14**
ONE–LINE CONSOLIDATION
  Consolidated financial statements **5.05**
  Equity method **14.03**
OPERATING CYCLE
  Current assets and current liabilities **8.01**
OPERATING LEASES
  Leases **26.25**
OPERATING LOSSES
  Carrybacks **19.04**
  Carryforwards **19.05**

Topical Index

OPERATING LOSSES (continued)
  Extraordinary items **19.05**
  Income taxes **19.04**
    Tax benefits **19.05**

PAID–IN CAPITAL
  Stockholders' equity **38.03**
    Definition **38.03**
    Sources **38.03**
PAST-SERVICE COST
  Pension plans **31.04**
PAY–AS–YOU–GO METHOD
  Pension plans **31.06**
PENSION PLANS
  Actuarial cost methods **31.03**
    Accrued benefit (unit credit method) **31.04**
    Actuarial assumptions **31.03**
    Actuarial valuation **31.03**
    Normal cost **31.04**
    Past-service costs **31.04**
    Pay–as–you–go method **31.06**
    Prior–costs **31.04**
    Projected benefit **31.05**
      Entry age normal **31.05**
      Individual level premium **31.05**
    Terminal funding method **31.06**
    Vested benefits **31.03**
  Actuarial gain or loss **31.06**
    Gain or loss from a single event **31.07**
    Interest assumption method **31.07**
    Realized and unrealized **31.06**
    Recognizing actuarial gains and losses **31.07**
      Averaging **31.07**
      Immediate recognition **31.07**
      Spreading **31.07**
  Amount of annual pension cost **31.09**
    Maximum **31.10**
    Minimum **31.09**
      Provision for vested benefits **31.09**
  Application of GAAP **31.06**
  Background **31.01**
    Coverage of GAAP **31.01**
  Comprehensive illustration **31.13**
  Disclosure **31.12**
    Illustration **31.12**
  Employee Retirement Income Security Act of 1974 (ERISA) **31.11**
    Basic provisions **31.11**
    Effective date **31.11**
    Primary concerns **31.11**
  Other considerations **31.08**

PENSION PLANS: Other considerations (continued)
    Change in accounting method **31.08**
    Income tax allocation **31.08**
    Interest on unfunded costs **31.08**
    Overfunding of pension plan **31.08**
  Overview **31.01**
    Accounting on the accrual basis **31.01**
    Contributory or noncontributory plan **31.01**
    Deferred compensation plan **31.02**
    Defined benefit plan **31.01**
    Defined contribution plan **31.02**
    Defined profit-sharing plan **31.02**
    Funded or unfunded plan **31.01**
    Limitation on legal obligation **31.02**
    Tax qualified **31.01**
      Pension plans **31.01**
      Profit-sharing plans **31.01**
      Stock bonus plans **31.01**
PERCENTAGE–OF–COMPLETION METHOD
  Long-term contracts **27.02**
PERIODIC INVENTORY SYSTEM
  Inventory pricing and methods **24.01**
PERMANENT DIFFERENCES
  Bad debts–savings and loan associations **19.04**
  Income taxes **19.03**
  Indefinite reversal criteria **19.07**
  Policyholders' surplus–stock life insurance co. **19.04**
  Types **19.03**
PERPETUAL INVENTORY SYSTEM
  Inventory pricing and methods **24.01**
PLEDGING
  Current–assets and liabilities **8.06**
POOLING–OF–INTERESTS METHOD
  Business combinations **3.15**
  Conditions for pooling **3.15**
  Disclosures **3.22**
  Disposal of significant assets **3.21**
  Effective date of consummation **3.17**
  Expenses of combination **3.21**
  Inconsistent transactions **3.21**
  Intercorporate investments **3.21**
  Reacquisition of voting stock **3.21**
  Restatement of prior years **3.21**
  Treasury stock **3.21**
PREFERRED STOCK
  Marketable securities **28.01**
  Stockholders' equity **38.01**
    Callable **38.01**
    Cumulative or noncumulative **38.01**
    Liquidation preference **38.01**
    Participating or nonparticipating **38.01**

Topical Index

PREFERRED STOCK: Stockholder's equity (continued)
    Preference **38.01**
    Voting rights **38.01**
PRICE INDEXES
    Financial reporting and changing prices **15.51**
    General price–level changes **17.03**
PRICE–LEVEL CHANGES
    Financial reporting and changing prices **15.51**
    General price–level changes **17.01**
PRIMARY EARNINGS PER SHARE
    Earnings per share **13.09**
PRIOR-PERIOD ADJUSTMENTS
    Earnings per share **13.02**
    Income taxes **19.02**
    Results of operations **36.04**
        Accounting changes **36.05**
        Definition **36.04**
        Interim **36.04**
PRIOR-SERVICE COST
    Pension plans **31.04**
PROFIT-SHARING PLANS
    Pension plans **31.02**
PROJECTED BENEFIT METHOD
    Pension plans **31.05**
        Entry age normal **31.05**
        Individual level premium **31.05**
PUBLICLY TRADED COMPANIES
    Accounting changes–interim periods **1.08**
    Interim financial reporting **23.03**
        Summarized interim reports **23.03**
PURCHASE METHOD
    Allocating cost **3.02**
    Amortization of goodwill **3.06**
    Business combinations **3.02**
    Contingent consideration **3.02**
    Determination of cost **3.02**
    Disclosures **3.05**
    Fair value **3.02**
    Net spread method **3.04**
    Recorded cost of an acquisition **3.02**
    Recording of goodwill **3.02**
    Registration and issuing costs **3.02**
    Separate valuation method **3.04**

QUASI–REORGANIZATIONS
    Accounting and reporting **32.02**
        Accounting procedure **32.02**
            Charge to retained earnings **32.03**
            Dating retained earnings **32.03**
            Effective date **32.03**
            New or additional shares **32.03**
            Parent and subsidiary **32.03**

QUASI-REORGANIZATIONS: Accounting and reporting (continued)
        Write-offs **32.03**
        Fair values **32.03**
        Formal consent **32.03**
        Provide for all losses **32.03**
        Report to stockholders **32.03**
        Tax benefits **32.03**
    Background **32.01**
        Corporate readjustment **32.01**
        Coverage of GAAP **32.01**
    Comprehensive illustration **32.04**
    Disclosure **32.04**
        Dating retained earnings **32.04**
        New retained earnings account **32.04**
    Overview **32.01**
        Accumulated deficit **32.02**
        Justification for reorganization **32.01**
            Alternative to legal steps **32.02**
            Assets require adjustment **32.02**
            Eliminate large deficit **32.02**
        New basis of accountability **32.01**
        Reduction of par value **32.01**
        Stockholders' equity **32.01**
        Turnaround point **32.01**

RAILROAD GRADINGS AND TUNNEL BORES
    Income taxes **19.09**
RAZING AND REMOVAL COSTS
    Depreciable assets and depreciation **11.01**
REACQUISITION PRICE
    Extinguishment of debt **15.02**
REAL AND PERSONAL PROPERTY TAXES
    Accounting and reporting **33.01**
        Adjustment to tax liability **33.01**
        Assessment date **33.01**
        Capitalization of real estate taxes **33.01**
        Consistent application **33.02**
        Recognition of tax liability **33.01**
        Reporting taxes in the income statement **33.01**
    Background **33.01**
REALIZED GROSS PROFIT
    Installment method of. accounting **20.02**
REALIZED INCOME
    Current value accounting **9.03**
REGULATED INDUSTRIES
    Accounting principles **34.01**
RELATED PARTIES
    Leases **26.34**
RELATIVE SALES VALUE COSTING
    Inventory pricing and methods **24.14**

Topical Index

RENEGOTIATION
Adjustment of selling price **18.02**
Disclosure **18.02**
Government contracts **18.02**
Provision for renegotiation **18.02**
REPORTABLE SEGMENT
Segmental reporting **37.04**
REPOSSESSED GOODS
Installment method of accounting **20.03**
RESEARCH AND DEVELOPMENT
Accounting and reporting **35.02**
   Acquired by purchase **35.02**
   Exceptions **35.02**
   Expensed when incurred **35.02**
   Inventories—research and development **24.17**
Background **35.01**
   Coverage of promulgated GAAP **35.01**
   Exclusions **35.01**
Disclosure **35.02**
   Amount charged to expense **35.02**
   Regulated industries **35.03**
      Accounting policies **35.03**
      Disclosure **35.03**
Overview **35.01**
   Conservatism **35.01**
   Definition of development **35.01**
   Definition of research **35.01**
   General and administrative **35.01**
   Market research and testing **35.01**
   Uncertainty of future benefits **35.01**
R & D computer software **35.03**
   Computer system **35.03**
   Developing **35.03**
   Improving **35.03**
   Internal developing **35.03**
   Leasing **35.03**
RESIDUAL VALUE
Depreciable assets and depreciation **11.02**
RESTRICTED OR LEGEND STOCK
Marketable securities **28.02**
RESTRUCTURING OF DEBT
Troubled debt restructuring **40.01**
RESULTS OF OPERATIONS
Backgound **36.01**
   Coverage of GAAP **36.01**
Disclosure **36.08**
Discontinued operations **36.05**
   Determination of gain or loss **36.06**
   Disposal date **36.06**
   Identifiable entity **36.06**
   Long-term leases **36.07**
   Measurement date **36.06**

RESULTS OF OPERATIONS (continued)
Extraordinary items **36.03**
   Characteristics **36.03**
   Items which are extraordinary **36.03**
   Items which are not extraordinary **36.03**
Overview **36.01**
   All–inclusive concept **36.01**
   Capital transactions **36.02**
   Current operating performance **36.02**
   Presentation of net income **36.08**
      EPS presentation **36.09**
Prior-period adjustments **36.04**
   Accounting changes **36.05**
   Definition **36.04**
   Interim-period adjustments **36.04**
RETAIL INVENTORY METHOD
Cost-to-retail ratio **24.09**
Inventory pricing and methods **24.09**
LIFO application **24.12**
RETAINED EARNINGS
Stockholders' equity **38.04**
   Appropriated **38.04**
   Unappropriated **38.04**
RULE OF PREFERABILITY
Accounting changes **1.02**

SALE LEASEBACK TRANSACTIONS
Leases **26.35**
SALES–TYPE LEASE
Leases **26.03**
SALVAGE
Depreciable assets and depreciation **11.02**
SAVINGS AND LOAN ASSOCIATIONS
Intangible assets **21.05**
   Net spread method **21.05**
   Separate valuation method **21.06**
SEGMENTAL REPORTING
Background **37.01**
   Coverage of GAAP **37.01**
Comprehensive illustration **37.10**
Determining reportable segments **37.05**
Dominant segments **37.08**
Foreign operations and export sales **37.09**
   Geographic areas **37.09**
Grouping products and services **37.06**
Information about major customers **37.10**
Information to be reported **37.08**
   Identifiable assets **37.08**
   Operating profit or loss **37.08**
   Other disclosure **37.08**
   Revenue **37.08**

Topical Index

SEGMENTAL REPORTING (continued)
  Nonpublic enterprise **37.03**
    Definition **37.03**
    Suspension of disclosure **37.03**
  Oil and gas producing companies **30.20**
  Overview **37.03**
  Restatement of previously reported segment information **37.10**
  Segment information not required **37.01**
  Selecting reportable segments **37.06**
    Comparability test **37.07**
    75% test **37.07**
    10% test **37.06**
  Terminology **37.04**
    Complete set of financial statements **37.02**
    Financial report **37.02**
    Foreign investee **37.03**
    Identifiable assets **37.05**
    Industry segment **37.04**
    Industry segment's operating profit **37.04**
    Interest on intersegmental receivables **37.04**
    Operating expenses of industry segments **37.04**
    Operating income of industry segments **37.04**
    Reportable segments **37.04**
    Revenue **37.04**
    Segmental information **37.02**

SELF–CONSTRUCTED FIXED ASSETS
  Depreciable assets and depreciation **11.04**
  Direct costs **11.03**
  Interest cost **11.03**
  Overhead costs **11.03**

STANDARD COSTS
  Inventory pricing and methods **24.06**
    Use of standards **24.06**
    Variations from standard **24.06**

STEP–BY–STEP ACQUISITION
  Consolidated financial statements **5.02**
  Intangible assets **21.04**
  Purchase method **3.14**

STOCK BONUS PLANS
  Pension plans **31.01**

STOCK DIVIDEND
  Stockholders' equity **38.07**
    Fair market value **38.07**
    Retained earnings capitalized **38.07**

STOCKHOLDERS' EQUITY
  Background **38.01**
    Capital changes **38.01**
    Capital surplus **38.01**
    Donated stock **38.01**
    Nonpromulgated GAAP **38.01**

STOCKHOLDERS' EQUITY: Background (continued)
    Preferred stock–liquidation preference **38.01**
    Regulated industries **38.01**
    Treasury stock **38.01**
    Profits or losses **38.01**
  Dividends **38.06**
    Cash dividends **38.06**
      Date of declaration **38.06**
      Date of payment **38.07**
      Date of record **38.06**
      Pro rata distribution **38.06**
    Stock dividends **38.07**
      Fair market value **38.07**
      Retained earnings capitalized **38.07**
    Stock splits **38.07**
      Amount to capitalize **38.07**
      Differences from a stock dividend **38.07**
      More than 20% to 25% **38.07**
  Legal capital **38.01**
    Authorized capital stock **38.02**
    Callable **38.01**
    Capital stock **38.02**
    Cumulative or noncumulative **38.01**
    Disclosures **38.03**
    Issued capital stock **38.02**
    Outstanding capital stock **38.02**
    Participating or nonparticipating **38.01**
    Par value **38.02**
    Preference in liquidation **38.01**
    Premium or discount **38.02**
    Stated value **38.02**
    Subscriptions **38.02**
    Treasury stock **38.02**
    Voting rights **38.02**
  Legal capital–disclosures **38.02**
    Call prices **38.03**
    Capital changes **38.03**
    Conversion rates **38.03**
    Dividends in arrear **38.03**
    Exercise prices **38.03**
    Liquidation preferences **38.03**
    Participation rights **38.03**
    Restriction on dividends **38.03**
  Minority interests **38.04**
    Disclosure **38.04**
  Overview **38.01**
    Legal capital **38.01**
    Minority interests **38.01**
    Paid–in capital **38.01**
    Retained earnings **38.01**
  Paid–in capital **38.03**
    Definition **38.03**

Topical Index

STOCKQUITY: Paid-in capital (continued)
    Sources **38.03**
  Retained earnings **38.04**
    Appropriated **38.04**
    Unappropriated **38.04**
  Stock rights **38.08**
    Accounting for issuer **38.08**
    Accounting for recipient **38.08**
  Treasury stock **38.04**
    Accounting and reporting **38.04**
      For other than retirement **38.05**
      To be retired **38.05**
      As an asset **38.04**
      Dividends **38.04**
      Gain or loss on disposal **38.06**
STOCK ISSUED TO EMPLOYEES
  Background **39.01**
    Coverage of GAAP **39.01**
  Common stock equivalents **39.09**
  Compensatory plans **39.03**
    Basic provisions **39.03**
  Comprehensive illustration **39.09**
  Disclosure **39.09**
  Measurement date **39.03**
    Distribution of treasury stock **39.05**
    Renewal of stock option **39.05**
    Stock option for current services **39.04**
    Stock options of convertible securities **39.05**
    Transfer of stock to a trustee **39.04**
    Variable awards **39.05**
    When the measurement date is **39.04**
  Measuring compensation costs **39.06**
    Combination of two or more plans **39.08**
    Future compensation costs **39.07**
    Option in convertible stock **39.07**
    Payment of cash to settle an earlier option **39.07**
    Reacquisition of stock issued **39.07**
    Stock option plan by principal stockholder **39.07**
  Noncompensatory plans **39.02**
    Characteristics **39.02**
    Definition **39.02**
  Overview **39.02**
    Compensatory stock option **39.02**
    Noncompensatory stock option **39.02**
  Recognition of compensation costs **39.08**
    Periods over which costs are recognized **39.08**
    Plans with past and future services **39.08**
    Substance of transaction **39.08**
    Unearned compensation costs **39.08**
  Related tax effects **39.08**
    Additional compensation costs **39.08**
    Tax deduction taken by company **39.08**

STOCK ISSUED TO EMPLOYEES: Related tax effects (continued)
    Timing difference **39.08**
  Types of plans **39.01**
    Combination and elective **39.02**
    Shadow or phantom stock **39.02**
    Stock bonus and award **39.01**
    Stock option and purchase **39.01**
    Typical fixed **39.01**
STOCK OPTIONS AND WARRANTS
  Earnings per share **13.04**
  Marketable securities **28.01**
STOCK RIGHTS
  Stockholders' equity **38.08**
    Issuer **38.08**
    Recipient **38.08**
STOCK SPLIT
  Stockholders' equity **38.07**
    Amount to capitalize **38.07**
    Differences from a stock dividend **38.07**
STOCK SUBSCRIPTIONS
  Stockholders' equity **38.02**
SUBSTANCE OVER FORM
  Common stock equivalents **13.03**
  Earnings per share **13.03**
  Leases **26.01**
  Nonmonetary transactions **29.01**
  Receivables and payables **22.01**
SUCCESSFUL-EFFORTS COSTING
  Oil and gas producing companies **30.07**
SUPPORT EQUIPMENT AND FACILITIES
  Oil and gas producing companies **30.04**
SYSTEMATIC AND RATIONAL ALLOCATION
  Depreciable assets and depreciation **11.06**
  Depreciation methods **11.06**
  Intangible assets **21.02**

TAXABLE INCOME
  Income taxes **19.26**
TERMINAL FUNDING METHOD
  Pension plans **31.06**
TERMINATION CLAIMS
  Determination of profit or loss **18.03**
  Disclosure **18.03**
  Disposal credits **18.03**
  Government contracts **18.03**
  Inventory for terminated contracts **24.17**
TIMING DIFFERENCES
  Deferred tax method **19.10**
  Depreciation **11.10**
  Foreign operations and exchange **16.08**
  Income taxes **19.02**

GAAP GUIDE / **42.25**

TIMING DIFFERENCES (continued)
 Indefinite reversal criteria **19.07**
 Losses of a subsidiary **19.07**
 Marketable securities **28.09**
 Measuring timing differences **19.02**
 Railroad gradings and tunnel bores **19.09**
 Stock issued to employees **39.08**
 Undistributed earnings of a subsidiary **19.06**
 U.S. steamship companies **19.09**
TREASURY STOCK
 Business combination **3.21**
 Dividends **38.07**
 Marketable securities **28.01**
 Stockholders' equity **38.04**
  As an asset **38.04**
  Dividends **38.04**
  Gain or loss **38.06**
  Other than for retirement **38.05**
  Profits or losses **38.04**
  To be retired **38.05**
 Stock issued to employees **39.04**
TREASURY STOCK METHOD
 Earnings per share **13.12**
TROUBLED DEBT RESTRUCTURING
 Accounting and reporting by debtors **40.03**
  Combination of types **40.04**
  Contingently payable amounts **40.04**
   Criteria **40.04**
  Disclosure by debtors **40.05**
  Incidental cost of restructure **40.05**
  Modification of terms **40.03**
  Transfer of assets **40.03**
  Transfer of equity interest **40.03**
 Accounting by creditors **40.05**
  Combination of types **40.06**
  Creditor disclosure **40.07**
  Modification of terms **40.06**
  Receipt of assets or equity **40.06**
  Related matters **40.07**
  Substitution of debtors **40.07**
 Background **40.01**
 Coverage of GAAP **40.01**
 Definition **40.01**
 Situation of troubled debt **40.01**
 Definition of terms **40.02**
  Receivable (or payable) **40.02**
  Situations not troubled debt **40.02**
  Time of restructuring **40.02**
 Overview **40.01**
TWO-CLASS METHOD
 Earnings per share **13.21**

UNAMORTIZED DISCOUNT OR PREMIUM
 Interest on receivables or payables **22.03**
UNAMORTIZED POLICY ACQUISITION COSTS
 Foreign operations and exchange **16.05**
  Translation–stock life insurance companies **16.05**
UNASSERTED CLAIMS
 Contingencies **6.03**
UNAUDITED FINANCIAL STATEMENTS
 Accounting policies **2.01**
UNCLASSIFIED BALANCE SHEETS
 Changes in financial position **4.01**
 Concept of funds **4.03**
 Marketable securities **28.06**
UNIT CREDIT METHOD
 Pension plans **31.04**
UNREALIZED GROSS PROFIT
 Installment method of accounting **20.04**
UNREALIZED PROFITS IN INVENTORY
 Consolidated financial statements **5.06**
 Inventory pricing and methods **24.19**
UNREALIZED PROFITS IN LONG–LIVED ASSETS
 Consolidated financial statements **5.08**
UNITED KINGDOM TAX BENEFITS
 Income tax **19.25**
U.S. STEAMSHIP COMPANIES
 Income taxes **19.09**

VALUATION OF ASSETS
 Depreciable assets and depreciation **11.01**
 Goodwill **3.06**
 Historical cost **11.02**
 Intangible assets **21.02**
 Inventory in business combinations **24.17**
 Present value **11.03**
 Price–level restatement **17.01**
 Replacement cost **11.02**
VESTED BENEFITS
 Disclosure **31.12**
 Pension plans **31.03**

WEIGHTED AVERAGE METHOD
 Inventory pricing and methods **24.08**
WEIGHTED AVERAGE SHARES
 Earnings per share **13.10**
WORKING CAPITAL
 Changes in each element **8.03**
 Current ratio **8.04**
 Definition **8.03**
 Changes in financial position **4.01**